AF515836

KAMALADEVI CHATTOPADHYAY

INDIAN LIVES

A series edited and curated by Ramachandra Guha

Ashoka: Portrait of a Philosopher King by Patrick Olivelle
Sheikh Abdullah: The Caged Lion of Kashmir by Chitralekha Zutshi

Forthcoming volumes include:
Akshaya Mukul on Jayaprakash Narayan
Aparna Kapadia on Kasturba Gandhi
Richard Jaffe on the Buddha
Srinath Raghavan on Subramanyan Chandrasekhar
Abhishek Kaicker on Anand Ram 'Mukhlis'
Harish Damodaran on Ramkrishna Dalmia
Prashant Kidambi on Bal Gangadhar Tilak
Richard Davis on Rajaraja Chola

Indian Lives has been made possible through the generous support of
Bajaj Auto Ltd and the late Rahul Bajaj
Forbes Marshall
R.G. Manudhane Foundation for Excellence

INDIAN LIVES

KAMALADEVI CHATTOPADHYAY

The Art *of* Freedom

NICO SLATE

An Imprint of HarperCollins Publishers

First published in India by Fourth Estate 2024
An imprint of HarperCollins *Publishers*
4th Floor, Tower A, Building No. 10, DLF Cyber City,
DLF Phase II, Gurugram, Haryana – 122002
www.harpercollins.co.in

2 4 6 8 10 9 7 5 3 1

P-ISBN: 978-93-5489-975-1
E-ISBN: 978-93-5489-960-7

Typeset in 11.5/15.2 Crimson Text at
Manipal Technologies Limited, Manipal

Printed and bound at
Thomson Press (India) Ltd

This book is produced from independently certified FSC® paper
to ensure responsible forest management.

For Emily Mohn-Slate—poet and teacher.

And for the artists of India—past, present and future.

'Beauty is the soul of freedom.'

Kamaladevi Chattopadhyay

Contents

Series Editor's Foreword

KAMALADEVI CHATTOPADHYAY WAS INDISPUTABLY THE MOST remarkable Indian woman of the twentieth century. Her life and work straddled so many fields: nationalist politics, socialist politics, feminist politics, refugee rehabilitation, the theatre, the renewal of handicrafts, and more. In all these areas she made significant, and often, transformative contributions. Along the way she wrote a series of influential books and founded a set of enduring institutions. Perhaps only Rabindranath Tagore matched her in the range of multiple careers she led and the diverse social worlds she enriched.

I have myself admired Kamaladevi for more than thirty years now. I first encountered her while working on the life of the anthropologist Verrier Elwin, with whom she forged an enduring friendship, based on their shared appreciation of tribal art and craft. As I turned to understanding the early history of the Republic, there was Kamaladevi again, a visionary social worker helping our country recover from the ravages of Partition. When I next went backwards in time to the 1930s, I found Kamaladevi challenging Gandhi for his refusal to allow women to participate in the salt satyagraha, a decision he reversed in part because of her eloquence and persistence. Then, when I came to settle in Karnataka, I met many men and women whom she had influenced in the state where she was born, raised and, in some senses, always considered 'home'.

I had thus, for both personal and intellectual reasons, much wanted a volume on Kamaladevi Chattopadhyay to feature early in this series. Fortunately, the best-qualified scholar for this task was known to me already. I first met Nico Slate when he was a graduate student—appropriately, in an archive, where he was exploring the papers of Kamaladevi. She turned out to be a central figure in his first book, a pioneering study of the connections between the Indian freedom struggle and the civil rights movement in the United States. I knew also from later conversations that his interest in Kamaladevi had only deepened. I was therefore delighted when he agreed to write on her for the Indian Lives series.

There have been other books on Kamaladevi, written by her disciples and admirers. Slate uses those earlier works judiciously, while going much further than them in the range of sources used, and in the richer and deeper understanding of the social and historical contexts in which her life was lived. This is as close to a definitive biography as we will get, paying proper attention to all aspects of her life and legacy. It is also beautifully written.

Kamaladevi resisted using the term 'feminist' to describe herself. Nonetheless, as the scholar Ellen Carol Dubois has pointed out, Kamaladevi 'consistently advocated virtually everything with which the term "feminism" is currently associated: independent women's organizations, equal political rights, equal pay for equal work, reform in marriage, divorce and inheritance laws, even birth control and "sex freedom"'. She was an early practitioner of what is today termed 'intersectionality'. As Kamaladevi herself wrote, she became conscious early in her public career that 'the women's struggle ... had to be an indivisible part of the larger political, social and economic struggle'. She was a feminist among the nationalists, challenging her male colleagues in the freedom struggle to take gender equality more seriously, as well as a socialist among the feminists, urging the middle/upper class leadership of the Indian women's movement to be more conscious of the divisions of caste and class that undermined their movement. She brought these interwoven sensibilities to the two institutions she was most closely associated with in the decades before Independence—the Indian National Congress and the All India Women's Conference.

Committed to the freedom of India from British rule, Kamaladevi nonetheless had a far more expansive idea of swaraj than that of most nationalists, who often saw the matter merely in political terms, as the handing over of power from the white rulers to the coloured subjects. Here, by way of contrast, is Slate quoting Kamaladevi as saying in December 1929: 'Freedom or swaraj can mean only one thing: absolute freedom for each individual as well as collective growth and evolution. It means the establishment of an order in the country which will give the fullest opportunity for each to grow physically, culturally and morally unhampered by such economic and social laws and conventions as demoralise human beings.'

Nico Slate reminds us that Kamaladevi's socialism was 'defined by a rejection of *both* rapacious capitalism and totalitarian communism'. Her younger colleague, Madhu Dandavate, praised Kamaladevi for helping nurture 'the aesthetic and ethical roots' of the Indian socialist movement. 'Even in the midst of [the] tumult and turmoil of political life,' wrote Dandavate of Kamaladevi, 'her vision of beauty was never blurred. To her aesthetic sense, inequality appeared quite ugly and immoral, because it stunted the free development of human personality.' In some ways she was to Indian socialism what William Morris had been to British socialism. That is to say, Kamaladevi brought joy and beauty to an otherwise austere and severely practical political tradition.

One of the many strengths of Slate's book is the close attention it pays to Kamaladevi's travels. Her political and social activism before Independence, and her nurturing of handicrafts before Independence, took her to every part of the subcontinent. There was no state and almost no district of India she did not visit or know. Yet she also travelled a great deal overseas, going to, among other places, Europe, the United Kingdom, China, Sri Lanka and Japan. She spent two intense years in the United States, interacting closely with women's activists and speaking out against racial prejudice and the ill-treatment of African Americans.

Kamaladevi Chattopadhyay's socialist comrade, Yusuf Meherally, who himself died tragically young, once said of her that in her travels she was always accompanied by her typewriter, when she had a free moment banging away on its keys in train compartment and ship deck alike. Slate presents careful assessments of the books she wrote and, perhaps more importantly, of the institutions she nurtured and founded. These included the Indian Cooperative Union, the Sangeet Natak Akademi, the All India Handicrafts Board, the Central Cottage Industries Emporium, the Association of Voluntary Agencies for Rural Development, the Crafts Council of India and the India International Council.

Kamaladevi's life touched many spheres and brought her in close touch with many people. Slate tells us of her relationships with nationalist stalwarts such as Gandhi, Nehru and Patel; with socialist activists such as Rammanohar Lohia and Jayaprakash Narayan; with other pioneers in the Indian women's movement such as Margaret Cousins and Sarojini Naidu. We also learn of her friendships with people overseas, among them crafts activists in America. Of all the people she met and knew it was Gandhi who had the most impact on her. And yet, though she admired the Mahatma, she was far from being a hero worshipper; for, as Slate writes, Kamaladevi 'was, and would remain, too independent to be a devotee of anyone'.

Nico Slate presents a full, rich and always nuanced picture of Kamaladevi Chattopadhyay's many-sided public career. Notably, he pays proper attention to her personal life too. He writes, with delicacy and care, about the problems she had as a child widow, and of her troubled marriage to her gifted and serially unfaithful second husband. The unhappy break-up of this marriage, the difficult relationship she had with her son Rama, made more complicated by her many jail terms—these are sketched with great sensitivity and honesty by Slate.

In its multifaceted-ness and its myriad-minded-ness, Kamaladevi's life bears comparison, as I have said, to that of Rabindranath Tagore. Like Tagore, she played an active role in nurturing the spirit of freedom under conditions of colonial rule. However, while Tagore died while India was still a colony, Kamaladevi lived on for more than four decades after Independence, always evolving, entering ever newer terrains, active and energetic till the end. (Some of her last writings were on the environmental challenges that confront humanity.) Slate's wonderful biography is therefore not just a moving and compellingly readable account of an extraordinary life, but also a uniquely illuminating window into twentieth-century Indian history as a whole.

Ramachandra Guha

Introduction

IN THE AUTUMN OF 1947, A FORTY-FOUR-YEAR-OLD WOMAN VISITED A cavernous building in New Delhi known as P-Block. The British Raj had just fallen. Two nations—India and Pakistan—had emerged from the wreckage of colonial rule. For generations, imperial authorities had stoked distrust between India's largest religious communities. As the colonial state retreated, that distrust turned violent on a staggering scale. More than half a million people died and more than 10 million fled their homes in one of the largest and bloodiest mass migrations in human history.[1]

Kamaladevi Chattopadhyay arrived at P-Block, the headquarters of the new Relief and Rehabilitation Secretariat, with a plan to resettle the hundreds of thousands of refugees who had arrived in Delhi. Known throughout the subcontinent by her first name, Kamaladevi had acquired a considerable reputation for her work in the socialist and women's movements and for having spent years in prison for her opposition to the British Raj. She worked closely with Mahatma Gandhi and with India's first prime minister, Jawaharlal Nehru. Yet the officials of the Relief and Rehabilitation Secretariat did not respond to her request that land be allocated to the refugees. Undeterred by the bureaucracy's indifference, she identified a patch of open terrain about 20 kilometres from the city and informed the authorities that if an appropriate alternative was not provided in the next three days, she would personally escort a group of refugees to claim the land. She hired trucks and worked with the refugees to gather all that was needed to build a temporary settlement. The night before they were to move, a letter arrived providing clearance for the land.[2]

Kamaladevi helped to organize a new city for refugees just outside of Delhi. Often described as a 'model' community, the new town of Faridabad would house 30,000 people on some 1,500 acres. 'From an unsightly settlement of ragged tents and squalid huts only a year and a half ago,' the *New York Times* declared in October 1951, 'Faridabad has become a model of combined suburban and rural development with homes, jobs, schools and public health service for all.' With its own electric powerhouse, 150-bed hospital and a range of small, collaboratively run businesses—from a dairy farm to a button factory—Faridabad testified to the hope and hard work of a multitude of uprooted people, the dedication of dozens of social workers, and the vision and determination of one indomitable woman.[3]

Kamaladevi's support for refugees was an act of empathy across many divides. Unlike most of the people she strove to empower, she had been born into wealth and status. Kamaladevi Dhareshwar entered the world on 3 April 1903 in Mangalore, a small city on the coast of the Arabian Sea in the present-day state of Karnataka. Her family belonged to one of the most affluent and educated communities in colonial India, the Chitrapur Saraswat Brahmins. Her life turned towards adversity when her father died without leaving a will. Most of the family's wealth was inherited by a male relative, leaving Kamaladevi, her sisters and her mother in a precarious position. At the age of eleven, Kamaladevi was married to an older boy from one of Mangalore's wealthiest families. Only a year later, the boy died, leaving Kamaladevi a child widow at a time when widows were often expected to live austere and secluded lives. With support from her mother, Kamaladevi broke social custom by pursuing her own education and, at the age of sixteen, falling in love and remarrying across lines of language, region and caste.[4]

With her new husband, she sang and acted in plays and films despite the fact that 'respectable' women rarely performed on stage or in front of the camera, and travelled to England to pursue a degree in sociology at a time when few Indian women studied abroad. After returning to India to support Gandhi's non-cooperation movement, Kamaladevi became one of the first women to contest a legislative election in colonial India. She played a key role in the creation of the All India Women's Conference (AIWC) and helped lead that organization as its first secretary. In 1930, when Gandhi launched a civil disobedience campaign while limiting the participation of women, Kamaladevi confronted him, helped to change his mind, and then herself became one of the first women arrested. She spent over two years in prison, some of that time in solitary confinement.

Kamaladevi emerged from prison to find that her husband had been having an affair. She broke yet another taboo by divorcing him. In 1934, she helped found a socialist group within the Indian National Congress and emerged as one of the most influential leaders of the left wing of the freedom struggle. She was also among the best travelled. During the Second World War, she journeyed across the United States, Japan and war-torn China before returning to India, where she was arrested yet again. After her release, she joined the Congress Working Committee—the party's highest body—at one of the most crucial junctures in the history of the freedom struggle. Along with her socialist colleagues, she opposed the partition of India, a stance that brought her close to Gandhi towards the end of his life. Kamaladevi brought Gandhi her plans to support refugees, and he offered his blessings along with one piece of advice: Don't depend on government support.

Kamaladevi's relationship with the Government of India was fraught. In many ways, she followed Gandhi's advice, refusing positions of high power and focusing instead on fostering grassroots social change. From the 1950s to the 1980s, she dedicated most of her time to supporting the arts and crafts, which she saw as vital cultural traditions and as sources of sustainable income, particularly for rural and indigenous communities. Her focus on handicrafts was very Gandhian—an extension of the Mahatma's emphasis on the spinning wheel, 'village industries' and a decentralized economy. Yet Kamaladevi was not averse to mobilizing the power of the government. She served as the director of the All India Handicrafts Board and held a variety of other governmental and quasi-governmental positions. She was an institution-builder. In addition to her work with the AIWC and the Handicrafts Board, she played a key role in founding and supporting the Indian Cooperative Union, Lady Irwin College, the National Theatre Centre, the Sangeet Natak Akademi, the India International Centre and a range of other institutions that continue to shape India's vibrant social and cultural life.

This is the story of Kamaladevi and of the making of modern India. Kamaladevi dreamt of a country that was free of much more than British rule; she demanded an end to poverty, sexism and caste oppression. She lived long enough to see many of her dreams frustrated, but hers is not a story of defeat. Indeed, Kamaladevi embodied the lasting promise of the Indian freedom struggle—understood not as a narrowly political campaign that ended in 1947 but as a confluence of dreams, community experiments and radical social movements. Here is the key lesson that Kamaladevi's story reveals about the making of modern India: It was the coming together of multiple causes that gave the freedom struggle its dynamic strength. By recognizing the intersection of different injustices and cultivating connections across movements, Kamaladevi fostered a pluralistic and inclusive India. It is the way she knitted together a variety of struggles that explains why the historian Ramachandra Guha has written that Kamaladevi 'has strong claims to being regarded as the greatest Indian woman of modern times'.[5]

Kamaladevi linked her bold vision for India to an expansive conception of solidarity across what would come to be known as the Global South. Her international connections were—among the most prominent leaders of the freedom struggle—rivalled only by Jawaharlal Nehru. It was not the sheer scale of her global ties that was most remarkable. Rather, it was in her combining of a global vision with local activism—and linking both to an inclusive nationalism—that Kamaladevi embodied the transnational potential of the Indian freedom struggle. When the novelist Raja Rao called Kamaladevi 'firmly Indian and therefore universal', he recognized one of her greatest feats—the way in which she forged connections across the borders of race, nation, class and gender, all while embracing the full powers of her own identity as an Indian woman.[6]

Kamaladevi's bridge-building—both within India and across the world—was a creative practice shaped by her love for handicrafts, drama, dance, music and all forms of art. Many histories of the freedom struggle and of independent India have little to say about art or artists. By contrast, Kamaladevi's life positions art—broadly understood—at the centre of India's history. Taking seriously the art of freedom requires doing more than respecting the imagination of political actors or the political power of artists; it requires reimagining, as Kamaladevi did, the meaning of both art and freedom.[7]

Kamaladevi's main art form was the written word. While often seen primarily as a social reformer, Kamaladevi understood herself as a writer and a thinker too, and she deserves to be recognized as one of the most creative and prolific public intellectuals in twentieth-century India. Consider this description of Kamaladevi offered by her socialist colleague Yusuf Meherally: 'She always carries a typewriter with her even on her travels, much to the exasperation of her friends, and sits in a crowded third-class railway compartment, typing out articles direct on the machine instead of writing them first by hand.' Over the course of her life, Kamaladevi authored over a dozen books and scores of essays on topics ranging from social policy to the arts to her own life. Her writings blend poetic vision with pragmatic detail. Many remain profoundly relevant. Kamaladevi wrote to advance specific ideas, to fight for the future of India and the world, and to cope with her own tumultuous life. 'No matter how great the depression or tension,' she explained in her autobiography, 'writing melts it away.' She deemed writing 'the only profession I can lay claim to in the constant turmoil I keep going through', and added, 'Moments of deepest distress or depression are lightened when I start writing.'[8]

Kamaladevi did not like to talk about the more difficult moments in her life. 'Whatever the modern trend may be,' she wrote in her memoirs,

'I do not think that in a life story one is required to lower the barriers of the discreet reticence which govern our everyday life and affairs.' Over the several hundred pages of her memoirs, she chose not to mention her son's birth or either of her marriages. This reticence was shaped by the ways her private life had long been used against her. As a divorced woman who refused to abide by the gendered expectations of her time, Kamaladevi's private life became a source of gossip and a weapon in the hands of her opponents. Her decision to keep many facets of her life private was not, however, solely a result of outward pressure. Kamaladevi explained her reticence as the result of a paradox in her personality, a paradox that makes it even more remarkable that she chose to participate in so many of the major events of her time. 'I seem bold, aggressive, out-going, having been a fighter all my life,' she wrote. 'But in reality, I am shy and retiring, rather averse to crowds and addressing large gatherings.' Rather than try to explain the origins of that contrast, she wrote simply, 'Some of us can be full of contradictions.' Along with her vision, her passion and her courage, it is Kamaladevi's contradictions that make her life so compelling.[9]

1

Born to Rebel

WALKING HOME FROM HER PRIMARY SCHOOL, KAMALADEVI noticed a man following her. The same man had verbally harassed her friends on a previous walk home. This time Kamaladevi was alone. She began to walk towards the central market where she knew a police officer was on duty. The stranger followed, coming closer with every step. Sensing that he was about to attack, she spun around to face him. He reached out, as if to grab the chain she wore around her neck. She screamed and ran towards the police officer, who managed to capture the would-be thief. When she returned home, Kamaladevi told her mother of the frightening experience. 'She gave me a pat,' Kamaladevi later recalled, 'with a proud look in her eyes, a very rare experience for me. I hardly ever seemed to measure up to her expectations.'[1]

As a child and as a young woman, Kamaladevi rebelled against sexism with courage and determination, and she rebelled against the woman who most inspired her determination—her mother. Their vexed relationship is more striking given that both mother and daughter rejected the social norms expected of an affluent woman in colonial Mangalore. Perched on the Arabian Sea, about halfway between Bombay and the southern tip of India, Mangalore was a strategic port that had been ruled by a variety of kings, emperors and sultans. After a series of wars that spilled across the final decades of the eighteenth century, the British East India Company wrested control from the fearsome Tipu Sultan, and the city had become a sleepy outpost of the British-run Madras Presidency by the time Kamaladevi Dhareshwar entered the world in the spring of 1903. Born into a prosperous family, young Kamaladevi had few opportunities to feel the weight of British rule. Instead, she rebelled against the customs of her own community and against her mother.[2]

Girijabai Dhareshwar, Kamaladevi's mother, was born into a wealthy landowning family. Although she followed social expectations in marriage and in motherhood, Girijabai found her own ways to buck traditional gender norms. As Kamaladevi later explained, 'My mother was acutely aware of the disabilities which women suffered and a great revolt built up within her—a feeling that these should be removed.' Towards that end, Girijabai helped to establish the first women's association in Mangalore, the Mahila Sabha, an organization that combined cultural activities with conversations about social and political topics. Women in dozens of cities and towns were developing their own local mahila samitis or women's clubs. These local groups were often connected to nationwide women's organizations, such as the Bharata Mahila Parishad (founded in 1905) and the Bharat Stree Mandal (founded in 1910). While some of these groups aimed to bring women together across the divides of caste and religion, many drew primarily from the ranks of high-caste, elite women.[3]

Kamaladevi admired her mother's commitment to women's freedom, but rebelled against her authority. The art critic Govindraj Venkatachalam later traced Kamaladevi's rebelliousness to her infancy. 'Her "infant-kicks", her mother will tell you, were unlike any other baby's,' he wrote. 'They were more vigorous and violent, more powerful and persistent.' The young Kamaladevi resisted her mother in ways large and small, including by trying to avoid the daily habits her mother enforced—from gargling with hot water after a meal to washing her feet before bed. Yet, regardless of how much she resisted, Kamaladevi was deeply shaped by her mother. Even towards the end of her life, she could not sleep without first washing her feet.[4]

Kamaladevi enjoyed an equally meaningful (and decidedly less rocky) relationship with her maternal grandmother. In her memoir, Kamaladevi called her grandmother 'a colossus who strode across my life'. She remembered her grandmother sitting with Sanskrit scholars, studying the ancient texts. Her grandmother loved books and taught the young Kamaladevi a lesson she would always remember: 'Books are lifelong friends, and will stay with you in faith, teach you many truths, and enrich your mind.' Kamaladevi connected her mother and her grandmother when she noted that both 'shared a love for books, and an almost insatiable hunger for knowledge'. Yet whereas Kamaladevi often came into conflict with her mother, she felt nothing but reverence for her grandmother.[5]

She had a similarly idyllic relationship with her father. Unlike her mother, Kamaladevi's father, Dhareshwar Ananthaya, was not born into an especially wealthy family. He worked his way up from an unpaid position to become the treasury deputy collector and the chairman of the Mangalore municipality. 'Emotionally, my father had been my closest companion,' Kamaladevi recalled later. 'He was of a gentle disposition, with a compassionate understanding of my rather rebellious spirit.' It was a profound shock when her father died suddenly. Life grew lonely for the young seven-year-old girl, deprived of her most emotionally supportive parent. She later told Jayaprakash Narayan, her close colleague in the freedom struggle, that her father had been 'the dearest thing I had in my life'. His death was 'the biggest loss I ever sustained and no one has ever been able to fill his place'.[6]

Her grief was compounded by the fact that her father had not left a will, and much of the family's wealth went to a male relative. Later, Kamaladevi would credit this calamity with deepening her opposition to sexism. 'All the vast property the largesse to no part of which we, the girls, qualified because of our sex, all went to a stepbrother whom we hardly knew except as a tycoon in a large, faraway city,' she wrote in her memoir. 'I woke up as from a daze. This was what mother had been alerting me about. Women had no rights and we should qualify to stake our claims and assert them. The question was not one of possessions but of principle.'[7]

Faced with economic uncertainty, and concerned about Kamaladevi's future, Girijabai arranged for her daughter to marry the son of one of

Mangalore's wealthiest men. She was eleven; the boy a few years older. Such child marriages were not atypical at the time but what unfolded after Kamaladevi's wedding was rare. First, just over a year later, her husband died. Within many communities, child widows were expected to spend their lives in austere seclusion. In her memoir, Kamaladevi noted that 'the word "widow" was then used as a term of *abuse.* "You son of a widow" was a term of withering contempt.' Tellingly, she made that comment in regard to a widowed aunt and said nothing about her own past. Her experience as a child widow would remain one of several major episodes in her life that Kamaladevi chose not to discuss publicly. In this case, her silence is especially striking given that she spent years fighting to raise the minimum age of marriage and to improve the conditions of widows. In *The Awakening of Indian Women,* a book she published in 1939, Kamaladevi described widows as 'souls in agony'. 'They were disfigured and relegated to a life of servility with scant regard for their feelings or needs,' she wrote. 'They are even regarded as objects of ill-omen.' Yet again she chose not to personalize her analysis. Years later, when asked about her experience of being a child widow, Kamaladevi stated, 'Life went on as before for me, but it was hard on my mother.' Did life go 'on as before' for the young Kamaladevi? We might dismiss such a statement as a form of psychological denial. Certainly, Kamaladevi's widowhood would play a significant role in her life. If nothing else, it would become a staple of how others perceived her. Yet there is reason to believe that, at least in many regards, life for the young Kamaladevi did go 'on as before'—a fact that testifies to the courage of her husband's family and of her mother.[8]

Rather than force Kamaladevi to don the white robes of widowhood and to withdraw from society, her mother and her husband's father agreed that she should continue her education and her social life. That decision caused tensions with less progressive members of the community. The Chitrapur Saraswats were renowned for being highly educated and 'modern' in regard to social questions. Such a reputation obscured persistent divisions within the community. In the 1880s, a group of socially liberal Saraswats living in Madras began to push for widows to have the right to remarry. They attracted supporters from among the most progressive residents of Mangalore, including Kamaladevi's father and Nayampalli Subbarao, a wealthy and influential figure who served as chairman of the municipality from 1905 to 1913. Subbarao's father had been excommunicated from the caste because of his liberal views, but that did not prevent him from continuing to support progressive causes—even when they concerned his own family. It was Subbarao's son whom Kamaladevi had married; his son who had died. By supporting Kamaladevi's independence, Subbarao refused to cater to the conservative members of his community. He could not have known that, in the process, he was empowering a young woman who would become one of India's most influential champions of women's rights.[9]

It was Kamaladevi's mother who played the most important role in protecting her daughter from the constraints of widowhood and who deserves primary credit for inspiring her abiding belief in the power of women. She taught Kamaladevi about leading women reformers, including Annie Besant, the British socialist and theosophist who was elected the president of the Indian National Congress in 1917. As a child, Kamaladevi met Besant. She later recalled being 'full of a kind of wonder' at having the chance to meet a woman she regarded as 'a political hero'. She also met Pandita Ramabai, who gained fame as a scholar and as the founder of the Arya Mahila Samaj (Arya Women's Society), an organization that focused on supporting women's education and opposing child marriage. Ramabai was a Brahmin from the same region as Kamaladevi. In her memoir, Kamaladevi called her 'the greatest Indian woman of our time' and recalled that her mother often reminded her that Ramabai 'was from our district and that I could become a crusader like her'. She did not mention that Ramabai had founded a home for child widows. It remains unclear how much that label—' child widow'—influenced Kamaladevi's self-perception during her youth. What is clear is that, with the support of her mother, she refused to be constrained by that label.[10]

Girijabai also exposed Kamaladevi to the nationalist cause. 'My mother was politically a very conscious person,' she later recalled. 'She was a voracious reader and kept abreast of current affairs.' The family subscribed to several nationalist journals, including Bal Gangadhar Tilak's *Kesari.* Indian nationalism came in a variety of flavours, not all of which dovetailed with the kinds of social reform pursued by figures like Pandita Ramabai. Part of the problem was that the British exploited social issues—particularly those relating to gender—in order to defend their 'enlightened' rule. In the years ahead, Kamaladevi would emerge as one of the most prominent voices blending social reform and anticolonial nationalism. She would argue that India's freedom required eliminating both British rule and the many inequities and divisions that existed within Indian society. She credited her mother with helping her develop such a robust 'nationalist feeling'. Importantly, that feeling was not anti-British. In an oral history, Kamaladevi later recalled that she developed 'kinship' with the British while attending an English-medium convent school, a kinship that helps to explain why she did not develop, in her words, 'any kind of prejudice toward the English as a people or toward England as a country'.[11]

Her awareness of India's own failings contributed to Kamaladevi's ability to embrace anticolonial nationalism without falling into xenophobic chauvinism. At the home of her maternal uncle, she met many social reformers, including the distinguished lawyer, Tej Bahadur Sapru, and the founder of the Servants of India Society, Gopalkrishna Gokhale. Her uncle was himself an active reformer who lent Kamaladevi books and encouraged her to learn more about India's problems. In addition to gaining awareness of sexism and patriarchy, she became increasingly concerned about poverty and class inequality. It does not seem to have troubled the young Kamaladevi that it was her class status that opened doors to the world of reform. She was grateful for the opportunity to learn from passionate advocates of change—even if most of those advocates came from the same upper-caste milieu into which she had been born.[12]

For a young widow, mingling with social reformers was itself an act of rebellion, an act that broadened her understanding of India and of herself. Kamaladevi's social and political world expanded even further in 1917 as a result of yet another family tragedy. Her oldest sister, Saguna, had long been abused by her husband. When Saguna developed life-threatening health problems, Girijabai decided to take her to Madras for treatment, and Kamaladevi relocated as well. One of colonial India's largest and most dynamic cities, Madras was a hotbed of social reform and artistic exploration. Kamaladevi enrolled at Queen Mary's College, but much of her education came through her social connections—especially her connections with one of the most dynamic families in modern India, the Chattopadhyays. The eldest daughter of the family had enrolled at Madras University at the age of twelve, had studied in London and Cambridge, and had gained fame as a poet and social reformer under her married name, Sarojini Naidu. The eldest son, Virendranath, had gone to Oxford to study for the Indian Civil Service but had become drawn to radical politics and had fled to France to avoid arrest. Several decades older than Kamaladevi, Sarojini and Virendranath would both play profound roles in her life. In 1917, it was younger members of the family who had the biggest impact: Suhasini, a fellow student at Queen Mary's; Mrinalini, who hosted a salon at her oceanside home; and Harindranath, often known as Harin, who was some five years older than Kamaladevi and who had become renowned as an actor and writer.[13]

Kamaladevi attended one of Harin's performances and was impressed by his many gifts. 'At first glance,' she later recalled, 'his talent struck me—poetry, music, acting, everything was given to him by the Lord.' She made these comments in conversation with one of her biographers, Kamala Ratnam. When Ratnam pressed Kamaladevi for more details regarding how she fell in love with Harin, Kamaladevi 'completely wrapped herself inside, taking all the light in'. After a moment of silence, she stated, 'Actually I was not attracted to him. Nor did I fall in love with him. Yes, his talent surely stunned me. It can be said that at that time both his liveliness and talent had overtaken me. I was mesmerized by them. But as I got acquainted with him, I noticed that he had a kind of personal instability.' It was, she explained, 'as if he could not stay in the same happy state of mind for long. Often it used to happen that now we are reciting poetry with laughter, but in the next moment absentmindedly he starts getting angry.' It is unclear how long it took for Kamaladevi to recognize Harin's 'instability'. At first, she was more focused on his many talents.[14]

For his part, Harin was struck by the 'young, rather attractive girl with large eyes which almost seemed to be conscious all the time of their own limpid quality'. That is how he would later recall his first glimpse of Kamaladevi. 'Her face was outstanding,' he added. 'I somehow guessed that that face was destined to play an important role in my life.' A few months later, the two were reunited at one of the Chattopadhyay family gatherings. Not long after, they became engaged. Neither Kamaladevi nor Harin offered many details regarding how they fell in love. While Kamaladevi ignored that question in her memoirs, Harin focused almost entirely on the physical beauty of the young woman with 'limpid' eyes. 'After opposition from some of her people, and support from a few members of her family who mattered,' he concluded, 'she became my wife.'[15]

The opposition came primarily from those who were against widow remarriage, although it was also an issue that this was an interregional and inter-caste union. The Chattopadhyays were originally from Bengal. They were Brahmins like Kamaladevi's family, but from a different community. Kamaladevi's mother supported the marriage, as did Harin's family, and the regional and caste differences would prove inconsequential. There were, however, other challenges awaiting the young Kamaladevi as she entered what was a tight-knit family. As she would later say, 'Marrying a Chattopadhya was to marry all.' That would prove to be a blessing and one of the greatest challenges of her life.[16]

~

Kamaladevi and Harin were married in 1919. They decided against a formal wedding, and no religious ceremonies were observed. 'We didn't even think about it,' Kamaladevi later recalled. It was in the court registry office that the two young people, both rebels in their own ways, became husband and wife. Harin was twenty-one years old. Kamaladevi was sixteen.[17]

Not long before the wedding, Kamaladevi contracted the deadly influenza virus that had swept through the world in 1918 and that continued to claim victims into 1919. Between 10 million and 15 million

Indians would die in that pandemic, many of them young people. Kamaladevi survived, of course, although she was still weak on her wedding day. This would not be the final time she escaped mortal danger. Her life would be shaped by struggles—many generated by Harin and by his family.[18]

Before the wedding, Kamaladevi and Harin had made plans to return to Mangalore so that Kamaladevi could continue her studies. After the wedding, Harin's sister, Mrinalini, demanded that the newlyweds move in with her in Madras. Even more gallingly, she insisted that Kamaladevi refrain from pursuing her studies, and she secretly made plans for Harin to travel to England to pursue his own education. It was only when those plans had been finalized that Kamaladevi was informed that her new husband would soon go abroad and remain overseas for several years.[19]

While coping with the challenges of Harin's family, Kamaladevi's own family contracted in a tragic way. Her sister Saguna died. Kamaladevi blamed the spousal abuse that Saguna had suffered. She had already lost a stepsister, Amba, who also died after years of abuse by her husband. In a pattern she would repeat throughout her life, Kamaladevi responded to these profound personal losses by redoubling her commitment to fighting injustice. She was determined to build a country in which no woman would need to fear her husband. From her mother's loss of the family property to her own experience as a widow to the deaths of her sister and her stepsister, Kamaladevi witnessed the multifaceted brutality of sexism and patriarchy. In the years ahead, she would develop a keen understanding of the interconnected nature of gender-based discrimination, and link the struggles of Indian women to global movements against sexism, colonialism and class inequality.

Kamaladevi's expansive activism had many sources, but she often traced the breadth of her social commitments to the influence of one man: Mohandas Karamchand Gandhi. Her relationship with Gandhi was intimate, dynamic and often rocky. More so than most Indian freedom fighters, she would challenge Gandhi to revise his views, especially in regard to women and women's activism. When she first came to know him, however, it was as a young woman inspired by his call for radical service to the nation.

On 6 April 1919, Kamaladevi arrived at Bombay's Chowpatty Beach where she found 'a sea of humanity'. 'One saw nothing but heads,' she later wrote. 'Like on a holy day, everyone had a dip in the water after which the vast concourse of people formed itself into a procession to move into the city.' Gandhi had asked Indians to stage a massive protest against colonial repression. During the First World War, over a million Indian soldiers had fought for the British Empire. In the aftermath of the war, many Indians—including Gandhi—had hoped that the British would reciprocate by granting representative government. Instead, modest constitutional reforms were paired with a series of repressive laws, the Rowlatt Acts, that allowed political prisoners to be held without trial and to be tried without a jury. It was in opposition to the Rowlatt Acts that Gandhi called for a day of 'fasting and prayer' and that Kamaladevi—just three days after her sixteenth birthday—joined that massive crowd at Chowpatty Beach.[20]

The following day, her new sister-in-law, Sarojini Naidu, took Kamaladevi to hear Gandhi speak. He was starting a new organization whose members would pledge to launch civil disobedience against the Rowlatt Acts. Gandhi had coined his own term for what was then often known as 'passive resistance'. There was nothing 'passive' about what he came to call satyagraha, a word that blended the Sanskrit for truth and for holding firm. Members of the new Satyagraha Sabha would hold firm to the truth in the face of injustice. Kamaladevi went to hear Gandhi unsure whether she would join his new organization. She had doubts regarding 'the practicability of maintaining complete non-violence' and wondered who in history had 'won freedom without violence and struggle'. Gandhi was persuasive. 'His words came slowly but emphatically,' she recalled, 'as though each word was weighed and phrased before it was uttered.' He told the audience, 'This is going to be a great struggle with a powerful adversary. If you want to take it up you must be prepared to lose everything and train yourselves to the strictest non-violence and discipline.' Convinced that Gandhi could foment the revolution India needed, Kamaladevi pledged to follow him.[21]

Her first act of civil disobedience was fitting for a lifelong reader and future writer—selling banned pamphlets authored by the Mahatma.

She expected to be arrested, but the police chose to ignore such acts of resistance. Meanwhile, Gandhi attempted to travel to the Punjab but was forced back towards Bombay. Kamaladevi joined the large crowd that gathered to meet him at the railway station. Suddenly, and without warning, the police charged on horseback. Kamaladevi escaped uninjured, if stunned by the brutality of the police. The violence in Bombay was traumatic but nothing like what happened in the Punjab, where a British brigadier-general ordered his troops to fire upon a peaceful crowd in Amritsar's Jallianwala Bagh, a public square bounded by walls. The firing continued for ten minutes. The crowd had no chance of surrender or escape. Colonial authorities counted 379 people killed. Others put the death count even higher. Could nonviolent protest work in the face of such organized violence? As Gandhi knew well and Kamaladevi would learn, nonviolence often works by eliciting violence from the oppressor. Anger at the Jallianwala Bagh Massacre inspired many Indians to join Gandhi's call for a nationwide non-cooperation movement. Beginning in the fall of 1920, many left their schools and jobs, and boycotted public transportation, courts of law and foreign-made clothing.[22]

Kamaladevi took to spinning cotton thread—one of Gandhi's most cherished anticolonial activities—and to organizing cultural events that raised funds for the movement. Her initial doubts about nonviolence quickly gave way to enthusiasm. 'The application of this concept of satyagraha as a political weapon was startling and exciting,' she later wrote. 'It was like gazing on a new instrument, complicated and powerful to operate.' In addition to deploying that instrument against foreign rule, Gandhi also called on Indians to confront their own social problems—including religious divisions and caste oppression. Kamaladevi was impressed by Gandhi's definition of freedom as more than the end of British rule. She had long been 'greatly puzzled and made unhappy by social differences and economic inequalities'. 'Now here came a leader who seemed troubled by the same injustices,' she recalled, a leader who had a 'programme of action'. That programme of action included empowering young women. In response to non-cooperation, Kamaladevi's family offered one of their homes as a temporary space for a new national school for girls, and Kamaladevi returned to Mangalore to help with the new school.[23]

The director of the school, the Irish social reformer Margaret Cousins, would have a major impact on Kamaladevi's life. In 1908, when Kamaladevi was five years old, Cousins cofounded the Irish Women's Franchise League. Her dedication to women's suffrage earned her several stints in jail. In 1915, she and her husband moved to India. Two years later, she cofounded the Women's Indian Association with Annie Besant. It was Besant who encouraged Cousins to serve as the founding director of the National Girls' School.[24]

Cousins quickly identified Kamaladevi as one of her most promising pupils. One morning, Cousins arrived at Kamaladevi's home with the news that a provincial legislature had introduced a bill to give women the right to vote. 'This is a great event, my dear,' Cousins declared, 'and I want to share it with you.' It was for good reason that Kamaladevi later called Cousins her 'guru', a teacher and mentor 'under whom I learned to do public work'. In addition to their commitments to social reform, the two women also shared a love for the arts. Cousins would often play the piano while Kamaladevi sang. It was Cousins who first taught Kamaladevi the patriotic song 'Jana Gana Mana', which Cousins had learned from its author, the poet Rabindranath Tagore.[25]

In late 1919, Cousins organized an unusual fundraiser for the National Girls' School, a fundraiser that drew upon the artistic passions that she and Kamaladevi shared. The plan was to stage a play written by James Cousins, Margaret's husband and himself a well-known writer and social reformer. The play focused on the sixteenth-century mystic poet Mirabai. Kamaladevi was chosen to play the lead role. According to Margaret Cousins, Kamaladevi was 'a mine of ideas and capability'. She set Mirabai's songs to music, memorized her lines and eagerly prepared for the performance. Acting remained a controversial activity for women, even teenagers like Kamaladevi. Many supporters of the school expressed opposition to the play, and a large segment of the community decided to boycott the event. Cousins could have cancelled what was obviously going to fail as a fundraiser, but as Kamaladevi later recalled, the play 'had become to us a *cause* and to abandon it would mean acknowledging that what we were trying to do was wrong'. In the words of Cousins, the play came to represent 'the cooperation of the sexes in the cause of artistic truth in drama'.[26]

Cousins decided to have a party at her house where the play could be performed privately, but under community pressure Kamaladevi's mother refused to allow her daughter to perform. In her memoir, Kamaladevi recalled that she was locked in a room until the play was over. Cousins remembered a different outcome. In her account, published several decades closer to the events themselves, Cousins wrote that 'at the last moment Kamala came in despair to say that she daren't act, as a relative had threatened to wreak vengeance if she did'. Cousins was forced to read Mira's part, but they found a way for Kamaladevi to participate. According to Cousins, 'Kamala sang Mira's songs very sweetly from behind a curtain.' Afterwards, everyone in attendance shared a meal. 'It was thrilling,' Cousins recalled, 'to have a big jolly Mohammedan, a hearty Indian Christian, Brahmins, non-Brahmins, two Hindu widows, a re-married Hindu widow, and a western woman, eating together and enjoying unrestrained laughter.' Kamaladevi shared the religious pluralism celebrated in this description of the meal, but it remains unclear how she felt being identified as a 're-married Hindu widow'.[27]

The Mirabai play was one of several incidents in which Kamaladevi came into conflict with Saraswat society in Mangalore—and with members of her own family. More trouble arose when a local newspaper ran a story on a performance by the classical vocalist Abdul Karim Khan. The story featured a photograph of Kamaladevi in the audience. An elderly relative took a clipping to Kamaladevi's mother and complained about the scandal of a young woman attending such a show. Girijabai deflected the criticism and tried to protect her daughter's independence, but Mangalore was simply too small for Kamaladevi. In 1921, she decided to join Harin in England. Some accounts suggest that she sold her own personal jewellery in order to pay for the journey. In any case, it was a daring move—to sail to the capital of the Empire, one of the largest cities in the world, to live with a man she still only barely knew. She was eighteen years old.[28]

Harin met her at the docks in London. Kamaladevi later recalled her husband admitting that it had been a mistake to leave her and promising that they would never again be separated. In his memoirs, Harin offered a different window to his emotions at that time. 'I had outgrown the first madness of early love,' he wrote. 'What I felt for her was a mixed feeling of joy to see her look so young and fresh and beautiful and a sense of sadness that my sanctuary had fled. Every real artist has a need of solitude and sanctuary which are sacred to him.' Harin's life in London had been far from solitary before Kamaladevi arrived. Indeed, he was known for having an especially active social life. While his claims regarding his 'solitude' ring hollow, he was certainly right that Kamaladevi's arrival was a big change for him. For one thing, her presence complicated his ability to court other women. His serial womanizing would come to define—and eventually to destroy—their marriage.[29]

It is telling that so many of Harin's memories of Kamaladevi focus on her physical beauty. According to one account, Harin told the Irish poet W.B. Yeats that 'the gods envied him when he moved about with Kamala'. Yeats replied, 'Young man, it is not safe to trifle with the gods.' This exchange reveals little about the relationship between Harin and Kamaladevi—two dynamic young Indians living in the heart of the British Empire. What it does reveal is that Harin valued the way others viewed him and his young and beautiful wife.[30]

For her part, Kamaladevi refused to be bounded by the standard expectations of an Indian wife. She met with a family friend who taught at Newnham Hall, one of two women's institutions affiliated with the University of Cambridge. The older woman asked the younger if she wanted to become an academic. 'No, I want to be educated to serve society,' Kamaladevi replied. She was advised to study sociology, and decided to do so at Bedford College in London. Unfortunately, the principal of Bedford College, a 'very elderly lady', told Kamaladevi that she could not admit her. 'You realise you will have to work in the East End of London and you simply cannot go there in that weird garb of yours,' she explained. Kamaladevi refused to change her dress and convinced the principal to allow her to enrol regardless. She thrived at Bedford, where much of her education was carried out via fieldwork. In the afternoon, she travelled to a variety of 'institutions, educational and corrective for adults and children'. She spent many of her evenings 'in workers clubs or institutes'. Just being in London was itself an education—and not just in regard to British culture. She also came to develop a new appreciation for her own identity as an Indian. It is telling, for example, that it was in the UK that Kamaladevi decided to have her nose pierced—an act that furthered her visual connection with Indian culture, at least as perceived through British eyes.[31]

Being Indian in the UK must have been especially complicated in the midst of the first major Gandhian civil disobedience campaign: the non-cooperation movement. It was hard on both Kamaladevi and Harin to be so far away from the epic struggles roiling their native land. In 1922, they decided to return to India to participate in the social transformations that had been generated by that struggle. Rather than return directly, however, they opted to travel through Europe. In Berlin, they met with Harin's older brother, Virendranath, who was widely known as Chatto. 'Talking to him was highly educative,' Kamaladevi later recalled. 'For the first time I became widely aware of the Indian economic conditions and its place as a colony in the British Empire. The imperialism I now spied was not merely a vast British Army holding our country, but so many other vital forces which were subordinating the Indian people.'[32]

Harin's memories of the trip do not include any of the conversations he shared with Kamaladevi. Rather, he recalled Chatto telling him in the Berlin train station, 'I am glad, fellow, that you have married a pretty person, and brought her along with you. We need beautiful women from India to visit Europe . . . It will be one of the finest forms of propaganda for our country.' Written down decades later, this may not be an accurate representation of Chatto's response to Kamaladevi. What is telling is the fact that Harin chose to repeat it—and not to record any of the conversations Kamaladevi shared with his older brother.[33]

Kamaladevi's own memoir provides a richer account of her intellectual and cultural explorations. She learnt from a variety of radical expatriates besides Chatto. Hasan Shahid Suhrawardy, the poet and art critic from Bengal, took her to galleries in Berlin. Kamaladevi was moved by a performance of Chekhov's *The Cherry Orchard* that featured the playwright's wife in one of the lead roles. She also learnt from Agnes Smedley, a radical American journalist and writer who, according to Kamaladevi, 'braved wars and shattering turmoil because of her single-minded devotion to the downtrodden'. Smedley would become a dedicated communist, but it was her independent spirit that Kamaladevi most admired. In her memoir, she quoted Smedley declaring her independence with words that applied equally well to Kamaladevi herself: 'I could never place my mind and life unquestionably at the disposal of leaders, become a mere instrument in the hands of men who believed that they held the one and only key to truth.'[34]

When she returned to India, the government demanded that Kamaladevi surrender her passport. She refused, and the authorities cancelled it. 'It did not disturb me unduly,' she later recalled. 'It was part of a subject citizen's life.' The active phase of non-cooperation had ended, but Kamaladevi and Harin found another way to contribute to India's freedom. They founded a travelling theatre group that performed Harin's plays, scenes from Shakespeare and folk dramas on the lives of popular saints. Many of their performances aimed to advance the cause of national freedom. Theatre was 'a most effective medium for communication', Kamaladevi later recalled. 'Now at last I was going to taste the fulfilment of my ambition to act on a real stage. I felt almost shaken by a new passion. I threw myself wholeheartedly into the theatre vortex.'[35]

Other than Harin and Kamaladevi, the other members of the troupe all had day jobs. Their friend Govindraj Venkatachalam travelled with the group, acting and helping in other ways. He later wrote that 'their plays performed in Madras, Bombay, Poona, Bangalore, Colombo and other towns to packed houses . . . Once in Bombay we broke all records by filling Excelsior theatre to overflowing and sending away hundreds without seats.' On 15 September 1926, the *Times of India* reported a 'crowded audience' at the Excelsior. After praising Harin's performance, the reporter added, 'Harindranath was ably assisted by his wife, Kamala Devi, whose acting and expression are simple and natural.' The following

March, the couple again performed at the Excelsior. Kamaladevi played the role of a dancer in the court of the caliph. Her performance was, according to the *Times*, 'magnificent'.[36]

While the content of the plays often broached controversial topics, even more daring was the fact that women were on stage. In addition to Kamaladevi, who both acted and sang, the troupe included two women dancers, one of whom, Leila Sokhey, would go on to become a renowned performer with the stage name Madame Menaka. In colonial India in the early 1920s, women performers were associated with the sexual promiscuity attributed to 'low-class' and particularly low-caste women. By performing on stage, Kamaladevi challenged customs at the intersection of gender, class and caste—but there is no evidence that she used her platform to forge solidarities with lower-caste performers, many of whom were from 'untouchable' communities now commonly identified with the term 'Dalit'. While she opposed untouchability throughout her life, Kamaladevi's relationship with Dalit women—and anti-caste movements more broadly—would remain limited.[37]

Some of Kamaladevi's transgressive acts were deemed rare for a woman of any caste or class. Even public speaking was a controversial feat in some conservative quarters. Although she rejected such constraints, Kamaladevi was not always a confident speaker. She would later credit V.S. Srinivasa Sastri, a scholar and liberal politician who was one of India's most celebrated orators, with helping her overcome her fears. A family friend, Sastri recruited Kamaladevi to speak with him in Mangalore soon after she had returned from the UK. She felt 'weak with fright' and stood up with 'trembling feet' but she managed to speak despite her fears. Acting helped her to overcome those fears. It also brought her closer to her husband. Their time on the stage is one of the few points in her memoir where we learn of her marriage: 'When poet-musician Harindranath and I teamed up it was for sharing of dreams and ambitions to devote ourselves to create a new theatre in India, for much of the existing theatre had degenerated even since my girlhood days.' It was the high point of their relationship.[38]

On 19 May 1923, Kamaladevi gave birth to a son, Ramakrishna. It is telling that the young couple, neither of whom would be known for traditional forms of religious devotion, chose to name their son after the Bengali mystic Ramakrishna Paramahamsa. Kamaladevi later credited her mother with inspiring her to choose that name. During Kamaladevi's pregnancy, her mother read her selections from ancient Hindu texts. Throughout her life, Kamaladevi rarely discussed her own faith, but a certain kind of devotion remained a vital—if largely private—facet of her approach to her work and her life. There is a parallel between her relationship to her faith and her relationship to her son. Both are barely mentioned in her memoirs and rarely make appearances in the official records of her life. Yet both were near the core of her identity.[39]

On the day Rama was born, Harin was in a foul mood. His temper was unpredictable. Alcohol often made it worse but even sober he could become suddenly angry over the smallest of things. A large contingent of his siblings had come to Mangalore and everyone was crowded under one roof. Kamaladevi's relations with the Chattopadhyays remained rocky. 'Compared to them,' she later recalled, 'I had come from a small village.' The contrast bred insecurity. 'I always felt my shortcomings in front of those people,' she explained. Even if Harin's family had been less challenging, it would have been difficult to all be together waiting for the child to arrive. The atmosphere was oppressive, so Kamaladevi decided to take a stroll. The May sun was hot and after walking for a long time Kamaladevi felt labour starting. She sat down on the side of the road. 'I was so disturbed and drowsy and my mind was torn between thousands of worries,' she later recalled. 'Was it my big mistake to bring this new innocent creature to earth?' She worried about the child, about how he would cope with the unpredictability of life—and of his father.[40]

The new mother quickly came to love her son, and that love helped to assuage Harin's failings as a partner. 'As the child started growing,' Kamaladevi recalled, 'I felt that he was filling the gap of heavy emptiness for me. God has now given me a person who will be my support, my companion and will fill my loneliness with the light of his innate affection.' Kamaladevi yearned to share all of her life with young Rama.

'Like a six year old girl,' she later admitted, 'I started waiting for him to grow up, so that we two become friends, play with each other and he becomes a participant in every activity of my life.' It was not easy to make Rama 'a participant in every activity' in her life. It was not easy to balance motherhood with acting or travelling. Kamaladevi's mother was able to help care for the child. As he grew older, little Rama often accompanied his parents on their many travels and even acted on stage with them. Still, fostering a healthy family life was a challenge, especially given Harin's unpredictable temper. 'I used to get very scared when the situation in the house unexpectedly deteriorated,' she later recalled of Harin's mood swings. 'I could not sleep at night. The fear that all this would have an impact on the child's future used to haunt me.'[41]

It did not help that several of Harin's siblings had strong opinions about how to raise a child. Of course, having extra hands can be useful when a child is born, but the Chattopadhyay family was often demanding and difficult. They tended to take Harin's side in any dispute, even when it became increasingly obvious that the birth of the child would not change Harin's serial womanizing. Soon after Rama was born, Harin began an affair with his son's nanny, a teenager named Seetha. When Kamaladevi learnt of the affair, Harin treated it as if it were a minor indiscretion.[42]

In a pattern that would be repeated, Kamaladevi responded to the tumult in her personal life by redoubling her commitment to her social and political work. In 1924, she was recruited by Dr Narayan Subbarao Hardikar to join a new organization originally called the Hindustani Seva Mandal (Indian Service Body) and later known as the Hindustani Seva Dal (Indian Service League). Hardikar had spent years in the United States organizing the expatriate community and cultivating American support for India's freedom. He envisioned the Seva Dal as a kind of nonviolent army. Jawaharlal Nehru served as the first honorary president of the dal, but its actual leadership fell to Hardikar and to Umabai Kundapur, a social reformer who ran the women's wing of the dal. Like Kamaladevi, Kundapur was from Mangalore and had been widowed. The two women also shared a love for theatre (Kundapur had written and produced a play). Together, Hardikar and Kundapur personally recruited Kamaladevi to the cause. They began by asking her to help organize the volunteers at the next annual gathering of the Congress, which was to be held in Belgaum in December 1924.[43]

A year earlier, Kamaladevi had played a similar role at the Congress meeting in Kakinada, a seaside town in present-day Andhra Pradesh, where she captained a 'lady volunteer corps'. 'I had no idea what being a volunteer meant,' she later wrote. 'I drew a romantic picture of soldiers of freedom marching with banners.' Instead, she found that many of her responsibilities were mundane, if important. Along with other volunteers, she cleaned the grounds, staffed entrances and exits, and completed a variety of small tasks that made the gathering possible. Her limited role at the conference was shaped by her gender. The Indian National Congress was open to women members from its founding. Annie Besant had served as its president in 1917 and Sarojini Naidu would be elected to that role in 1925. But the membership and leadership were both overwhelmingly male. Women who attended were often asked to perform service roles that sidelined them from the main work of the conference. There is no evidence that Kamaladevi was disappointed by the limitations of her role. She was proud to have been of service. In the words of one of her biographers, Jamila Brijbhushan, 'The fact that her political life began with a broom and a basket has always been a matter of pride to her.' When Hardikar and Kundapur asked her to volunteer again, this time at Belgaum, Kamaladevi agreed with enthusiasm.[44]

A hilly town, perched in the foothills of the Western Ghats, Belgaum is roughly halfway between Mangalore and Bombay. In December 1924, Kamaladevi made the journey to Belgaum to help organize the volunteers and to ensure that the conference, the only one in which Gandhi would preside, went smoothly. Kamaladevi's work with the Seva Dal was, in her words, 'a far cry from the art and theatre world'. She missed the creativity and energy of the stage. 'But I drew a different nourishment from the volunteer's career,' she added. 'It filled me with a new sense of robustness, and earthy freshness, an opening out into wider worlds, almost obliterating my little self.' That 'almost' matters. In the 1920s, Kamaladevi would develop a new level of self-confidence, even as she threw herself into the struggle for India's freedom. Self and society were inseparable, she came to believe, but the freedom of the individual should not be subsumed within visions of collective liberation. After all, freedom did not just mean independence from British rule but also liberation from sexism, casteism and other forms of inequity and discrimination.[45]

As a young woman, Kamaladevi had already bucked the conventions of widowhood, pursued her own education, and remarried, choosing for herself a man and a marriage that crossed the lines of region, language and caste. She had travelled across Europe, met with radical thinkers and activists, and returned home to help organize a mass movement. She had used all of her talents to contribute to that movement, defying gender norms yet again by singing and acting on the stage and choosing to balance her career with the responsibilities of motherhood. All of these rebellious acts were expressions of her desire to change her country and the world, but they were also efforts at self-realization. The freedom she sought was for her country but also for herself.

2

Bridging Revolutions

IN THE AUTUMN OF 1926, KAMALADEVI GAVE A SPEECH IN HER hometown of Mangalore. Before an audience of over 2,000 people, she offered an idyllic portrait of gender equity in ancient India and declared, 'Never in the history of any country, at any time, has woman been so honoured as she has been in this country.' Her use of 'has been' suggested that things were not as rosy as they once were. By invoking a utopian antiquity, Kamaladevi deployed a common rhetorical strategy among Indian nationalists, a strategy that she would return to repeatedly in the years ahead—to contrast the past with the present in order to inspire new ideas for the future. The challenge was to do so in a way that did not appear too critical of the men who made up the majority of her audience. This was, after all, a campaign speech. Kamaladevi was attempting to become the first woman to be elected to a provincial legislature in British India. As she knew well, the electorate was overwhelmingly male.[1]

Through her campaign, Kamaladevi contributed to a long struggle to empower women as voters and as elected officials. In India, suffrage advocates had to fight on multiple fronts—to enfranchise Indians within a colonial system designed to maintain power in the hands of the British; and to enfranchise women, the poor and other marginalized communities that were excluded even when the franchise was gradually extended to property-owning Indian men. In 1908, the *Indian Ladies Magazine* declared that 'the educated men are so far away from getting the votes for themselves that the idea that women in India could ever imagine any such power being lodged in their hands is but the vainest of dreams'. Yet even then some women voted in certain municipal elections, and many were working to extend the right to vote. In 1920, Madras became the first province to grant suffrage to women. Bombay Province followed the next year and, over the course of the decade, several other provincial councils extended suffrage to affluent, property-holding women. Still, only a tiny fraction of women—less than 1 per cent—were eligible to vote. If Kamaladevi was to win the election, she would need to convince men to vote for her.[2]

While idealizing ancient India and avoiding direct attacks on patriarchy in modern India, Kamaladevi did not hesitate to draw attention to her gender. 'I stand for no party or community,' she told her audience in Mangalore. 'I stand as a representative of women.' She encouraged women to 'come forward and share the responsibilities equally with men'. Rather than a matter of claiming rights, this was a question of duty—the duty of women to help build a better society. 'All over the world,' Kamaladevi told her audience, 'women are now taking a keen and an active part in all departments of life.' Linking her campaign to this global trend, she appealed to the patriotic sentiments of her audience. 'If women in other countries have proved competent enough to handle these problems,' she declared, 'I do not think an Indian woman will prove an exception.'[3]

Although she framed her campaign as a call to duty, Kamaladevi understood that she was pushing the boundaries of what women were seen as capable of doing. Her campaign was about women's rights—the right to vote, the right to run for elected office, the right that all Indians had to serve their nation. As she would throughout her life, Kamaladevi linked her advocacy on behalf of women to an inclusive Indian nationalism. That was especially important—and especially difficult—given that the 'woman question' had long been used to defend British imperialism. Practices like sati—the burning of a widow on her husband's funeral pyre—had allowed colonial officials to suggest that Indian society was too barbaric for self-rule. Even British suffragists paired feminism with imperialism by portraying Indian women, in the words of historian Antoinette Burton, 'as the victims of heathen religious practice and as powerless in their own society'. In 1927, one year after Kamaladevi ran for office, American journalist Katherine Mayo published a bestselling book called *Mother India,* in which she argued that colonization was necessary to save 'backward' peoples. Mayo focused much of her argument on the oppression of Indian women. Kamaladevi knew that as a child widow and as a champion of women's rights her own story could be distorted by imperialists like Mayo. In rejecting the idea that Western do-gooders would save Indian women, Kamaladevi also rejected the appropriation of her own life narrative. She remained committed to women's struggles and to the nationalist cause.[4]

In her election speech, Kamaladevi traced her interest in politics to the influence of Gandhi. She explained that she and Harin were in England during the non-cooperation movement. 'Our hearts throbbed to the cries of the great nation,' she declared. 'Gandhi's message of love thrilled us, and we felt that we should not be led away by the glamor of foreign degrees.' Thus, she positioned herself and her husband as patriots willing to sacrifice their own educational opportunities in order to serve the nation. She recounted a conversation at the Belgaum Congress in which she and Harin had told Gandhi of their plans for a travelling theatre aimed at inspiring patriotic service. 'He gladly assented to our plans and with his blessings we started upon our work,' she stated. 'We have been trying to wake up the political consciousness of the country through poetry, through music and through drama. It was just a month ago that we met Mahatma Gandhi in Bombay and he said: "Though I am pressed with heavy work, I have found time to watch with pleasure your progress. Though I cannot be with you in person, let me admire you from a distance. When you have a little leisure come to my Ashram and show my boys the beauties of your art."' By linking herself and her campaign to Gandhi, Kamaladevi attempted to win votes from those committed to Gandhi's cause—a challenge given the fact that it was her opponent who was running under the aegis of the Indian National Congress.[5]

Her opponent's status as the Congress candidate—and as a popular incumbent—was only one of the obstacles facing her campaign. At the start of the campaign, Kamaladevi was not even a registered voter. The franchise was based on property ownership and she did not have any property of her own. As she later recalled, 'A long term lease of some property was hurriedly arranged to enable me to pay the tax on property and be entitled to vote.' In the face of long odds, Kamaladevi attracted a band of volunteers who referred to themselves as the 'Knights of the Blue Lotus', a reference to the fact that Kamala means 'lotus' in many Indian languages. Harin travelled from village to village singing patriotic songs and encouraging audiences to support his wife. Margaret Cousins also canvassed for Kamaladevi and drafted an election manifesto in which she declared that Kamaladevi's election would 'publish to the World the honour in which India holds her womanhood, and be a refutation of the criticisms so often levelled at India that she holds her women in contempt'. The greatest strength of the campaign was Kamaladevi herself. Many who heard her speak in those years commented on her powerful oratory. One observer declared, 'I have heard her keep a large audience—men, women, Asians and Europeans—spellbound for the great part of an hour.' Much had changed since she had been 'weak with fright' at the idea of speaking in public.[6]

Kamaladevi lost the election, but by a small margin—only a few hundred votes. Her supporters refused to abandon hope—not just for Kamaladevi the candidate but also for the cause of women's participation in politics. On 21 November 1926, the Hindu Social Reform League of Madras passed a resolution requesting that the government nominate 'a few ladies' to the Madras Legislative Council, one of whom was Kamaladevi. The resolution was sent to the governor of Madras and was also published in the *Indian Social Reformer*. In the end, Kamaladevi was not nominated, but other women were. As Margaret Cousins noted, Kamaladevi helped establish a 'custom' of women candidates that would lead to 'the appointment of women Ministers and Ambassadors' and to women gaining office through the ballot box. Her campaign was seen as trailblazing outside of India as well. From London, the *International Woman Suffrage News* praised Kamaladevi as 'a worthy representative of the new era of womanhood—young, talented, travelled, full of patriotic, artistic, feminist ideals'. Hers was a 'heroic defeat' and 'a matter of pride to all who support the progress of women'.[7]

Her campaign also opened doors for Kamaladevi herself. In 1927, one year after losing the election, she was invited to the first All India Women's Conference on Educational Reform. The gathering, held in Poona, was the brainchild of Margaret Cousins, who had written to prominent women across the nation suggesting that they gather to draft 'an authoritative and representative memorandum by women on educational reforms'. At the start of the gathering, Sarojini Naidu welcomed the delegates by celebrating their diversity:

> Literally from the Himalayas to Cape Comorin, from the Indus to the Brahmaputra they came, the gifted representatives of Indian womanhood of all ranks, all races, all creeds, old women, young women, women signally successful in all departments of public life—in literature, art, science, education, law, medicine, philanthropy, social service, administration, brave women, proud women, dedicated to the regeneration of India, bound by an indivisible bond of womanhood.[8]

Naidu's hyperbole obscured the class homogeneity of the women, most of whom came from elite, educated backgrounds. Yet while the diversity of delegates had its limitations, Naidu had good reason to celebrate the ways in which the gathering was representative of the diversity of India. The historian Mrinalini Sinha has argued that 'the new gender identity of Indian women' that emerged in the interwar period did so 'not in opposition to men but in opposition to the collective identity of communities, defined by religion, caste, ethnicity, and so on, which had formed the typical building block of colonial Indian society'. The challenge—for the AIWC and for Kamaladevi in particular—was how to craft such an inclusive identity without obscuring the deep inequities within Indian society, inequities that were reproduced within the AIWC itself.[9]

The AIWC would go on to become the most influential women's organization in pre-Independence India. Even at the first AIWC gathering there were already signs that the group's ambit would expand beyond education. Delegates discussed how to improve primary education for girls and urged that scholarships be given to women interested in studying 'law, medicine, social science and fine arts'. As the delegates quickly realized, expanding education for girls and women required grappling with a range of other challenges, including controversial topics such as child marriage and the age of consent.[10]

The most decisive step towards expanding the AIWC was the decision to select Kamaladevi as its first secretary. Near the conclusion of the conference, Sarojini Naidu told Kamaladevi that she had been selected for that vital role. 'I became panicky and quickly declined,' Kamaladevi recalled. Naidu told her, 'Don't be silly now. Did you not want to be a social worker, and here when your services are sought, you refuse. You better accept it.' Kamaladevi's relationship with Naidu, her sister-in-law, would become increasingly fraught as a result of Harin's behaviour and the different temperaments and political commitments of the two women—arguably the two most prominent women nationalists in the decades before Independence. Those tensions should not obscure the fact that Naidu played a vital role in shaping Kamaladevi's early career. So did Harin himself. When Kamaladevi asked for his advice, Harin encouraged her to accept the position of AIWC secretary. At the urging of Harin and Naidu, Kamaladevi took on that important responsibility. Publicly celebrating Kamaladevi's new role, Naidu praised her sister-in-law for her historic electoral campaign. 'Her spectacular performance blazed a new trail for Indian womanhood,' Naidu declared. Kamaladevi may have lost the election but 'the loss of one State now means the gain of the entire country'.[11]

Even after she accepted the position, Kamaladevi remained nervous about 'disgracing myself before these grand women'. It was Margaret Cousins who reassured her. Kamaladevi came to refer to Cousins as her spiritual mother. The historian Barbara Ramusack has chronicled the 'maternal imperialism' that shaped the influence of older European women such as Cousins and Annie Besant. Yet for Kamaladevi the mother–daughter nature of her relationship with Cousins felt natural, perhaps because her relationship with her own mother remained fraught.[12]

There was a degree of 'maternal imperialism' built into the relationship between the AIWC membership—nearly all of whom were affluent elites—and the vast mass of Indian women for whom they claimed to speak. Kamaladevi strove to bridge that divide. As AIWC secretary, she travelled across the country, in her words, 'carrying on continuous propaganda among the public for social and legal changes to give women their rights'. To prepare for her work, Kamaladevi learnt shorthand and typing and began her tradition of taking her typewriter everywhere. 'Whether it was in a train or a waiting room,' she later recalled, 'I could always manage to do my own work.' While her speeches attracted large audiences, much of her contribution to the AIWC involved the more mundane but equally important organizational work needed to turn what began as a one-time gathering of women into 'a live and vibrating body which would become dynamic enough to revolutionalise the scene'. To 'revolutionalise the scene' meant connecting the women's cause to other struggles. As she later wrote, 'Obviously women were not the only victims of social and economic disabilities and discriminations, others were equally oppressed socially, and depressed economically. It was dimly growing on me that the women's struggle had therefore to be an indivisible part of the larger political, social and economic struggle.'[13]

Kamaladevi rejected the label 'feminist'. In this she was not alone. Sarojini Naidu famously declared, 'I am not a feminist', and many Indian women would similarly distance themselves from a label seen as essentially Western. As Ellen Carol DuBois has pointed out, Kamaladevi 'consistently advocated virtually everything with which the term "feminism" is currently associated: independent women's organizations, equal political rights, equal pay for equal work, reform in marriage, divorce and inheritance laws, even birth control and "sex freedom"'. Yet the term 'feminist' would remain anathema to her. 'Like many non-western women activists, in her time and ours,' DuBois explained, 'she insisted that feminism was a western tradition, inappropriate to the conditions and challenges of the women of India and Asia more broadly.'[14]

To build a women's movement that was 'an indivisible part of the larger political, social and economic struggle' required collaborating with men; it also required creatively pushing the boundaries of what was expected of women. While travelling for the AIWC, Kamaladevi often presented short dramatic performances in the style that she and Harin had pioneered. As she later recalled, such performances 'provided a channel for the creative elements within me, an outlet for my surging emotions'. They also gave her a creative platform of her own. With Harin, she had always performed supporting roles. Now, she had the stage to herself. She was free, in her words, to 'do my work in my own way'.[15]

Within days of Kamaladevi joining the AIWC, Harin left on a three-year journey to the UK and the US. There is no evidence that Kamaladevi missed him. She must have been grateful to not have to worry about his unpredictable moods and the impact of those moods on Rama. She had long been a single parent. Sometimes, she would take little Rama on her journeys, but it is unclear how often Rama travelled with her. Girijabai often took care of him while Kamaladevi was travelling or otherwise busy. Kamaladevi also relied on the support of the Seva Sadan, a women's organization in Poona, Maharashtra, that she later described as 'a rock on which you could rest'. The women who ran the Seva Sadan became like an extended family. 'If I had any problems,' Kamaladevi explained, 'they were able to help me; they were very sympathetic and experienced.' Kamaladevi made Poona her home base for much of 1928 and 1929, and she enrolled Rama in a school there. Finding a way to work and to travel while raising a child, she demonstrated the possibility—if also the challenges—of the increased freedom she hoped to achieve for all women.[16]

~

Aware that most poor women had no choice but to work within and outside of the home, Kamaladevi became increasingly committed to fighting poverty and class inequity as well as sexism and colonial rule. Her own class and caste status empowered her activism while remaining a barrier between her and the majority of Indian women. Kamaladevi could not escape the tension between the universality of certain gender norms and the divisive inequities of class and caste. Consider her love for that traditional emblem of Indian womanhood—the sari.

The journalist J.N. Sahni met Kamaladevi in 1928 and later remembered her as a 'charming, refined young woman artistically dressed in a green silk sari, flat chappals and a champagne rose becomingly fixed in her hair'. Throughout her life, Kamaladevi would maintain her love for colourful saris, for wearing flowers in her hair, and for elaborate but inexpensive jewellery. Sundari Shridharani, the director of the Triveni Kala Sangam in Delhi, recalled the first time she heard Kamaladevi speak in Karachi in the early 1930s: 'She seemed to me the optimum of the typical Indian beauty. She wore a typical Maharashtrian saree, pearl tops and a big bindi.' Kamaladevi saw no hypocrisy in fighting inequity while collecting an expansive wardrobe; neither did she see a contradiction in embracing traditional women's fashion while challenging the ways tradition limited women. Later in life, she recognized that others might find it odd that she rejected 'those restrictions and sentiments of the society that women should not do this, should not do that', while herself embracing 'a feeling of pure femininity' and the sartorial adornments associated with femininity. Many observers recognized that Kamaladevi rejected the stereotypes associated with her taste in clothes and jewellery. As Sahni recalled just after describing Kamaladevi in her green silk sari, 'This was no butterfly but a dynamite of emotions, full of lightning and thunder who spoke of the degradation to which men had compelled women in India.' Shridharani similarly remembered the power of Kamaladevi's oratory. 'The huge audience listened to her spellbound,' she recalled, 'and my own reaction was that whatever happened I must join the movement.'[17]

In 1927, Kamaladevi was asked to organize a new volunteer corps for the upcoming Indian National Congress session. She agreed and, in addition, decided to become a member of the Congress. In December, she attended the annual meeting of the Congress and of the Indian Social Conference in Madras. Founded in 1887, the Social Conference gathered annually as a kind of subgroup of the Congress, to focus on problems within Indian society such as untouchability and child marriage. Members of the Social Conference had long struggled to combat such 'backward' practices without providing ammunition to colonial officials or imperialists like Katherine Mayo. Kamaladevi was elected one of the national secretaries of the Social Conference and, the following year, in December 1928, she was selected to the All India Congress Committee.[18]

While deepening her ties to nationalist politics and to the Congress, in particular, Kamaladevi also bridged women's struggles with the fight against economic inequality. In Madras, she joined with Margaret Cousins to fight for three months of guaranteed maternity leave. Despite fierce resistance from employers, the campaign succeeded. Further south, in Madurai, Kamaladevi gave speeches and offered organizational support to unionized women workers in textile factories. When the owners declared that the union had to be dissolved, some 3,000 women workers held firm and maintained the union. Kamaladevi brought her commitment to unions back to her home region. According to one biographer, Kamaladevi 'was the first organiser of trade unions in Mangalore district and launched a number of unions of both men and women, that of transport workers being the largest'. She also helped organize women labourers in cashew-processing plants near Mangalore. Under Kamaladevi's leadership, the AIWC began to investigate the conditions facing women workers, particularly in mining and agriculture. Kamaladevi led the investigation in Bengal and Assam, where women worked long hours on tea plantations. After gathering data, the AIWC drafted legislation aimed at improving work conditions for women and lobbied to have such legislation passed.[19]

There was a tension between Kamaladevi's union activism and her work with the AIWC, many of whose members were elite women not inclined to support union organizing. A similar tension existed between her work with the AIWC and her anticolonial activities. The leaders of the AIWC were aware, in the words of the historian Geraldine Forbes, that 'their work was taking them in two directions: one that would benefit women specifically and one aimed at helping the entire nation'. Those two directions sometimes conflicted. As Forbes explained, 'Their interest in women's status in law propelled them towards collaboration with British officials and members of the legislature while the Gandhian emphasis on village uplift and untouchables involved work at the grassroots level as well as a totally different interpretation of the dynamics of social change.'[20]

These tensions came to a head in 1928 when a parliamentary commission, led by Sir John Simon, arrived in India to prepare recommendations concerning the future of India's government. The commission did not include a single Indian member, and many organizations—including the Congress and the Muslim League—boycotted the commission and launched protests. Young people were at the forefront of the protests and Kamaladevi participated in a planning meeting in Delhi to help organize the 'Simon go back' movement. She had come to Delhi to serve as the general secretary of the AIWC at their annual conference, a comparatively staid affair that Lady Irwin, the wife of the viceroy, was to inaugurate. As Kamaladevi later wrote, 'On the morning of the opening we were informed that the Vicerine could not possibly patronize an organization whose General Secretary was participating in activities intended to embarrass the Government.' Margaret Cousins tried to convince the vicerine's advisers that the AIWC was not involved in the protests. If Kamaladevi participated in the protests, it would be as an individual rather than as a representative of the AIWC. The argument worked, and the vicerine agreed to open the conference. Kamaladevi joined other AIWC leaders in sharing lunch with the vicerine, who was surprised that a young Indian radical would be willing to eat with her. This outcome could be interpreted as revealing the limitations of the AIWC. Why did the organization fail to take a stand against the Simon Commission? Yet Kamaladevi recalled these events as an example of courage and independence. She attended that protest meeting regardless of her position with the AIWC. She recalled Cousins telling her, 'Don't let anyone muscle or bully you, my dear. We stand for freedom all through.'[21]

In the second week of February 1928, some 200 women gathered in Delhi for the second AIWC gathering. In keeping with the celebration of diversity that Sarojini Naidu had offered the previous year, delegates came from as far apart as the northwest provinces, Trivandrum in the south, and Calcutta in the east. Yet again, they represented multiple religious identities: Hindu, Muslim, Parsi, Christian. They had been selected as delegates via local elections that involved more than 15,000 women. According to Margaret Cousins, the conference proved to be a 'brilliant success' but it remained unclear what impact the AIWC would have on the lives and futures of most Indian women.[22]

One of the chief efforts of the AIWC was to raise the minimum age at which girls and boys were allowed to marry. That goal had been discussed at the first meeting of the AIWC. Since then, a legislator and former judge, Har Bilas Sarda, had introduced a bill to raise the age of marriage. A separate bill, introduced by Sir Hari Singh Gour, aimed to raise the age of sexual consent. Kamaladevi had underscored the need for such legislation when, in September 1927, she published an article in *The Hindu* decrying the case of a young girl who was physically abused by her husband because she refused his sexual advances. The girl went to the authorities but, as Kamaladevi explained, 'the law could not give her redress since she could not prove the case against the husband as there were no visible marks upon the body, nor could she get any witnesses on her side since the incidents took place in the husband's house and none of his party would, of course, bear testimony against him'. 'These are not isolated cases,' Kamaladevi wrote. That so few became publicly known was a result of the fact that 'such atrocities on the part of the husbands are hushed up even by the parents of the girls for fear of public opinion'.[23]

During the 1928 AIWC gathering, 176 delegates visited the Legislative Assembly, packing the visitors' gallery. The agenda for that day included a discussion of Gour's Age of Consent bill. According to Margaret Cousins, 'The mover's fine speech and the Government's open opposition to the Bill made a vivid impression on the mind of every delegate. The statement that a Committee might be formed by Government to investigate the question of child marriage and age of consent satisfied no woman present. Each came out after the debate burning to press women's views directly on those responsible and powerful in the Legislatures.'[24]

Within twenty-four hours, a delegation of AIWC members led by the Rani of Mandi lobbied the viceroy and the leadership of the most prominent political parties. The memorial prepared by the delegation to the viceroy declared, 'Until the abolition of child marriage is brought about by Legislative action India cannot fit herself to take her place in the comity of civilized nations.' Kamaladevi took a similar message to the Congress powerbroker, Motilal Nehru. In the years ahead, Kamaladevi would develop a close relationship with Motilal's son, Jawaharlal, who would become one of the most important figures in Kamaladevi's life. While Jawaharlal was known as a progressive, Motilal was one of the leaders of the Congress establishment. Kamaladevi was not intimidated. She asked the elder Nehru whether he would support the Sarda bill. He responded testily with his own question: 'Are you trying to instruct me and my colleagues how to vote, you chit of a girl?' Kamaladevi refused to back down. 'If your objection is to my age,' she replied, 'I will bring a batch of old women to seek your vote!' Her courage impressed the elder Nehru. 'Far from causing a breach,' she later wrote, 'the incident led to a softening of his encounters with me.'[25]

Kamaladevi spearheaded the AIWC's campaign in support of the Sarda and Gour bills. On 15 September 1928, the *Times of India* reported that she was in Simla giving evidence before the Age of Consent Committee. She argued that legal changes would need to be paired with educational efforts focused on 'popularising the advantages of the law'. Kamaladevi asserted that 'the right of complaint should rest with the girl, her parents, social reform associations and societies and village panchayats; but on no account with the police'. The *Times* left unclear why Kamaladevi was opposed to the police initiating a complaint, but it seems likely that she was concerned about the overreach of the colonial government. As the scholar Philippa Levine has argued, most age of consent laws underscored 'women's apparent incapacity to choose or reject sexual advances without the help of the state'. Such laws could be seen as depriving women of agency. For Kamaladevi and her colleagues in the AIWC, however, protecting girls from unwanted sexual encounters involved empowering young women, if also their parents, social workers, and—perhaps regrettably—the colonial state.[26]

In November 1928, the *Servant of India* published Kamaladevi's review of a book on coeducation. She praised the book for defending 'the principle that boys and girls should be educated on an equal footing and given sufficient scope for free intercourse and association with each other'. The notion that boys and girls should receive an equal education was seen as radical within more conservative factions of Indian society, and the idea that girls and boys would attend school together was even more controversial. Kamaladevi softened the radicalism of her statement by adding that the book 'does not countenance the foolish ambition of eliminating sex-differences'. This was more than an effort to blunt conservative opposition. She was, after all, writing in a leading journal of progressive reformers. Her desire to advance a radical women's movement without undermining 'sex-differences' would remain an important element of her approach to social reform.[27]

With time, Kamaladevi would come to prioritize equality across gender lines above the potential benefits of sex-specific protections. Her shifting views were bound up with her increasing participation in a range of causes that went beyond the aegis of 'women's struggles.' On 9 December 1928, she attended the Bihar Provincial Political Conference in Patna. Later that month, she also participated in the All India Trade Union Congress (AITUC) held at Jharia, Bihar. She was invited by Dewan Chamanlal, a young assembly member, who told her, 'Women are not the only sections of society exploited. It is worse in industrial establishments, and there are lots of women among the workers.' The president of the AITUC that year was a young Congress member with socialist leanings—Jawaharlal Nehru.[28]

From Bihar, Kamaladevi travelled to Calcutta, where she spoke on 'the rights of women' at a meeting of the Bengal Social Reform League. 'We have to bring about a very strong revolutionary change in our social life,' she told the audience. 'If you want social reform it is to begin in the homes.' She stressed that women's advancement should not be understood only in regards to ending 'child marriage or purdah'. More fundamental change was necessary. 'We have got to change the whole mental attitude towards women,' she declared. 'If we can do that fundamentally then alone can we achieve any sort of real social reform.'[29]

While Kamaladevi pushed male social reformers to confront sexism, she also challenged her colleagues in the AIWC to broaden their conception of the women's movement. From Calcutta, she returned to Patna for the third session of the AIWC, where she moved a proposal to expand the focus of the organization to include a broader commitment to social welfare. In the words of a report on the gathering, Kamaladevi 'expressed a hope that their movement would soon revolutionize the life of the society'. Her resolution sparked 'a very animated discussion', and some conservative delegates moved an amendment 'suggesting that the conference should restrict its activities only to educational matters'. Aware of the importance of organizational unity, Kamaladevi helped to broker a compromise. The AIWC created two sections: one focused on education and the other on social work.[30]

In her address to the delegates, Kamaladevi connected the unity of the AIWC to the unity of India. She told the delegates, as the *Times of India* reported, that 'the most important work achieved by the conference . . . was that it had established for the first time a real all India women's movement so as to include women of all stages of progress'. That quote, which reeks of paternalism, might not have been Kamaladevi's actual words. In any case, the sentiment was more aspirational than factual. The AIWC remained an elite organization. As the debate over Kamaladevi's resolution made clear, many delegates preferred not to extend its activities, lest the organization be pulled into the increasingly radical movement for independence—precisely, of course, what Kamaladevi hoped would occur.[31]

~

In the spring of 1929, Kamaladevi witnessed one of the most dramatic events in the history of the freedom struggle—an event that revealed both the extent and the boundaries of her radical politics. She was living in Delhi, lobbying legislators on behalf of the AIWC. The assembly Speaker, Vithalbhai Patel, had granted her office space, and she often went into the gallery of the assembly to observe the proceedings. One day, while she sat in the gallery, a loud bang shook the floor and smoke filled the room. Everyone rushed to the exits, where Kamaladevi was stopped by security and questioned before eventually being released. Later, it became known that bombs had been thrown by two anticolonial revolutionaries, Batukeshwar Dutt and Bhagat Singh. Kamaladevi had strong sympathies for Dutt and Singh's politics, and her memories of that particular incident are largely positive. Still, it is telling that she was in Parliament that day as a lobbyist and not as a bomb-throwing radical.[32]

It was as a nonviolent radical that Kamaladevi sailed for Europe in the summer of 1929. Her understanding of the Indian freedom struggle had been shaped by her time abroad in the early 1920s, and this trip would prove equally impactful. In June, she was in Berlin attending a gathering of the International Alliance of Women for Suffrage and Equal Citizenship. The newspaper of the International Alliance, the *International Woman Suffrage News*, had reported on Kamaladevi's trip in advance, telling its readers that 'India will be well represented wherever this her worthy daughter goes'. Founded in 1904 by leading American and European suffragists, the alliance had grown to become a massive organization and the gathering in Berlin included over 1,000 delegates from some forty-five countries. Despite such numbers, Egypt and India were the only non-Western nations to have their own representation. 'Other colonial countries were represented by their *rulers* and not the country's nationals,' Kamaladevi later explained. Egypt's delegation was led by the pioneering feminist Huda Shaarawi, who would become a longtime friend and colleague of Kamaladevi's. India's delegation was led by Ṣarojini Naidu, who gave a powerful speech that, in Kamaladevi's words, inspired 'mighty pride' in 'we who seemed to be otherwise rather statusless'.[33]

Their 'statusless' condition was made evident by the fact that the Indian delegates did not have a national flag representing them at the gathering. Kamaladevi joined her fellow women in rectifying that injustice. 'The Indian delegates pulled out their saris,' she recalled, 'cut up pieces to form the colours of the Indian National Congress flag, i.e. red, green and white. No one grudged tearing up their fineries. In fact, we felt free and liberated at the gala opening function watching our flag fluttering proudly amidst others.' The Indian delegation championed a resolution in support of increasing the minimum age of marriage, a resolution that the British delegation opposed. The result, according to Kamaladevi, was that 'India was thus able to not only create a favourable impression but also remove to some extent the false impression abroad that India is too orthodox and uneducated to favour progressive ideas'.[34]

Kamaladevi's time at the conference should not be framed in terms of a narrow Indian nationalism. For one thing, the Indian delegation included Dorothy Jinarajadasa, the British-born feminist and theosophist who had become a leading figure within the Indian women's movement. Moreover, the conference was an opportunity for Kamaladevi to forge ties with several American women with whom she would have lasting relationships. Perhaps the most significant of these relationships for Kamaladevi was her friendship with Molly Ray Carroll, a labour law advocate who worked for the American Department of Labor. Carroll would remain a supporter and friend in the years ahead. At Carroll's invitation, Kamaladevi travelled to Prague to attend a gathering of the Women's International League for Peace and Freedom, a pacifist organization that had grown out of opposition to the First World War. At the gathering, Kamaladevi met with the American social worker Jane Addams, with whom she conversed about Gandhi and nonviolent social change. Many Western feminists used an 'imperialist rhetoric', in the words of historian Leila Rupp, that 'assumed that Western women needed to take care of indigenous women in the colonized countries'. But not all Western women advanced such an imperialistic feminism, and Kamaladevi enjoyed deep and lasting relationships with several British and American women.[35]

In addition to forging ties within the international women's movement, Kamaladevi used her time in Europe to explore her interest in education. She travelled to Geneva for a gathering of the World Federation of Teachers and then to Copenhagen for a different educational conference hosted by the New Education Fellowship, an organization dedicated to advancing progressive education. Kamaladevi's philosophy of education fit well with the student-driven approach popular with many of the participants in both conferences. A few years later, she was quoted saying that 'education is no mere "teaching" but a gradual unfoldment of the child leading to the establishment of its relationship with the world harmoniously'. The Indian delegation to the Copenhagen conference was led by a celebrated educator and social reformer from Poona named Dhondo Keshav Karve. A leading Copenhagen newspaper carried a front-page photo of Karve with Kamaladevi, along with the caption, 'The venerable Indian professor and his young wife.' When Kamaladevi protested, she was told that the photo revealed 'the general impression that an Indian women [sic] only travelled under the protection of her husband'.[36]

While Kamaladevi challenged stereotypes of Indian women and of India itself, her experience abroad also sharpened her desire to change the social, political and economic realities facing her homeland. Consider Kamaladevi's response to the education conference in Denmark. 'It is in such gatherings that our humiliating position is brought home to us more poignantly than ever,' she declared in the *Modern Review*. What was 'humiliating', she made clear, were not the foolish stereotypes of India that were embraced by some Europeans but the fact that India remained under foreign rule. 'It is time indeed that Indian women realized their responsibility in the political struggle of the country,' she proclaimed. 'We waste so much of our time and energy on petty reforms and let it run into non-essential channels that we but ruffle the sandy surface leaving the hard rock beneath untouched.'[37]

In addition to bringing her anticolonial politics to gatherings of women reformers and educators, Kamaladevi also linked her anticolonialism to worker's movements and the radical left. While in Berlin, she attended a large gathering of workers organized by socialist labour unions. In Frankfurt in July, she attended a meeting of the League against Imperialism, a left-wing organization that had formed the year before under the leadership of the German communist Willi Münzenberg and with the backing of the Comintern. Kamaladevi was invited by her brother-in-law, Chatto, who helped organize the gathering. In stark contrast with the quiet civility of the other conferences she attended in Europe, the League against Imperialism was marked, in her words, by 'sharp expressions, violent language, loud demonstrative delivery'. It was not the vibrant atmosphere that most impressed Kamaladevi; it was the ideas that were being debated and the fact that, despite her age and gender, she was treated as an equal. 'It was a novel experience for me,' she later recalled, 'to be received as a mature political personality whereas in India I had been treated as a youth with condescension by elders.'[38]

Many of the ideas she encountered at the league's gatherings would have already been familiar to her. It is likely, for example, that she had discussed the relationship between imperialism and capitalism when she visited Chatto nearly ten years before. A voracious reader, Kamaladevi had also explored anti-imperialism and socialism through books. In 1926, the educator Kota Lakshminarayan Karanth visited Kamaladevi at her home in the Kodialbail neighbourhood of Mangalore. Karanth recalled seeing 'a vast collection of books' that included Trotsky's *History of the Russian Revolution.* Kamaladevi agreed to allow Karanth to borrow that particular volume but reminded him to return it within a week. Her extensive reading and her personal connections with radicals like Chatto prepared Kamaladevi to make the most of her time at the League against Imperialism and at the other gatherings she attended in Europe. She later wrote Chatto that 'this trip to Europe has made a great difference to my whole work'. As she put it in her memoir, she returned to India 'full of renewed enthusiasm, astir with new ideas'.[39]

She arrived in Bombay in September eager to bring her new ideas to the many organizations and initiatives she had left just a few months earlier. The day after she arrived, members of the Youth League took her to inaugurate 'a Khadi and Swadeshi Bazaar' that they had founded at the People's Hall. The hand-spun and handwoven cloth known as khadi was central to Gandhi's vision of an economy based on locally produced goods. As Gandhi saw it, products that were swadeshi ('of one's own country') would fuel swaraj—a word often translated as independence but that literally means 'self-rule'. Both Gandhi and Kamaladevi believed that true self-rule—true swaraj—was about more than political independence from the British. It is unclear, however, whether Kamaladevi had Gandhi in mind when she told her young audience in Bombay that swaraj 'was an economical proposition and not merely a sentimental one'. That idea, which would have resonated with Gandhi, would also have found eager acceptance—and a more socialist spin—at the League against Imperialism. Kamaladevi's belief in the economic underpinnings of freedom would long be inspired by a blend of socialism and Gandhian philosophy, but her time in Europe pushed her towards a more socialist understanding of the economic revolution necessary to achieve swaraj.[40]

Kamaladevi knew that swaraj would also require major social and cultural changes, and she continued to focus on dismantling patriarchy in particular. She had reason to be hopeful in regard to that struggle. The same month that she returned to India, the Sarda bill, officially known as the Child Marriage Restraint Act, was passed by the central legislature. Kamaladevi heralded the news as a result of the tireless lobbying of the AIWC. In her words, 'The great achievement of the Conference and one which it regards as a personal triumph is the passing of the Sarda Act.' In the short term, the impact of the law on marriage practices proved minimal, in part because the government issued a circular restricting its implementation. More significant was the confidence that this victory gave to Kamaladevi and the other leaders of the AIWC. As Kamaladevi noted at the time, in order to advance such social legislation 'the Conference had to face much severe criticism and attacks from some on grounds of orthodoxy and from others on grounds of impracticability'. The Sarda bill survived because 'the women's practical sense stood by and helped to render this then impossible dream an actual reality.'[41]

The Child Marriage Restraint Act demonstrated that women could come together across the divides of caste and religion. As the historian Mrinalini Sinha has noted, it was not only 'the first piece of social reform legislation in colonial India that was enabled in large part by the efforts of autonomous all-India women's organizations themselves'; it was also 'the first, and since then also the only, uniform law on marriage that cut across separate religious personal laws affecting marriage for different religious communities in India to be applicable universally'. The uniform nature of the Act mattered deeply to Kamaladevi, whose vision of the women's struggle would always be bound up with the unity of India.[42]

Her vision of India's unity was not limited to the regions of India governed directly by the colonial state. More so than most Indian anticolonial activists, she was deeply concerned about the future of the hundreds of 'princely states' that covered more than a third of the subcontinent. Officially governed by rajas and other assorted potentates, the princely states were indirectly controlled by the British. As Kamaladevi saw it, the people of the princely states were doubly oppressed—by the British and by their 'native' allies. Soon after returning from abroad, Kamaladevi travelled to Bangalore, a city controlled in part by the maharaja of Mysore, one of the largest and most powerful of the princely states. There, she gave three talks organized by three distinct groups: the District Congress Committee, the Textile Labourers Union and the Bangalore Youth League. According to one biographer, the content of her speeches 'was officially reported as being so objectionable that she was served with an order by the State Government forbidding her to speak in public'. One official report quoted her telling the Bangalore Congress Committee that 'Britain cannot give freedom to India'. The Indian people had to claim their freedom. It was, Kamaladevi asserted, a 'delusion' to expect the British 'to grant responsible government to India'.[43]

It was also a delusion to believe that getting rid of the British would bring India true freedom. It was in pursuit of an expansive freedom that Kamaladevi continued to dedicate much of her time to social reform. In retrospect, some of her reformist efforts might seem to conflict with her commitment to ending British rule. Consider the history of Lady Irwin College in New Delhi. Combining her interest in education with her attention to the everyday realities of life for many women, Kamaladevi floated the idea of a new educational institution focused on 'domestic science'. Lady Irwin, the wife of the viceroy, agreed to chair the fundraising effort, and the institution would eventually become Lady Irwin College. This was the same Lady Irwin who had been concerned by Kamaladevi's opposition to the Simon Commission. By collaborating with her, Kamaladevi was yet again attempting to advance the women's movement by partnering with colonial authorities—even while calling for an end to colonial rule.

The focus of the educational institution might seem to be in tension with Kamaladevi's radical vision of gender equality. Founding a college for women that focused explicitly on domestic science risked suggesting that women were not capable of pursuing other vocations. Kamaladevi did not see it that way. She would defend the importance of domestic work throughout her life. In her AIWC presidential address in 1944, she would recognize 'the tremendous labours of the housewife' and would declare that 'the housewife is as much of a working woman as a factory worker'. Kamaladevi herself was far from a traditional housewife, and she fought for women to have the freedom to pursue multiple careers. As she said in 1944, 'The entrance of women into extra-domestic activities has to be welcomed, for it provides a wider field for the women's talents, breaks the relative segregation of the woman as a sex, relaxes the restrictions that otherwise narrow women's functions.' Nevertheless, Kamaladevi felt that too much emphasis on public careers could blunt the importance of what many women did within the home. Advocates of equality between men and women might celebrate the fact that the curricula of Lady Irwin College, now a part of the University of Delhi, eventually expanded beyond 'home science' and that the college is now considered to be among the most prestigious educational institutions in India. For Kamaladevi, however, the shift towards a more standard liberal arts curriculum diluted the original emphasis on providing a practical education that would touch the lives of poor and working-class women.[44]

In 1929, Kamaladevi wrote the introductory chapter for an edited volume, *Women in Modern India,* that was published in Bombay. In her chapter, Kamaladevi returned to the strategy she had deployed three years earlier in her campaign for elected office—praising ancient India in order to challenge contemporary patriarchy. 'In those beautiful days of the Vedic period of India,' she wrote, 'women took part freely in the social and political life of the country.' Her rose-tinted history allowed her to offer a collaborative vision of the women's movement. 'This movement cannot in any sense be said to be a rebellion or a revolt against man,' she wrote. 'It is not actuated by any spirit of competition nor marked with violence; it is a movement of calm assertion.' She tried to walk a fine line—challenging patriarchy without besmirching Indian society. Despite her caution, she did not hesitate to decry the 'supreme overlordship of man' and to declare that 'women seek to have their own free choice in the selection of partners in life, the right to enter the state of motherhood, when and if they desire, to seek divorce if necessity arise'.[45]

Her defence of divorce would later become personal. Had she already pondered ending her marriage? Her recorded memories are silent on that question, but in the years ahead it would become clear that Harin's extramarital affairs and his growing dependence on alcohol were causing her great sadness and bringing uncertainty into many facets of her life. She had been a teenager when she had fallen in love with Harin. By 1930, they had been married for a decade. Their son, Rama, would be turning six. His future must have weighed on her when she pondered her own options. What she could not have known as the decade of the 1920s came to an end was just how profoundly turbulent and transformative the year 1930 would be—for her, for her family and for her country.

~

On 14 December 1929, some 4,000 young people crowded a massive outdoor pavilion in Ahmedabad for the Bombay Presidency Youth Conference. The pavilion was adorned with banners. 'Long Live Revolution,' one declared. Another called for 'All Power to the Soviets'. The conference began with the participants singing 'Vande Mataram', after which a twenty-one-year-old student named Rohit Mehta took the stage. Mehta had helped lead a three-month student strike at Gujarat College in opposition to a rule prohibiting students from engaging in political activity. Before the massive crowd, he nominated Kamaladevi as the chair of the gathering. According to one account, 'She took up her seat amidst vociferous cheers.'[46]

Yusuf Meherally then stood to speak. Born into an affluent Muslim family in 1903, the same year Kamaladevi was born, twenty-six-year-old Meherally had long gravitated to radical activism. Kamaladevi later described Meherally in words that applied to her too: 'Fearless and sincere he inspired the young and the old alike with fire and fervour. But happily his basically pragmatic nature worked out a satisfactory balance.' In Ahmedabad, Meherally moved a resolution that urged the Congress Party to declare complete independence at its upcoming gathering in Lahore. The resolution passed with a strong majority, but what did 'independence' mean?[47]

In her speech, Kamaladevi offered a radical vision of independence—radical in its breadth and depth. 'Freedom or Swaraj can mean but one thing,' she declared: 'absolute freedom for each individual as well as collective growth and evolution. It means the establishment of an order in the country which will give the fullest opportunity for each to grow physically, culturally and morally, unhampered by such economic and social laws and conventions as demoralise human beings.' She warned against replacing British rule with indigenous forms of oppression and linked that danger to India's foreign policy. 'A free country is one which does not permit exploitation of the masses either by foreigners or by a handful of its own people,' she stated. A free country also should not 'become a party to the exploitation of other weaker nations.' She turned abroad to demonstrate the importance of achieving a fully inclusive freedom. 'We have the case of South Africa,' she declared, 'which is supposed to have practically full freedom—yes; but freedom for whom? For the White rulers. The Negroes, the children of the soil, and the Indians who are settlers there, are alike trodden down and exploited ruthlessly.' Her global understanding of racial exploitation sharpened her critique of British rule, which she noted was built upon 'deep-rooted contempt for the coloured people'. By employing an expansive conception of 'coloured people', Kamaladevi linked India's struggle to antiracist movements in Africa, Asia, and elsewhere.

Her transnational understanding of the racial dimensions of the Indian struggle dovetailed with her socialist concern for class inequity. 'India's struggle has to be against world Imperialism,' she declared, 'for Imperialism is a united force that has its roots in Capitalism and is preserved by Militarism.' India would not be truly free if the British ceded power to a small group of wealthy Indians. 'I cannot imagine a free India,' she explained, 'where poverty and oppression still linger, where exploitation holds sway or medieval forms of autocratic rule of monarchy continue.' The Indian freedom movement was 'not merely a war against the White man,' she argued. 'It is a fight against all exploitation, no matter whether it be White or Brown.' She made clear that 'in a free India there cannot be any caste or sex discrimination or inequality'. What was needed, she told the students, was 'an all-embracing revolution—political, social and economic'.[48]

As to how to achieve such a revolution, Kamaladevi's vision was equally bold. Radical students had been drawn to violence, inspired by figures like Bhagat Singh. Kamaladevi rejected that approach as impractical. 'The term "revolution" is much abused and misunderstood,' she explained. 'It usually means fighting with guns, but with us it can only mean a great upheaval through moral force, for a disarmed nation has no choice in the matter, even apart from the ethical, moral or the practical view point.' In a different record of her speech, this key sentence ends 'even apart from the ideal of nonviolence which we have adopted as our ideal'. Regardless of which version accurately represents the words she spoke that day, their discrepancy frames a vital question: did Kamaladevi embrace nonviolence as her ideal? What is clear is that she rejected as impractical both armed rebellion and individual acts of antistate violence; recognized the limitations of legal and constitutional methods of reform; and believed in the power of civil disobedience. The students must, she asserted, 'start civil disobedience, declare an independent republic, establish a parallel Government, do it at any cost and any sacrifice'. Her rejection of violence could be seen as a sign of moderation, but the colonial authorities did not see her position that way. The police monitored her speech and recorded her declaring that 'if the political leaders and the Congress fail to fulfill our expectations and their own at the coming Congress, the Youth League will take the initiative in starting work of its own'.[49]

The Congress did not disappoint the students—at least not in Lahore the following week when Jawaharlal Nehru presided over the annual gathering of that august body. On 19 December, the Congress passed what came to be known as the Purna Swaraj Resolution, demanding the end of British rule and full independence or 'purna swaraj'. For years, Kamaladevi had advanced an expansive conception of swaraj that embraced economic, political and social change throughout India—including when it came to the status and rights of women. In the years ahead, she would continue to fight both to end British rule and to achieve true swaraj—true freedom.

On 20 January 1930, the fourth session of the All India Women's Conference met in Bombay. Sarojini Naidu served as president and Kamaladevi as the organizing secretary. 'Within the last 3 years,' Kamaladevi wrote in a report, the AIWC had 'grown into a responsible and consolidated organization to voice the united opinion of the women of India'. Whether the women of India could be said to be united was a tricky question that involved questions of caste, class, creed and language. Kamaladevi noted that the organization had taken to publishing reports in different languages, but she tended to assume the unity of women, with one major exception: class inequity. 'The field of labour work is a new one that the Conference has entered upon,' Kamaladevi told the delegates in Bombay, 'and its first venture has been the cooperation with the Labour Commission.' The AIWC had failed to get a woman on the commission, but Kamaladevi was working 'to put up women witnesses to give evidence on behalf of the women industrial workers'. She urged delegates to visit Bombay's textile mill area in order to 'get first hand information'. The AIWC would, she declared, make labour reform 'a special item in its future programme of work'.[50]

A week after the AIWC conference, on 26 January 1930, Kamaladevi joined a massive crowd at Bombay's Azad Maidan to celebrate what had been deemed 'Independence Day' in recognition of the decision of the Congress to fight for Purna Swaraj. Just after the national flag had been raised, a group of communist activists attempted to replace it with the hammer and sickle. Kamaladevi ran to the flagpole to defend what she saw as India's honour. The sun had set and a confused skirmish erupted in the darkness. 'My hands became bruised in the struggle to hold on to the flag,' Kamaladevi later recalled, 'and probably drew some blood that kept trickling, but I was not conscious of anything except that I must save the flag from defilement.' That moment would be celebrated in poems and songs and would strengthen Kamaladevi's nationwide reputation.[51]

It is striking that an act through which she embodied the nationalist cause was not directed at the British but at communist trade unionists. Only a few months had passed since she had been hosted by Chatto and had written to him expressing her desire to leave India in order to work with him.[52] The colonial authorities continued to associate her with communism and with violent revolutionaries. One police report claimed that Kamaladevi had declared, at a gathering of the Nagpur Youth League in February 1930, that violence was 'inevitable in a struggle for liberty and every means must be employed'. This assertion seems more in line with official stereotypes of the radical activist than with Kamaladevi's other public statements. It sounds more like her to declare that it was 'the duty of youth to bring about revolution' or to shout 'Long live Bhagat Singh, Dutt and Rajguru', as the police report alleged that she had. It seems likely that she would tell a group of railway strikers in Nagpur 'that they were the owners of the country and all its industry', but highly unlikely that she would add that 'the usurping foreigners must be exterminated'. A less biased report quoted her telling the Central Provinces Youth Conference in February 1930 that while young people should 'be prepared to sacrifice their lives and property in the battle for Swaraj', they should commit to 'avoiding violence and maintaining strict discipline'. The police suggested to the Bombay Presidency Home Secretary that 'Kamaladevi Chattopadhyaya is a dangerous person whose speeches to youth and students are resulting in an increasing truculence of manner and recklessness of speech and would have to be curbed'. The Bombay Home Department, in turn, warned the central government that 'the lady is an enthusiastic communist and will utilize her passport for getting into closest relations with one of the most dangerous centres of communism'. Her passport was subsequently cancelled, despite the fact that she was neither 'an enthusiastic communist' nor an advocate of violence. Kamaladevi's own socialism had yet to fully form, but it would be defined by a rejection of both rapacious capitalism and totalitarian communism.[53]

From when she first ran for office in 1926 until she clutched that flagpole in 1930, only four years had elapsed. In those years, she developed strong connections across a variety of struggles—the women's movement, the youth movement, the Indian National Congress, and the labour movement. She understood all of these struggles as interconnected efforts to gain freedom, and her refusal to give all of herself to any one movement or organization was itself an expression of that freedom.

Kamaladevi embodied the inclusivity that scholars such as Michele Louro and Carolien Stolte have identified as a pillar of anticolonial politics in the 1920s—not just in India but throughout the colonial world. Kamaladevi's international reputation was shaped by her inclusive politics. In March 1930, for example, the *India & Canada* newspaper of Vancouver published a photo of Kamaladevi alongside a glowing tribute to her 'energetic, aggressive and talented' contributions to the AIWC and the Youth League. Her decision to eschew violence, to reject communism and to embrace the AIWC, the Youth League and the Congress should not obscure her radicalism. In the 1930s, Kamaladevi would continue to advance radical conceptions of freedom that transgressed the borders of movements and nations.[54]

Kamaladevi claimed a similar freedom in her personal life as she strove to balance her responsibilities as a mother with her career. That balance would prove difficult to sustain. She had planned to attend the Lahore session of the Congress in December 1929, the session at which the Purna Swaraj Resolution was passed, but Rama fell ill. It would have been hard to balance motherhood with her social and political career even if Harin had been a more supportive partner. In 1930, he came back to India after several years abroad. Instead of embracing the responsibilities of a husband and a father, he returned with a married woman with whom he had absconded. By then, Kamaladevi was in a British jail after playing a vital role in a civil disobedience campaign that shook all of India and made news throughout the world. She had long been a rebel—both politically and personally. Refusing to live the widow's secluded life and remarrying a man of her own choice had set her apart in ways that were related to her campaign for elected office and to the organizing work she did with the AIWC. As her marriage became increasingly untenable, Kamaladevi would decide to yet again take radical action in her own personal life, and yet again that action would both empower her and complicate her political career.[55]

3

Salt and Solitary

On 12 March 1930, Gandhi began his most celebrated march—a 386-kilometre trek from his ashram in Ahmedabad to the Arabian Sea. His plan was to scoop up a handful of salty sand and thus break the government's monopoly on the production of salt. The sixty-year-old Mahatma strode forward, walking stick in hand, accompanied by seventy-eight carefully selected satyagrahis who were diverse in nearly all ways—religion, caste, region, language—except for one glaring exception. They were all men. Gandhi had decided that the most confrontational protests would be reserved for men, and he held firm to that decision until Kamaladevi helped to change his mind.

At first, Kamaladevi was baffled by the very idea of the salt satyagraha. 'At least to several of us,' she later recalled, 'the concept of breaking the salt law to initiate and launch a revolution was rather hazy.' When Jawaharlal Nehru explained the plan, she asked, 'Is that all our Great Leader could devise?' Nehru replied, 'We cannot always grasp his ideas in their entirety. But rest assured there is a method in what people think is madness.' Kamaladevi would eventually embrace the salt satyagraha and become one of its leaders, but she did so in a way that consistently pushed beyond Gandhi's vision—nowhere more dramatically than when it came to the question of women's participation.[1]

Kamaladevi was 'flabbergasted' when she learnt that women were going to be marginalized within the satyagraha. 'I had built up a whole edifice of hopes of involving women in this great adventure,' she later recalled. 'This was to be their breakthrough. They simply had to be in it.' Many women felt similarly. Khurshedbehn Naoroji, the granddaughter of the pioneering anticolonial figure Dadabhai Naoroji, wrote Gandhi to protest the exclusion of women, and Margaret Cousins penned a protest in *Stri Dharma*. But it was Kamaladevi who rushed to Gujarat to speak with Gandhi directly. She caught up with him on 22 March between the small towns of Jambusar and Amod. Walking at his side, she challenged him to recognize that women could and should contribute to every facet of the struggle. In 1919, she had humbly pledged to follow India's new leader. In 1930, she was still following him but as a colleague who was not afraid to question his decisions. That is why Gandhi's grandson, the scholar and diplomat Gopalkrishna Gandhi, sees Kamaladevi as 'crucial to the political life of Mahatma Gandhi'. Unlike many of his followers and devotees, she challenged him.[2]

Gandhi explained to Kamaladevi that he envisioned women contributing to the struggle by picketing shops that sold alcohol and foreign cloth. He saw the roles he had assigned women as 'a tribute to the high qualities they possess' and told Kamaladevi that 'the call for them was not for slogan shouting or marches, but utter dedication, which was a natural quality in women'. She rejected such patronizing limitations. 'Let them do all this,' she replied, 'and also participate in direct action.' Kamaladevi used the prevailing view that women were 'weaker' to argue for their inclusion. 'The significance of a non-violent struggle,' she told Gandhi, 'is that the weakest can take an equal part with the strongest and share in the triumph as you have yourself said.'[3]

Gandhi relented. He agreed to allow women to participate in all facets of the struggle. Before Kamaladevi left, she made one more request—that Gandhi issue a public call inviting women to join the struggle. 'His eyes twinkled as he gave a hearty laugh,' she recalled. 'You don't know your sisters,' he said, 'if you think they need a special message.' She persisted, and he wrote out a message: 'All are free and those who are ready are expected to start mass Civil Disobedience regarding the Salt Law from April 6th.' Kamaladevi was elated. 'I felt I had won the world,' she recalled.[4]

The *Times of India* offered a different version of this exchange, one in which Gandhi told Kamaladevi that 'if impatient sisters will be a little patient, they will find ample scope for their zeal and sacrifice in this national struggle for freedom'. According to the *Times*, rather than directly reject the idea of women waiting patiently, 'Mrs Kamaladevi asked Mr Gandhi what women with children should do.' In this version of the conversation, Gandhi said 'he neither desired nor expected women to neglect children. They would have to wait and bide their time and be of use in other ways.' He added, however, that those women 'who could make some satisfactory arrangements to have their children well looked after should join the struggle'. This account of the conversation, while suggesting a less dramatic confrontation between the Mahatma and Kamaladevi, reveals her courage in an especially personal light. While fighting for women to have the right to risk imprisonment, Kamaladevi was also weighing her responsibility to her son, who would turn seven in May.[5]

In the wake of Kamaladevi's conversation with Gandhi, a formal appeal was circulated, signed by the leaders of the women's wing of the Seva Dal: Umabai Kundapur, Lakshmipathi and Kamaladevi. 'The call has come forth for a strong force of seventy lakhs to fight the battle of freedom,' the appeal declared. 'The cooperation of women at this stage is of supreme importance and invaluable to the welfare of the world at large.' While calling for women to join the struggle, Kamaladevi continued to grapple with what her own involvement would mean for her personal life—and for her family. 'I was leaving behind all that the past decade held for me,' she later wrote: 'the buoyance and glamour of the theatre, music, games, sports; the deep human involvement with women, building intimate channels for love, affection and mutual confidence to flow; above all there would henceforth be precious little of a personal life to envelop one in its warm comfort, soothe the bruises, provide the pillow on which to rest.' Many of her closest supporters understood her need to join the salt satyagraha. When she wrote Margaret Cousins to resign from her position at the AIWC, Cousins replied, 'I had always believed I would some day hold you to my heart as my daughter. Now you are on the march to prison and to freedom, I can do so.' While her actions solidified her ties with her 'spiritual mother', they risked straining her ties with her biological mother and with her son. If Kamaladevi were arrested, she could not know how long she would be away from her family.[6]

On 6 April, Kamaladevi joined a small team of seven satyagrahis chosen to be the first to break the salt laws in Bombay. 'I was yet raw and felt privileged and self-conscious in my spotless khadi,' she later remembered, 'conspicuously displaying the badge with the national flag colours: orange, white and green, proud to have a place in the first batch of Law-Breakers!' Walking towards the sea through the streets of the city, Kamaladevi and her fellow satyagrahis were showered with rose petals. Huge crowds lined the path to the beach. Once she had reached the sand, Kamaladevi lit a small fire to boil saltwater, while friends created a protective circle in anticipation of police interference.[7]

The police charged the circle, beating the nonviolent protesters with batons. 'I could hear the dull thud as the blows fell,' Kamaladevi recalled, 'faint moans as the wounded struck the ground.' While tending a young protester with a cracked skull, Kamaladevi was kicked to the ground. Her arm slammed into the burning coals of the fire, and the pain overwhelmed her. When she opened her eyes, she found a police officer staring down with 'kindly eyes'. 'Can I take you to a hospital?' he asked. Although the officer seemed 'genuinely solicitous', Kamaladevi refused to leave. He tried to reason with her: 'According to Mahatma Gandhi you should not regard me as an enemy.' Despite her wounds, Kamaladevi recognized the irony of the situation. 'I could hardly forbear a smile,' she later wrote, 'to find this police officer attempting to interpret the Gandhian philosophy to me after perhaps having battered a good few people.'[8]

Kamaladevi was not arrested and, having recovered from her wounds, she awoke the next day eager to again challenge British rule. Soon after dawn, she joined a bustling procession that left Congress House bound for Mahalaxmi, a seaside neighbourhood named in honour of a temple perched on the shore. The group was led by Khurshed Framji Nariman, a Parsi lawyer and Congress leader. The group stopped at a public park near the ocean, and four volunteers retrieved large pots of seawater.

Kamaladevi and her friend Avantikabai Gokhale lit fires beneath the pots, and in less than an hour the water had boiled away, leaving behind a fine white powder that was presented to the approving crowd. That evening, a crowd of some 10,000 people gathered at Chowpatty Beach to celebrate. Kamaladevi was one of the featured speakers. She later recalled that the beach was 'more full of people' than sand.[9]

The salt satyagraha combined vast marches and epic gatherings with profoundly intimate forms of protest. The scale of the struggle ranged from 10,000 people together on a beach to one woman crouched on the ground tending a boiling pot of seawater. Kamaladevi thrived in both settings. By 1930, she had overcome her fear of speaking. While she remained generally taciturn and was not known for lighthearted chitchat, she had no hesitation climbing on to stage after stage to address massive crowds. Yet, equally important to her was the opportunity to get down on the ground and do the hands-on work of making salt. This was an early form of the embodied, hands-on politics that would define much of her career. From tending a stove to gathering saltwater to knocking on doors to recruit volunteers, Kamaladevi embraced the kinds of seemingly mundane labour that had long been relegated to women. But she refused to be limited by that labour. It was the full range of her activism that inspired her to locate herself within a long tradition of courageous women. 'Although India has a long illustrious tradition of women warriors,' she wrote in her memoir, 'this was their first appearance in any modern militant political campaign and I could hardly suppress my excitement to be amongst the first.'[10]

Kamaladevi quickly earned the attention of the police. On 9 April, at a mass meeting in Ahmednagar, the police noted the sale of 'some contraband salt supposed to have been sent by Mrs Kamaladevi Chattopadhyaya'. The following evening, a police contingent stormed Bombay's Congress House with orders to destroy anything that could be used to produce salt. They found two large concrete salt pans full of seawater. The pans were guarded by some fifty satyagrahis who, according to the police report, were 'headed by Mrs Kamaladevi Chattopadhyaya and Y.J. Meherali'. Six months earlier, Kamaladevi and

Meherally had stood together on the dais at the Bombay Presidency Youth Conference and urged young people to rise up and claim their independence. Now, they were putting their words into action. When the satyagrahis refused to move, the police shoved them out of the way and destroyed the salt pans. Meherally was arrested but the police chose not to arrest Kamaladevi.[11]

On 11 April, Kamaladevi presided over a public meeting attended by some 300 people. The following morning, 500 satyagrahis left Congress House in groups of ten to sell contraband salt in different parts of the city. Kamaladevi led her group door to door at Bazaar Gate. That afternoon, she entered the Share Bazaar and sold salt packets to the traders. Many cheered her on, yelling 'Mahatmaji Ki Jai'. According to the police, one of the packets sold for the extravagant sum of Rs 500. In total, she earned over Rs 4,000 for the cause, and the *Bombay Chronicle* reported her exploits. A few days later she repeated the experience at Marwadi Bazaar, again reaping a huge sum, with one trader paying Rs 701 for a single packet of salt.[12]

At the outset of the salt satyagraha, Kamaladevi had worried about losing touch with her artistic and theatrical passions. She need not have worried—the salt satyagraha proved full of drama, some of which was even lighthearted. Along with two colleagues, Kamaladevi entered the Bombay High Court and sold salt before encouraging the lawyers and judges to dress in homespun fabric. Her days filled with marches, speeches and acts of civil disobedience. On the morning of 13 April, she spoke to 3,000 people gathered at Chowpatty for a meeting presided over by Sarojini Naidu. That evening, she returned to the same beach to speak before a massive gathering of some 50,000 people. On the afternoon of 16 April, she spoke to 300 workers at the Mulji Jetha Market. That same day, she visited Cotton Green where, according to the police, she 'induced the cotton brokers to contribute large sums of money in aid of the salt satyagraha'.[13]

Despite the large amounts she raised from traders and merchants, she increasingly focused on mobilizing workers. On the evening of 18 April, Kamaladevi presided at two large meetings outside the Dinshaw Petit

Mills in Lalbaug. She spoke to about 1,500 people, mostly millworkers. According to the police, she urged the workers 'to join the Congress if they wanted to find a solution to their troubles and grievances', and appealed to 'women workers to come forward as volunteers'. The following night, she presided over a similar event for 200 millworkers at the Cement Chawls in Naigaum. Her efforts among the millworkers could be seen as a challenge to the communists, but Kamaladevi focused her criticism on the mill owners and the government. On the evening of 22 April, she told some 400 millworkers that 'the workers did not succeed in their fight against the capitalists because the latter were supported by the British Government and their police'.[14]

To mobilize Bombay's workers, Kamaladevi worked closely with C.K. Narayanswami, a veteran Gandhian activist with strong ties to textile and railway workers unions. On 22 April, the *Bombay Congress Bulletin* announced that Kamaladevi and Narayanswami had 'started a vigorous campaign in the labour area with a view to carrying the message of the Congress to the workers and to explain to them their duty in the present nonviolent war for Independence'. Kamaladevi spoke at Gold Mohur Mills and Sewri Cement Chawls, declaring, in the words of the bulletin, that 'the struggle for Independence meant nothing but the struggle for bread'. The police noted that 'Mrs Kamaladevi and C.K. Narayenswami are doing their utmost to bring the millworkers under the Congress flag'. Together, the two activists addressed several large gatherings on the evening of 23 April, speaking to nearly 2,000 millworkers. The next day Kamaladevi again presided over two meetings of millworkers, one in the morning and one in the evening. On 28 April, the *Bombay Congress Bulletin* counted fifteen recent meetings of workers, at all of which 'Shrimati Kamaladevi Chattopadhyaya presided'.[15]

Kamaladevi also focused on recruiting women to the struggle. At a special meeting of women held in Bombay's Parel neighbourhood, she offered a hands-on lesson on how to make sea salt. That evening, she offered 'a stirring speech' to a large crowd. According to the *Bombay Congress Bulletin,* she 'declared that the breaking of the Salt Law was not the end of the struggle but it was only the beginning of the end.

It was sowing the seeds of a mass revolution which was inevitable'. At the end of the meeting, Mrs Gangaben Patel 'paid a glowing tribute to Mrs Kamaladevi Chattopadhyaya and expressed the hope that the women would join in the large numbers when the campaign of foreign cloth boycott and liquor shops picketing begins'. Kamaladevi believed in such picketing. As she made clear to Gandhi, however, she did not want women to limit their contributions to the struggle. Indeed, she was planning a protest that was more radical in scope than any that had yet to occur—and she wanted women to play a central role in it.[16]

The protest would occur at Wadala Salt Works. Located to the northeast of Bombay on land that had been reclaimed from the sea, Wadala Salt Works consisted of a series of small shallow ponds, or salt pans, in which seawater was allowed to evaporate, leaving behind salt. On 16 April, Kamaladevi led a group of 500 satyagrahis to Wadala, where they gathered natural salt and sold it on the spot. The trip served as a trial run for the much larger protest that Kamaladevi was planning.[17]

While Kamaladevi was recruiting women, Gandhi seemed to backtrack on women's involvement in the most dangerous facets of the struggle. On 17 April, writing in his journal *Young India,* the Mahatma praised Kamaladevi by name and declared that women volunteers had 'acted with rare courage and calmness'. He followed this praise with a major caveat. 'But they would allow me to say,' he added, 'that they would have done better to remain outside the venue of the men's fight. For women to be in the midst of such danger as they put themselves in was against the rule of chivalry.' Kamaladevi might not have found Gandhi's words as patronizing as they sound today. She believed in his leadership and was able to see past his shortcomings. Yet it must have rankled to read that only 'when there are no men left to fight the battle of free salt' should women then 'take up the work deserted by men'. It is unclear how Kamaladevi responded to this particular editorial. What is clear is that she would decide for herself when, where and how to 'fight the battle of free salt'. The same day that Gandhi's editorial was published, Kamaladevi led 275 satyagrahis to the Churchgate seafront to collect saltwater in earthen pots.[18]

While the salt satyagraha complicated Kamaladevi's relationship with Gandhi, the struggle brought her closer to her sister-in-law, Sarojini Naidu. On the evening of 20 April, Kamaladevi and Naidu spoke together at a mass meeting at Chowpatty Beach. The police recorded 8,000 people in attendance, but the *Bombay Chronicle* put the number at 1,00,000. A few days later, the two women again shared the stage at Esplanade Maidan, where some 3,000 people heard them speak. On 27 April, Kamaladevi and Naidu were at Shivaji Park, where Naidu hoisted the national flag to the delight of 1,000 onlookers.[19]

On 21 April, some 500 police officers descended on Bhatia Baug where a group of about 600 satyagrahis had gathered to make salt under the direction of K.M. Munshi. When the police arrested Munshi, Kamaladevi assumed leadership of the protest. The police commissioner ordered Kamaladevi to stand aside. She refused. 'It is an awful nuisance when women interfere,' the commissioner remarked. Even before the salt satyagraha, Kamaladevi's gender had influenced government debates about whether to arrest her. One official had noted that 'the prosecution of a woman for incitement to violence would perhaps be inadvisable; nevertheless Mrs Chattopadhyaya is a dangerous person whose activities will have to be curbed sooner or later'. Kamaladevi's 'appeals to youths and students' were 'resulting in an increasing truculence of, manner and recklessness of speech and it is not difficult to imagine what the ultimate result will be; the first case suitable for prosecution will be sent up to Government'. Yet now that Kamaladevi was openly defying the law, the government remained hesitant to arrest her or the other women leaders of the movement. In Bhatia Baug, the police forced their way through the volunteers and kicked over the salt pans, but they again decided not to arrest Kamaladevi. Once they had left, the pans were put back in place, the fires were relit and salt was 'prepared in large quantities'. According to one account, 'Mrs Kamaladevi auctioned the salt for fabulous sums. The women began to offer the jewels on their persons and they were auctioned for large sums. All the jewels were returned to Mrs Kamaladevi by the purchasers to be re-auctioned over and over again until it was impossible to get rid of those jewels.'[20]

On the afternoon of 26 April, a 'victory procession' set out from Esplanade Maidan with Kamaladevi, Naidu, Narayanswami and several other prominent Congress members leading the way. As the procession moved through the city, spectators joined the group, swelling its ranks to nearly 10,000. Such mass enthusiasm for the movement extended well beyond the city centre. In the suburbs, volunteers gathered seawater every morning and prepared salt, which was then sold in the surrounding neighbourhoods and even in more remote villages. According to a Bombay Presidency Police report, women in these areas were showing 'greater interest in the movement. This appears to be the result of the speeches of Mrs Kamaladevi Chatopadhyaya of Bombay.'[21]

On 29 April, Kamaladevi presided over a large gathering of railway workers. She declared, in the words of the *Bombay Congress Bulletin*, that 'the Congress programme and principle would not become real unless it was a programme of swaraj for the masses'. This quote suggests a critique of Congress moderation, yet most of Kamaladevi's speeches indicate that she was more focused on bringing workers into the movement than criticizing how the movement was defined. That would not always be the case. Later in the decade, Kamaladevi would direct much of her effort to advancing a radical vision of India's freedom. In the early 1930s, by contrast, she shared with more conservative Congress leaders a belief in the overriding importance of ending British rule. To be clear, she was already a radical—both in her methods and in her vision of swaraj—but the salt satyagraha was so dynamic and multifaceted that there was space for Kamaladevi to pursue her own approach to India's freedom without focusing on the limitations of the Congress.[22]

The *Bombay Congress Bulletin* of 30 April demonstrates Kamaladevi's multifaceted vision of the struggle for freedom. She had joined Naidu in having an 'interesting talk with a large number of Muslim ladies who had assembled to hear about the importance and nationwide implications of the Congress movement'. The same issue also noted that 'two women's meetings were held at Parel on Tuesday when Smt. Kamaladevi Chattopadhyaya and Smt. Gangaben Patel explained to the women the implications of the Salt Civil Disobedience and the need for boycott of foreign cloth'. The *Bulletin* noted that 'great enthusiasm was shown when Smt. Kamaladevi demonstrated the preparation of contraband salt from sea water'. Lastly, the *Bulletin* reported that 'two mass meetings of workers were held on Tuesday in the labour area. Smt. Kamaladevi Chattopadhyaya, Dr Choksey, C.K. Narayenswami and others addressed the meeting.' Thus, in the same *Bulletin,* we see Kamaladevi building bridges with Muslim women, teaching others how to prepare salt, and speaking to large gatherings of workers.[23]

Her efforts to mobilize workers yielded mixed results. According to the *Bulletin* of 1 May, 'The continuous propaganda in the working class area is bearing good results. The labourers have, in no uncertain terms begun to respond to the Congress call.' This statement reveals more about the hopes of Congress leaders than the realities of working-class support for the movement. Large numbers of workers were willing to attend meetings, but it was more difficult to inspire them to risk imprisonment or the loss of their jobs. As April gave way to May, Kamaladevi must have wondered what it would take to generate a mass strike—to inspire not thousands but hundreds of thousands of people to risk their livelihoods and their lives for India's freedom.[24]

Late at night on 4 May 1930, Gandhi was arrested. When the news reached Bombay the following morning, volunteers spread out across the city urging merchants to shutter their stores and encouraging workers to leave the mills. According to the police, 'The millhands and the railway workshop people are at work. Mrs Chattopadhyaya's attempts to get them out failed.' She did not stop trying, however. That evening, a massive crowd gathered at Esplanade Maidan. The police estimated the attendance at 25,000 but the real number was likely higher. Six platforms were constructed and Gandhi's portrait was garlanded amidst cries of 'Mahatma Gandhi Ki Jai'. Speeches were offered by Sarojini Naidu, Acharya Kripalani, Moulvi Muhammad Ali Kasuri and several other leaders. Kamaladevi's speech was one of two that the police deemed worthy of analysing in detail. According to the official report, 'Mrs Kamaladevi Chattopadhayaya said that the arrest of Gandhi was a signal to break all the sections of the Indian Penal Code. She added that the British Government was based on laws, the transgression of which would bring them Swaraj.'[25]

The next day's *Bulletin* included messages from six leaders. Naidu argued that Gandhi's arrest revealed the government's fear, and she called for 'concerted action, discipline, non-violence and self-suffering'. Kamaladevi's note was more militant and more explosive. 'Imperialists are so cowardly that they never dare to face the broad daylight,' she began. 'And true to their tradition, they stole upon Gandhiji while the world around slept and darkness hid from watchful eyes this dastardly crime. How can these lawless bandits then face an open trial in a Court of law?' In keeping with her global perspective, she wrote, 'India's honour has been brought into serious question before the world by the arrest of Gandhiji ... All humanity is watching India with expectancy to see how she will vindicate this outrage perpetrated not only on herself but on all human justice and honesty.' Kamaladevi personified India as feminine and declared that, 'India has received insult after insult from her foreign oppressor the British and too long has she let these insults go by. But this challenge to her self-respect can only be accepted by dealing the final death blow to the British Raj.' 'The world shall know no safety from such terrorism,' she concluded, 'until this imperialism is completely destroyed and every vestige of its power wiped out.'[26]

Whereas Naidu had struck a typically Gandhian tone with her emphasis on discipline, nonviolence and 'self-suffering', Kamaladevi's message left unclear her own commitment to nonviolence. In early May, she told volunteers 'that they should not abuse the police who were after all their brethren and who would be won over [to] the movement [if] they were convinced of the justice of the people's cause'. This was a very Gandhian point—that even the 'enemy' must be treated with respect. Kamaladevi's nonviolence was less visible when she praised the Seva Dal as 'the Indian National Army', 'a finely equipped army' and 'the rising Indian Army'. Gandhi often used military metaphors to describe his campaigns, but he made clear that he was talking about a nonviolent force. By contrast, the conspicuous absence of the word 'nonviolent' adds a different character to Kamaladevi's repeated descriptions of the dal as an army.[27]

The nonviolent character of the movement was in question. Gandhi himself was accused of violence, particularly in regards to his plan to 'raid' government salt works. On the evening of 8 May, Kamaladevi left Bombay for Gujarat to inspect Dharasana Salt Works and help plan the protest there. On 13 May, the police reported that she had returned to Bombay and was 'busy selecting 100 able-bodied volunteers to go to Jalalpore to take part in the raid on the Dharasana salt depot'. While in Dharasana, she and Kasturba Gandhi had challenged the police to arrest them. On 14 May, the *Bombay Chronicle* published a photograph of their protest along with the question, 'Will government arrest the ladies?' Meanwhile, Kamaladevi returned to Wadala to plan a similar protest there. The police closely surveilled her visit, and noted that the Bombay Provincial Congress Committee had decided to launch the raid at Wadala on 18 May. Kamaladevi would lead a group of some 2,000 volunteers. The plan was to leave Congress House on the evening of 17 May, and to camp at Gowari, near Wadala. At dawn, some of the volunteers would march towards the salt works, while others would encourage nearby residents to join the protest.[28]

On the evening of 15 May, Kamaladevi helped to lead a procession of approximately 3,000 volunteers that set out from Esplanade Maidan. The procession was organized by the Bombay Youth League in solidarity with the Afghan Youth League, the members of which were being arrested in the Northwest Provinces. According to the police report, 'All the processionists wore red badges and a paper badge bearing the inscription "Inquilab Zindabad, we are all outlaws".' Some communist flags were also seen by the police. Kamaladevi carried a national flag. She envisioned her efforts, and especially the plans to march on Wadala Salt Works, as part of a massive revolution, but one fought in the name of India's freedom. For over a month, she had worked tirelessly to create a broad-based struggle in which women and working people would be at the forefront. She envisioned the Wadala march as an opportunity to demonstrate the power of a truly enormous protest, but she would not be able to lead that protest—at least not at Wadala. Before dawn on the morning of 16 May, Kamaladevi was arrested.[29]

~

Upon her arrest, Kamaladevi offered a parting message that was characteristically defiant in spirit and global in vision: 'Carry on the fight until British Imperialism becomes only a dark shadow of the past; India's freedom will open the gate for world freedom.' Even at a moment of great personal uncertainty, Kamaladevi's thoughts expanded beyond herself, beyond Bombay, beyond even India. It was 'world freedom' for which she was fighting.[30]

Her arrest sparked immediate protests. According to the police, 'A large number of volunteers on hearing of her arrest came up from the Congress House and became very excited roughly handling the Police officers present and breaking down the hood of the Inspector's car in which Mrs Kamaladevi was seated.' Once the crowd was dispersed, Kamaladevi was taken to a nearby jail. 'I found myself in a dark gloomy room,' she later recalled, 'full of murky air and putrid smell; bats hanging from the ceiling occasionally startled the room by sudden flights from corner to corner.' There were no toilets in the room, nor any lights. The police passed the time by mocking the women prisoners. 'I was the first political prisoner,' Kamaladevi wrote, 'and the other inmates were rather dubious when they heard for what purpose I had chosen to enter this asylum.'[31]

From jail, Kamaladevi wrote to Makund Ramrao Jayakar, a prominent lawyer and politician, who had refused to participate in civil disobedience. 'So here I am at last,' Kamaladevi began. 'Rightly or wrongly Govt have realised I am too dangerous for public safety.' Jayakar had issued a public statement opposing the planned protest at Wadala Salt Works. Kamaladevi replied with sarcasm, issuing a defiant challenge worthy of quoting in full:

> The immediate cause of my arrest was the contemplated 'Raid' that you chose to ridicule in your statement. I expect you are somewhere in the cool beautiful hills which hold many a sweet & bitter memory for me. I hope you will enjoy them if it is possible to do so when this cruel & grim war is being fought out. I wish it had been possible for one to say to you finish what I could not finish, as I have said to so

> many other friends of mine. But I make no appeal. If these prison bars that hold me today can speak to you what one tongue cannot perhaps you will still throw in your lot with this movement.

Thus, Kamaladevi challenged Jayakar to join the struggle. While her anger comes across with nearly every word, the fact that she chose to write Jayakar on the very day of her arrest suggests that she had not lost hope that he could be converted. She had not lost hope in the many Indians who were, through their actions and their inactions, preserving foreign rule.[32]

To protest Kamaladevi's arrest, many shops and markets were closed. That day, 17 May, the *Bombay Congress Bulletin* carried the headline: 'KAMALADEVI IS ARRESTED'. Readers learnt that Kamaladevi had been arrested because of her leadership in planning the Wadala civil disobedience. 'The only reply therefore that the citizens of Bombay can give to the insolent, mad and shameless Government,' the article declared, 'which by laying their hands on our dear sister have challenged the manhood of Bombay is to join in large numbers the Congress army and carry on the raid at Vadala and carry on a relentless fight on as many fronts as possible and make it impossible for the Government to function or to exist.' Such a gender-based rallying cry obscured the many women in the movement. As Kamaladevi had long argued, the salt satyagraha depended on the participation of as many people as possible. Would Kamaladevi's arrest help inspire the kind of massive protest she had planned for Wadala?[33]

In the evening, a public gathering was held on Esplanade Maidan at which the arrest of Kamaladevi served as a rallying cry. Protests against Kamaladevi's imprisonment erupted outside of Bombay as well. In Poona on 18 May, at a meeting of 1,000 women, Kamaladevi was 'congratulated' for having been arrested. In Sholapur, near the border with present-day Karnataka, the police recorded thirteen meetings held 'in connection with the arrest of Kamaladevi Chattopadhyaya and the Civil Disobedience Movement'. Jawaharlal Nehru recorded Kamaladevi's arrest in his jail diary, and it garnered international attention as well.

An Australian newspaper featured a large photo of Kamaladevi carrying the national flag and described her as a 'leader of the Indian Women's League'. In the United States, an article by the *United Press*, published in a range of newspapers, explained that Kamaladevi was the second woman to be arrested in India since the start of the campaign. Jayaprakash Narayan wrote about Kamaladevi's arrest in a letter to John Haynes Holmes, an American pastor and ardent supporter of India's freedom. Not surprisingly, given his own left-leaning politics, Narayan described Kamaladevi as 'one of the Indian representatives at the Frankfurt Congress of the Anti-Imperialist League'. Perhaps the most touching—and heart-wrenching—protest featured Kamaladevi's son, Rama, marching in a protest to carry forward his mother's legacy.[34]

Kamaladevi's arrest occurred just two days before Rama's seventh birthday, and the fact that she could not be with him must have added to the many worries in her mind as she was taken from her jail to the courtroom for her trial. The presiding magistrate scolded her: 'You have been more responsible for people breaking the law than almost anyone else.' She replied, 'Neither I nor any single person can be held responsible for the power Gandhiji has given us all.' She was convicted and sentenced to at least six months' imprisonment. In a statement she issued to the press after her conviction, Kamaladevi declared, 'There can be no doubt that the immediate cause of my arrest was the contemplated raid on Wadala. I make this appeal to Bombay to carry the raid to a finish.'[35]

On 17 May, a group of satyagrahis camped near Wadala. Before dawn the next morning, a contingent of armed police officers descended on the camp to arrest the volunteers. Many evaded arrest and moved towards the salt pans. They would easily have been captured if not for the fact that thousands of nearby residents joined the effort. In the words of the *Bombay Congress Bulletin*, 'Men, women and boys of all ages, rank and position threw to the wind their lurking notions of respect for this Government and rushed through the police cordon and snatched away the salt.' The protest continued for hours, at which point some thousands of kilograms of salt had been liberated. Another raid was launched the following day. This time, the police responded with brutality, and one protester had his skull fractured. That evening, another public meeting was held at Esplanade Maidan in order 'to congratulate Mrs Kamaladevi Chattopadhyaya and the other satyagrahis who were arrested in connection with the Wadala salt raid'. K.F. Nariman praised 'the dauntless spirit of Mrs Kamaladevi who had joined the struggle after leaving her home and child'. The brutality of the police did not prevent an even larger raid at Wadala on 1 June when nearly 15,000 people swarmed the salt pans. Yet while police brutality could not stop the movement, the monsoon rains proved to be a more effective deterrent. The most intense phase of the salt satyagraha ended in June with the onset of the monsoon season.[36]

While protests continued to roil Bombay, Kamaladevi was sent to Yeravda Jail, outside of Poona, where she was housed with Sarojini Naidu. In many ways, her new living situation was dramatically better than the dark cell she had been given in Bombay. Naidu and Kamaladevi were kept apart from the other prisoners. They had their own toilets and access to a garden and were given a curtain they used to divide the room in two. Whatever privacy that curtain offered could not have been enough for the fiercely independent Kamaladevi, now forced to live with her domineering sister-in-law. In her memoir, Kamaladevi offered this careful and revealing assessment of this time with Naidu: 'She had always been kind, showing something of a family proprietorship as its head. Now we were on a different footing as political prisoners, which at least for me made companionship easier.' Easier, perhaps, but not always easy.[37]

Kamaladevi received support from Margaret Cousins. From jail in Bombay, Kamaladevi had written her, 'Today I lay forward my claim to be your spiritual daughter and disciple.' In October, Cousins visited Kamaladevi in prison, as did Harin. He had just returned from his long stay in the United States, and had made his own plans to join the freedom struggle, plans he shared with Kamaladevi. In addition to such visits, Kamaladevi found meaning in the way her arrest continued to galvanize resistance to British rule. In Poona on 10 August, at a gathering of some 400 people, Kamaladevi's imprisonment was repeatedly denounced. According to a police report, speaker after speaker 'mentioned the names of Sarojini Naidu, Kamaladevi and other women leaders who were rotting in jail for the sake of their country'.[38]

Sporadic protests continued until 5 March 1931, eleven months after the salt march had begun, when Gandhi and the viceroy signed an agreement that allowed Indians to produce their own salt for domestic consumption. Many protest leaders, including Kamaladevi, yearned for more dramatic changes. For those who had marched and been beaten and spent months in jail, a partial repeal of the salt tax seemed a paltry reward. Kamaladevi's vision of the salt satyagraha accords with the way scholar Erin Pineda has framed civil disobedience as a 'decolonial praxis', an act of radical imagination that envisioned far more than piecemeal reforms. From her demand that women be included in all facets of the struggle to her efforts to enlist the millworkers of Bombay to her vision of the Wadala protest, Kamaladevi strove to build an inclusive movement that would transform Indian society. Her vision, like Gandhi's, went far beyond the right to gather sea salt.[39]

Yet although swaraj had not been achieved, Kamaladevi would come to see the salt satyagraha as transformative—especially for women. 'It is not what the women actually did in the Satyagraha movement which matters so much as what the movement did to her,' she wrote in 1944. 'The status of women was completely transformed.' In her memoir, Kamaladevi praised Gandhi for using the cause of salt to energize so many Indians. 'By some extraordinary alchemy Gandhiji had used common salt to galvanise the age old inertia stemming from a sense of hopelessness, into self-confidence,' she wrote. 'The under current of fear evoked by a mighty weight sitting on our chest had evaporated, leaving us with a spirit of fearlessness.' Freed from jail, Kamaladevi quickly set about using that 'spirit of fearlessness' to continue the struggle for freedom.[40]

On 6 March 1931, Kamaladevi presided over the All Bengal Students' Conference in Calcutta. The conference hall was 'packed to suffocation'. In her address, Kamaladevi offered a powerful vision of freedom, not just as independence but as the responsibility to pursue justice. She said, 'No man ever remains free who acquiesces in what he knows to be wrong.' True freedom entailed fundamentally transforming Indian society. 'Unless there is a definite and radical reconstruction of society as it stands at present,' she declared, 'freedom will be only a dream. A mere transference of power from one group to another will leave the average toiler just where he was.' Kamaladevi drew on her travels in Europe to inform her argument. In the new nations formed after the breakup of the Austro-Hungarian empire, she found that conditions had 'improved considerably as a result of their getting rid of foreign rule but one cannot say that they have attained real freedom'. Even in a country like France, a country which had once inspired the world with its 'struggle for freedom,' Kamaladevi wrote, 'the very mention of the word liberty seems such a mockery to-day when one sees the miserable condition of the workers and the peasants.' The key to attaining true freedom, according to Kamaladevi, was 'organizing into a strong, powerful central body the workers and the peasants so that the power of the new Government may radiate from their co-operation'. The students would learn more from such organizing than they could ever learn in college. 'This organizing work,' she told the students, 'shall be your University.'[41]

To help define 'real freedom', Kamaladevi joined a small youth committee that included Yusuf Meherally and C.K. Narayanswami. 'It was necessary,' Kamaladevi wrote, 'that when we are calling upon the people to wage this big struggle for freedom, they should be guaranteed something of what that freedom would mean, the substance of it, and we should pledge ourselves—the Congress should pledge itself—that this is what you will get; this is what the essence of freedom will mean.' According to Kamaladevi, the committee asked the Bengali economist Nalinaksha Sanyal to produce a draft statement that Kamaladevi herself then took to Nehru, who added his own thoughts, wrote a preamble, and passed the resulting document along to Gandhi. This draft eventually became the landmark fundamental rights resolution that would be passed at the Congress session in Karachi in March 1931. While echoing long-standing demands for civil liberties, the resolution also called for social and economic rights, including free primary education and the right to form unions. While it is unclear who deserves credit for authoring the resolution—most accounts credit Nehru—what is clear is that Kamaladevi helped to advance a radical vision of a free and independent India.[42]

She did so in the midst of a personal crisis. Harin travelled with Kamaladevi to Karachi. On the return journey, he became drunk and made such a scene that other passengers felt compelled to intervene. Jawaharlal Nehru later enquired of Kamaladevi if there was some way he might help. Harin had become well-known for his drinking and for his womanizing. Indeed, one of his many affairs had become a topic of conversation throughout elite Indian circles.[43]

Sometime in 1929 or early 1930, Harin met Esther Luella Sherman in Brooklyn, New York. Born in Michigan in 1893, Sherman had taken the name Ragini Devi and had begun telling anyone who asked that she was from Kashmir and was a leading expert on Indian dance. Her performances were popular and, by the time she met Harin, Sherman was widely known as Ragini Devi and as a talented Indian dancer. The main problem for their relationship was not the fact that she was actually a White American woman; it was the fact that both were married. Ragini Devi had married Ramlal Balaram Bajpai, a chemist and Indian nationalist. That did not prevent Harin from pursuing the dancer. When Bajpai left on a trip to California, Harin and Ragini sold all of the furniture in the apartment and boarded a ship for France. This was in April 1930, at the very time that Kamaladevi was helping to lead the salt satyagraha in Bombay. While Kamaladevi was facing police violence and the threat of imminent arrest, Harin was sauntering across Paris with a married woman.[44]

Rather than travel to India together, where Harin feared arrest, he and Ragini hatched a plan to travel separately to Colombo, Ceylon (present-day Sri Lanka). The plan fell apart when Bajpai, the abandoned husband, alerted the colonial police and they refused to allow Ragini to disembark. She was forced to stay on the ship as it headed towards India, carrying with her a secret she had concealed from both Harin and Bajpai: she was pregnant. Before the ship reached India, she had given birth to a baby girl.[45]

While Ragini and Harin were travelling through Europe, Bajpai launched a letter-writing campaign, spreading news of the scandal across elite Indian society. Perhaps to redeem himself, Harin returned to India and threw himself into the salt satyagraha. He was arrested in

November 1930. Meanwhile, Ragini found herself alone with a newborn child. News of her plight made its way to Kamaladevi, who was still in jail. From her cell, she arranged for money and clothes to be brought to Ragini and her baby. As Sukanya Rahman, the daughter of that baby (and the granddaughter of Ragini), later wrote of Kamaladevi, 'Motivated by her respect and admiration for Ragini the artist, and perhaps by her feminist ideology, this remarkable woman rose above any ill-feelings or jealousy, and from her prison cell directed her network of friends, relatives, colleagues and theosophists like Annie Besant, to assist Ragini and her baby in every possible way.'[46]

After she was released from jail, Kamaladevi met Ragini in Bangalore. Ragini encouraged Kamaladevi to divorce Harin and offered to testify in court that Harin had broken his marital vows. When Kamaladevi challenged Harin about his relationship with Ragini, Harin denied everything and said that Ragini was lying. 'I was now very tired of all these matters,' Kamaladevi later recalled, 'and I did not have the strength to deal with their intricacies.'[47]

All of this happened before Kamaladevi and Harin sailed for Karachi in March 1931. If anyone had good reason to get angry on that ship, it was Kamaladevi. Yet she still maintained hope in Harin and in their future together. In Calcutta a month earlier, she had told the participants in the All Bengal Students' Conference that 'suffering and sacrifice are two magic coins that freedom demands from every one of us'. She ended, in her words, 'by quoting the following two lines that my husband sang to me the other day when I saw him in prison—"I am the flame that comes to heart out of long centuries of pain".' While the 'long centuries of pain' weighed on all Indian patriots, Kamaladevi had her own pain that was more private, a wound that she still hoped she and Harin could find a way to heal.[48]

~

Kamaladevi had little time to resolve her familial crisis. Not long after returning from Karachi, she left on a trip to Ceylon, where she was scheduled to preside at the annual meeting of the Jaffna Youth Congress.

She made plans that Harin and Rama would follow her. Perhaps the three of them would have a chance for a restorative family holiday, a chance to overcome the pain of the past.

On 23 April 1931, Kamaladevi arrived in Jaffna, a vibrant urban settlement on the northern tip of Ceylon. She boarded a carriage drawn by three white horses and was taken in a grand procession led by several musical bands. The procession, which included a crowd of volunteers all wearing khaddar and Gandhi caps, culminated at the Jaffna Esplanade, where a large pavilion had filled with young people eager to hear from Kamaladevi. 'Under the guise of a beneficial rule,' she declared, 'the imperial lords loot rich lands for the benefit of their own kinsmen.' The 'imperial lords' were hungry for resources and for markets. 'The British nation,' Kamaladevi explained, 'must find fresh fields for investing its capital and once again our lands come to their help.' She decried such 'economic enslavement'. According to Handy Perinbanayagam, the educator and anticolonial activist who had founded the Jaffna Youth Congress, Kamaladevi's address 'would have done justice to an academic lecture on the nature of Capitalism and Imperialism and exploitation of subject peoples in the colonies'. Perinbanayagam felt that Kamaladevi's intervention helped generate 'a turning point among the radicals in Jaffna who in course of time adopted a socialist anti-imperialist approach to politics'.[49]

Kamaladevi's time in Ceylon overlapped with a visit by Jawaharlal Nehru. In a speech at the inaugural meeting of the All-Ceylon Youth Congress in Wellawatte in May 1931, Nehru dismissed a rumour that he and Kamaladevi were secretly directing a boycott of the state council elections. Meanwhile, more intimate rumours were also circulating through Ceylonese society. Nehru was accompanied by his daughter, Indira, and his wife, who also happened to be named Kamala. The Sri Lankan architect Minnette De Silva later recalled that high society was abuzz with gossip regarding the relationship between Nehru and Kamaladevi and that Kamala Nehru was unhappy that Jawaharlal took Kamaladevi rowing on the lake in Kandy. Such tensions might not have arisen if Harin and Rama had joined Kamaladevi in Ceylon. Despite their plans to share a family trip, Harin never showed up with the child. Kamaladevi had to rush back to Madras to try to find them. She eventually located them in a small fishing village. Harin had not thought to tell her of the changed plans. As Kamaladevi later explained, he 'had no idea how much pain he had inflicted on others'.[50]

Kamaladevi and Harin might have reconnected through their shared passion for the arts. In 1931, Kamaladevi performed in a new art form, one that Harin would later make his own—the cinema. She had a role in *Vasantsena*, a silent film based on a well-known Sanskrit drama. According to the film scholar Bhagwan Das Garga, 'A salient feature of the production was that it brought members of the educated classes—Enakshi Rama Rau, Kamaladevi Chattopadhyay, Nalini Tarkhud and J.K. Nanda—to the screen, thus doing away with social prejudice against the profession.' As Kamaladevi put it in her memoir, the idea of educated women performing was still 'frowned upon by society'. The film was produced and directed by Mohan Bhavnani, a rising star in Indian cinema. Filmed at some of southern India's most storied temples, *Vasantsena* revolves around the romance between a man named Charudatta and a glamorous courtesan named Vasantsena. Kamaladevi played Charudatta's dutiful wife, a strangely fitting role given that she had her own wayward husband.[51]

In her own life, Kamaladevi rejected the role of the quiet, obedient wife. Her rebellious independence often put her at odds with the older men who guided the Congress, men like Sardar Vallabhbhai Patel. More than twenty-five years older than Kamaladevi, Patel was known as a tough pragmatist who was aligned with the more conservative elements of the national movement. In 1931, he published a critique of young radicals. Kamaladevi was upset by what she later called Patel's 'wholesale condemnation of all youth,' and in a published reply she 'hit back in scathing terms'. Not long thereafter, she visited Nehru in Allahabad, and found Gandhi there, holding the article she had written about Patel 'marked darkly by a red pencil'. Gandhi asked if she wrote it. She answered that she had. He replied, 'Did you really? When I read it I could hardly believe that.' Kamaladevi felt a 'pang' that she had hurt Gandhi, which was 'the last thing' she wanted to do. 'But I had no regret for what I had written,' she later explained, 'and I meant to make that clear.' After she defended herself, Gandhi put the article away and did not raise it with her again. 'He had a way of closing a topic like locking a box,' Kamaladevi recalled.[52]

Despite their ideological and personal differences, Kamaladevi had to find a way to work with Gandhi and Patel, especially after the Congress Working Committee decided to assume control of the Seva Dal. Kamaladevi's worries about the future of the dal are evident in a letter she sent to Gandhi from Poona on 26 July. She had travelled to Poona to organize local women to picket foreign cloth shops. She wrote Gandhi that she and Yashodabai Bhat had begun the picketing at the start of the month and had attracted two more volunteers to work with them. Together, they had convinced 101 shops to stop selling foreign cloth. Kamaladevi was proud of their work, but wished that more local women had rallied to the cause. She hoped that Gandhi would support such grassroots organizing and that 'the new organization which is to come into existence should give us every facility, opportunity & encouragement to carry on the work of organizing & training women volunteers'. After asking for a chance to meet Gandhi in person in Bombay, she closed her letter to him formally in a way that indicated the distance between her and the Mahatma at that time: 'With kindest regards, sincerely yours, Kamaladevi Chattopadhyaya.'[53]

Kamaladevi's commitment to defending the independence of the women's movement also led to tensions with Nehru, tensions that were on public display when, in early August, she travelled to Bombay for a meeting of the All India Congress Committee. Building on the economic rights resolution passed in Karachi in March, the AICC members debated a draft statement, 'Fundamental Rights and Economic Policy', Article Four of which called for the 'protection of women workers, and specially adequate provisions for leave during the maternity period'. Kamaladevi argued that many women would object to the word 'protection', as it suggested that women were weak. According to one record of the proceedings, she explained that 'her past experience had showed that women were shut up and disabled and crippled under the false guides of "protection". She added that she was sure there would be some conservatives in the swaraj government who would exploit the word "protection" and continue to keep women under their thumb.' Nehru was dismissive of these arguments. He replied, 'There could be no better instance of inferiority complex than Mrs Kamaladevi's objection to the word "protection". I do not understand what is humiliating in "protection".'[54]

Nehru won this debate, but Kamaladevi was more successful when moving an amendment to make primary education compulsory. Nehru argued against the amendment, explaining that he supported compulsory education 'but the Working Committee thought it would be difficult to enforce it in the whole of India'. Despite such practical complications, Kamaladevi's amendment passed. That proved a rare victory, however, as several other amendments she supported were rejected. Each rejection revealed how Kamaladevi's evolving views conflicted with the dominant Congress attitude. For example, Clause Nine read, 'The State shall observe religious neutrality regarding all religions.' Kamaladevi suggested adding 'except regarding social legislation affecting the progress and welfare of the people'. This suggestion revealed her awareness that religious orthodoxy often stood in the way of social reform, particularly in regards to the rights of women. The debate regarding when and if the state should become involved in matters of religion would be played out again after Independence in connection with the possibility of a uniform civil code. Presaging the challenges facing such a uniform code, Kamaladevi's amendment was rejected.[55]

She also lost when it came to land reform. Depending on the vantage point of the speaker, 'land reform' could include anything from gradual improvements in the tax system to massive land redistribution. The delegates discussed Article Seven, which could be seen as aiming for a middle ground by calling for 'immediately giving relief to the smaller peasantry by substantial reduction of agricultural rent'. The article left unclear exactly what would constitute 'substantial reduction of agricultural rent'. A delegate from Andhra suggested a more radical amendment: 'The system of reform shall aim at the gradual elimination of all intermediaries between the cultivators and the state.' Kamaladevi seconded the amendment and argued, in the words of the report, 'that under the present system of land revenue the cultivator was being exploited and crushed by these intermediaries who were sucking their life-blood like horse-leeches'. A more conservative delegate denounced both the original article and the amendment as 'sovietism in disguise'. Ultimately, delegates took the middle path, passing the original article but rejecting the more radical amendment that Kamaladevi had supported.[56]

On 9 August, one day after the conclusion of the AICC debates, Kamaladevi attended a special conference of the Seva Dal to decide whether to accept the Congress Working Committee's plan to bring the dal under Congress control. Gandhi opened the proceedings and Patel presided. Nehru, Hardikar, Khan Abdul Ghaffar Khan, Avantikabai Gokhale and Rajendra Prasad also attended. With such a luminous cast of Congress leaders, it is not surprising that the gathering voted to confirm Congress control of the dal. In Ahmedabad in September, the Working Committee officially accepted the plan to create a women's wing of the dal and to appoint Kamaladevi as the lead organizer. After the meeting, Nehru informed Kamaladevi of the Working Committee's decision. He expected her to be delighted with the news. Instead, she surprised him by replying, 'Don't you think you should have consulted and taken my prior approval?' Nehru agreed and apologized. Having asserted her autonomy, Kamaladevi accepted the appointment.[57]

She and Hardikar remained worried that the Congress would limit the activities of the dal. She decided to visit Patel. 'He received me with an unusually friendly smile,' she later recalled, and he surprised her by suggesting that their first priority should be 'training Sevikas in thousands—hundreds of thousands'. Delighted by such an ambitious plan, she suggested that the dal launch an 'All-India national camp to train instructors who in turn will train the women in their own regions'. Patel agreed, saying, 'I want to assure you I will never interfere. And any time you need my help, never hesitate to contact me.' In October 1931, the police reported that Kamaladevi was working 'to organize a Central

Women's Camp at Hubli to train 10–15 women instructors from all provinces'. Towards that end, 'Mrs Chattopadhyaya has made a brief tour of the Karnatak and is shortly to make an all-India one.'[58]

In her travels, Kamaladevi split her time between women's organizations and student groups. In October, she was in Lahore presiding over a student conference. Gandhi was at the Round Table Conference in London, but Kamaladevi remained sceptical that the British would voluntarily relinquish power. 'Let us remember,' she told the students, that those 'who are banqueting with Mahatmaji in London today, will send him to Yeravda Prison tomorrow.' She condemned the education system as 'a frame that ill fits us for it is cast in a sinister mould'. Her own approach to education is evident in her work with the Seva Dal. As she travelled the country setting up local organizations of desh sevikas, she demonstrated her belief in the power of a politically engaged mass education that linked learning and liberation.[59]

With liberatory education as the goal, Kamaladevi helped to organize the national training camp at Borivali, a suburb of Bombay. Patel inaugurated the camp on 16 December, but it was not his support that meant the most to Kamaladevi. It was the enthusiasm of the many women who volunteered to make the camp a success. 'I was swept off my feet by the response from the women,' Kamaladevi later wrote. 'An age limit had been put, from the age of 16 to 45, for the recruits. But our efforts to try to adhere to it became a battleground, young kids on one side, and real old women on the other tugged at our recruitment line.' Kamaladevi chose Sophia Somji, a seventeen-year-old Khoja Muslim, as her main assistant. The overall responsibility for the camp was shared. In December, Nehru wrote K.F. Nariman, 'I understand that Kumari Lajjavati of the Punjab has been appointed by Hardikar as the commander of the women's camp. I think this is a good choice. Lajjavati is a capable and enthusiastic woman and she should do well. Kamaladevi of course will be there to help but she was not prepared to take entire charge.' For her part, it is unlikely that Kamaladevi wanted full responsibility for the camp, as that would have limited her ability to travel. On 22 December, she was in Poona at the Maharashtra Youth Conference, where she shared the stage with Subhas Chandra Bose, the Bengali firebrand and future leader of the Indian National Army.[60]

The government kept a watchful eye on her travels, as did others invested in the status quo. An officer of the European Association of Calcutta wrote the Home Department to denounce Kamaladevi's efforts to create a cadre of young people and women who would 'go among all classes of people as theoreticians, as propagandists, as agitators, and as organisers'. Meanwhile, the colonial government was making plans for a new campaign of repression—a campaign that would target not just the dal but the entire Congress leadership.[61]

In early January 1932, the government declared the Congress illegal. Gandhi was arrested, as were several other leaders. The arrests set off protests throughout much of India. In Bombay on 6 January, Kamaladevi led a group of desh sevikas dressed in orange saris to picket shops selling foreign cloth. After a half-hour of picketing, the shops closed. Kamaladevi had little time to celebrate, however, as she was soon arrested. The authorities chose not to detain her for long—at least not yet. On 6 April, a crowd of some 3,000 people gathered in Bombay for an event designed to encourage women to join the freedom struggle. Kamaladevi organized a procession and had just begun leading it when she was again arrested, along with eight others, two of them teenage girls. 'On their arrest,' the police reported, 'the crowd showed some excitement and were dispersed by a mild lathi charge.'[62]

Kamaladevi was brought before a magistrate who demanded to know her address. She gave the address of the Borivali camp, which had recently been dismantled. 'So you have no residence,' the magistrate replied. 'You were picked up on the road, you are a vagrant.' He sentenced her to one year of rigorous imprisonment. Was it a source of support or of pain that Sarojini Naidu brought little Rama to witness the verdict? It must have been deeply painful for both mother and son to know that they would be separated yet again.[63]

~

Kamaladevi was taken to Arthur Road Jail in Bombay. Finding it dirty and crowded, she drafted a memo demanding improvements. The warden identified her as a troublemaker and isolated her from the other prisoners. 'The black prison van took a quick round,' Kamaladevi recalled, 'and within minutes I was in a barrack at the back of where I had left.' She was greeted by 'a tall white figure, holding out both hands and a warm smile'. It was Mirabehn. Born Madeleine Slade, the daughter of a British admiral, Mirabehn had become one of Gandhi's most devoted disciples. Seeing that her new cellmate would be Mirabehn brought Kamaladevi great relief. 'I felt like a storm-wrecked boat being docked in a secure cove,' she later recalled.[64]

Mirabehn and Kamaladevi were kept apart from the other prisoners. During the day, they were allowed to make use of a small open space that featured a tree and a few flowers. When Kamaladevi picked a red flower and put it in her hair (a practice she would maintain throughout her life), she was scolded by the prison matron. The prisoners were not allowed to sleep outside, despite the stifling heat and 'the endless variety of evil smells' that wafted in through the drains and from beyond the prison wall. The two women made the best of their situation. Mirabehn cooked their food and shared her books and her spinning wheel with Kamaladevi. They also took to praying, singing and exercising together. Kamaladevi suggested skipping as a good way to exercise in a small space, a fact that Mirabehn included in a note she wrote to Gandhi. He replied, 'I am delighted that you have Kamaladevi with you and that she joins you at the morning prayer and sings bhajans in the evening. Her vigorous skipping reminds me of the time when I used to skip for the same reason as Kamaladevi.' Imprisonment was bringing Kamaladevi closer to Mirabehn—and to Gandhi, as well.[65]

Kamaladevi would not be able to enjoy Mirabehn's company for long, as she was soon transferred to Hindalga Jail in Belgaum. When Gandhi learnt of the transfer, he wrote Mirabehn, 'A prisoner has no choice. His or her body is not in his or her own keeping.' Saddened that she would be separated from Mirabehn, Kamaladevi found one silver lining in her forced transfer. Somehow, she managed to arrange for Rama to be brought to the train station at the moment she was to be transported to Belgaum. If it brought her comfort to see her son, it also brought increased anxiety and perhaps guilt. 'For the first time I saw him look very forlorn and depressed,' she later wrote. 'No doubt he was one of thousands of his age going through this trauma.' By universalizing the experience of her son, she distanced herself from the sadness and fear he must have felt and avoided discussing her own emotions as she left her son to go to prison without knowing for how long they would be apart.[66]

Kamaladevi was a Class B prisoner. Most anticolonial leaders were given either Class A or Class B status. They were allowed books and newspapers and could often cook their own food or decide on their own clothes. By comparison, most poor women were Class C prisoners who were denied these privileges. At Hindalga, Kamaladevi was interned with Gauramma, the wife of Sardar Venkataramiah, a Seva Dal leader. Venkataramiah later recalled that Kamaladevi shared the extra milk, butter and bread that she received as a Class B prisoner with Gauramma and other local women, most of whom were Class C prisoners. Many were from poor forest villages. While Kamaladevi shared food with them, they in turn shared their experiences of struggle—not just during the satyagraha but also in the course of their daily lives. Their experiences left a lasting mark on Kamaladevi and her commitment to combating poverty and inequality. 'These were the poorest women I had occasion to live in close contact with and get glimpses of their everyday life of want and hunger,' she wrote in her memoir. It was not solely their experiences of poverty that touched her. Equally important was their expansive conception of freedom. 'Their concepts of what they wanted was not just mere food, better houses, proper clothes, etc.,' Kamaladevi wrote. 'Yes, they needed these but it was more than that, they explained. They wanted freedom, not only for them, but all who were today in bondage like them.'[67]

Kamaladevi was housed with other Class B prisoners, including committed activists like Mridula Sarabhai. Rather than do hard labour, they were allowed to spend their days spinning, reading, writing and talking. Yet even for the Class B prisoners, the conditions were crowded, bedbugs and mosquitoes were rampant, and the food was meagre, monotonous and lacking in nutrition. One of the biggest challenges for Kamaladevi was the cold, Belgaum being several thousand feet in elevation. The prisoners were given two thin blankets, one to be used in lieu of a mattress. Kamaladevi 'shivered all night'. Whether because of an infection or the diet, she developed jaundice, and her health quickly deteriorated. 'The days flitted past like grey shadows that formed a kind of a monotonous moving curtain,' she recalled. 'It was as though everything was receding further and further behind this shadowy curtain.' In late November 1932, Margaret Cousins visited Kamaladevi in jail and found her 'shrunken in body, but strong in nerve, and indomitable in will'. News of her illness escaped the prison, pressure mounted on the authorities, and a senior doctor authorized a more nutritious diet. Kamaladevi recovered and, in typical fashion, responded to her struggles by helping others. She set up a makeshift hospital ward in an abandoned shed. 'The floor was ordinary raw ground,' she recalled. 'I begged of those who were getting released to donate to this hospital some essentials like cotton, bandages, disinfectants.' Slowly, she amassed enough materials to treat sick prisoners, including a woman with typhoid and a pregnant woman whose baby Kamaladevi helped to deliver.[68]

Kamaladevi remained in jail in Belgaum throughout the fall and winter of 1932–33. When she emerged from jail in the spring of 1933, she learnt that Harin was living in the far south of India with their former nanny, Seetha—and they had kept Rama with them. It remains unclear exactly at what point Kamaladevi decided to seek a divorce. 'I could not imagine leaving Harindranath even after suffering so much,' Kamaladevi later told Kamala Ratnam. 'In spite of all possible efforts to make the marriage a success in every possible way, there was a feeling in my mind that there was some flaw in me, due to which our family was not able to run normally. Somewhere I had failed.' Her guilt prevented her from initiating the divorce. She felt that if only she tried harder, she might be able to set Harin on a better path. 'I can bring stability in his life,' she thought. 'I will be able to help him in finding a direction.' Harin exploited Kamaladevi's sense of responsibility by telling her that he felt differently about her than he did the other women with whom he had affairs. 'Your attraction has taken me beyond the male–female relationship,' he explained, 'and that's why I think my relationship with you will be permanent.' Harin's words seem hollow and obviously self-interested, but Kamaladevi still found hope in them. 'I felt then,' she recalled, 'and still feel that the relationship he had with me was different from his relationships with other women.'[69]

The decision to seek a divorce was made even more difficult by Kamaladevi's role in the movement and the danger that the scandal would jeopardize her reputation. Divorce was extraordinarily rare, and many of Harin's family members—including Sarojini Naidu—blamed Kamaladevi for her marital problems. As Kamaladevi recalled, 'Harindranath's brothers and sisters used to treat his love affairs very lightly.' They also charged Kamaladevi with the responsibility for policing Harin's behaviour. Several members of the family, including Naidu, took to warning Kamaladevi to keep Harin away from particular lovers. They saw Kamaladevi's interest in divorce as a dereliction of duty. Naidu remained among the most prominent women in India. Alienating her would be a tremendous risk for Kamaladevi. She had already strained her ties with Gandhi, whose own opposition to divorce was well known.[70]

On 26 March 1933, a week before her thirtieth birthday, Kamaladevi wrote Gandhi from Mangalore. 'Dear Revered Mahatmaji,' she began, 'Since you were kind enough to take so much interest in my affairs and to very generously offer to help me in my immediate work and the course of action I should follow, I take this liberty of writing to you . . . So much has happened since I last saw you,' Kamaladevi continued, 'and I am rather perplexed and disturbed as to what I should do. May I implore you to help me to arrive at some decision? It would mean so much to me.' Kamaladevi hoped Gandhi could find the time for an in-person meeting. As she explained in her letter, a face-to-face conversation 'would save my giving these unpleasant & rather intimate details through letters . . . You must forgive my troubling you thus,' she wrote. Kamaldevi knew that Gandhi had 'weighty & serious problems to tackle,' and wrote, 'I feel most guilty when I approach you thus. It is only your kindly assurance &

generous offer that has emboldened me.' Her distance from Gandhi was again made clear by the way in which she closed her letter: 'With kindest regards, yours sincerely, Kamaladevi Chattopadhyaya.'[71]

Unlike Mirabehn and many other Gandhian activists, Kamaladevi would never become a disciple of the Mahatma. As Margaret Cousins later wrote, while others were dedicated to Gandhi as a person, 'Kamaladevi followed what she regarded as principles, not personalities'. Kamaladevi had challenged Gandhi when it came to women's involvement in the salt satyagraha, but she continued to respect him. In 1932, Kamaladevi penned an essay entitled 'Enter Gandhi' for an edited volume called *India's Case for Swaraj*. 'Gandhiji has prepared a case not merely for India's Freedom,' she wrote, 'but for a vaster and more comprehensive morality and in his own inimitable way he has shown that there cannot be two moral codes, one for the individual and one for the nation.' Could the Mahatma's moral code make room for divorce? By seeking freedom for her nation and for herself, Kamaladevi embodied the moral integrity that she credited Gandhi with advancing. It remained unclear if he would see it that way.[72]

Kamaladevi's next letter to Gandhi, sent on 5 May 1933, offers evidence of a growing closeness between them. Importantly, the letter does not concern her struggles but his. He had vowed to commence a fast against untouchability. 'Dear Mahatmaji,' Kamaladevi wrote, 'I realise that your decision to make this stupendous sacrifice is final & irrevocable. But I have a conviction that you will pass through it.' She added, 'Perhaps the very strength and intensity of our need of you will keep you amidst us. Our thoughts and prayers are ever with you.' The warmth of her wishes was mirrored in the way she closed her letter: 'Your ever devoted Kamaladevi.' She no longer felt the need to sign her full name.[73]

Her growing closeness with the Mahatma would be tested by a letter that Sarojini Naidu sent Gandhi that fall. Naidu accused Kamaladevi of wanting a divorce in order to marry someone else and asked Gandhi not to involve himself in Kamaladevi's 'affairs'. Disregarding that request, Gandhi wrote several colleagues seeking additional opinions on Kamaladevi and her trustworthiness. Having gathered more information, he then arranged to speak with Kamaladevi directly. In a gesture that demonstrated his commitment to transparency as well as his trust in Kamaladevi, Gandhi showed her the letter he had received from Naidu. We do not know what Kamaladevi thought or felt reading that letter in Gandhi's presence. Despite their frictions, Kamaladevi had long respected Naidu. She would later praise the poet as 'one of those rare beings who is never defeated or frustrated in the most trying circumstances'. But the two women were not close. Towards the end of her life, Kamaladevi wrote of Naidu, 'The closer one got to her, the more one saw her, the more bewildered one felt. There were many conflicting and contradictory forces working within her.' According to Gopalkrishna Gandhi, Kamaladevi 'never said a word about Sarojini Naidu, neither in praise nor in disparagement, and her silence said everything'.[74]

In her memoir, Kamaladevi recalled that her conversation with Gandhi focused on Rama. She remembered the Mahatma asking, 'What do you propose to do with your son?' Gandhi had met with the boy in Mangalore during Kamaladevi's imprisonment. According to Kamaladevi, Gandhi told her, 'Either you take control of the situation, set a proper course for him or decide to abandon him to an existence of disruption and drift and feel you don't care what happens to him ultimately. I want you to realise that if you can't have a grip on your own life and shape it, how do you think you can break our country's bondage?' According to the scholar Julie Laut Barbieri, Gandhi's advice 'eerily echoes the imperialists' demands on their Indian colonial subjects to put their house in order before assuming political rights'. It doesn't seem as if Kamaladevi saw it that way, at least when she penned her memoirs. Her framing of the interaction with Gandhi is generally positive. Tellingly, she chose not to write anything about Naidu's letter or Gandhi's thoughts on the prospect of her divorce. There is evidence, however, that Gandhi's advice confirmed her decision to move forward with the divorce. 'Sitting near Bapu,' she told Kamala Ratnam, 'I felt at that moment that we cannot fight for freedom without being free ourselves.'[75]

Kamaladevi might have courted Gandhi's support by promising not to remarry. Instead, she stated, 'Only time will tell whether I marry another man.' Kamaladevi was accompanied at the meeting by Dr Hardikar. It is unclear exactly what role Hardikar played in the conversation, but Kamaladevi would later express gratitude to him for the fact that he 'stood nobly by her' when 'the clouds were very dark in my sky'. It is also unclear what advice Gandhi offered her regarding her marriage. On 20 October, he wrote Mathuradas Trikumji, 'There is no alternative but to guide Kamaladevi. One cannot go by rumours. I asked her many frank questions. But she only declares her innocence. I am not trying to stop the divorce. It has become necessary.' What is clear is that Gandhi advised her to take a break from her political work and to go home so she could be with Rama, who was ill at the time. Returning home seemed like a wise next step, but the journey would prove much harder—and much longer—than anyone could have expected.[76]

On the train from Wardha to Mangalore, Kamaladevi was joined by Kaleshwar Rao, a lawyer and Congress leader who would later become the Speaker of the Andhra Pradesh Assembly. Rao invited her to break the journey at Vijayawada and to accompany him on a short trip to his native village. When they reached the village, all the residents gathered to greet them. Suddenly, the police arrived and arrested both Kamaladevi and Rao. When their trial began, Rao demanded to know the charges. The police had no good answer, and the magistrate was about to close the case when the government's attorney managed to have the proceedings shifted to another village where Kamaladevi and Rao were kept in jail for several days in harsh conditions. In typical fashion, Kamaladevi managed to laugh at the situation. She wrote a colleague, 'I have had the most glorious experiences in Gudivada—two days to get a change of clothes, four days to get toothpaste, five for a comb and on to the sixth day a cake of soap actually arrived! All these were withheld on grounds that they are luxuries. Fruit was refused because the paternal magistrate feared it would give me indigestion! Once I asked for a glass of water. He consulted the police and law books to see if the Indian Penal Code has a Section permitting the accused drinking water.'[77]

Kamaladevi's arrest quickly became news among Congress leaders. 'I have just seen that Kamaladevi has been arrested in Gudivada,' Nehru wrote Hardikar on 28 October. 'This was rather unexpected. I suppose that probably she will be let off soon. But one never knows. This kind of thing is bound to continue. People talk of our withdrawing our offensive but they forget that the other party's offensive is continuous and unrelenting.'[78]

Yet another trial was held. While the judge was considering his verdict, Kamaladevi penned a letter to the editor of the *Bombay Chronicle*. Dated 4 December 1933, Kamaladevi's letter demonstrates her belief in helping people whenever possible. 'I am writing this during my trial,' she began. 'The judgment is expected to be delivered in an hour's time.' Rather than discuss her case, she asked the editor to help a young journalist who was hoping to publish a weekly letter in the *Chronicle*. Facing another term of imprisonment, Kamaladevi made time to write a letter of recommendation for a young man she barely knew.[79]

The new magistrate again dismissed the case and the prisoners were discharged. It seemed as if this latest nightmare was coming to an end. But as they left the courtroom, the police arrested them again. This time, they were offered a way out. If they would sign a bond promising good behaviour, they would be released. Rao signed the bond. Kamaladevi refused. Why should she be forced to sign a bond promising good behaviour when she had done nothing wrong? Such a request was an infringement on her rights and she refused to play along. According to Reena Nanda, 'Her imprisonment was unnecessary since she could easily have signed the bond like Kaleshwara Rao. Her young son needed her but she gave no heed to that.' Yet the fact that Kamaladevi refused to sign despite her familial responsibilities testifies to her commitment to her principles and her fierce opposition to official malfeasance.[80]

It was her concerns for Rama, including the impact of Harin on the boy, that finally convinced Kamaladevi to move forward with the divorce. At first, Harin was shocked. According to Kamaladevi, 'Harindranath probably thought of me as a part of the decorations of his house.' If it was hard for him to accept the necessity of divorce, the overall process was much harder for her—both because of the special burdens placed on divorced women and because she saw the divorce as a personal failure. She later described the process as akin to 'coming out of a small hole full of thorns . . . the soul bleeds in the process'.[81]

During her imprisonment in Gudivada, she was given special parole in order to offer evidence in the divorce case in Bombay. She had to leave jail and travel 1,000 kilometres by train to participate in an even more difficult courtroom proceeding. For someone as private as Kamaladevi, it must have been painful to discuss her marital life in a public courtroom. Of course, she had long advocated for divorce as a fundamental right. 'It was surprising,' she later recalled, that 'I was feeling so much difficulty in reaching the same solution for myself.' But it is one thing to affirm a general right and something else to exercise that right in one's own life. Kamaladevi asked that the divorce proceedings be completed in a closed court. The English judge in the Bombay High Court refused her request, and the proceedings went forward in open court. Harin chose not to attend. 'Standing in the court and accusing him was a very difficult task for me,' Kamaladevi recalled. At least the divorce was granted.[82]

Years later, Kamaladevi would offer a vivid portrait of Harin's strengths and failings, a portrait that reveals much about Kamaladevi herself. 'Deep inside him, somewhere very profound, there was an alive-element,' she explained to Kamala Ratnam. Asked what attracted her to Harin, she replied, 'I was attracted to his roots. These roots were visible in all his works.' She liked that his roots 'were deeply Indian', but they did not provide stability. He was 'as fickle and directionless as a gust of wind, utterly unsteady'. He was 'like an instrument receiving the broadcasts of All India Radio, whose hold on the sound-waves has become loose. Even after repeatedly moving the needle to a certain place, it would not settle there.' A gust of wind, a faulty radio—Harin's instability demanded multiple metaphors. 'It was as if,' Kamaladevi declared, 'the gems of his genius had been scattered here and there without any thread.'[83]

The range of poetic metaphors she deployed to describe Harin is fitting given that it was art, broadly understood, that brought the two together. Kamaladevi told one interviewer that her relationship with Harin was defined by their 'common interest in art', adding that 'I would not call it a marriage in the purely emotional sense'. She suggested that their connection was driven primarily by their desire to work together. 'We had great dreams of doing things together and we thought it would be difficult to work together unless we were married,' she explained. 'Perhaps, in a way, that was helpful because, in spite of many difficulties, we were able to work together.'[84]

No matter how much Kamaladevi tried to separate her public and private lives, they remained linked together. Even those who were supportive of divorce played a role in keeping her private life linked to her public activism. On 21 November 1933, Jawaharlal Nehru wrote Kamaladevi, 'Your arrest seemed to me to give point to my argument that those who are likely to act or speak aggressively in public are not going to be tolerated.' 'We have a strong conservative element which dislikes divorce,' he added. 'I don't know why anyone should object to a divorce proceeding?' Many did object, and as a single woman Kamaladevi would long be dogged by rumours of sexual impropriety, rumours that were rarely directed at single men. Kamaladevi's relationship with Nehru had already generated gossip. Certainly, she and Nehru were close despite their many disagreements. In 1933, she wrote Nehru of his 'smile with its exquisite melting quality' and said no camera captured 'these divine glimpses'. It remains unclear what her relationship with Nehru meant to Kamaladevi, but his support must have been especially meaningful as she dealt with conservative opposition to divorce and the threat of an interminable prison sentence.[85]

Kamaladevi was sent to Vellore Jail, a few hours west of Madras. In Belgaum, she had shivered through the cold of the hills. In Vellore, she suffered the intense heat of the plains. 'All day the sun beat down and at night the day's heat absorbed by the rocks oozed out, penetrating into my very bones,' she later wrote. 'The nights became pretty nightmarish.' Her cell was 5 feet wide by 8 feet long. It had a single door made of iron bars. There was no window. At night, it became suffocating. She asked for permission to sleep outdoors, but her request was denied. Unlike previous periods in jail, the authorities kept her in solitary confinement. She was allowed to send and receive but one letter per month. Even the women who brought her food were instructed not to speak with her.[86]

The greatest burden was the fact that she could not be with her son. 'It was my misfortune,' Kamaladevi recalled, 'that in the midst of the troubles of the break-up of the marriage, I had to go through the troubles of going to jail and being separated from my family.' Although it was her concern for Rama that had convinced her to seek the divorce, she was now unable to be there to guide him. 'The dear son for whose sake I had bothered to get a divorce,' she lamented, 'after the divorce, he was no longer with me. The one whose delicate body and lovely face I wanted to embrace to fulfil my cut-off limbs, was now away from me. Far from loving him, I could not even see him.'[87]

Kamaladevi's ordeal in Vellore reminds us of the suffering of many colonial prisoners and draws special attention to the experience of women separated from their children. Colonial authorities publicized the special care they gave to Gandhi when imprisoned, displaying for reporters, for example, 'a dozen woolly animals of the purest strain, purchased by His Majesty's Government to supply the prisoner with his favourite beverage: goat's milk'. Kamaladevi's experience undermines such imperial propaganda by revealing the brutality of colonial jails and the bodily and psychological suffering of many prisoners. 'I can't say that I didn't feel sad, hopeless or helpless during this period,' Kamaladevi later remembered of her time in Vellore Jail. 'Those who say that prison life elevates man, elevates him to a higher level of spirituality,' she added, 'they want to paint a very painful atmosphere with the colours of their imagination. In my understanding, the body surrounded by constricted conditions also makes the mind constricted.'[88]

At times, Kamaladevi maintained her sense of humour. 'Oh Bhai,' she wrote her colleague Acharya Kripalani, 'do write when you can give me news from your part of the world—of course news such as will reach me.' Only some letters survived the prison censors. 'I had a letter from Elwin,' she wrote, referring to the anthropologist Verrier Elwin. 'He says even the bears and lions have been quiet this year. I don't wonder. General Depression I suppose.' Such an oblique reference to the state of the country must not have troubled the authorities, but Kamaladevi was not always so cautious in her prison correspondence. 'You and I will stick to the plains and its gloom,' she told Kripalani, 'while our very illustrious friends rush to the Imperial Capital of the cool hill-station of

Simla. Don't you wish they would settle down there forever and never come down again?' One wonders what the prison censors made of such a direct criticism of the British. Kamaladevi concluded, 'I am feeling as fit and well as ever. It is lovely being alone—just books and books and books. I wonder if you envy me.' A testament to her passion for reading, this note also reveals her fierce determination. But neither passion nor determination could protect her body from the harsh conditions of her imprisonment. She might have been having an unusually good day when she told Kripalani that she was 'feeling as fit and well as ever'. Or perhaps she did not want to worry him with the brutal nature of her ordeal. The unrelenting heat and the inadequate diet both took a heavy toll on her health. Twice she was found unconscious in her cell before she was finally released on medical grounds.[89]

4

Democratic Socialism

On 21 October 1934 some 150 delegates gathered in Worli, Bombay, for the first All India Socialist Conference. The delegates included such prominent figures as Ram Manohar Lohia, F.H. Ansari, Achyut Patwardhan and Jayaprakash Narayan. Kamaladevi was one of the few women present. If that fact bothered her, she chose not to mention it, neither then nor later. At women's conferences, she had long been one of the few socialists. At socialist gatherings, she was often one of the only women. Perhaps she saw it as an opportunity to bridge struggles. She must have approved when delegates envisioned a free India in which 'the State shall not discriminate between sexes'. Yet there is no evidence that she chose to speak on behalf of women's struggles, or to urge delegates to focus on combating sexism. By 1934, she had become convinced that the two most fundamental goals of the Indian struggle needed to be wresting political power from Britain and economic power from landlords and capitalists.[1]

Her political and economic views positioned Kamaladevi in opposition to both communism and the conservative wing of the Congress. With the communists, she shared a belief in the necessity of sweeping economic redistribution, and a willingness to use state power to achieve such redistribution. She parted ways with many communists when it came to the importance of democracy and nonviolent change. By contrast, her dedication to democracy and nonviolence connected her with even the most conservative Congress leaders. With them, it was her commitment to economic equality that made her stand out. Like Kamaladevi, many Congress Socialists positioned themselves between the communists and the conservative wing of the Congress. Their support for both democracy and socialism distinguished them from either extreme of the political spectrum.

The first All India Socialist Conference was briefly disrupted when a truckful of Communist Party members drove up shouting slogans. The conflict between communists and socialists went back well beyond when Kamaladevi had protected the national flag from the hammer and sickle, and it would continue to play a major role in shaping Kamaladevi's understanding of her politics. It was not the communists, however, but conservative Congressmen like Vallabhbhai Patel who Kamaladevi had in mind when she moved a resolution that was widely covered in newspapers, including several overseas. As far away as Perth, Australia, readers learned that 'Mrs Kamaladevi Chattopadhyya, a militant Congress leader just released from prison on completion of a sentence for civil resistance, moved that the conference urge on the Congress that the goal of independence should mean the establishment of an independent State and complete separation from the British Empire. The resolution was adopted.'[2]

Most of the socialist leaders remained members of the Congress, and worked to shift its priorities. Their gathering had been timed to coincide with the 48th Annual Session of the Congress which also met in Bombay. The socialist conference attracted some 150 delegates, a tiny number compared to the thousands of people who attended the Congress session. Yet the socialists had influence beyond their numbers. In his opening speech at the Congress gathering, the chairman of the reception committee, K.F. Nariman, declared, 'This is the first session in which an organised political group within the Congress makes its appearance with a radically different outlook and fundamentally different programme. The Congress Socialist Party, born only a few months ago, has emerged with an ambitious programme.' In his presidential address, Rajendra Prasad also discussed the socialists. 'My friends,' he stated, 'the socialists are keen on a more inspiring ideology and would hasten the elimination of all that stands for exploitation. I should like to tell them in all humility but with all the force at my command that there is no greater ideology than is expressed by the creed of truth and non-violence and the determination of the country not to eliminate the men that stand for exploitation but the forces that do so.'[3]

The Congress Working Committee had passed a resolution that opposed 'loose talk about confiscation of private property and the necessity of class war' as 'contrary to the Congress creed of non-violence'. The socialist leader Narendra Deva moved an amendment that aimed to delete that resolution. Kamaladevi seconded Deva's amendment and declared, 'A Parliamentary programme will have no effect unless linked up with dynamic mass action in the country.' Referring to the Working Committee resolutions on socialism, she added, 'I was shocked at that exhibition of colossal ignorance on the part of India's Nationalist Cabinet.' She then proceeded to explain why the resolutions reflected ignorance. 'Class war is inherent in the present capitalistic society,' she began. 'Nobody created it. It simply exists by itself and will continue to exist as long as the present social and economic system continues.' It was silly for the Working Committee to treat 'class war' as a policy under consideration; it was a reality of life under any capitalist system. Kamaladevi then asked a series of questions: 'Why should the instruments of production be controlled by a small coterie to the detriment of the masses? Why should a few people be rolling in wealth while millions upon millions have not even plain food to eat, much less clothes to wear?' She linked her critique of inequality to an overemphasis on markets. 'A society that is regulated by the motives of the market deserves to be demolished,' she declared. Rajendra Prasad had contrasted socialism with Gandhian nonviolence. Kamaladevi responded by linking capitalism with violence. She asked, 'Can there be a more organized and systematised kind of violence than the one that permitted a few to exult in the miseries of the many?'[4]

Kamaladevi and her socialist colleagues struggled to recruit other delegates. Even Acharya Kripalani, who would later become a leading socialist, declared that 'the Congress Socialists have misunderstood the problems of class-war and confiscation of property'. He cited the French and Russian revolutions in order to argue that 'class hatred' would lead 'to massacres and a reign of terror'. When it came to a vote, a large majority rejected the socialist amendments. Yet the Congress Socialists would have a lasting impact on the future of the Congress and thus on the future of India. The hope and idealism that Kamaladevi shared with her socialist colleagues would combine with their trenchant critique of inequality to inspire a range of initiatives—from small-scale community efforts to massive state-directed institutions. Over time, Kamaladevi would come to realize the dangers of state power, and would move towards a blend of socialism and Gandhian anti-statist activism. What remained at the core of her socialism throughout her life was perhaps the most striking achievement of the Congress Socialists more generally—the way they blended a revolutionary vision of a new society with a principled commitment to deliberative democracy. As important as what Kamaladevi argued at the Congress gathering was the simple fact that she was there—debating ideas with colleagues across the political spectrum—and not building bombs or organizing armed peasant revolts. Embodying Amartya Sen's celebration of the 'argumentative Indian', Kamaladevi demonstrated a commitment to nonviolence that had grown stronger over time, rooted not in devotion to absolutes but in tolerance, humanism and the joy of a good debate.[5]

~

Kamaladevi's political journey would dovetail with the evolution of India's most renowned socialist, a man who was one of her mentors and a good friend—Jayaprakash Narayan. Born a year before Kamaladevi in present-day Bihar, Narayan became a socialist in the United States, where he lived, worked and studied from 1922 to 1929. While attending courses at the University of California and the University of Wisconsin, Narayan survived by picking grapes, waiting tables and washing dishes. His courses and his work experiences together inspired his commitment to socialism. 'Strangely enough,' he later remembered, 'it was in the land of resilient and successful capitalism, in the United States of America . . . that I became a convert to Marxism.' Narayan was inspired by another well-known Indian Marxist, Manabendra Nath Roy, who also spent time in the United States. After being targeted by American authorities as 'one of the most violent revolutionaries India has produced', Roy escaped to Mexico where he helped found the Mexican Communist Party. In addition to Narayan and Roy, colonial India was home to a variety of other prominent socialists and communists, many of whom had their own distinct approach to socialism. The historian John Patrick Haithcox divided the Congress Socialists of the 1930s into three groups, with Narayan and Acharya Narendra Deva being most influenced by Marxism; Minoo Masani and Asoka Mehta being 'democratic socialists'; and Achyut Patwardhan and Ram Manohar Lohia sharing 'Gandhi's faith in governmental and economic decentralization and nonviolent revolution'. Kamaladevi spanned many of these divides. She helped bridge different socialist factions, just as she had long helped connect women's movements to other facets of the freedom struggle.[6]

The inclusivity of Kamaladevi's socialism came from her broad reading, her blend of idealism and pragmatism, and her ability to see multiple perspectives on a particular question. Madhu Dandavate, the physicist and socialist politician, praised Kamaladevi's 'total and integrated view of life'. He paired Kamaladevi with Yusuf Meherally. It was their 'fascination for Indian culture' and their interest in the 'cultural aspects of socialism' that shaped the 'aesthetic and ethical roots' of their socialist politics. Speaking of Kamaladevi, Dandavate wrote, 'Even in the midst of tumult and turmoil of political life her vision of beauty was never blurred. To her aesthetic sense, inequality appeared quite ugly and immoral because it stunted the free development of human personality.'[7]

Dandavate had good reason to emphasize the importance of beauty and that 'aesthetic sense'. Yet in the 1930s Kamaladevi was equally known for her ferocity. She did not hesitate to speak her mind. 'That's my trouble,' she wrote Acharya Kripalani in 1934, 'blunt language like a blunt knife is more exasperating than a sharp one.' Part of her ferocity was a response to what was expected of women. As she told Kripalani, she was not one of those 'Bapu-worshipping females who loll comfortably in their armchairs'.[8]

Kamaladevi was also known for supporting a range of grassroots organizations. In 1933, she had joined a march of farmers and peasants led by N.G. Ranga. In October 1935, Ranga asked Kamaladevi to inaugurate the All India Peasants and Workers Conference. Kamaladevi encouraged Ranga to expand his efforts beyond his base in contemporary Andhra Pradesh to include leaders from Bihar and the United Provinces.[9]

Kamaladevi continued to bring her organizing talents to the Congress as well. She focused on her own region by working to revitalize the Mangalore District Congress Committee. 'I am getting the District Committee firmly established,' she wrote to N.S. Hardikar. She was planning a tour of the district but worried that she wouldn't be able to do it physically. 'My leg is bad,' she explained, 'and I can't walk.' Health problems created by her harsh imprisonment would continue to challenge her for years. It was from her bed that Kamaladevi organized new elections in order to bring in 'new men who have proved earnest workers and are reliable'. 'They have been elected,' she wrote, 'but the old block is up in arms . . . they want to sit tight on their offices.' She told Hardikar, 'I know these people would be only too glad to be rid of me and my politics.'[10]

In May 1935, she chaired the reception committee at the Karnataka Political Conference in Mangalore and was elected president of the conference. She celebrated the fact that 'the women of India are once again taking their place in the service of their country. No organization can call itself truly National unless it has men and women working in it side by side.' She rejected the meagre constitutional reforms offered by the British as distractions and declared that 'the so-called Reforms should be resisted and the entire machinery paralysed by a powerful mass movement.' Her vision of the 'entire machinery' extended beyond British India to include the princely states. According to the *Servant of India*, Kamaladevi 'criticized the Congress sharply for neglecting the subjects of Indian States'. She was quoted as declaring, 'It is obvious that there cannot be a free India, as long as there are over seven crores peoples in the States under a discredited feudal system.'[11]

Kamaladevi's opposition to the princely states resulted, in part, from the proximity of Mangalore to Mysore State. Kamaladevi repeatedly crossed Mysore with Dr Hardikar urging people to join the Congress. In 1930, they both attended the first Mysore State Youth Conference in Bangalore despite the fact that they were banned from offering speeches. Their silent presence testified to the repressive nature of the state government. In 1936, Kamaladevi visited several cities in Mysore State, managing to give speeches despite the fact that her meetings were routinely banned or broken up by the authorities. Many of her talks concerned socialism, a subject which, according to one account, 'had assumed importance and had become the topic of the day'. Kamaladevi had sent Hardikar a Marathi translation of the *Communist Manifesto* and had asked that it be translated into Kannada. She opposed princely rule, British rule and the economic rule of landlords and the wealthy. Her broad radicalism continued to attract the attention of colonial officials. One intelligence report stated, 'Kamaladevi is down over this side [Karnataka] for socialist propaganda and is delivering lectures on Socialism with a view to create awakening in the masses.'[12]

While she served as an active member of the Congress and of the Congress Socialists, Kamaladevi devoted much of her time in the mid-1930s to the Seva Dal. In the eyes of the British, the dal was itself revolutionary. Whereas the official ban on the Congress had been lifted, the government continued to ban the dal. In February 1935, a colonial official defended that policy in the Central Legislative Assembly by claiming that the dal 'taught the use of weapons'. This was a peculiar claim given the dal's commitment to nonviolence. Pressed for details, the government claimed that the dal sometimes encouraged its members to train with air rifles. Kamaladevi refuted these charges in the *Bombay Chronicle* with scathing sarcasm. 'Every militant organization is no more a terrorist body,' she wrote, 'than every dead rat is charged with plague bacilli—the government sees a terrorist in every Indian of any stuff these days.'[13]

Her radicalism remained an issue for many Congress conservatives, including Gandhi and Vallabhbhai Patel. On 21 March 1935, Kamaladevi wrote Hardikar from Mangalore that Patel had asked her to speak out against the government's policy on the dal. 'I told him he had a far greater responsibility than any of us as he was President at that time,' she explained, 'and we only worked under his direction. So if anyone was expected to send a refutation, it was he.' Patel replied that 'something ought to go from the Women's Section'. Kamaladevi replied defiantly. 'I said No,' she told Hardikar. 'I would like the Government to believe (not that they do) that Indian women were plucky enough to handle rifles.' As to Patel, she explained, 'I am afraid he irritates me and puts my back up. I had long chats with him this time. He and I had adjoining rooms at Wardha, and he used to come and chat. He can be very sociable, I find. What is the idea—or is it just his way?'[14]

Patel continued to speak out against the socialists, at one point suggesting that they were contributing to immoral views of sex. In the pages of the *Congress Socialist*, Kamaladevi denounced Patel's 'bracketing of sex and socialism' as 'characteristic of the old irrational medievalism against the new, national and scientific spirit'. She reminded readers that 'sex has never been taboo in the orient.' 'It has always been treated as an important human force, its potentialities recognised as invaluable, and its interplay in human life vested with all the beauty and dignity it deserves.' While importing Western conceptions of sexual propriety, Patel's real mission, Kamaladevi argued, was defending 'vested interest' and the 'status quo'. 'The old order is certainly passing,' she wrote. 'That is what old Sardar is railing against . . . He is of the band of conservatives who would turn their backs against the rising golden light and try to envelop themselves in the vague security of mediaeval twilight.' Kamaladevi parodied the position of conservatives like Patel:

> The rich must go on being richer. No one shall disturb their deep slumber of luxury, which means the poor to be where they are. They are the children of God, safe under the trusteeship of the pious rich. Are not the rich god-fearing? Do they not wear *khaddar* and

> sometimes even ply the *charkha*; what if they pay a little less to the workmen and extract a little more from the peasant? Poverty is a virtue, for it is simplicity. The rich too play the humble devotees of this cult. They even travel third class. It does not affect their amassing wealth out of thousands of their half-starved workmen.

Kamaladevi's condemnation of Patel could be seen as an attack on Gandhi as well, but she avoided directly criticizing the Mahatma. 'The Vallabhbhais of this world would naturally run away from healthy adventurous youths who are breaking old idols and creating new ideals,' she declared. 'But the hope and future of India lies with iconoclasts, and it is the strong unswerving hand of youths that will break the old and carve the new.'[15]

~

In 1935, Kamaladevi acted in a film called *Bikhare Moti* ('Scattered Pearls') that was written and directed by Jayant Dayal, a young socialist colleague from Gujarat. The film failed to attract much attention, and some of the attention it did receive was negative. The manager of one cinema complained 'that the screen was polluted by this film being shown'. It is unclear how much the manager's opinion was shaped by the politics of the film. In any case, Kamaladevi herself grew increasingly critical of cinema. 'Film acting failed to attract me,' she later wrote, 'while the drama theatre filled me with a passionate fervour; acting in a studio seemed like performing in a void without the warm sensitive communion with a responsive audience.'[16]

Kamaladevi remained committed to theatre and a range of other art forms, but had little time to pursue those interests. Politics had become her stage. At the AICC meeting in Madras on 17–18 October 1935, Kamaladevi worked to achieve greater democracy within the Congress and, in particular, to push power from the Working Committee down towards the grassroots membership. She was joined by Yusuf Meherally, who worked with her to challenge Congress policy on the princely states. Kamaladevi recognized that fighting the Congress old guard would be an uphill battle—especially given that the socialists were themselves far from unified. In October 1935, she wrote Meherally, decrying the 'disorganized, leaderless radical elements'. The socialists needed to disabuse themselves of any 'illusions about our strength'. The Congress was set to meet again in April 1936 in Lucknow. It would be 'suicidal to meet only at Lucknow, unprepared and unorganized'.[17]

On 29 January 1936, Kamaladevi presided over a meeting of the Congress Socialist Party in Meerut. She was only thirty-two years old, yet her achievements, skills, knowledge and dedication had garnered the admiration of her colleagues. In her presidential address, Kamaladevi noted that opponents of the socialists argued that 'our struggle today is against a foreign power and the talk of class-war confuses the issue and gives rise to internecine fights'. She rejected such an argument, noting that 'imperialism is the outcome of capitalistic production'. Under her leadership, the delegates paired such high-level debates with more pragmatic discussions of urgent social problems. They passed resolutions in support of unemployment insurance, free compulsory primary education, and 'free milk for the children of the unemployed'.[18]

In April 1936, in an article entitled 'Sex and Social Struggle' published in the *Congress Socialist*, Kamaladevi declared that 'those who oppose change and fear upheavals in society invariably plead and fight in the name of social morals'. As she often would in her writings, Kamaladevi turned to ancient history to buttress her argument. She asked her readers to imagine 'the dawn of Christianity' and 'to visualise the demoralised society of Rome' in which women became seen as 'the cause of sin' and sex had to be 'hidden, suppressed, tabooed'. Kamaladevi linked the history of sex to the history of sexism, and brought a class-conscious perspective to that history. 'While the leisured class degraded the woman of its own class by rendering her helpless and depriving her of her economic and social rights,' she wrote, 'it degraded the woman of the working class by dispossessing and disinheriting the entire class as a whole.' Kamaladevi offered a sharp critique of patriarchal systems in which the typical wife is 'man's private property' with 'no existence or significance apart from man'. She linked such oppressive patriarchy to imperialism through an analysis of the rhetoric of reproduction. 'The Imperial State needs men,' she wrote, and 'a woman who can't fulfil this function can be discarded by the husband though today science teaches us that the responsibility for barrenness in a couple may be as much with the man as with the woman'.

In typical fashion, Kamaladevi did not discuss her own life, even when writing that 'a widow is of no use to such a society or State, for it is the male counterpart that counts for without him she can have no progeny and the emphasis is all on reproduction. Minus him, she becomes an object of abhorrence and ill luck—an outcast in society.' Rather than discuss her own experience of widowhood, she turned to global affairs, adding that 'in the newly rising Fascist society fired by inordinate dreams of world conquest, similar codes are being instituted'. In keeping with Marxist theory, Kamaladevi found hope in the 'advent of industrialism' and its role in generating 'new standards, new ethics, new attitudes towards sex, woman and the emotional relationship between man and woman'.[19]

Her rejection of social and economic conservatism linked her work with the Congress Socialists to her older organizing with the All India Women's Conference. She had grown increasingly critical of the limitations of the AIWC and of the women's movement more generally. In another article published in the *Congress Socialist* in 1936, she lamented the limitations of the women's struggle. 'The feminist movement in India,' she continued, 'as in most other countries' was 'in the hands of the few bourgeois women who colour it with their own needs and reactions. It does not reflect the demands and problems of the large mass of women.' She urged reformers to realize that 'they can do little to free the women if they are to carry on their activities within the framework of capitalism. If they mean business, they will have to chalk out an entirely new line of work among the peasants and the workers to secure for these toiling women, their husbands and children, complete economic freedom by the establishment of a non-exploiting socialist society.'[20]

In April 1936, Kamaladevi sat on the dais at the Lucknow session of the Indian National Congress. She had come a long way from the days when she had been a volunteer, broom in hand, unable to even hear the proceedings. As a socialist and as a woman, she was still outside the centre of power, but she was able to give the socialists a rare victory when she proposed an amendment that would protect proportional representation, an arrangement that helped boost the numbers of socialists on the AICC. According to one record of the proceedings, Kamaladevi 'said that she was moving the amendment not because she happened to be a Socialist, but because she wanted to ensure representation of any minority on the A.I.C.C.' Her amendment was approved but only by twenty votes. According to the *Times of India*, the socialists were helped by the fact the vote was undertaken at one in the morning, 'many delegates having left to eat or sleep'. Still, the Congress Socialists were 'extremely jubilant over their surprise victory at the last moment on Mrs Kamaladevi Chattopadhyaya's amendment'.[21]

Nehru, the Congress president, had spoken in support of Kamaladevi's amendment and, in addition, had offered a forceful defence of socialism. In his presidential address, he stated that socialism was 'the only key' to India's future, a key that would require 'vast and revolutionary changes' including 'the ending of private property, except in a restricted sense, and the replacement of the present profit system by a higher ideal of co-operative service'.[22] Nehru and Kamaladevi had much in common—a general commitment to socialism, a close but complex relationship to Gandhi, and a broad, international perspective on India's struggles. Did they also share a romance of some kind? As we have seen, as early as 1931, there were rumours about their time together. Kamaladevi later praised Nehru as 'the finest jewel of India, most beloved of all youths and rivalled but by one as the greatest leader of the country'. She offered a strikingly intimate portrait of Nehru:

> The far-away look in his eyes speaks of hidden dreams. Once that deep-set mouth must have broken into smiles oftener; those firm lips melted into softer lines; the stern eyes danced with a more tender light. Those delicately shaped hands, the exquisitely chiselled feet, all so eloquent of a dream-laden soul, are today masked by the hard relentless marks of terrible struggle, which he so characteristically

embodies in himself as the representative of a nation in the throes of a fierce battle.

There is a tenderness in the details she noticed, as well as in the way she went beyond physical observation to offer a more psychological portrait. 'One cannot help wishing sometimes that he were a little less serious,' she wrote of Nehru. 'There is something almost terrifying in that intense concentration of all life-force and energy into one unrelieving objective,' she added. 'It tempts one to want to seduce him into other interests, into softer moods, see that mouth relax and the eyes shade off into a milder light. For when the transformation does come, one is gripped by its beauty and wonder. It is like a rainbow breaking through a heavy sky.'[23]

In February 1936, Nehru's wife died of tuberculosis. In the years ahead, rumours circulated that Nehru planned to marry a socialist colleague who was a college graduate. As Reena Nanda has pointed out, 'There were not many graduate, socialist Congresswomen!' There is no solid evidence that Kamaladevi's connection to Nehru went beyond friendship, and excessive speculation can distract us from appreciating the rich complexity of the relationship that grew between Nehru and Kamaladevi. In February 1937, in preparation for the upcoming elections to provincial assemblies, Kamaladevi travelled with Nehru on a campaign tour. One photograph shows them in a vintage car, looking like a royal couple. Their schedule was demanding. They spoke at a midnight meeting in Hubli, for example, and then left at five in the morning for their next destination. At one point, they had to get out of their car in order to push a cart out of the path. Such shared struggles brought them together—visionaries who liked to get their hands dirty. In the years ahead, even when their politics diverged, Kamaladevi and Nehru would remain connected by their shared past, as well as by the way they combined hands-on pragmatism with a global conception of the struggle for freedom.[24]

Kamaladevi's global vision was on display in Karachi in January 1935 at the annual gathering of the AIWC. She encouraged the delegates to connect the struggle for women's rights to efforts at radical social, political and economic change throughout the world. According to the *Indian Social Reformer*, 'Mrs Kamaladevi Chattopadhyaya cited the example of Turkey, where a radical transformation had been effected by Mustafa Kemal.' Kamaladevi often used her knowledge of international events to shape her activism within India, as well as to encourage other Indians to deepen their knowledge of global affairs. In Bombay in August 1935, she inaugurated a series of lectures, organized by the Congress Socialist Party, that focused on 'dealing with the international situation'. In her own lecture, entitled 'Twilight of Capitalism', she declared that 'the failure of the World Economic Conference two years ago has shown the way the world under Capitalism is going'.[25]

In the fall of 1936, she applied for a passport to do 'cultural work' in a range of countries, including South Africa, Australia, the UK, Japan, China and Turkey. The Secretary to the Government of Madras warned the Foreign Secretary of the Government of India that it was 'a reasonable assumption that if Mrs Kamaladevi Chattopadhyaya is permitted to go abroad she will engage in activities in furtherance of the communist movement'. The government denied her request for a passport.[26]

Given the fierce tensions between communists and socialists in India, it is unlikely that Kamaladevi would have engaged in 'activities in furtherance of the communist movement'. According to the *Servant of India*, Kamaladevi was planning to attend an international women's conference, most likely the gathering of the World Committee of Women against War and Fascism, which had been founded by the French feminist and pacifist Gabrielle Duchêne. 'If Mrs Chattopadhyaya wants to visit a foreign land,' the *Servant of India* opined, 'we fail to see why she should be prevented from doing so.' 'Her movements in India are under no restriction whatever,' the editorial added. 'If she is looked upon as safe enough for India, why should she be regarded as dangerous for any other country?'[27]

Kamaladevi's right to travel was debated on the floor of the British Parliament. On 30 November, the Welsh Labour politician and conscientious objector Morgan Jones asked the Under Secretary of State for India, R.A. Butler, why Kamaladevi had been denied a passport. 'The matter would appear to be one for the authorities in India,' Butler replied, 'and I have no information beyond what I have seen in the Press.' Jones refused to allow the matter to be dropped so quickly. He asked, 'May we take it that persons who regard themselves as Socialists are on that account precluded from coming to England or to Europe?' Butler replied, 'Not on account of their Socialist activities as distinct from Communist or revolutionary activities.' Jones shot back, 'Has the hon. Gentleman any evidence to show that this lady was open to this charge?' Butler answered, 'I imagine that the authorities in India were satisfied.'[28]

The authorities chose not to prevent her from all travel. At the end of March 1937, Kamaladevi returned to Ceylon. Six years had passed since she had been warmly welcomed at the Jaffna Youth Congress. This time, she was the guest of the Lanka Sama Samaj Party, a socialist party that had been founded in December 1935. She would give eighteen speeches in seventeen days, speaking in English with simultaneous translations into Tamil and Sinhala. She offered one address on 'women's part in the Indian struggle', but most of her talks focused on anti-imperialism and socialism. On 28 March, 1,000 people gathered at the Colombo Town Hall to hear her. On 1 April, she spoke to 5,000 people at Galle Face about how to 'smash imperialist might'. On 5 April, at Wembley Theatre in Kandy, she cited the American Revolution, the ongoing Irish freedom struggle and the British failure to protect Ethiopia from Italian aggression. On 6 April, she told an audience of 2,000, many of whom were dockworkers, 'No power on earth can oppress you or exploit you unless you allow yourselves to be exploited.' On 11 April, she gave a similar message to textile workers. 'You are the producers of wealth and if you realize this no one can keep you in bondage,' she declared. 'History shows that wherever the workers organize themselves and struggle for their freedom no power can obstruct them.'[29]

Her travels attracted the attention of the local authorities. One British intelligence officer wrote secretly that 'the fact that a great Indian leader like Mrs Kamaladevi has come to Ceylon at the invitation of the Lanka Sama Samaja Party . . . will no doubt give a fillip to this Party's activities and to the spread of Socialism generally in Ceylon'. Ultimately, it wouldn't be Kamaladevi herself who would cause the greatest controversy during her visit. On 4 April, a crowd that had gathered for Kamaladevi heard a young White man offer a speech that would become a major flashpoint. Mark Bracegirdle had met Kamaladevi when she arrived and had accompanied her to several of her events. Born in the UK, Bracegirdle had joined the Young Communist League in Australia before travelling to Ceylon. His speech earned the ire of the planter class and the authorities ordered that he be deported. Instead, Bracegirdle went into hiding and his case became a rallying cry for the anticolonial left.[30]

It remains unclear if Kamaladevi knew that Bracegirdle was a communist—or if she cared. In the middle of the 1930s, left-leaning activists were building antifascist coalitions in many parts of the world. Kamaladevi was open to such coalitions. She had always been a bridge-builder as well as a rebel, and she remained eager to forge solidarities of struggle across borders of many kinds—including the borders that divided British India from the princely states.

~

In 1937, Mysore did something unusual for a princely state: it held an election. The election was for the assembly, a body that had little power and was loaded with nominated members. Nevertheless, the Congress selected candidates and the Mysore Congress Party invited Kamaladevi to help launch the campaign by speaking in Bangalore and Mysore. Within hours of her planned Bangalore speech, the Mysore Police notified her that she had been prohibited from making public speeches for at least the next six months.[31]

The ban earned widespread condemnation. Nehru released a statement to the press attacking the gag order and noting that it had been 'extended even to the proprietor of the hotel where a tea party had been arranged'. The *Servant of India* declared the ban 'ill-advised and unjustifiable' and based on 'ill-informed, prejudiced and one-sided police reports'. The authorities held firm. The dewan (chief administrator) of Mysore state, had long targeted Kamaladevi, perhaps because she had recruited his wife to the AIWC. It did not help that Kamaladevi had repeatedly denounced the autocratic rule of the princes—and of the Mysore authorities in particular. The ban inspired her to fight even more forcefully to shift Congress policy on the princely states. First, she had to deal with her reputation as a troublemaker within the Congress itself.[32]

Kamaladevi's strained relationship with Gandhi came to a head in the spring of 1937. Nehru had proposed that Kamaladevi join the Congress Working Committee, but Gandhi was opposed. 'I think I told you that I used to like her,' Gandhi wrote Nehru. 'Her ability is unquestioned. But I have known things which have worried me about her.' He added, 'You may show my objection to Kamaladevi if you know her sufficiently. For I do not say this behind her back. I believe she knows my opinion.'[33]

What were the 'things' that Gandhi had come to know? Were these related to Naidu's letter and Kamaladevi's divorce? In her memoirs and in an interview in 1967, Kamaladevi traced Gandhi's decision to the article she had written criticizing Patel, as well as to Gandhi's general impression that she was not 'a very disciplined and manageable person'. It is possible that Gandhi shared his reasoning with Kamaladevi herself. On 5 April 1937, he again wrote Nehru concerning the Working Committee. 'Kamaladevi travelled with us from Wardha to Madras,' he explained. 'She came to my compartment twice and had long chats. At last she wanted to know why Sarojini Devi was excluded, why Laxmipati was being kept away by Rajaji, why Anasuyabai was excluded, and so on.' It is revealing that Kamaladevi did not ask about her own case but rather why so many other talented women had been excluded. Her concern extended even to Naidu. It was Gandhi himself who raised Kamaladevi's own career. 'I then told her of my part in her exclusion,' he wrote Nehru, 'and told her almost all that [I] could remember of the note I wrote for you on that silent Monday.'[34]

Excluded from the Working Committee, Kamaladevi focused on building the socialist movement and on exerting influence on the Congress in other ways. On 27 April 1937, she presided over the second session of the Provincial Congress Socialist Conference of Gujarat. Some 4,000 people attended. According to the *Times of India,* she 'dwelt on the drawbacks of Imperialism and Capitalism', and declared, 'The Governors may say "nay", but it is the Congress which is the people's raj.' In late October 1937, she urged members of the Bengal Congress Socialist Party to confront the princely states. A few days later, at the AICC meeting in Calcutta, she moved a resolution protesting the 'repressive policy of the Mysore Government' and extending greetings to 'the people of Mysore in their struggle'. She noted that the Congress had been charged with 'interfering' in the affairs of Mysore state. In fact, she argued, it was the Mysore government that was 'interfering with the normal day to day activities of the Congress'. She offered as evidence, in the words of one report of the proceedings, that 'she herself had been perpetually pursued by the police and persecuted in the most insulting and vulgar manner'. In April 1936, the Congress had reiterated a long-standing policy of 'non-interference' in the affairs of the princely states. Kamaladevi rejected that policy. 'We do not recognize insider and outsiders,' she declared. 'It is the inherent right of every Congress worker to be able to go everywhere.' The delegates approved Kamaladevi's resolution 'amidst applause', prompting one leading newspaper to call it a 'red letter day'.[35]

Not every Congress leader was happy with the outcome. Writing in *Harijan*, Gandhi called the resolution 'offensive' and stated that it was '*ultra vires* of the resolution of non-interference'. He did not single out Kamaladevi by name but added that 'the speeches were full of passion and without regard to the facts of the case'. Gandhi's article prompted a letter from Nehru, who agreed that the resolution was 'very badly worded'. Nevertheless, Nehru defended the resolution and challenged Gandhi with a series of pointed questions: 'Are we to refrain from condemning repression in a State in future whatever the nature of this repression? If this repression consists in attacking the Congress itself, insulting our Flag, or banning our organization, are we to remain silent?' Kamaladevi had galvanized a necessary debate within the Congress. Later, she would praise Gandhi for recognizing 'that confrontation with state rulers at that time would have been very awkward, aggravating other problems of the independence movement'. There was good reason, however, for her to feel that the leaders of the princely states had to be challenged. In the years ahead, she would play a pivotal role in shifting Congress policy towards a more direct confrontation with the autocratic rulers of those states.[36]

On the second day of the AICC conference, a resolution was moved noting that 'there are several political prisoners in the provinces where Congress Cabinets exist' and calling for 'the immediate release of all political prisoners'. The issue at stake was portentous: how would the Congress act now that it was in power in several provinces? A few months earlier, in an article in the *Modern Review*, Kamaladevi had communicated her support for the Congress assuming control at the provincial level so long as the party remained focused on 'the overthrow of imperialism and the establishment of complete independence'. Now, Kamaladevi supported the civil liberties resolution and challenged the Working Committee to provide 'all the necessary facts'.[37]

She had little hope that the Working Committee would take the kind of aggressive action necessary to achieve true freedom. The greatest hope for the future, she believed, resided with India's youth. On 8 November 1937, Kamaladevi presided over the UP Students' Conference in Kanpur. She declared that 'the rights of the students must be recognized' and encouraged the students to engage in politics. 'Education after all cannot be divorced from life, from our day to day existence and struggle,' she declared. On 1 January 1938, Kamaladevi inaugurated the All India Students' Conference in Madras. In a large pavilion on the Medical College grounds, she discussed, in the words of one report, 'the important role which the students had to play in the national life'. She rejected 'the idea that the moment they were free from political domination by a foreign country, all their problems would be solved'. True freedom would require confronting sexism, casteism, class inequality and other 'social problems'. She lamented the fact that 'many young men who displayed great extremism in politics, were not broad-minded in their social ideas'. The task facing all Indians was 're-shaping and re-building society' which was why, according to Kamaladevi, 'Socialism had come to attract the youthful mind.' Her primary goal was not, however, to recruit students to become Congress Socialists. 'Students should not identify themselves with any political party,' she argued, but should 'support all progressive and democratic elements'.[38]

In February 1938, at the annual Congress session in Haripura, Kamaladevi renewed her opposition to the princely states. The Government of India Act of 1935 had suggested a federation in which the princely states would retain disproportionate power. Kamaladevi proposed an amendment demanding that if federation were enforced, the Congress would respond with 'direct action for the overthrow of the constitution and preparation for convening of a constituent assembly'. Nehru spoke against the amendment. 'There is no need to say that we are going to fight federation,' he stated. That was obvious. 'Regarding the suggestion of direct action,' he asked, 'what other weapon have we in our armoury?' He described Kamaladevi's amendment as 'irresponsible' and as 'reckless and undignified' but left unclear how the Congress should respond to the ongoing injustice of princely rule.[39]

Kamaladevi forced the issue of the princely states in true Gandhian fashion—by getting arrested. In August 1938, she was invited by the Travancore State Youth body to open a conference in Trivandrum. The dewan of Travancore, C.P. Ramaswami Iyer, was an old family friend. He was also a ruthless administrator who despised the Congress, and his ties with Kamaladevi's family did not prevent him from banning her from entering the state. She ignored the ban and entered Travancore via rail. As long as she remained on the train or in a station, she was technically under the jurisdiction of the central government. Thus, ironically, it was the British colonial government that shielded her from being arrested by a nominally Indian government managed by a family friend. A huge crowd met her at the station in Trivandrum, which she promptly transformed into a hotbed of rebellion by hosting meetings with local freedom fighters like Annie Mascarenhas. After spending a night at the station, Kamaladevi could have decided that her point had been made and could have boarded a train for the (relative) freedom of British India. Instead, at around 4.30 in the afternoon of 20 August, she defiantly strode out of the railway station and was immediately arrested.[40]

The jail superintendent told her that the dewan regretted having had to arrest her, and passed along a question posed by the dewan: why had Kamaladevi chosen to enter Travancore knowing she would be arrested? 'That is an absurd question,' she replied. 'I have broken no law, nor committed any violence. I entered Travancore with a valid railway ticket, legally and peacefully.' According to the *Indian Social Reformer*, 'The Dewan has explained that it was the reputed Communism of Mrs Kamaladevi that led to the ban on her entry. Reputations often belie facts. Mrs Kamaladevi is not a Communist. She is a Congress Socialist, a small party which is regarded by Communists as even worse than Capitalists for the purpose of the proletariat dictatorship.'[41]

In his journal *Harijan*, Gandhi called the arrest of Kamaladevi 'a first-class tactical blunder'. Gandhi noted that the dewan was himself not a native of Travancore. 'It passes comprehension how Sir C.P. Ramaswami Aiyar [sic], himself a foreigner,' Gandhi wrote, 'prohibited the entry of a distinguished Indian lady on the grounds, according to him, of her being an outsider.' By calling Iyer a 'foreigner', Gandhi mocked the very idea that the princely states were separate from the larger Indian polity. 'I thought it was only reserved for the English administrators to treat Indians going from one province to another as foreigners,' he wrote. 'It ill becomes the Indian Princes and their advisers to follow the pernicious practice of the English administrators—a practice of which many Englishmen are heartily ashamed.' When Kamaladevi had spoken out against the rulers of Mysore, Gandhi had worried that her radicalism was alienating the princes. Now, her arrest forced him to take a bolder stand in defence of the fundamental unity of India.[42]

Kamaladevi continued to advocate on behalf of freedom struggles in the princely states. In January 1939, the *Indian Student* published an article in which she argued that the 'severe repression' in Mysore had raised 'the very ticklish and intriguing issue of the Congress policy in the Indian States'. The Congress resolutions on the topic were 'so beautifully vague that the deity and the devil can quote them alike with equal impunity and exuberance'. For Kamaladevi, the issue was clear: 'the Indian problem is one and indivisible'. She recited her own history to demonstrate the extent of repression in Mysore. 'A prohibitory order was served on me while I was merely passing through the State and had declared no programme,' she wrote, 'and the authorities thought it fit to send down to the frontier a posse of 17 policemen for this silly job!' The way in which the order was served might have been "silly," but there was nothing humorous about the denial of freedom of speech and other basic democratic rights. 'The affairs of the State are the main concern of the people themselves,' Kamaladevi declared, 'and not the monopoly of knighted satraps.'[43]

Kamaladevi continued to press for a stronger approach to the princely states at the annual gathering of the Congress in Tripuri in March 1939. Rajendra Prasad moved a resolution that heralded 'the awakening of the people of Indian States in many parts of the country' and reiterated the commitment of the Congress to 'complete independence' for 'the whole of India, inclusive of the States, which are integral parts of India and which cannot be separated'. Prasad's resolution revealed the impact of Kamaladevi and other radicals in pushing the Congress towards a firmer stance, but it did not fully discard the existing policy which entailed encouraging 'the peoples of the States to organize themselves and conduct their own movements for freedom'. Kamaladevi wanted more. She argued, in the words of one record of the meeting, 'that the Congress should take a direct interest in States' affairs and actively be in charge of the conduct of movements in the various States'. Her socialist colleague Achyut Patwardhan seconded Kamaladevi's amendment, as did K.C. Reddy, a leader from Mysore. In response, Prasad argued that 'the Congress had always said less than what it had intended to do. Nothing could be achieved by indulging in high-sounding words.' Kamaladevi's amendment was rejected.[44]

A month later, in April 1939, the *Times of India* reported that she had yet again been banned from speaking in Mysore. She had travelled to Bangalore to attend the Mysore State Congress, after which she had planned to preside over the All-Karnatak Socialist Conference at Vidhuranagar. In Bangalore, the deputy commissioner of Kolar sent her a letter explaining that she had been banned from making any public speeches. The deputy commissioner had the gall to add that he hoped she would receive this ban 'in a friendly spirit'.[45]

The harassment she suffered in the princely states haunted her even during family vacations. When Rama was eleven, Kamaladevi took him on a trip to Kashmir. Just as they were about to board a *shikara* for a tour around Dal Lake, they were stopped by the police and Kamaladevi was interrogated in front of her son. She received similar treatment in Gwalior, where Rama was studying at a boarding school. She had barely entered the state when she was stopped by the police and required to answer a barrage of questions about what was supposed to be a short visit to see her son.[46]

Kamaladevi did not get enough time with Rama. According to Reena Nanda, the boy often showed a preference for Harin. 'It is understandable,' Nanda wrote, 'that a young boy of 11 would be drawn towards a father who did not believe in his going to school, took him to the seaside, and lived a life of wanderlust, poetry, music, and song.' Often, Harin would appear unexpectedly and abscond with Rama without telling Kamaladevi where they were going or how long they would be gone. Such episodes left Kamaladevi in 'dreadful doubt' given that she had no way of ascertaining her son's health and wellbeing. It was to give Rama more stability that she enrolled him in the Scindia School in Gwalior. Harin could still visit Rama but there were more safeguards in place to guarantee their son's safety and education. Despite her many professional commitments, and despite her reluctant decision to send Rama to Gwalior, Kamaladevi refused to allow her son to drift too far away from her. In 1937, she wrote Jayaprakash Narayan that Rama was 'the dearest thing I ever had in my life'.[47]

It was not easy to be a divorced mother sharing custody with an unpredictable man. Friends encouraged Kamaladevi to consider remarrying. Some well-meaning acquaintances even brought her marriage proposals. Kamaladevi did not appreciate the interest in her private life. 'After divorce,' she explained, 'when someone would talk about marriage in front of me, I would feel seriously humiliated and my heart would get hurt.' The suggestion that she remarry only 'created a lot of bitterness in my mind'. Later, Kamaladevi would reconsider her opposition to such proposals and would blame the 'influence of tradition' and of 'the old thinking' on her decision to remain single.[48]

Her understanding of her own gender identity might also have played a role in Kamaladevi's decision to remain single. 'Although I loved working with women,' she told Kamala Ratnam, 'I still have a masculine feeling within me. The feeling of being a sort of alternative human being separated from both the male and the female genitalia made me closer to men and allowed me a camaraderie with them.' Kamaladevi linked her gender identity to the breadth of her politics. 'Because of this male–female spirit,' she explained, 'I have been able to participate in many kinds of projects and initiatives with men and that too at a time when women and men in our country had no freedom to mingle.'[49]

Kamaladevi knew that her family life would never be traditional, regardless of whether she chose to remarry. She strove to balance her commitments as an activist and writer with her responsibilities as a mother and brought to her family life the same stubborn determination that she had long brought to her public work. One might compare her commitment to the freedom and unity of India to her desire for wholeness within her family. Such an analogy obscures, however, as much as it reveals. Whereas she hoped to provide Rama as much stability as possible, she believed the only way to India's freedom was through revolution.

~

At the end of December 1938, Kamaladevi was in Delhi for the annual session of the AIWC. Over the course of the 1930s, she had become increasingly disengaged from the organization. By the middle of that decade, as the scholar Nandini Deo has written, the AIWC was 'dangerously close to being perceived as collaborating with the British'. Towards the end of the decade, however, the leadership began to shift towards closer alignment with the freedom movement. Kamaladevi worked hard to strengthen that alignment. On 1 January 1939, delegates debated a new draft constitution that stated, 'The A.I.W.C. shall not belong to any political organisation nor take an active part in party politics but shall be free to discuss and express its opinion on all questions and matters whether social, educational, economic or political, especially where they affect the interests of the women in India.' Some delegates objected to the word 'political' out of worries that it might 'cause disunity'. A representative from the Northwest Frontier Provinces declared, 'We should not follow the footsteps of men and introduce politics in our organization. Today people will join the Indian National Congress and others the Muslim League or the Maha Sabha and where will it lead us?' In response, Sarojini Naidu moved an amendment that would expand the AIWC's mission 'to include everything except party politics'. Kamaladevi supported Naidu's amendment and 'the idea of widening the scope of this Conference'. She did not want to threaten the less politically-engaged members of the AIWC. 'Clearly associated as I am with politics and political organisations,' she stated, 'I assure you that it is not my desire to convert this into an essentially political body.' But she urged the delegates to not avoid the word 'politics', which she defined as 'government of the people for the welfare of the people for their future progress, growth and development'. Such a broad definition of politics meant that the AIWC had never been apolitical. 'We cannot get away from this aspect of politics,' she explained, 'because administration and legislation are essentially a part of social work, a part of our own activities and are necessary if we want our women to progress.' The delegates voted unanimously for Naidu's amendment, but it remained unclear how many supported Kamaladevi's expansive understanding of politics.[50]

That same day, 1 January 1939, the *Congress Socialist* published an article by Kamaladevi entitled 'Freedom'. 'Social legislation all the world over is changing,' she wrote, 'making deeper and sharper indents into the old social fabric.' She offered a variety of explanations for these changes: 'The West has come with its own modes and ideologies. Science has opened up new visions and newer worlds. The machine has with its colossal fangs eaten into the tired foundations of an old civilization.' While acknowledging the power of these social forces, Kamaladevi made clear that 'progress' was not bound to happen. With fascism spreading across Europe and beyond, 'the forces of reaction' had been let 'loose once again' and the 'semi-emancipated' were 'being forced back into the dark cellars and the cold gloomy pavements'. The only way to check the spread of fascism was to create solidarities across 'the socially dominated classes', which Kamaladevi defined, notably ignoring race and caste, as 'the labouring class, rural and urban, and the women'. 'The women's movement is by nature militant,' she declared, 'like the labour or the peasants movement.'[51]

Two weeks later, Kamaladevi again wrote on 'women's rights' in the pages of the *Congress Socialist.* She declared that the Delhi session of the AIWC 'marks a new epoch in the history of this Conference' which has 'now broken all its former bounds and decided to take up all questions affecting the nation'. 'The problems of women and children,' she wrote, 'are inextricably part of the national problems of the country.' Turning to the risk of religious division, Kamaladevi declared that 'communalism is merely the creation of a small class which wishes to exploit the major people for its own selfish ends'. The AIWC had a responsibility to confront the threat of communalism. 'It is by our close contact with the masses,' she argued, that AIWC members could help build bridges across divides and thus 'that Communalism can be destroyed'. She praised the AIWC's growing support for labour but argued for a 'change in its composition so that it represents much more the average Indian woman'.[52]

For over a decade, Kamaladevi had fought for Indian independence and for the full emancipation of Indian women. As her politics became increasingly radical, she focused on linking the women's movement to labour activism and socialist organizing. Her vision of the women's movement as interconnected with other freedom struggles was bound up with her opposition to what she saw as the divisive nature of Western feminism. The relationship between the two pillars of her approach to women's struggles—opposing multiple injustices and working with men rather than against them—was made clear in the chapter she contributed to Shyam Kumari Nehru's *Our Cause: A Symposium by Indian Women,* an edited volume published in 1938.

Although it was entitled 'Future of Indian Women's Movement', Kamaladevi's chapter began, like many of her essays, with history. She rejected the idea that 'the history of woman' runs 'from the dark winter of primitivism to the exuberant spring tide of Americanism'. Within 'so-called civilized society', she argued, all women remained oppressed but in different ways depending on their class positions. 'While the millions of toiling women are being sealed up in darkness and hunger,' she explained, 'the rich are being sealed up in luxurious prisons of marble and precious stone equally doomed only to pompous idleness.' She linked her critique of capitalism to her belief that feminism was a Western idea. 'The feminist movement in the accepted sense is a symptom of Capitalist society,' she declared, 'and has no place or reality in a mass class struggle.' 'The right to work is essential to human happiness,' she added, 'but the need of the mass of Indian women to-day is not the "right to work" but the "right to the legitimate fruit of their labour".' It would not be enough to gain political freedom from the British. The right to vote meant little, she argued, 'so long as power is entrenched safely in the hands of vested interest which draws its wealth out of the sweated labour of the masses'. In opposition to such exploitation, Kamaladevi envisioned a multifaceted social movement. 'They who would win freedom for women, vindicate their rights and give them perfect equality,' she declared, 'must work for the larger freedom of the exploited and the oppressed.' Evoking the language of human rights, she proclaimed, 'India must therefore look to a revolutionized future, when class shall have been wiped out and man and woman will have obtained not only their sex rights but their human rights as well.'[53]

Several of the policy changes Kamaladevi demanded on behalf of the women of colonial India were intimately connected to her own lived experience. In her contribution to *Our Cause,* for example, she called for publicly funded childcare and, without mentioning her own life history, stated that 'divorce has to be as simple and as private a concern of the parties concerned as marriage'. In the article on freedom that she published in the *Congress Socialist* in January 1939, she defended divorce as 'a human right'. Again, she chose not to cite her own experience. Although she routinely dismissed 'feminism', her attention to the political dimensions of familial life epitomized one of the key facets of feminist movements in many parts of the world.[54]

In 1939, Kamaladevi edited *The Awakening of Indian Women,* a book that provided a sweeping assessment of the Indian women's struggle—

its past, present and future. The book included essays by Margaret Cousins, Shyam Kumari Nehru, the maharani of Indore, and several other influential Indian women. Kamaladevi wrote the two opening chapters: one on the 'women's movement in India' and the other on 'imperialism and class struggle'. She offered a class-based critique of the movement. 'The women's movement (in the accepted sense) in India as in the other countries is in the hands of the few bourgeois women who must necessarily maintain it within the framework of present society,' she wrote. 'It is consequently coloured by their own problems and needs and does not correctly reflect the demands or the problems of the large mass of women.' 'While the toiling masses are exploited as a class by the upper class,' she wrote, 'the women in their turn, even within that class, are oppressed and exploited by men.' Echoing her contribution to *Our Cause,* she concluded, 'Those who would will freedom for women, vindicate their rights and give them perfect equality, must work for the larger freedom of the exploited and the oppressed and wipe out the society which keeps the few in luxury at the expense of the many. The women's problem is the human problem.'[55]

The Awakening of Indian Women received mixed reviews. A glowing appraisal in the *Servant of India* praised Kamaladevi for emphasizing 'the fact that the women's problem is the human problem' as well as for detailing how 'imperialism and its Indian allies—Princes, capitalists, middlemen, moneylenders—are pressing heavily upon a subject country'. Her fellow socialist Aruna Asaf Ali offered a more critical assessment in the pages of the *Indian Social Reformer.* Kamaladevi and Ali had personal differences and would remain estranged despite their overlapping politics. Their rocky relationship helps to explain why Ali decried the 'hurry and haste evident in most of the chapters' and concluded that the book left 'the impression of a scrappily compiled series of newspaper articles'. Nevertheless, Ali found the overall treatment 'creditable' and stated that the book would 'certainly go a long way to educate those who are eager to know how thinking women are approaching their problems'.[56]

Despite Aruna Asaf Ali's criticism, *The Awakening of Indian Women* solidified Kamaladevi's reputation as one of the leading voices of the women's movement, and positioned her to return to a more prominent role within the AIWC. She already maintained a central position within the Congress Socialist Party, and she continued to forge links with student activists, labour leaders, and all those struggling against the autocratic princely states. Despite being denied a place on the Congress Working Committee, Kamaladevi had the potential to enter the 1940s as a key leader at the nexus of many of India's most progressive struggles. Instead, in the summer of 1939, she chose to take her son abroad for his studies. After completing two years at the boarding school in Gwalior, Rama had returned to Mangalore to prepare for the Senior Cambridge examination. After passing the exam, he expressed a desire to pursue an education in radio engineering, a field best studied in Europe or the United States. Kamaladevi's decision to take her son abroad could be understood as a choice to focus on her family rather than her politics, but she brought her politics abroad with her.[57]

The AIWC had asked her to represent it at a gathering of the International Alliance of Women for Suffrage and Equal Citizenship, which was to be held in Copenhagen in July 1939, and her activism abroad would extend well beyond the women's movement. Kamaladevi's expansive internationalism was shared by many left-leaning Indian anticolonial figures—including Jawaharlal Nehru. She was relatively unique, however, even among Indian radicals, in both the breadth of her commitments and the depth of her opposition to sexism and racism in particular. Recognizing the danger of sending such an eloquent troublemaker abroad, colonial officials at first denied her a passport. Kamaladevi approached her old colleague C. Rajagopalachari, who was serving as Prime Minister of the Madras Presidency. Rajaji intervened, and her passport was granted. Colonial spies would shadow her throughout her travels, and the government made a point of noting that the passport had been granted 'for travelling to certain countries for sight seeing'. They must have known that Kamaladevi was never one to passively observe.[58]

5

Freedom Abroad, Prison at Home

On 2 June 1939, Kamaladevi and Rama left Bombay on the Italian ship *Julius Caesar*. Kamaladevi was thirty-three and Rama had recently turned sixteen. The *Bombay Chronicle* published a photo of mother and son, ringed by friends, ready to depart on their shared adventure. The *Chronicle* noted that 'Mrs Kamaladevi's tour has a political value for India. Her participation in the International Conference of Women will bring into broad relief the far-sighted vision that India takes of world problems.' Kamaladevi would be gone for over two years in a tour that would take her around the world—from Egypt to Europe to the United States, Japan and China. In the course of her travels, she would have many opportunities to demonstrate her own 'far-sighted vision'. She would attack imperialism—both the British and Japanese varieties. She would decry fascist aggression while refusing to allow the US and the UK to ignore their own hypocrisies. She would build solidarities of resistance with African Americans that demonstrated her expansive conception of the struggle for freedom. Throughout her travels, her central focus would remain the power of women to combat sexism as well as other social and political injustices. She fought for women to have the freedom to be all of who they were—a struggle she embodied by travelling as a freedom fighter, as an ambassador for her country and as a mother.[1]

Her first stop was Egypt, where she was a guest of the nationalist Wafd Party. Kamaladevi and Rama stayed at the home of the feminist leader Huda Shaarawi. Kamaladevi gave a speech about India at Port Said and was feted in Cairo, where 'an address was read to her on behalf of the women of Egypt'. So reported the president of the AIWC, who described Kamaladevi's travels in a speech to the delegates at the annual convention. On 9 July, Kamaladevi offered her own 'View of Egypt' in the *Bombay Chronicle.* Her new Egyptian friends had urged her to recognize 'the need for a common language for our country', which Kamaladevi called 'a puzzle I have not been able to solve'. This was the kind of self-reflection Kamaladevi would demonstrate throughout her travels—taking something she had learnt abroad and using it to reflect on struggles within India.[2]

Often, such comparisons were implicit. She must have been thinking of home when she told readers of the *Chronicle* that in Sweden 'the trade unions are powerful and have a more effective voice in the Government'. The power of the unions had combined with 'the taxes steadily imposed up on the richer class', levelling incomes and 'ridding the country of those two unbearable extremes'. The articles she penned abroad revealed her broad curiosity and wide-ranging interests, as well as her talents as a travel writer. She called Italy 'a land of aggression' where even the birds 'seemed stilled into a deathlike silence'. By contrast, Denmark was a peaceful land where 'people neither hurried nor hurled you through life' and 'everybody is shaking hands with everybody else'.[3]

Her positive impression of Denmark did not carry over to the proceedings of the International Alliance of Women (IAW), which gathered on 8 July in Copenhagen. Delegates adopted a 'declaration of principles' that located their work within 'the great struggle against oppression of creed, race, class and sex'. When it came to being specific about where such oppression was to be combated, however, the metropolitan biases of the organization, which had long been based in London, became obvious. 'While righteous wrath was directed against Nazism,' Kamaladevi later wrote, 'a tight curtain was drawn over imperialism.' Kamaladevi and Dr Malini Sukthankar, the honorary secretary of the AIWC, penned a joint note denouncing the fact that most delegates 'could not think of Eastern people except as primitive and backward needing the protective wing of some European power or other'. They encouraged the AIWC to leave the Alliance. Instead of wasting time at such imperial gatherings, it would be better for Indian women to forge ties 'with the Eastern countries . . . and thus be able to form a solid block to be able to make its impact felt on the Alliance'. Convinced by Kamaladevi and Sukthankar, the AIWC president, Rani Lakshmibai Rajwade, wrote the IAW president, British feminist Margery Corbett Ashby, denouncing the Eurocentric bias of 'a body which claims to be a world organisation'.[4]

Kamaladevi's critique of Eurocentrism was never anti-Western nor even anti-British. She arrived in London just before Hitler's armies invaded Poland in September 1939. Earlier that year, she had made clear her own view on the origins of the war. In an article for the *Congress Socialist,* she praised the AIWC for condemning imperialism, recognizing 'economic exploitation and the lust to possess colonies as the root causes of war' and urging 'the women of the world, especially those in imperialist countries, to join hands with those who are fighting for the freedom of every nation and country for then alone can real peace be established'.[5]

In August 1939, the *Bombay Chronicle* published a letter from Kamaladevi to Gandhi in which she urged the Mahatma to 'voice the attitude of India and of the exploited peoples of the East' on the growing crisis in Europe. She also sent her appeal directly to Gandhi. 'The present conflict is mainly centred round the usual scramble for colonies,' she wrote. She praised India (and implicitly Gandhi himself) for demonstrating 'to the world a superior technique of struggle whose moral value the world is bound to appreciate some day' and she urged all Indians to 'speak not only for themselves but all the exploited peoples of the world'.

In October, Gandhi published Kamaladevi's letter in his journal, *Harijan.* He stated, 'I agree with Kamaladevi's analysis of the motives of the parties to the war.' He distinguished between the US and the UK on the one hand and the fascist powers on the other hand. 'However incomplete or equivocal the declarations of the Allies are,' he wrote, 'the world has interpreted them to mean that they are fighting for saving democracy.' He agreed with Kamaladevi, however, that it was imperative 'that the peace this time is not to be a mockery designed to share among the victors the spoils of war and to humiliate the vanquished'.[6]

This exchange reveals a rapprochement between Kamaladevi and Gandhi, a rapprochement advanced by their shared views on the world war and the urgency of Indian independence. In October, Kamaladevi gave a short lecture about Gandhi on the BBC Empire service. She focused on nonviolence, declaring that 'even at this dark, grim hour, his call evokes a responding chord within the heart of humanity and offers a new path for the liberation of the world'. She left uncharacteristically vague what the 'liberation of the world' meant for the British Empire, but by lauding Gandhi as a prophet of nonviolence she helped buttress the reputation of the Empire's most renowned critic.[7]

Colonial authorities recognized Kamaladevi as a threat to the Empire. Their surveillance extended to Rama, who was summoned for police questioning soon after mother and son arrived in the UK. If the authorities hoped such tactics would intimidate Kamaladevi, they were wrong. Throughout her time in the UK, she defiantly argued the case for India's freedom, and lobbied a range of Labour Party leaders, including Fenner Brockway, James Maxton and Sir Stafford Cripps. V.K. Krishna Menon, the secretary of the India League, hosted a welcoming gathering for Kamaladevi that attracted over a hundred guests. As Europe descended into war, Menon suggested that Kamaladevi travel to the US to raise American awareness of British imperialism and thus 'strike a few blows for India'. As a first step, Kamaladevi and Menon contacted key figures in the Indian American community. Kamaladevi corresponded with Basant Kumar Roy of New York, who helped to arrange her travel plans. Menon asked filmmaker K.S. Hirlekar to discuss Kamaladevi's schedule with Indians living in the United States. Hirlekar, in turn, contacted Ramlal Bajpai, the very same chemist and veteran anti-imperialist whose wife had absconded with Harin nearly a decade earlier. In a demonstration of anticolonial solidarity—and perhaps the solidarity of abandoned spouses—Bajpai agreed to help Kamaladevi when she arrived in the US.[8]

British officials closely monitored her travel plans. A representative of the Royal Empire Society wrote Lord Zetland, the Secretary of State for India, that Kamaladevi was 'distinctly anti-British'. Across the top of the letter, Zetland scribbled a question: 'Can we take any action to prevent this woman going to the U.S.A.?' The answer appeared in a note one intelligence official sent another, arguing that although Kamaladevi was a 'keen Socialist and an ardent champion of the Women's Movement', she was not 'sufficiently fanatical to be classed as "Left-Wing"'. Moreover, the official explained, 'She has powerful friends in the United Kingdom who would, no doubt, object if she were refused permission to go to the United States.' Those powerful friends included Agatha Harrison, a pacifist and social reformer who strongly supported the Indian independence movement. On the advice of the British, the US consulate at first denied Kamaladevi a visa. Harrison intervened, the decision was reversed, and Kamaladevi and Rama sailed for New York.[9]

They arrived in November 1939. To welcome Kamaladevi, a gala dinner was organized that included leading Indian Americans, including the businessman and community advocate Jagjit (J.J.) Singh, and the sociologist and veteran Gandhian activist Krishnalal Shridharani. Singh and Shridharani championed Indian independence and the rights of Indian Americans. They were supported in both causes by liberal Americans like the Unitarian minister Charles Francis Potter, and by socialists like Mary van Kleeck—both of whom also attended the welcoming dinner. Van Kleeck would prove to be an especially important resource for Kamaladevi. The longtime director of the Russell Sage Foundation's Department of Industrial Studies and the first head of the US Federal Women's Bureau, Van Kleeck had connections that spanned many of the same causes Kamaladevi championed in India—especially women's rights and labour activism. She was twenty years older than Kamaladevi but the two women quickly became friends. Kamaladevi wrote letters connecting Van Kleeck to Jawaharlal Nehru and to the Servants of India Society. In turn, Van Kleeck became one of Kamaladevi's most important contacts. It was Van Kleeck who arranged a meeting between Kamaladevi and Franklin and Eleanor Roosevelt despite concerns at the White House that such a meeting would complicate diplomatic relations with the UK.[10]

It appears that Kamaladevi first met with Eleanor at the Roosevelt home in Hyde Park, New York, and later came to the White House as the First Lady's guest. The two women had much in common: a passion for social causes; a history of being attacked (wrongly) as communists; an independence that defied prevailing gender norms; and marriages strained or, in Kamaladevi's case, broken by faithless, philandering men. There is no evidence that the two women discussed their personal lives, but it appears they warmed to each other quickly. In her memoir, Kamaladevi remembered Eleanor as 'breathing solidity, power, with an air of informality, and kindly manners', and credited the First Lady with extending her visa so that she could stay in the United States indefinitely. Kamaladevi's memories of Franklin Roosevelt were also generally positive. She remembered the President telling her, 'You may be aware that I feel strongly on India's right to freedom. It is one of the questions on which Churchill and I have clashed.' She would later offer a balanced account of President Roosevelt's response to the Great Depression, crediting him with launching 'important and far-reaching reforms' but also noting that his goal was 'to save the capitalistic order'. Her writings on Eleanor, by contrast, offer a more glowing portrait, one that reveals Kamaladevi's own ideas about national service. She must have been thinking of India, for example, when she quoted Eleanor that 'a country is a collection of human beings. It is this element we have to touch if we desire to serve the country, for it is the most important.'[11]

We don't know what the Roosevelts made of Kamaladevi, but many Americans would soon have opportunities to learn from Kamaladevi and to hear her take on India's struggle. On 26 November, the *New York Times* published one of the first of many American newspaper articles on Kamaladevi, an article entitled 'India Advanced in Equal Rights: Mrs Kamaladevi, Visiting Here, Tells How Men and Women Cooperate'. In an effort to debunk imperialist claims that British rule protected Indian women, Kamaladevi risked underplaying the reality of sexism within India. Readers learnt that 'sex antagonism in political and economic life is unknown in India'. Only a few years earlier, Kamaladevi had challenged Gandhi regarding the rejection of many women from the Working Committee. Her own career continued to be complicated by her reputation as a rebellious (divorced) woman. Yet in the US she would consistently dismiss what she saw as imperialist myths regarding the prevalence of 'sex antagonism' within India.[12]

On 17 December, Kamaladevi lectured an audience at New York's Community Church on 'India, the British Empire and the War'. According to the *New York Times*, Kamaladevi explained that the people of India would first have to free themselves from the 'imperialistic dictatorship' of British rule before they could consider joining a war that was supposedly on behalf of 'world freedom'. She was introduced by the minister, John Haynes Holmes, who had long championed Indian independence and had been instrumental in having Mahatma Gandhi's autobiography published in the United States. On 3 January, Kamaladevi was hosted by the War Resister's League, a pacifist organization led by another radical Christian, A.J. Muste. On 26 January, she participated in a celebration, organized by J.J. Singh's India League of America, to mark the anniversary of the Purna Swaraj Resolution.[13]

Kamaladevi clashed with Singh and the other men who had established themselves as the leaders of the Indian American community. Sexism likely played a role in these conflicts, although there is also evidence that Kamaladevi's prickly disposition strained ties as well. According to Roger Baldwin, the leader of the American Civil Liberties Union (ACLU) and a fierce supporter of Indian independence, Kamaladevi had refused to speak at the India League's celebration. In a letter to Nehru, Baldwin suggested that Kamaladevi suffered 'some not too worthy sentiments of jealousy' inspired by Bhicoo Batliwala, a Parsi lawyer who was in the midst of her own tour of the United States. 'Miss B. made an excellent speech,' Baldwin wrote Nehru, 'but Mrs K. would not talk.' He lauded Kamaladevi as 'a most effective spokesman for India' but added that she was 'a bit difficult'. J.J. Singh echoed these criticisms in a private letter in which he decried Kamaladevi's 'lack of social graces'.[14]

Singh overlooked the fact that Kamaladevi's 'lack of social graces' could, at times, help to advance India's cause. Consider how she responded to a speech by Alfred Duff-Cooper, who had served as the British Minister of Information and was in the US to prop up American support for the British war effort. After Cooper concluded his comments, Kamaladevi rose to challenge him. According to one account, Kamaladevi 'wanted to correct some of Mr. Duff-Cooper's points about India'. The organizer of the event attempted to end the meeting, but the audience demanded that Kamaladevi have the right to speak, and she seized the opportunity to offer a spirited defence of India's freedom.[15]

In addition to her many speeches and interviews, Kamaladevi used her talents as a writer to shape American views of India. In January 1940, the popular magazine the *Living Age* published Kamaladevi's thoughts on women's contributions to the independence movement. The title of the piece, 'Women Reform India', could easily be misread to suggest an essay on issues like sati or widow remarriage that had long animated imperialists. Instead, Kamaladevi focused on the ways women were contributing to the fight for India's freedom. 'Passive resistance is a powerful weapon when used with skill,' she wrote. In using that weapon, Indian women had been 'the equal and the comrade of man'. Kamaladevi did not want her defence of equality to be seen as somehow dividing men and women. 'The Indian Women's Movement is not a sex war,' she wrote. At the same time, she did not want to understate the importance of confronting social problems internal to Indian society—from sexism to casteism. Indeed, she argued that it was imperialism that prevented Indian reformers from combating those problems. 'Those who rail against Indian society for certain of its unpleasant aspects,' she explained, 'ignore the reason for them: that the Government tries to torpedo every fundamental social reform.' That is why fighting British rule was key to achieving a freedom that went beyond political independence. That is why so many Indian women were dedicating their lives to the freedom struggle. 'The authorities in India,' she concluded, 'have grown to fear women far more than men, for their ranks cannot be disrupted nor their morale corrupted.'[16]

In Washington, DC, Kamaladevi spoke at a meeting of the National Conference on the Cause and Cure of War, a pacifist women's organization founded by the suffragist Carrie Chapman Catt. One of the delegates at that gathering, Cairine Wilson, the first woman to serve as a senator in Canada, later recalled how Kamaladevi explained 'that Indian women are active in the nationalist movement and hoped by non-violence to gain their freedom'. Kamaladevi also stressed the need to fight economic inequality, and her message resonated with many delegates. The American peace activist Georgia Lloyd wrote her, 'Your struggle in India is an inspiration, and should be a great help to those Americans who would like to see more economic democracy in this country.'[17]

A brochure advertising Kamaladevi as a potential speaker called her 'the only person at present in America who can speak on India as one who comes from the Inner Circle of the India National Movement'. While not entirely inaccurate, this was an ironic claim given Kamaladevi's exclusion from the Working Committee. The flyer included testimonials from a range of figures, including Carrie Chapman Catt, who called Kamaladevi 'a very remarkable woman'. Another flyer, titled simply 'Kamaladevi', called her 'India's foremost woman' and quoted Nehru: 'She will do good to our cause and will bring India and America near to each other.' American newspapers echoed the language of these flyers, with the *Washington Post* describing her as 'one of the country's leading women political leaders' and a 'distinguished Indian woman leader'.[18]

At first, Kamaladevi planned a short stay in the US, but Secretary of Labor Frances Perkins arranged for her to gain an extended visa. She made good use of the extra time. She met with Supreme Court justices and members of Congress. She visited Sing Sing prison, where she was introduced to the warden as a 'distinguished prisoner from India'. She gave a convocation address at the University of Kansas and attended the Republican Party's national convention, which she later recalled as 'noisy beyond description, garish, chaotic, people dressed up in weird costumes, more like a typical vaudeville show'.[19]

In March 1940, a professor of sociology at Hobart College wrote Nehru after hearing Kamaladevi speak before a large audience. 'She lectured in the Coxe Hall auditorium to a capacity house,' the professor wrote, 'and when she finished there was the most prolonged cheering I ever heard there.' He concluded, 'This wonderful woman inspired us with the spirit of the Indian movement for independence and we shall do our best to carry its meaning to others.' In Chicago, she told an antiwar meeting that India's freedom was central to 'the immediate and future destiny of human affairs'. At the University of Illinois, she linked India's poverty to colonial rule, discussed nonviolence, and praised Indian women for picketing shops selling foreign cloth. Asked about her bindi, she replied, 'It used to mean something, but now the Indian women wear them for vanity, much like you women make your lips red.' The League of Women Voters and local women's groups helped to arrange many of Kamaladevi's speaking engagements. Not all of these events went according to plan. Kamaladevi wrote Georgia Lloyd about a women's meeting she had been asked to address, a meeting in which 'the men did all the talking'. Kamaladevi left the event without delivering her speech. 'The men's talk gave me such a pain,' she explained, 'I simply got up and walked out after the second speech.'[20]

In addition to establishing connections with women reformers, Kamaladevi also forged ties with African Americans. In December 1939, she met with the executive director of the National Association for the Advancement of Colored People (NAACP) at a special gathering in Harlem. 'We condemn imperialism and oppression in South Africa and in any other part of the world,' she declared. 'Because of our color we feel a racial kinship with the other colored peoples.' Her solidarity extended beyond words. On a trip to the American South, Kamaladevi chose to stay with an African American family. The *Bombay Chronicle* called Kamaladevi's interactions with African Americans in the South 'a daring and unusual procedure because of the strong prejudices against Negroes in that part of the country'.[21]

In the spring of 1941, Kamaladevi had an especially 'daring and unusual' encounter with Jim Crow racism. She was travelling by train from Mississippi into Louisiana. As the train crossed the state line, the ticket collector told her that she had to leave what was a 'Whites only' section of the train. She refused to move. After storming off, the collector recognized that Kamaladevi was not African American. According to the peculiar norms of the Jim Crow South, dark-skinned foreigners were sometimes exempted from the racial codes that separated 'White' from 'Black' but Kamaladevi refused to use her identity as an Indian to defuse the situation. When asked where she was from, she replied, 'New York.' 'I mean which land do you hail from,' the ticket collector clarified. Rather than declare her status as a distinguished Indian freedom fighter or list the many powerful Americans she had met in New York and Washington, DC, Kamaladevi answered, 'It makes no difference. I am a colored woman obviously and it is unnecessary for you to disturb me for I have no intention of moving from here.' The ticket collector grumbled, 'You are an Asian,' but he did not bother her again. By refusing to move, Kamaladevi defied the racism of the American South. By proclaiming herself 'colored', she expressed solidarity with the millions of African Americans who struggled on a daily basis with the brutalities of segregation.[22]

This was more than a passing gesture of sympathy. Throughout her time in the United States and afterwards, Kamaladevi repeatedly advanced solidarities between Indians and other 'dark' or 'colored' peoples. On 23 February 1941, for example, she lectured a New York audience on 'Culture and the Future of the Darker Races'. Her solidarity with other people of colour became an important facet of her identity. The African American newspaper the *Chicago Defender* announced one of Kamaladevi's talks by describing her as 'Gandhi's Aide' and 'India's foremost woman leader'. A woman, an Indian, a person of colour—all of these markers of identity infused her interconnected approach to freedom struggles throughout the world.[23]

Kamaladevi forged ties with African American socialists. In March 1941, she spoke at a meeting of the Council of African Affairs alongside Paul Robeson and Max Yergan. Robeson and Yergan, both left-leaning activists, had already developed connections to India. Yergan had travelled to India in 1928, where he met a young Jawaharlal Nehru. Robeson had also formed strong connections to India, in part through his friendship with Nehru and also through his interactions with Rajni Patel, a young Indian law student who volunteered for the India League in London. When Kamaladevi and Rama had sailed to the US, Patel had travelled with them. During his time in the US, Patel would, like Kamaladevi, work to connect Indian and African American struggles. He would also provide yet another point of connection between Kamaladevi and Nehru. When Patel returned to India and was immediately arrested, it was Nehru who wrote Kamaladevi about the arrest. Perhaps conscious of the fact that their correspondence would be censored, he focused on their shared love for travel. 'From your letters and other accounts, which we have been following with great interest,' he wrote, 'you have had an extraordinarily interesting time in America.'[24]

Kamaladevi had seen vastly more of the US than originally planned, and had shared much of her travels with readers at home via the *Bombay Chronicle*. On 12 January 1941, for example, the *Chronicle* published a photograph of a party given for Kamaladevi in Hollywood. While sparking interest in the US among readers back in India, Kamaladevi's main focus was on shifting American opinion of India. She sat for countless interviews, gave dozens of talks across the country and, in April 1941, spoke on the radio in New York City. In an article in *Asia* magazine, an American woman named Hilda Wierum Boulter declared that 'there are so many stories told of Kamaladevi that she has become almost legendary'. Boulter also praised Kamaladevi before Indian audiences. In an article for the *Bombay Chronicle*, she praised Kamaladevi as 'absolutely tireless'. Boulter explained that Kamaladevi 'would make and keep as many appointments for one day as the average busy person makes for a week'. Boulter had served as Kamaladevi's assistant during her American travels. After praising Kamaladevi as an organizer, Boulter lauded her potential as a leader. She told her Indian readers that 'a free India in the hands of such leaders as Kamaladevi will be a tremendous force for true progress, civilization and democracy'. By serving as an unofficial ambassador for the Indian struggle, Boulter suggested, Kamaladevi had demonstrated her promise as a leader within India. Whereas Katherine Mayo had used gender and caste inequity to promote imperialism, Kamaladevi reversed that specious argument by trying to persuade Americans that the anti-imperial struggle was the better path towards a more equitable India. She was uniquely suited to make that claim. No other prominent Indian visitor to the United States connected so many social struggles. By forging ties with socialists, women's advocates, African American civil rights leaders and a range of other social reformers, Kamaladevi embodied the progressive inclusivity that she hoped to convince Americans was at the core of the anticolonial movement.[25]

As Kamaladevi's stay in the US stretched towards two years, she began to make plans for the next leg of her journey—a trip to Japan and China. Rama would stay in New York to continue his studies. Kamaladevi tried to entice several of her American friends to travel with her, writing one, 'I hate traveling alone—and I am so helpless on the sea.' Her efforts proved unsuccessful, and she would start the next phase of her journey solo.[26]

It must have been hard for her to leave Rama. Mother and son had already spent many years apart, whether because of Kamaladevi's stints in jail, her many travels, or the decision to send Rama to boarding school. Their physical distance had contributed to an emotional distance that also had roots in the divorce and in Rama's closeness with his father. According to Kamaladevi, Rama had 'a lot of sympathy in his heart' for Harin. At times, Kamaladevi resented the concern Rama showed for his father. 'The fact was that I equally needed affection and closeness,' Kamaladevi explained. She often felt 'neglected and lonely, but in front of the boy I didn't talk about that. The wounds of my soul were always stitched in front of him, their closure never loosened.' It remains unclear whether their travels in Europe and America had helped to bring them closer. In any case, Kamaladevi knew that when she left Rama in New York it would most likely be years before she would see him again.[27]

Mary van Kleeck raised over $250 for Kamaladevi to take home with her and surprised her with the gift at a special birthday party held on 3 April 1941. It was in the company of her American friends that Kamaladevi celebrated her thirty-eighth year. It must have been a bittersweet occasion—both because she was so far from home and because she would soon need to say goodbye to the many friends she had made in the United States. By 16 April, she was in San Francisco, and from there she left for Hawaii en route to Japan.[28]

In Hawaii, she told a university audience that 'freedom is not something which can exist in one part of a country and not in the other; in one half of the world and not in the other'. Her speech was reported by a Japanese American newspaper the *Nippu Jiji,* under the headline 'Britain Flayed by Indian Woman Leader in Talk'. The Japanese American community would suffer racist internment in the aftermath of the attack on Pearl Harbor in December of that year. In April, tensions between Japan and the United States were already high. To many colonized Asian peoples, Kamaladevi later wrote, Japan 'had become a sort of a Mecca'. By contrast, her time in the country would confirm her belief that Japan was yet another imperial power hungry for conquest. 'A complete totalitarian pall lay tightly over the entire country,' she later wrote. That 'totalitarian pall' did not prevent her from speaking her mind. Indeed, just as she had in the United States, Kamaladevi championed India's freedom while opposing inequities and injustices wherever she found them.[29]

~

Kamaladevi arrived in Kobe, Japan, in May 1941. She wrote Georgia Lloyd that she had received 'a very good reception here' and that 'there is very genuine sympathy for the Indian cause'. That sympathy did not assuage Kamaladevi's sadness at having left behind so many friends and loved ones. 'I miss U.S.A. a great deal though,' she wrote. 'I miss all my friends. I felt very sad to leave and I miss Rama a lot.' Kamaladevi expressed similar feelings in other letters. 'I feel very lonely here and miss the U.S.A. and friends,' she wrote in a letter to Mary van Kleeck and Van Kleeck's longtime partner, Mary Lambertine Fleddérus. 'I keep missing you all an awful lot. I am just so home-sick for America.' Her association of America with home testifies to the closeness of the bonds she had formed in the United States, as well as her rejection of Japanese imperialism. 'It is impossible for us to look upon the fascist powers as the champions of liberty,' she told her American friends.[30]

A few days after she arrived in Japan, a reporter for the *Japanese American News* interviewed Kamaladevi in Tokyo. 'Mrs Kamaladevi declared India's immediate hope was acquiring complete independence,' the reporter explained. According to the article, Kamaladevi 'contradicted rumors of anti-Japanese feeling existing among the natives, adding that Indians abhor quarrelling among Asiatics and prefer a quick end to the war in Asia'. That may have been true, but as Kamaladevi would make clear, she believed it was Japan's responsibility to withdraw its forces from China and other occupied Asian countries.[31]

Kamaladevi did not hide her opposition to Japanese militarism, but she focused her public pronouncements on India's struggle for freedom. From Aomori, on the northern tip of Honshu, Japan's largest island, she penned a letter to Van Kleeck and Fleddérus describing huge crowds coming to hear her speak even in rural areas. 'For the first time they hear the real story of India and they respond so spontaneously,' she declared. 'This has been a great education to me and I feel in many ways compensated for all the want and ache in my own heart.' But even if speaking on behalf of India gave her purpose, that 'want and ache' remained. 'I feel so lonely and lost,' she admitted. 'It is a new and different world to anything I have known. I feel considerable irritation, but above all I feel blind and dumb not being able to get a grip on things.' Some things were familiar. When told that Japan wanted to create a 'family of nations', Kamaladevi replied that 'this had a very familiar ring for us because it is the very argument used by British imperialists'.[32]

While she kept private her sharpest criticisms of Japanese imperialism, Kamaladevi generated controversy by commenting on sexism within Japan. At a dinner with prominent intellectuals, she challenged the idea that women, many of whom had taken on jobs created by the war effort, should abandon 'their newly acquired profession' and go 'back to the kitchens'. 'This nearly caused an explosion,' she wrote. Most Japanese men were 'not used to "Oriental" women arguing like them.' Challenging such stereotypes was meaningful but did nothing to help Kamaladevi feel more at home in Japan. 'I feel so alone and solitary here,' she wrote Van Kleeck and Fleddérus. 'Wish you folks were somewhere around.'[33]

In the same letter, Kamaladevi explained that her travel plans had been complicated after she admitted to her Japanese hosts her desire to visit Chungking, where the Chinese Nationalists were still resisting the Japanese occupation. To her American friends she criticized Japanese leaders for 'presuming to look on such an immense continent with such diversities as Asia, as though it were a backyard to breed a brood of chickens'. It's unclear how much of her criticism she shared with her Japanese hosts, but it was enough to make them wary of her. 'Maybe I should have been less frank and direct and more politic,' she mused. 'I am not a politician and no good at such games. My frankness usually costs me a lot.' She explained such bluntness as something of a national virtue. Speaking as an Indian, she wrote, 'We love discussions, debates. It is almost the bane of our life, so it seems at times. That is why we don't hesitate to differ even with such a leader as Mr Gandhi.' Her use of 'we' is striking. Her willingness to disagree with Gandhi and other Congress leaders had not always been advantageous to her career. Indeed, it had been only five years since she had been denied a position on the Working Committee. Perhaps her travels abroad made her appreciate the degree to which Congress leaders tolerated dissent. Compared to the rulers of imperial Japan, even the stodgiest Congress conservatives appeared liberal.[34]

Even during her time in Japan, Kamaladevi did not hesitate to speak her mind. 'Everywhere I made the Indian point of view clear,' she wrote in the *Bombay Chronicle*. 'As long as Japan remained an aggressor and continued the war with China, India could have no sympathy with Japan.' Japanese rule was 'no different from rapacious imperialism'. In a statement that revealed Kamaladevi's ability to critique Western imperialism without attacking the West more generally, Kamaladevi criticized Japan for being 'vitiated by a continuous artillery of hatred against the West'.[35]

From Japan, Kamaladevi travelled to Shanghai, a divided city, parts of which were under Japanese rule and other parts of which, the 'foreign concessions', were controlled by European powers. Kamaladevi received permission from a local official to visit Nanking, controlled by the Japanese. In the book she would publish the following year, *In War-Torn China*, she recalled the harrowing train journey. 'The devastation everywhere was great,' she wrote. 'Every few yards stood a soldier with a pointed gun.' After returning to Shanghai, she sailed for Hong Kong, from where she hoped to travel to Chungking. She was aware that the British authorities might arrest her. Before she left the United States, she had written Georgia Lloyd about the possibility of being imprisoned in Hong Kong. 'For a while the thought depressed me,' she wrote, 'but I am reconciled. So long as the food is not too bad and the heat not too great, I think I shall survive it long enough to kick once again and harder than ever.'[36]

As her boat approached Hong Kong, a group of British soldiers boarded and locked her in her cabin. She was allowed to come ashore but was denied the right to communicate freely and was required to report to the police daily. Local Chinese leaders had arranged several events for her that had to be cancelled. 'The British authorities in Hong Kong gave me a very warm welcome as anticipated,' she wrote sarcastically to Georgia Lloyd. Despite the restrictions on her movement and communication, Kamaladevi arranged a flight to Chungking and convinced the British authorities that it would be politically riskier to detain her than to let her go. Ironically, she would find more freedom in a city being bombarded by Japanese air raids than she had in a peaceful city under British rule.[37]

'Chungking balances itself on the hill tops, steep and severe like a fortress,' she later wrote. 'The plane as it approaches the City, heaves over peaks, curves dangerously and bends in and out of hills and suddenly slips on to a narrow stony strip of land along the Yangtse River.' According to Kamaladevi, the aerial bombardment of Chungking was even worse than what London received from the Luftwaffe. 'Streets, lanes, and shops and civilian quarters were turned into heaps of charred ruins,' she wrote, 'and in between them stood a forest of gaunt walls bearing testimony to the city that once was.' She wrote Georgia Lloyd that she 'was impressed not merely by the general morale of the people but also by their stupendous efforts to adjust themselves to impossible conditions'. She was also impressed with the Chinese leadership. On a visit to the 'mountain hide-out' of Chiang Kai-shek and Madame Chiang, she found Madame Chiang especially compelling. 'A vivacious personality' and 'a fascinating talker', Madame Chiang 'made the air hum'.[38]

She also met Zhou Enlai, but the communists seemed to her a small and insignificant force and her praise of the Chinese resistance offers little sense of the internal divisions within China. Later, she would write, 'When I arrived in Shanghai I started hearing disturbing reports about the Chiang Kai Shek regime, the exploitation of the peasantry, the concentration and growth of wealth and consequently power in the hands of a group.' At the time, she offered favourable comments on the nationalist government, although it was the heroism of Chinese women that most attracted her praise. In her travelogue *In War-Torn China,* she dedicated a chapter to the role of women in China's defence.[39]

Kamaladevi sent gifts from Madame Chiang to Nehru, who was in jail at the time. On Friday, 10 October 1941, Nehru recorded the following in his prison diary: 'Kamaladevi has sent me a letter from Madame Chang [sic] and a pot of marmalade which she [Madame Chiang] made herself. Delicious stuff.' He felt 'very happy to receive these gifts' and wrote that 'Madame Chiang's letter was moving and I was deeply touched. These instances of affectionate remembrance from afar make life worth while and jail is forgotten.' Nehru left unclear if hearing from Kamaladevi also helped him feel that life was 'worth while'. What is clear is that Madame Chiang's letter and gift demonstrated how Kamaladevi's travels strengthened her ties with Nehru. In his diary, Nehru recorded the note Madame Chiang had sent with the marmalade: 'I am sending you a Szechwan product which symbolises to me what life holds—the rind, the juice, the seed—the sweetness, bitterness, and spice which comprise life.'[40]

Kamaladevi had her own experience of the 'sweetness, bitterness, and spice which comprise life'. When she returned from Chungking to Hong Kong, she decided to take a new approach to British harassment. 'This time I was determined I would not be coerced or bullied,' she recalled. 'I completely ignored the regulations which I was given to understand were still in force.' As she wrote Georgia Lloyd, 'I am by instinct & habit a very law abiding person & refuse to be treated as a criminal.' The China

Defense League organized an event for her presided over by Madam Sun Yat-sen, and Kamaladevi attended despite the possibility that she would be arrested. She wrote Mary van Kleeck and Mary Fleddérus that she told the police that 'they could do their worst, but I would not submit to these insults. I may not be the terror they wish to make me out to be, but I can be what your slang would describe as a "tough guy" on such occasions.'[41]

On her way back to India, she made plans to stop in several other Asian countries. In the Philippines, she addressed a women's group on 'The Women of India'. The *Bombay Chronicle* published a photo of her with the president of the Philippines, Manuel Quezon. While her stop in the Philippines was a success, the rest of her journey home proved frustrating. The British authorities refused to allow her to disembark in Singapore or in Ceylon. Her boat came to feel more and more like a prison. What would happen when she returned to India itself?[42]

On 24 September, she wrote Georgia Lloyd from her ship, the SS *President Garfield.* 'I will be in Bombay tomorrow,' she began. 'I don't know what is in store for me after the recent experiences—the detention in Hong Kong with so many regulations and restrictions. And since then I have not been allowed to land at any British port.' She mused that 'an unarmed woman's presence even for a day at a place is considered dangerous,' adding, 'I must be some dynamite!' Of course, Kamaladevi knew that her reputation, her intellect and her gifts as an orator were all potent threats to colonial rule. She also knew that the authorities were committed to maintaining control. 'The situation in India seems very depressing,' she told Lloyd. 'Roughly about 90 thousand are in prison.' Churchill had made it clear that India would not be granted the rights guaranteed by the Atlantic Charter, such as the right of a country to choose its own government. Kamaladevi denounced American policy as equally 'disheartening' and asked, 'Is there any ray of hope somewhere?' As if to answer her own question, she concluded by restating her own determination. 'I feel at moments so disheartened,' she wrote, 'and then my irrepressible optimism spurts forth again.'[43]

~

Much had happened in India during Kamaladevi's absence. In March 1940, the Congress Socialist Party had expelled communists from its ranks, and the communists then took control of the All India Kisan Sabha, the All India Students Federation, and the All India Trade Union Congress. That same month, the Muslim League met in Lahore and passed what would come to be known as the Pakistan Resolution demanding 'independent states' where Muslims were in the majority. In October 1940, Gandhi called for certain leaders to take up individual satyagraha and several were imprisoned, including Jawaharlal Nehru. In January 1941, Subhas Chandra Bose, who had by this point left the Congress, escaped house arrest and made his way to Nazi Germany and then onward to Japan. Kamaladevi was aware of all that had changed and all that was still changing—both in India and abroad. In a postcard she sent Georgia Lloyd, she wrote, 'We need all our faith in our convictions to face the world today.'[44]

A few days after returning to Bombay in late September 1941, Kamaladevi gave a press conference in which she told reporters that 'the politically minded American public took some sort of interest in India and her problems, but no party was willing to make that an issue in any political programme'. Part of the problem was that 'the average American had got the idea that India was a country torn into religious groups'. Passionately committed to India's unity, Kamaladevi had failed to recognize the severity of religious divisions within India. Her desire to counter imperialist propaganda drove her to underestimate religious divides—just as, at times, she underestimated sexism and casteism, motivated by an overriding desire to defend India's readiness for self-rule. Her belief in the fundamental unity of India was a kind of faith—a hopeful vision for the future of her country—that received 'a very sympathetic hearing' from American audiences. She praised the poet Rabindranath Tagore and the dancer Uday Shankar for similarly improving American opinion of India during their visits to the US and 'stressed the need for sending more cultural messengers to America'.[45]

Not all Indians were convinced of the efficacy of such diplomacy. An editorial in the *Indian Social Reformer* criticized Kamaladevi for advocating 'the organizing of propaganda on behalf of India in the States' and added that such efforts had 'not advanced the cause of India'. The editorial returned to the confrontation between Kamaladevi and Duff-Cooper, who the anonymous authors argued 'could have pointed to Kamaladevi herself as the outstanding proof of what British rule has done for India'. The editors went on to declare her 'one of the most emancipated women of India' and stated that 'the like of her would have been an impossibility under Hindu or Muslim rule'. This specious reasoning gave the British too much credit for advancing the cause of Indian women, while discounting the ability of Kamaladevi to speak for herself—not as a two-dimensional icon of the 'emancipated woman'.[46]

In contrast to the scepticism of the *Indian Social Reformer*, many Indians understood the importance of Kamaladevi's travels. Not surprisingly, her closest colleagues were especially vocal in praising her efforts. At the Bihar Provincial Congress Socialist Conference, Purshottamdas Tricumdas 'stressed the need of the presence abroad of a few Indian representatives like Mrs Kamaladevi Chattopadhyaya'. In her book *Indian Womanhood Today*, published in 1941, Margaret Cousins praised Kamaladevi for 'getting into touch with colonies of people from India who settled early in the States, such as some hundreds of Indians who are employed in the Motor works in Detroit, especially in Ford's Factories'. Cousins was aware that 'the future of a Woman Socialist is impossible to forecast despite gifts of the highest quality'. 'Her sex weights the scales against her,' she wrote, 'especially when the woman has taken advantage of modern laws to secure marital freedom.' Regardless, Cousins predicted that Kamaladevi would 'be a Constructor of a New Order for New India'.[47]

It was not only Cousins and socialists like Purshottamdas Tricumdas who believed in Kamaladevi's leadership. Indeed, one of the first people to contact Kamaladevi after she arrived in Bombay was Sardar Vallabhbhai Patel. He happened to be in Bombay as well and asked Kamaladevi for a meeting. The two shared a long and warm conversation in which Patel expressed admiration for Kamaladevi's efforts abroad and urged her to visit Gandhi as soon as possible. On 3 October 1941, Gandhi himself wrote Kamaladevi from his ashram, 'I am glad you have returned home after a long absence.' He invited her to his ashram and ended his letter by saying, 'I hope you are quite well. Love, Bapu.' The warmth of his note suggested that the time apart had helped to smooth over the tensions that existed when Kamaladevi was denied a place on the Working Committee.[48]

Kamaladevi visited Gandhi at his ashram on 9 October. While we do not know much of their conversation, we do know that Gandhi wrote her again on 8 November, inviting her to return to the ashram whenever she wished. She returned a week later, just in time to help Gandhi with a challenging task. Jayaprakash Narayan had launched a hunger strike from his jail cell, and some 200 other prisoners had joined the strike. Gandhi asked Kamaladevi to press a mutual friend and colleague, C. Rajagopalachari, to intervene with the authorities. Gandhi also asked her to help convince Narayan to end the strike. He was joined in these requests by Sardar Patel. Kamaladevi agreed to help and spoke with Rajagopalachari. On 17 November, Gandhi telegrammed Narayan: 'Kamaladevi here. She and I consider your demand . . . literal execution.' Kamaladevi's efforts did not convince Rajagopalachari or Narayan, but they did create an opportunity for rapprochement between Kamaladevi and the Congress old guard, especially Patel and Gandhi. Afterwards, Gandhi encouraged her to stay with him at Patel's house in Bardoli. Kamaladevi later recalled Patel giving her a tour of his 'well-kept garden and the orchard in which he showed special interest'. Her time with Patel changed her understanding of him. 'Here was a personality other than the renowned Iron Man,' she wrote, 'handling seedlings with incredible sensitivity, and with a rare soft light in his usual stern eyes.'[49]

While her time away seemed to have strengthened ties with Gandhi and Patel, Kamaladevi's warmest reception came from her colleagues in the AIWC. At the end of December 1941, she travelled to Kakinada, a seaside town on the Bay of Bengal, for the sixteenth annual gathering of the AIWC. She brought with her a gift from Madame Chiang—a banner depicting an eagle (China) fighting a rising sun (Japan). Kamaladevi explained to the delegates that the image symbolized 'China carrying on her struggle to the women of India who are also carrying on a similar struggle for the freedom of their country'. Kamaladevi was greeted with a standing ovation. In her presidential address, Vijaya Lakshmi Pandit declared, 'I should like to express my gratification at the presence of Shrimati Kamaladevi in our midst today after her long absence abroad where she has so ably represented India's cause in many countries.' Such praise was especially significant coming from Pandit, who would go on to become one of India's most influential diplomats and was already, like her brother, Jawaharlal Nehru, among India's most cosmopolitan figures.[50]

The AIWC had moved closer to the anticolonial struggle in ways long championed by Kamaladevi. At Kakinada, the delegates approved a resolution on civil liberties that Kamaladevi warmly supported. 'It has been said that we are creating a Charter of liberty for the future generations,' she declared. 'This is not true. The Charter has been laid out by others before us. It has been evolved through centuries and generations.' She broadened the focus beyond the borders of India by declaring, 'The Charter is there in the minds of thousands of people all over the world.' As always, Kamaladevi was keen on action. She did not want the delegates to content themselves with 'talking in the air, or indulging in high-sounding phrases simply as echoes'. She chaired a subcommittee on economics and health that focused on securing maternity leave for more women. The committee also discussed vocational training and a 'big co-operative scheme, both for production and marketing' that would bring more industries into the villages. The delegates passed a proposal for a village reconstruction project but it was a different plan that would have a larger influence on Kamaladevi—a plan to create a training camp for provincial organizers.[51]

The camp opened on 20 March 1942 under Kamaladevi's leadership. It was located in Abrama in the Surat district of Gujarat, not far from Dandi, where Gandhi's salt march had reached the sea a dozen years earlier. Much had happened in the freedom movement and in Kamaladevi's life since those heady days. Indians were yet again entering a period of dramatic confrontation with the Raj. In 1930, Kamaladevi was just emerging as a national figure. Now, as she approached her thirty-ninth birthday, she was an established leader, tasked with directing a camp that would train the next generation of freedom fighters. In keeping with the capacious understanding of radical education that Kamaladevi and Gandhi shared, the camp combined physical exercise, lectures on politics and social reform, and hands-on training in everything from midwifery to beekeeping. 'In introducing and explaining the curriculum to the campers,' one visitor reported, 'the fact was stressed that most, if not all, social problems are inter-related and that the range of subjects had to be wide enough to cover problems arising in all strata of society.' In order to confront the interconnection of social problems, students travelled to nearby villages and observed a range of community development projects. The Tata Graduate School of Social Work sent lecturers, and a dozen university students participated in the camp. On 15 March, Kamaladevi had given the opening address at the Third Social Workers Conference at the Tata School. She believed in expanding the number of academically trained social workers. But the focus of the Abrama camp was not on academic training; the focus was on grassroots social work and hands-on community building.[52]

Located in a mango grove, the camp became a model of rural development. Kamaladevi's old prison roommate Mirabehn helped erect small grass and bamboo houses, and the site took on the feeling of a Gandhian ashram. Another similarity to Gandhi's ashrams was the explicit effort to bridge India's religious divides. Most of the fifty women who attended the camp were Hindu, but eleven were Muslim and several other faith traditions were represented. One visitor praised the harmony of the group, writing that she would not have 'believed that different communities could live together as if belonging to one sisterhood'. Such sisterhood was central to the camp's mission—to prepare young women to become leaders in the struggle for India's freedom from British rule and from inequities of class, caste, religion, language and gender.[53]

According to one visitor, Kitty Shiva Rao, the campers 'formed a very happy family with Kamaladevi at its head'. Austrian by birth, Shiva Rao had married an Indian journalist and politician, and had become a dedicated supporter of India's freedom. She offered a revealing portrait of Kamaladevi's leadership:

Watching over the day's work of the Camp in letter and spirit was Kamaladevi. She inspired, organised, advised and supervised everything from the academic work down to the office and the kitchen. Her eyes during the day were ever on the clock, lest the bell which directed the day's activity be a minute later than the appointed time, with the result that everything and everybody was punctual to the minute. But that was not all. In a Camp like this, emergencies arise almost every day which have to be coped with, from visiting lecturers who did not arrive on the appointed day (so that the next day there are four of them instead of two) down to, let us say, the vegetable man who failed with his supply because he had gone to attend a marriage! However, all that did not seem to ruffle her or if it did, she did not show it. The Campers respected and adored her, and she in her turn was always ready to help them however big or small their problems.

As this description suggests, Kamaladevi combined an ambitious vision with the pragmatic scrappiness needed to respond to unexpected challenges. The camp was a deeply meaningful experience for many of the campers, but the question remained what impact it would have on the larger struggle.[54]

The campers did not have to wait long to put into practice their training. In March 1942, as Kamaladevi launched the Abrama training camp, Sir Stafford Cripps was sent to India to arrange a plan for a transition to dominion status. Kamaladevi had met with Cripps a few years earlier during her time in the UK. A prominent liberal and a friend of Nehru's, Cripps was seen as sympathetic to the Congress, but he proved unable to broker a workable agreement in the face of fierce resistance from the viceroy and other colonial administrators. In July 1942, the Working Committee met at Wardha and passed a resolution that demanded full independence. When the British rejected this demand, Gandhi prepared to launch civil disobedience from Bombay, where the All India Congress Committee was to meet in early August. Colonial intelligence intercepted a letter from Khurshedbehn Naoroji to Kamaladevi: 'Bapu has sent two impressive resolutions . . . hope you will see it and get a move on . . . Congress can only function as a revolutionary movement.' Gandhi and Kamaladevi had remained close ever since she had returned from abroad. When Kamaladevi had a minor accident in February 1942, Gandhi wrote her a warm note. 'You had no business to have the accident,' he jokingly scolded her. 'I hope, however, you are out of the wood now.' Gandhi invited her to visit his ashram whenever she wanted. Ties between Gandhi and Kamaladevi would grow even stronger as a result of colonial India's last massive wave of nonviolent resistance.[55]

On 6 August, Kamaladevi addressed the Bombay Students' Union. According to an intelligence report, she 'salvaged the students from the Communists for the Congress cause'. That same day, she presided over a meeting of the National Executive of the All-India Congress Socialist Party. The group included Acharya Narendra Dev, Yusuf Meherally, Achyut Patwardhan, Ram Manohar Lohia, Asoka Mehta and Purshottamdas Tricumdas, at whose Malabar Hill house they met. The group issued a resolution that was published in the *Bombay Chronicle*: 'If Britain and America are genuine for helping Russia and China, the biggest step in this direction would be for Britain to shed her Imperialism, and thus to make it a struggle of free peoples for the defence of their freedom and for a new International Order based on freedom and the co-operation of democratic peoples.' They were not going to wait on the British to realize their hypocrisy. The time had come to claim their freedom. 'We offer our homage to Mahatma Gandhi,' the socialist leaders declared, 'and pledge ourselves without reservation to the great struggle which the Congress has determined to launch under his inspiring leadership.'[56]

On 8 August, at Gowalia Tank Maidan in central Bombay, Gandhi gave one of his most renowned speeches. 'Here is a mantra, a short one, that I give to you,' he declared. 'You may imprint it on your hearts and let every breath of yours give expression to it. The mantra is "Do or Die". We shall either free India or die in the attempt; we shall not live to see the perpetuation of our slavery.' Gandhi reiterated his commitment to nonviolence, but there was a new militancy in his call—and in the movement that ensued. As Kamaladevi would later write, 'the bell of freedom' had begun to ring. 'The 1942 revolt differed in many respects from previous fights,' she wrote. 'People moved unerringly forward guided by almost an elemental feeling towards seizure of power.'[57]

On 9 August, Gandhi was arrested along with many Congress leaders. The government banned all public meetings and, in the months ahead, imprisoned more than 1,00,000 nonviolent protesters. Knowing that she was a target for arrest, Kamaladevi escaped Bombay and travelled to Bangalore, a decision that revealed her commitment to bringing the struggle into the princely states. In Bangalore, she joined old friends including the Seva Dal leader Sardar Venkataramaiah, and the Congress leader Srinivas Malliah. They took refuge in the Canara Bank building on Avenue Road and from one of its windows watched mounted police chasing demonstrators as people threw ragi porridge onto the road in an effort to slow the horses.[58]

Kamaladevi managed to escape the authorities for a month. On 7 September, she was arrested by the Mysore police. She was prepared for a long prison term in Bangalore, but the state authorities suddenly released her. As she left the prison, she was informed that she had to leave the state immediately. She walked towards a group of friends, but the Mysore police suddenly changed their story; they explained that they were under orders to transfer her into the custody of the British police. A chaotic scene unfolded, as Kamaladevi protested that she had only just been released and was in the process of obeying the order to leave the state. The Mysore police remained firm, and Kamaladevi was separated from her friends and forced into a van driven by officers of the British Raj. She was taken to a military cantonment from which she was transferred to Vellore Jail, the scene of her harsh solitary confinement some seven years earlier.

Kamaladevi's arrest became news across India and abroad. One Indian newspaper condemned the arrest as 'autocratic, unconstitutional and illegal'. In the United States, an Indian American journalist, Kumar Goshal, penned an editorial in which he decried Kamaladevi's imprisonment and criticized the US and the UK for claiming to fight for 'democracy' while denying democratic rights to African Americans and Indians.[59]

Kamaladevi would spend the next eighteen months in jail. 'This term in Vellore proved even more difficult than the previous,' she later wrote, 'for my body began to act adversely even from the early days.' Her health 'began to deteriorate rapidly'. The authorities did little to relieve her suffering, and 'time ticked on, slowly, agonisingly'. Finally, in the late spring of 1944, a doctor advised her release on medical grounds. As she sat in the railway station, preparing to travel home to Mangalore, a messenger arrived with the news that Margaret Cousins had suffered a stroke. Kamaladevi rushed to the bedside of her 'spiritual mother'. Cousins had lost much of her mental capacity. 'She recognised and clung to me almost like a child,' Kamaladevi later wrote. She arranged for Cousins to receive the best possible care and then returned to the many other struggles at hand. Her time in Vellore would be her last stint in any jail, but she did not know that when she was released. Indeed, despite her own weak health, she soon risked arrest yet again.[60]

~

The AIWC was scheduled to meet in Bombay in April 1944. Kamaladevi had been elected president of the group early in 1942 but had not been able to serve in that capacity due to her arrest. Now, she wanted to preside over the annual gathering, but the police issued an order barring her from entering Bombay. She decided to disobey the order and, a few days before the conference, 'slipped into Bombay at night'. In accord with Gandhi's emphasis on transparency in nonviolent protest, she then called State Home Secretary H.V.R. Iyengar to announce that she had broken the order. An old acquaintance, Iyengar promptly rescinded the order and added that he hoped they would soon have the opportunity to share dinner. The mayor of Bombay, Minoo Masani, organized a reception for Kamaladevi that he publicly celebrated as a gathering organized 'by a jail bird to a jail bird'. The hospitality of Iyengar and Masani demonstrated the shifting political realities of the Raj. The days of British rule were numbered. The balance of power had shifted. As president of the AIWC, Kamaladevi aimed to exploit those new realities in order to speed up the attainment of independence and bring to fruition the radical social transformation she had long argued was necessary to achieve true freedom.[61]

On Friday, 7 April 1944, the seventeenth session of the AIWC opened on the grounds of Vanita Vishram on Sandhurst Road in Bombay. The retiring president, Vijaya Lakshmi Pandit, opened the conference. Pandit lauded Kamaladevi, declaring that 'her work for women both in India and abroad had done much to raise the prestige of Indian women'. Lady Premlila Thackersey, who chaired the reception committee, then spoke directly to Kamaladevi: 'You are the embodiment of world womanhood. You have done the greatest service to your sisters in this country by the most favourable impression you have created abroad.'[62]

In her own address, Kamaladevi began by sending greetings to Margaret Cousins, who was still 'on her sick bed'. She then turned to one of her oldest themes: that the women's movement 'operates as an integral part of the progressive social structure in the broadest sense, and is not a sex war as so many mechanically believe or are led to believe'. Kamaladevi acknowledged that some traditionalists had challenged whether the women's conference should engage in politics. 'To a subject people politics is its very life breath,' she countered. 'To deny that urge is to deny life. Weighed down though we may be by chains, we continue to live on dreams and thoughts of freedom.' Such freedom dreams could not be contained by the boundaries of any one country. It was with a global perspective that she declared, 'The world cannot be divided into islands of slavery and freedom.' Freedom was indivisible. 'Just as national freedom is but an extension of the social freedom the Conference is fighting for,' she declared, 'the establishment of the same principle all the world over is of equal interest to us.' Kamaladevi championed national independence and global interdependence. As she put it, the goal was to achieve 'the right of every nation to determine and rule its own destiny but in a co-operative world order'.[63]

As president of the AIWC, Kamaladevi set about putting her transformative vision into action. She established a central office and a small library in Bombay at Gilder Tank Building, Lamington Road. To help manage the office, she hired Avabai Bomanji Wadia, a Parsi lawyer who had been born in Ceylon in 1913 and educated in England. The position came with a small salary. 'I baulked at this,' Wadia later recalled. She told Kamaladevi that she would 'gladly work free of charge,' but Kamaladevi explained 'that the underlying idea was to demonstrate that there was nothing derogatory even in well-off women getting paid, and that it was a part of women's rights'. Wadia agreed and quickly became a vital contributor to the AIWC. She later recalled that Kamaladevi offered 'many gestures of friendship ... which not only sweetened my labours but brought me many new insights and experiences and raised my whole level of comprehension and understanding of working for one's country.'[64]

As president of the AIWC, Kamaladevi often echoed the Gandhian rhetoric of service to the nation. At a mass meeting in Calicut, for example, she 'stressed the need for more selfless workers to serve the country'. In keeping with that call, she embarked on a variety of 'constructive' initiatives. She created a plan to provide milk to children and nursing mothers. The plan was shared with the AIWC branches, most of which organized 'milk campaign weeks' and set up 'free milk centres' for children. She also helped establish a medical van that travelled to poor areas outside Bombay, as well as an employment section of the AIWC to help women who needed jobs.[65]

Kamaladevi described her vision for the women's employment bureau in an interview with Homi Taleyarkhan, a journalist who wrote for the left-leaning journal *Blitz* and would later become the governor of Sikkim. Kamaladevi explained that 'she did not want the twelve thousand and odd women now employed directly or indirectly in war jobs to think that they were being ignored and forgotten'. The bureau would help such women find employment in a range of fields, including teaching, nursing and midwifery. According to Taleyarkhan, Kamaladevi was recruiting women for such professional roles and just 'as constantly agitating for improving the conditions of the working women, their pay, their quarters'.[66]

Kamaladevi also continued the AIWC's long-standing efforts to advance progressive legislation. She submitted a statement to the Hindu Law Committee in support of divorce rights, inter-caste marriage, and 'the daughter's right to a share in the father's property'. While the statement was designed to undo generations of patriarchy, it was framed, in keeping with Kamaladevi's vision, as an effort at equality rather than special protection. 'We, as a conference,' the statement read, 'are emphatically of the opinion that the law should not permit of any difference in regard to sex and should provide for complete legal equality between man and woman.'[67]

In April 1944, the *Indian Social Reformer* published a long piece on Kamaladevi and the AIWC. 'For many years since its inception,' readers were told, 'presidents of the Conference were chosen for their social, economic or official status.' By contrast, Kamaladevi was the first president 'who owes her position to no extraneous circumstance'. The editorial added praise worth quoting in full:

> She has practically fought her way to the Presidentship of the premier women's organization in India by sheer hard work, indomitable faith in herself and against a load of prejudice under which most other women would have broken down. Without any advantages whatever, except that of her own engaging personality, she has travelled widely, studied at first hand the questions which agitate the human mind and equipped herself for her role as a national leader.

This assessment of Kamaladevi as a hardworking, widely travelled, highly knowledgeable leader contrasted with another portrayal offered in the same journal just two weeks later. Juxtaposing the two pieces reveals the difficulties many female leaders faced. The second editorial compared Kamaladevi with Kasturba Gandhi, who had died two months earlier. 'Kamaladevi is the antithesis of Kasturba in every respect,' the anonymous author declared. 'Complete self-effacement was the key-note of Kasturba's character. Kamaladevi is all self-assertion.' Of course, self-assertion could be seen as a virtue, but contrasting Kamaladevi with Kasturba, who was widely idolized, was bound to cast Kamaladevi in a harsh light. It did not help that the editorial compared Kamaladevi to the Goddess Kali, 'red in tooth and claw'. The editorial was not entirely negative. Readers were told that 'the common trait of Kasturba and Kamaladevi is their infinite capacity for endurance'. But overall Kamaladevi was presented as harsh, demanding and self-aggrandizing.[68]

We do not know what Kamaladevi made of these conflicting editorials, but that same year she published an essay on Kasturba that serves as a fitting rebuttal of the way the *Indian Social Reformer* contrasted the two women. She wrote of Kasturba that the Mahatma's 'strong will was matched by hers. To the last she retained her own individuality.' Marriage did nothing to diminish that individuality. 'She was not the wife who walked in his shadow,' Kamaladevi declared, for 'she was one who shed a light of her own.' A few years later, she offered another tribute to Kasturba in a syndicated article. 'What she signifies is not just a simple quality or trait,' she wrote of Kasturba. 'When she died they called her sati, and it brought before us the picture of a strong proud woman who willingly offered her all—her very life—on the altar of an ideal.' It was not Kasturba's sacrifice that Kamaladevi celebrated; it was the way in which she gave her life to the struggle while retaining her own independence. 'That was the test of her strength,' Kamaladevi explained, 'that she could be part of that mighty force yet keep her individuality intact.'[69]

Kamaladevi's most important tribute to Kasturba was her decision to work for the Kasturba Gandhi National Memorial Trust, a new organization created by the Mahatma to promote 'the general welfare of poor and needy women and children in rural areas in India'. Working for the Kasturba Trust strengthened Kamaladevi's increasingly warm relationship with Gandhi. In June 1944, she wrote Gandhi to arrange a meeting. The date she proposed happened to fall on his regular 'silent day'. In his reply, Gandhi explained that he had resisted the 'mischievous' urge to let her come on that day. 'But I shall be good,' he wrote. 'You can come on 27th instant [sic] and see me at 5 p.m. With love, Bapu.' The following month, he again wrote Kamaladevi. 'I am glad you thoroughly realize the virtue of the wheel and the importance of the village programme,' he stated. 'Mridula is coming here. Khurshedbehn is already with me. With two such stalwarts by my side, I am not likely to go wrong. My dream is to have India's women to lead the world of men who have led women up to now. Yours, Bapu.' Kamaladevi was not a Gandhian 'stalwart', at least not like Khurshedbehn Naoroji or Mridula Sarabhai. She was, and would remain, too independent to be a devotee of anyone. But as the reference to the wheel makes clear, she was drawing closer to several of Gandhi's fundamental beliefs. As his comments on gender indicate, he had also been influenced by her.[70]

On 5 April 1945, Kamaladevi joined Sarojini Naidu and Mridula Sarabhai at the opening of a training camp for women in Borivali, a suburb of Bombay. The camp had been organized under the aegis of the newly created Kasturba Trust. The camp would offer 'instruction in Social work, Hygiene, Medical relief, Village industries etc'. The *Indian Social Reformer* criticized the camp as an example of the 'segregation of women in society and in schools' but still praised Kamaladevi as 'a strenuous worker' who was 'sure to impress her personality on whatever she may undertake'. For her part, Kamaladevi continued to believe in the importance of women's organizations and initiatives and did not believe the camp constituted 'segregation'. She saw nothing wrong with women organizing as women while also working with men to confront the nation's problems.[71]

She demonstrated the inclusivity of her vision during yet another tour across India. On 22 April 1945, she spoke before some 2,000 people in Ujjain, an ancient city located on the banks of the Kshipra River in what is now Madhya Pradesh. According to a colonial intelligence report, Kamaladevi 'spoke of the shortage of food grains in the State and that several people died of starvation'. She told the audience to 'co-operate in bringing about a compromise between the Hindus and Muslims' so that they could eliminate poverty and achieve 'a free India'. On 6 May, she was in Belgaum at a conference of Karnatak Congress workers. She accepted responsibility for a new 'women's organization' subcommittee. On 12 May, she spoke to some 200 people at the Nanavat Congress House in Surat. She 'described the economic and social conditions of various countries and advised her listeners to implement the Congress Constructive Programme if they wanted to be free and happy'. On 16 June she was in Dharwad in present-day Karnataka, opening a training centre under the aegis of the Kasturba Trust. While Kamaladevi remained committed to shaping nationwide policy and her vision of freedom continued to stretch throughout the world, her attraction to Gandhian constructive work called her to smaller-scale, grassroots efforts at creating sustainable social change.[72]

In the summer of 1945, Kamaladevi visited Gandhi during his silent day. He scribbled her a warm note: 'I have imposed silence on myself today. I hope you do not mind it. But ask questions and I would answer.' The full scope of their conversation is unknown, but we can glean much from the different notes Gandhi scribbled on used envelopes, all of which Kamaladevi kept in her records. In one note, he wrote, 'If I went to a village as a worker I would expect the villagers to fund my expenses and I would make it worth their while to do so. I began life thus.' This comment suggests that Kamaladevi had asked about the practicality of scaling up the grassroots social work being done under the aegis of the Kasturba Trust. Much of the conversation concerned Kasturba herself. 'Though herself a vegetarian, she did not insist on it for others,' Gandhi wrote. 'Prayers she lived in and for. Therefore if I was a woman worker I would conduct prayers for all religious-minded people and for all religions. Neither Christians nor Muslims nor others would be excluded.' Such tolerance was yet another point of connection between Kasturba and Kamaladevi—and between Gandhi and Kamaladevi as well.[73]

While many held up Kasturba as a model, others celebrated Kamaladevi as a different kind of model—in ways that were complicated and not always comfortable for Kamaladevi herself. Although she rarely mentioned her past marriages in public, she was still used as an example of a successful widow—and at times, of a successful divorcée as well. On 30 December 1944, Australian newspaper the *Advertiser* published an article headlined 'The Problem of India's Women' in which Kamaladevi was cited as evidence that 'the widow's lot is improving'. Readers learnt that she was 'the president of the All India Women's Congress' and 'a widely-travelled member of the Congress Socialist Party'. Her achievements were more remarkable given her personal struggles. 'She was widowed when young,' the article explained, and 'not only did she re-marry, but she divorced her second husband.' It is unlikely that Kamaladevi found meaning in being held up as a token of the successful divorcée. For one thing, such descriptions infringed upon her privacy. Moreover, her divorce had been deeply painful and it remained to be seen what lasting damage it would cause to her political career. Fighting for the freedom of her country, Kamaladevi also fought for her own freedom.[74]

~

Even as she threw herself into the endgame of India's struggle for freedom, Kamaladevi maintained her commitment to global freedom struggles—and, in particular, to solidarities of resistance within what would later be called the Third World or the Global South. In 1944, as president of the AIWC, she sent a message of support to the pan-Arab Feminist Conference in Cairo: 'Remember during your deliberations the struggle of India and her participation for the sake of the entire East.' That same year, she published *Uncle Sam's Empire* with Padma Publications, a left-leaning publishing house headed by Yusuf Meherally. *Uncle Sam's Empire* sampled American history with an eye to its increasingly imperial role in the world. In the chapter 'The Negro Slave Trade,' she stated, 'Human history is stained with many a dark patch but few can compare with the blot left by the trade in "Black Ivory" as the negro slaves were termed.' According to the *Hindustan Times*, the book was 'objective, free from bias, and well balanced'. *Janata* magazine similarly praised the work as 'impartial and objective' and the *Illustrated Weekly of India* told readers, 'This book should very definitely find a place on the bookshelf of anyone with pretensions to a knowledge of international affairs.'[75]

A few years later, Kamaladevi published another book on the United States, this one entitled *America: The Land of Superlatives.* Yet again, she dedicated an entire chapter to American racism. 'The biggest blot on the fair name of America is the problem of the Negro,' she declared. She located African American social movements within a global 'struggle between the dispossessed colored world and the ruling white'. She also offered an extended analysis of the economic bases of racial prejudice. At the root of racism she found 'the inevitable alliance between the new industrial kings and the old land monarchs, against the rising democratic forces of the masses'. Of African American art, she wrote, 'When it speaks for economic equality and social justice, it speaks for the peoples of the world.' For an example of the expansive power of African American artists, she concentrated on Paul Robeson:

> For when Paul Robeson sings he becomes something more than a singer. He transcends all human limitations and becomes the disembodied melody, which knows neither colour nor race. He interprets the ageless, deathless spirit of his lost land of Africa, his priceless heritage, before which even the hooded order of bigotry and hate spontaneously retreat.

In her praise for Robeson, Kamaladevi demonstrated the complexity of her commitment to the solidarity of 'dark' or 'colored' peoples. She congratulated Robeson for transcending 'colour' and 'race' before lauding him for interpreting 'the deathless spirit of his lost land of Africa, his priceless heritage'. Kamaladevi linked a sweeping humanism to a strong belief in the importance of social and cultural roots. She wrote:

> Soon Africa too, will come back, and come into her own, and the dark ones will cease to be the 'untouchables' of the world. The international colour line has been challenged and stormed by Asia. No more the colonials will allow themselves to be jim-crowed the world over and their country looted under pseudo-slogans. The Negro problem will only cease when the colourline of imperialism vanishes, when Science becomes the benefactor of man and knowledge his friend, and human respect for each other and for the sanctity of life are observed as the codes of our daily life.

By juxtaposing colonization and Jim Crow, Kamaladevi offered a vision of solidarity between different struggles for freedom.[76]

Kamaladevi's reference to 'untouchables' did not reveal a deep concern with caste inequity. Although she consistently opposed untouchability and caste more generally, casteism was never a major focus of Kamaladevi's activism. In 1928, at the All-India National Social

Conference in Calcutta, she moved a resolution 'that inter-caste and inter-communal dinners be encouraged' and 'that freedom be given for inter-marriage among the several communities inhabiting in India'. In December 1929, she declared that 'in a free India there cannot be any caste or sex discrimination or inequality'. But the limits of her approach to caste were evident a few years later when she told a gathering of students that it was through 'union and fullest co-operation among all classes of people' that Indian patriots could 'solve far more easily our communal and caste differences'. She called for 'a definite organized rebellion . . . against all social oppression' but she warned against being diverted 'into minor channels' that 'side-track' the main issues. 'Take, for instance, the depressed classes who are now agitating for temple-entry in certain places,' she stated. 'This question is merely one of the many aspects of the whole social system which is based on tyranny and exploitation and it is against this system itself that we have to fight.' Such an approach to caste—locating it in relation to imperialism, class inequality and other injustices—was common among socialists and could become an excuse for inaction.[77]

Like many upper-caste Indian nationalists, Kamaladevi believed that the worst manifestations of casteism were already receding. In 1940, she declared that 'untouchability and caste prejudice are fast becoming past memories'. Given that this statement was made in an American magazine, it should be understood in part as an effort to combat British propaganda that labelled India as caste-ridden and thus in need of foreign rule. Nevertheless, such a statement also revealed a kind of optimistic blindness when it came to the depth of casteism. Such optimism did not always prevent Kamaladevi from speaking out against caste inequity. In April 1944, during her presidential address at the AIWC gathering in Bombay, she stated that the women's movement was 'a comrade to the struggle of the backward castes and the long oppressed classes seeking alike to regain the lost inheritance of man's inalienable rights'. Her decision to frame the 'struggle of the backward castes' as a matter of human rights suggested that she had begun to move away from the socialist dogma that put class above caste when it came to social reform. But caste would never become a major focus of her activism.[78]

Her failure to attack caste with the same passion she brought to opposing class inequity, imperialism and sexism could be excused as a result of the limitations of her time and energy. Yet Kamaladevi herself was dismissive of activists who focused too narrowly on only one set of injustices. During her tenure as president of the AIWC, for example, she wrote the International Alliance of Women calling upon Western feminists 'to take a clear and strong stand on the question of freedom for all peoples'. On 12 May 1945, the *Bombay Chronicle* published a letter from Kamaladevi to Corbett Ashby, the president of the IAW, calling upon the organization 'to throw its full weight in favour of instituting a world order in which political and economic domination of one people over another will find no place'. Kamaladevi quickly lost hope in the IAW. In 1946, she declared the more radical Women's International League for Peace and Freedom 'the only organization that gave her hope and faith'.[79]

That must have been an overstatement, given how many causes and organizations she supported—and the profound hope she brought to a variety of struggles. On 4 January 1945, she was in Ahmedabad where she met with local Congress members and 'advised workers to implement the constructive programme wholeheartedly'. The following day, she told an audience at Gujarat College that 'it was a matter of doubt whether real democracy would be established in the world'. In a conversation with local journalists, she 'advocated the forming of Kisan and Majdoor Mandals [peasant and worker unions] and advised the avoidance of a conflict with the Communists'. On 6 January, she challenged some 400 students 'to carry on the "Torch of Knowledge" to the villages in order to bring about their social, political and economic uplift'. That same day she also addressed a local women's group, calling on them to work against female illiteracy and in support of the Hindu civil code. On 21 January and then again on 27 January, Kamaladevi addressed large meetings in Solapur, a city in what is today southern Maharashtra. Hundreds of people, many of them students, flocked to hear her stress the importance of 'the Congress constructive programme'.[80]

While travelling the country giving speeches and meeting with local groups, Kamaladevi continued writing as well. With the help of Avabai

Wadia, she launched a 'research, investigation and information bureau' and a series of publications written by AIWC members, with most of those works published in English, Hindi and Marathi. One of the first publications was by Kamaladevi herself: *Towards a National Theatre*. Although she had moved away from her own stage career, Kamaladevi remained a passionate advocate of the theatre. In Bombay, she helped a group of younger artists establish the Indian National Theatre (INT) in the spring of 1944. While she has often been credited as founding the INT, Kamaladevi used the pages of *Towards a National Theatre* to praise the 'young people, mainly students' who had founded the group 'with exemplary devotion and selfless industry'.[81]

She was less upbeat about the state of theatre more generally. 'It is a strange as well as a tragic fact,' she wrote, 'that the general national awakening in India resulting, amongst other things, in a tremendous revival in fine arts and various aesthetical pursuits, should have so completely bypassed the drama and the stage.' Most theatrical works, she lamented, dealt 'mostly with the intellectuals, usually ignoring the vast masses'. It was not just the topic or themes of dramatic works that concerned her. She wanted to democratize the writing and production of theatre as well. 'The State must establish Theatres,' she wrote, 'and make them available at nominal cost . . . to the people for their use.'[82]

Kamaladevi's vision of a grassroots, politically engaged theatre dovetailed with the efforts of the Indian People's Theatre Association (IPTA), an organization that had been founded a few years earlier by a group of left-leaning activists, many of whom had strong ties to the Communist Party. In *Towards a National Theatre*, she praised the IPTA for doing 'much to stimulate, encourage and foster cultural work all over the country.' She added that the IPTA had 'started as the cultural front of a political faction—the Communist Party of India' and concluded that 'art when it functions as the propaganda arm of political ideologies becomes constrained and limited'. Her critique of the IPTA was noteworthy given her deep admiration for Soviet theatre. In *Towards a National Theatre* she reproduced language from Huntly Carter's *The New Theatre and Cinema of Soviet Russia*. 'Our primary need,' she wrote, 'is of writers who will take the challenges of today and give adequate expression to the vivified impulses and emotions, the surging thoughts and actions of a vast human mass slowly stirring like a huge elephant rising to its feet. Then alone will the theatre cease to be a reserved enclosure and become an open creative playground for all, an organic part of the national life, expressing the individuality of the people as a whole.' Carter had written of the theatre as 'an open creative playground for everyone instead of a reserved enclosure for shopkeepers, gamblers and egoists' and had declared that 'the theatre had an extreme value as an organic part of social and national life' that expressed 'the individuality of the people'. In the years ahead, Kamaladevi would often recycle her own writings and would occasionally also draw upon the writings of others without proper attribution. Given her many commitments and the fact that she was not writing as a scholar, she might be forgiven for these practices. What is most striking in this case is not the fact that she borrowed language from Carter but the fact that she reproduced a homogenous conception of 'the people' drawn from an account of Soviet theatre. Her vision of the future Indian nation often suggested, in the words of the scholar Aparna Bhargava Dharwadker, 'a classless community whose collective identity is self-evident and unproblematic'. In this case, her vision of 'the people' was meant as a critique of the upper-class bias of contemporary theatre. Still, as scholars of Indian citizenship have demonstrated, homogenous conceptions of a united Indian people risked erasing or excluding minorities and perpetuating the inequities of religion, region, class and caste.[83]

Kamaladevi embraced the diversity of India and of Indian theatre, yet not always in ways that transcended the limitations of her own upper-class, upper-caste background. Consider her assessment of the performer she knew best: Harin. Kamaladevi lauded Harin as 'unique amongst actors and producers' and 'endowed with many rare gifts and talents'. Her praise at times hinted at why he was not as good a husband as he was an actor. 'He was like an elemental being,' she wrote, 'an unspoilt child of nature and of the people.' The phrase 'unspoilt child of nature' seemed positive, but by comparing Harin to a child Kamaladevi gestured towards his limitations. For one thing, his talent fostered a certain egotism. 'Perhaps the only drawback was that he was so rich, varied, scintillating and vivacious a personality as an artist,' she explained, 'that he rather overpowered the group, and often his show was like a one-star performance.' Nevertheless, she declared, 'One of his greatest contributions to the Indian Theatre is the re-introduction of women to the stage, starting with his own wife and family members.' 'The Chattopadhyayas,' Kamaladevi wrote as if she were an unbiased observer, 'helped to draw out many talented women who might otherwise have been completely lost to this great art.' While recognizing the important precedent she and Harin set by performing together on stage, Kamaladevi overlooked the rich traditions of female performance within Dalit communities. Writing about herself in the third person was an act of humility but perhaps also a way to maintain distance from her own class and caste position—as well as from Harin and what remained an unsettled dimension of her life.[84]

So much had happened since Kamaladevi had ended her marriage while suffering through solitary confinement in Vellore Jail. She had travelled across the world and returned to an India seething with rebellion. She had given all of herself to the Quit India movement and had struggled through yet another long period of imprisonment. Now that Indian independence seemed imminent, perhaps the many struggles of the past—both personal and political—came to feel safely distant. But as Kamaladevi knew all too well, the scars of the past never fully heal, and one could never know when the burdens of history would suddenly collapse upon the present and darken the promise of the future.

6

Triumph and Tragedy

SPEAKING IN BOMBAY IN AUGUST 1945, KAMALADEVI DECLARED, IN THE words of the *Times of India*, that 'a time had come to form an organisation for utilising the vast potentialities of the theatre in the country and thereby releasing a flood of creative energy that may inspire every class and strata of society into purposeful activities so that the whole nation may be enriched'. After Independence, Kamaladevi would take a leading role in building the kind of national theatre she envisioned. In the late 1940s, however, her contributions to theatre were less organizational and more intellectual—and they were bound up with her efforts to achieve independence and to reimagine what independence would mean for India. Kamaladevi saw many connections between art, theatre, politics and constructive social work. In her interview with Homi Taleyarkhan, she declared that the ideal social worker would need to 'have a general all-around knowledge, without necessarily an expert's knowledge on any one topic, so that when teams of social workers go out on their jobs, each will know something about the work of the other'. To explain the importance of such generalized knowledge, Kamaladevi offered the example of 'the producer who must have a smattering of everything pertaining to the screen or stage, before he can put up a successful show'. In the final push for freedom, Kamaladevi wanted to be more than a lead actor; she wanted to help write the script. Ultimately, however, she wanted the people of

India—all of them—to decide how the tragedy of the Raj would end and a new drama, full of hope and promise, would begin.[1]

As a writer and a thinker, Kamaladevi shared her broad vision for the independence struggle. In *Roshni,* the journal of the AIWC, she wrote on 'The Principles of Health Insurance'. In the prestigious Calcutta-based journal the *Modern Review,* she published articles on topics ranging from the film industry to industrial strikes. Many of her articles examined current affairs in Europe, the United States, Africa and other parts of Asia. Often, she drew connections between international events and Indian affairs. Her piece on 'The Struggle of Viet Nam against French Imperialism', for instance, compared French divide-and-rule tactics with the way in which 'territorial disruption is being encouraged in India under a sinister caption of "special responsibilities" of the British towards the minorities, tribal peoples and the Indian princes'. In a piece on 'Full Employment', she quoted the progressive American politician Henry Wallace, and discussed the UK's Beveridge Plan before arguing for the necessity of centralized, state-directed economic planning and the 'socialization of the national economy'.[2]

A few common threads link most of the articles Kamaladevi published: a vision of Indian independence bound up with world affairs; a deep concern with class inequity; and the belief, as she put it in an essay on the 'Goals of Social Reconstruction', that 'democracy in life is only possible when, the principle is observed in every phase of our life', including within the family. In an article on 'The Place of Women in the New Society', published in the *Modern Review* in July 1946, Kamaladevi defended 'woman's right to any profession' and 'equal payment for equal work, free from the present sex discriminations'. She attacked sexual double standards that expected men 'to be licentious' while women were forced to remain 'the repository of social morals'. She argued for divorce, lamenting the fact that in many cases the law still prevented 'two intelligent people from separating if their union had in reality ceased to be' and had 'become a burden or a mockery'. In a striking analogy that linked her own personal life to India's freedom struggle, she declared that a 'man has no more rights over his wife than an Imperialist country over a colonial'.[3]

On 23 September 1945, at a gathering of the AICC, Kamaladevi moved an amendment that the Congress contest the upcoming elections to the central and provincial assemblies—but only to reveal 'the will of the people on the issue of immediate transfer of power and the framing of a Constitution for an Independent India'. She asserted that all adults should be able to vote, that the constituent assembly should have 'sovereign authority' without interference from the colonial government, and that the princely states should be represented by delegates chosen in free and fair elections. That same month, Kamaladevi published an article in *The Leader* declaring that 'the hour of confabulations and conferences, speeches and debates, is gone . . . Now we can make our moves with only one purpose,' she wrote: 'the carving of a free India, functioning under its own constitution and controlling its own economy.' She decried the fact that the proposed elections would be 'fought on a hopelessly restricted franchise enjoyed by a meager 23 per cent, or so'.[4]

Such limited elections could not usher in true freedom. The key, Kamaladevi believed, was to use the elections to spur grassroots organizing across the country. In the fall of 1945, she travelled across India, visiting AIWC branches wherever she could. The Mysore branch invited her to visit, but a police inspector travelled from Mysore to warn her that an old order prohibiting her entry into the state was still active, and that she would 'be committing a penal offence by going against it'. In response, she sent a letter of protest to the Chief Secretary of the Government of Mysore. 'Sir,' she began, 'I was surprised to find that an old order served on me in 1942 December not to enter the State of Mysore has been kept alive . . . By the time that I next move in your enlightened state, I expect the bar sinister to have been removed.' She also alerted all AIWC members to this injustice, explaining that 'no case has been stated, no explanation given of the why and wherefore, or of any specific circumstances on which the order is sought to be enforced'. She criticized the Mysore branch for suggesting that she ask 'permission' to enter the state and that she promise in writing to not make any political speeches.

'To give an undertaking not to make political speeches,' she explained, would be impossible. 'The term is very sweeping,' she explained, 'for politics is not merely party politics, but may include any discussion or speech about elections, franchise, the Constituent Assembly, the future Constitution for India, etc. all of which fall within the purview of the AIWC, which actively deals with them on nonparty lines.'[5]

In early December 1945, Kamaladevi wrote Gandhi asking his opinion regarding how she might challenge the restrictions on her travel in Mysore state. He encouraged her to wait until she had work that needed to be done there. At that point, she should give 'due notice' of her plans and then 'should enter the State and take the consequences'. Eight years earlier, Gandhi had been troubled by Kamaladevi's insistent desire to challenge the princely states. Now, he wrote, 'If the State presumes to interfere with your activities, it might be worth while to test the legality of such action.' He also offered some advice regarding Kamaladevi's own future. 'I would much like to see you settle down in a village,' he wrote, 'and put your hand not to the plough which may be too hard for you but to the wheel which is hard for nobody.' He concluded, 'Love Yours, BAPU.' This was a well-intentioned suggestion, but Kamaladevi was, like Gandhi himself, too committed to widespread social change to 'settle down in a village'. She would continue travelling the country organizing resistance to colonial rule and advancing a broad, democratic vision of Indian independence. That same month, she offered the inaugural address at the Morris College centenary in Nagpur. 'Perhaps no other branch of human affairs has been treated as so exclusive a class possession as education,' she declared. True education should contribute 'to the construction of a new society which will answer to the three main qualities that are indispensable, for in our conception of a moral social order, it should be classless, cooperative, democratic'.[6]

Classless, cooperative, democratic—would a free and independent India live up to such a radical vision? While fighting to end British rule, Kamaladevi continued to broaden the definition of India's freedom. In the last days of 1945, she travelled by train from Bombay to Karachi and then on to Hyderabad, Sind, for the annual AIWC gathering. She was accompanied by Avabai Wadia and by Wadia's mother. 'When we reached Karachi,' Wadia later recalled, 'there was a huge, milling crowd of thousands' that had gathered to welcome Kamaladevi. 'It was almost impossible to move,' she stated. The three women had to wait until a group of Congress volunteers locked arms and created a path of escape. 'My mother and I were quite frightened,' Wadia wrote, 'but Kamaladevi was used to such adulatory crowds. She firmly got hold of my mother's arm and, with me close behind, led us outside and to the car.' They stayed at the house of a shipping magnate where visitors came to see Kamaladevi 'at all times of the day and early night'.[7]

Did Kamaladevi feel any psychic tension staying at the home of a wealthy businessman while demanding a classless society? Like Gandhi and many other prominent Congress leaders, Kamaladevi often relied on the generosity of wealthy supporters—especially during travel. Unlike Gandhi, she had long challenged Congress leaders to attack inequity by redistributing land and wealth. It remained unclear how a political entity like the Congress—in debt to wealthy and landed interests—would approach the profound poverty and inequity of India once it was in power. It also remained unclear how Kamaladevi would reconcile her radical vision for India with her own class status, her pragmatism and her abiding belief in the importance of national unity.

On 25 December, Kamaladevi ceremonially hoisted the national flag at a large gathering in which she encouraged the audience to find strength in unity. Her own strength was complicated by ongoing health problems, many of which had been caused by her years of harsh imprisonment. 'Due to her present state of health,' the *Times of India* reported, Kamaladevi had 'cancelled all her other programmes' and would return to Bombay after the AIWC conference in Hyderabad. She refused to miss that gathering of women activists, at which the delegates unanimously approved a resolution denouncing Mysore's ban on Kamaladevi.[8]

Kamaladevi spent the early months of 1946 resting and recuperating. By April, she was travelling again. At the Workers' and Peasants' Conference at Jabalpur, she defined 'the immediate task before the country' as 'the organising of the peasants and the workers, for through them alone the struggle for Freedom can achieve its purpose'. As usual, she offered a radically broad vision of freedom. 'If one is to visualise a free India,' she explained, 'one has to think in terms of the complete wiping out of all forms of exploitation, whether it be of one class over another, one caste over another or one sex over the other.' In June, she spoke at the Socialist Conference at Gadag in present-day Karnataka. 'All Asia is in ferment,' she declared, 'and the colonial people are making one supreme effort to throw off the old yoke.' She warned against India becoming 'a monotonous repetition of every Western State, a capitalist-democracy in which the power of the masses, if not emasculated as in a totalitarian state, is certainly in danger of being crippled'. Her socialism shaped how she approached the most portentous question facing all those eager to achieve Indian independence—how Indian unity could be maintained despite profound tensions between religious communities and, in particular, despite the divide between the Muslim League and the Congress. 'It is socialism alone that can destroy the canker of communalism from its very roots,' she declared.[9]

Kamaladevi had long seen religious divisions as a danger to Indian unity, a danger deliberately stoked by the British via such tactics as allowing 'separate electorates' for Muslims. In May 1935, she told one audience that 'separate electorates have served to reinforce all the disintegrating tendencies'. Ten years later, she insisted that 'the communal conflict' had been 'created and built up over decades for the perpetuation of third party rule'. She dismissed 'phrases and slogans such as self-determination and plebiscite for minorities'. The Muslims of India were, she insisted, 'Indians first and last.' Her views were shared by most socialists. In 1942, Ashoka Mehta and Achyut Patwardhan had published a volume entitled *The Communal Triangle in India* in which they argued that religious divisions were 'largely a creation of the British'. In June 1945, Narendra Dev argued that 'the communal problem will have to be tackled only by laying emphasis on the economic issues which equally affect Hindu and Muslim masses'. Whereas many socialists remained outside the locus of power, Kamaladevi would bring her opposition to Partition to the Working Committee, that elite group charged with deciding Congress policy, at precisely the moment when its decisions were most fateful.[10]

In the summer of 1946, the fate of India's unity hinged on what was known as the Cabinet Mission Plan, a complex agreement that had been created by three British cabinet members. The Muslim League had accepted the plan and it seemed the Congress had as well. But on 10 July Nehru gave a speech in which he suggested that the Congress would not be bound by the terms of the plan. Fearing majoritarian rule, the Muslim League withdrew its support. It was just at that moment, when it seemed India's hopes for unity were dissolving, that Nehru nominated Kamaladevi to the Working Committee. It had been ten years since Gandhi had blocked her from that select and powerful group. Now his 'doubts' about her had been removed, and it was Kamaladevi herself who was unsure she wanted to join the committee.[11]

On 11 July, one day after Nehru's explosive comments, Jayaprakash Narayan issued a statement in Bombay supporting the idea of Kamaladevi joining the Working Committee despite the distrust between the socialists and the old guard of the Congress. It was JP, more than anyone, who convinced Kamaladevi to accept the role despite her grave concerns about Congress policy. It remained unclear if she would be able to do anything to preserve India's unity or to ensure that when swaraj came it was not a pale shadow of the freedom for which she, JP and so many others had long fought.[12]

~

In early August 1946, Kamaladevi was in Wardha with the other Working Committee members. They passed resolutions on Goa, Hyderabad, Indian migration to East Africa and Indian migrant laborers in Malaya. Their main focus, however, was on communal violence and the spectre of Partition. The Muslim League and its leader, Mohammad Ali Jinnah, had declared 16 August as 'direct action day'. In Calcutta, what began as a hartal (a shutdown of shops and businesses) quickly escalated into widespread violence, and thousands died. Soon after, Kamaladevi travelled to Delhi for another round of Working Committee meetings.

In response to the violence in Calcutta, the committee expressed 'deep sorrow' and extended 'their sympathy to the innocent sufferers of whatever community'. In late October, the group met again after yet another round of brutality. After blaming both the Muslim League and the colonial government, the committee declared 'it hard to express adequately their feeling of horror and pain'. In November it was the massacres of Muslims in Bihar that filled the Working Committee members with 'horror and pain'. They concluded, 'Deeds of loot, arson, murder and other forms of gruesome brutality have been committed on such a wide scale that they must create grave concern in the minds of all lovers of freedom and humanity.'[13]

What could be done to stop the violence? Some argued that the partition of the subcontinent had become inevitable, and that separating the main religious communities was the only path to permanent peace. Kamaladevi forcefully disagreed. In February 1947, she wrote an article for *Blitz* on 'Pakistan and the Shifting of Populations'. She analysed population exchanges between Greece and Turkey in 1923 and Nazi 'compulsory population shifts' in order to argue against relocating large numbers of people across hastily drawn borders. 'It is well to remember,' she wrote, 'no matter with what care frontiers are drawn, that they are bound to be prone to changes sooner or later, until some World Federation comes into operation which will tone down ultra-nationalism and curb the present fanatical insistence on the fetish of national sovereignty of every single national group.'[14]

While Kamaladevi worked against Partition on religious lines, she also pursued India's unity by promoting democracy in the princely states. Towards the end of February 1947, at the fifth annual gathering of the Congress Socialist Party in Kanpur, she seconded a resolution that 'demanded an immediate end of personal rule in every State and the establishment of unrestricted civil liberties and full transference of power to the people'. On 18 April, she was in Gwalior at the All-India States' Peoples' Convention, a gathering dedicated to 'the establishment of full Responsible Government in the States'.[15]

Her vision of a united democratic India included Goa, a Portuguese-controlled enclave on the west coast where a freedom movement was being viciously repressed by the colonialists. In 1946, in the *Modern Review,* she called it 'absolutely intolerable that such atrocities as are taking place in Goa should be inflicted on our kith and kind and what is even more outrageous, within the frontiers of our own country'. Along with the socialist firebrand Ram Manohar Lohia, she made plans to stay in a new training camp for 'Satyagrahis for the resistance movement in Goa' that was to be opened outside of Belgaum in January 1947. In June, she inaugurated a political conference on Goa at Sunderabai Hall, Bombay. The conference featured prominent Goans and leading political figures including her fellow Congress socialist Purshottamdas Tricumdas and the president of the Bombay Provincial Congress Committee, S.K. Patil. Kamaladevi declared that 'India's freedom must simultaneously mean freedom for the people of Goa'. As a Konkani speaker, she shared a native tongue with many of the people of Goa, but it was not her regional pride that she invoked when attacking colonial rule there; it was her vision of a united India. 'Goa belongs to the heart and soul of Hindustan,' she declared. She praised the people of Goa for fighting against a 'foreign regime' and concluded that 'the Goan public must share with the rest of India in this great struggle to bring freedom to the common man, to make freedom a living reality, so that men and women can lead freer, happier and nobler lives'.[16]

Kamaladevi saw that 'great struggle to bring freedom to the common man' extending across borders of many kinds—both within and beyond the nation-state. In March 1947, she was in Delhi for the Asian Relations Conference, a gathering that brought representatives from across Asia to discuss the imminent collapse of colonial rule. It was in triumph that the official president of the gathering, Sarojini Naidu, greeted an audience of thousands at the Purana Qila in Delhi. 'Fellow Asians,' Naidu declared, 'remember the night of darkness is over. Together, men and women, let us march forward to the Dawn.' In his welcoming address, Nehru declared that 'the idea of such a Conference arose simultaneously in many minds and in many countries of Asia'. For her part, Kamaladevi had long championed solidarities between colonized peoples. In addition to helping build the groundwork for such solidarities—and thus for the conference—Kamaladevi made two more unique contributions to the gathering.

First, she helped transform the conference from a meeting of national representatives, focused on diplomatic or international relations, into a gathering of social activists who cared about transnational ties between social movements. Towards that end, she submitted a report on the 'Status of Women in India'. She had written a chapter with the same title nearly twenty years earlier. As she had then, she began by praising the Vedic period as a time when 'women seem to have enjoyed equal rights with men'. Turning to the present, she deployed a range of statistics to criticize the government for underfunding education and healthcare. She also examined women's labour in agriculture, mining, the textile industry and in government services—arguing throughout that women should be paid the same salaries as men doing the same work. She discussed marriage and divorce and asserted that 'above all, what a national India aims at is a single national code, uniform for all communities irrespective of their religion'. In a concluding section called 'Our Common Aim', she noted that different Asian countries had long influenced each other, and she called for 'a renewed comradeship in the glad hour of our dawning freedom'. She expanded on that transnational vision in another piece written in conjunction with the conference. Entitled 'The Awakening of Asia', that essay argued that 'the political and economic emancipation . . . of Asia and Africa' had 'a direct bearing upon the question of world peace'. She celebrated 'the mighty continental shift from West to East', discussed the shared experience of colonialism, and called 'for the Asian countries to enter upon a joint plan for the purpose of pooling together economic resources as well as experience'.[17]

In addition to offering a gendered framework for transnational anticolonial solidarities, Kamaladevi also brought to the conference her passion for the arts—and particularly for drama. Nehru asked her to organize a cultural programme. She agreed and, along with Damu Jhaveri, the general secretary of the Indian National Theatre, she produced a theatrical dance interpretation of *The Discovery of India*, Nehru's bestselling history of the subcontinent. Presented with a list of available talent, Kamaladevi worried aloud that 'these are all communist boys'. She hired them anyway, putting together a talented group including the dancer and choreographer Shanti Bardhan. In setting aside the tensions between socialists and communists, Kamaladevi tried to heal the even more glaring divides facing India, especially the divides of religion. Nehru's book celebrated Hindu–Muslim collaboration across generations, and a dramatic performance of the text offered an opportunity to spread that message of tolerance to new audiences.[18]

Kamaladevi herself also continued to spread the message of tolerance. In Mangalore, she gave a talk entitled 'The Communal Problem—A Socialist Perspective' at the Provincial Socialist Convention. The communal problem was, according to Kamaladevi, 'a device conceived and carried out by British imperialism to maintain itself'. Across the world 'the elements of reaction' used distinctions 'of religion or of race' in order to divide people and to defend the status quo. 'The very findings of anthropology and ethnology are perverted to reinforce brutal reactionary forces,' she declared, 'as in the case of the Nazi rule; the oppression of the coloured peoples in Asia and Africa; the discrimination against negroes in America and the Harijans in India; the widespread anti-Semitism in Europe.' Despite the pervasive nature of such discrimination, Kamaladevi found hope in the interconnected nature of social reform. 'Every effort to combat and mitigate the social problems—poverty, unemployment, illiteracy, scarcity—is a blow against communalism,' she declared. She also found hope in the rich plurality of Indian culture. She offered an inclusive vision of India as 'a land of many customs, faiths, languages, costumes and styles of cooking'. Her cultural pluralism was balanced by a strong belief in the fundamental unity of all Indian cultural forms. 'The Muslims of India today are as much Indians as the Hindus,' she stated, and 'the lovely mosques and mausoleums of India are as Indian as the temples or the stupas.'[19]

In retrospect, Kamaladevi's vision appears hopelessly unrealistic. Many Muslims had become convinced that only a separate Muslim-majority nation would guarantee their safety and freedom. Many Hindus had come to embrace a vision of India as a fundamentally Hindu nation. Many Congress leaders, while sharing Kamaladevi's vision of a pluralistic India, had come to accept Partition as the inevitable price of freedom. At the end of May, the Congress Working Committee met to discuss the question of Partition. Kamaladevi was there along with a roster of prominent freedom fighters including Gandhi, Nehru, Patel, Acharya Kripalani, Khan Abdul Ghaffar Khan, Sarojini Naidu, Maulana Azad, Rajendra Prasad, Chakravarti Rajagopalachari, Jagjivan Ram and Jayaprakash Narayan. It was Narayan who raised his voice in opposition to Partition. He argued that the Working Committee could not commit to Partition without consulting with the AICC. His challenge was dismissed. Kamaladevi later recalled that on the question of Partition 'the majority were of one view' and 'did not have any open mind at all'.[20]

On 3 June 1947, the viceroy of India, Louis Mountbatten, announced the partition of the British Raj in a radio address. On 8 June, the national executive of the Congress Socialists met and publicly opposed Partition. On 14–15 June, when the AICC met to discuss the Working Committee's decision in support of Partition, the Socialists abstained from voting. They had lost faith in the process and had begun their own separation—not from India but from the Congress. In a revealing shift in nomenclature, they dropped the word 'Congress' and became just the 'Socialist Party'. In May 1947, JP had written Nehru recommending that Kamaladevi and six others join the Constituent Assembly. In response to Partition, the Socialists decided to boycott that influential body and instead to embrace their opposition status. Kamaladevi later called that strategy 'unrealistic'. She would maintain strong ties with the Congress and with Nehru in particular. But during the endgame of the Raj, it was a different Congress leader to whom she turned with the greatest hope.[21]

The only person who could prevent Partition, she believed, was Gandhi. At the Working Committee meeting in May, the Mahatma explained that he remained opposed to Partition but would not stand in the way of the majority decision. Kamaladevi pleaded with him to intervene. 'Why did you let it happen?' she asked him. 'Even now if you refuse to accept this monstrous decision, the people will support you.' He replied, 'It is too late. If it had been ten years earlier . . .' At that, Kamaladevi recalled, Gandhi's 'voice trailed off for a while as though lost in some thought'.[22]

On 15 August 1947, as India celebrated its independence, Gandhi was in Calcutta, where he would fast against the religious violence many worried would return to that city. Nehru was in Delhi, celebrating India's 'tryst with destiny'. Where was Kamaladevi? What was she feeling and thinking? Her memoirs are silent in regard to that historic day, but she did reflect on Indian independence more broadly. 'What my own contribution was worth to the sum-total of it all,' she wrote, 'it is hard to say nor is it relevant. But certainly the struggle brought out the best in me. I was the finer for having gone through the experiences, with all their hopes and disappointments, the aspirations and the disillusionments.' Those disillusionments came quickly, as the birth of India and Pakistan led to violence on a vast and brutal scale.[23]

~

Kamaladevi responded to the violence of Partition by focusing on the widespread abduction of women and the millions of refugees crossing the borders. At least 70,000 women had been abducted. In November 1947, in a rare example of common ground, the governments of India and Pakistan agreed that 'every effort must be made to recover and restore abducted women and children'. Yet many families refused to accept such 'dishonoured' women. As the historian Urvashi Butalia has written, 'So acute was the problem that both Gandhi and Nehru had to issue repeated appeals to Hindus asking them not to refuse to take the women back into the family fold.' Some women, afraid of being ostracized within their families, did not want to be 'rescued', as Kamaladevi learnt firsthand when she travelled to Pakistan with Rameshwari Nehru and Mridula Sarabhai to help oversee the process of identifying abducted women and bringing them to India. In Peshawar, she met with a group of women who had been abducted, one of whom explained that she did not want to return to her family. In her memoir, Kamaladevi wrote, 'God how many messes we had created! I sat dumb ... I had no words to say to her.'[24]

The refugee crisis was equally complex and even larger in scale. In Delhi alone, hundreds of thousands of refugees had arrived during the fall of 1947. Sucheta Kripalani, Rameshwari Nehru and several other

A family portrait. Kamaladevi is on the right between her mother and father. Courtesy of the Delhi Crafts Council.

In Berlin with another Indian delegate to the gathering of the International Alliance of Women. Courtesy of the LSE Library, 2IAW/1/J/1/5/14.

Delegates to the gathering of the International Alliance of Women in Berlin in 1929. Kamaladevi is in the front row, second from the left. Courtesy of the LSE Library, 2IAW/1/J/1/5/1.

Speaking in the United States. Courtesy of the Library of Congress, 'Speaking for the independence of India—noted woman leader, Kamaladevi Chattopadhyaya, photographed at recent demonstration', LC-USZ62-138185.

Kamaladevi and her son, Rama. Courtesy of Nina Menon and Neel Chatto.

With Sarojini Naidu. Courtesy of the Delhi Crafts Council.

With Jawaharlal Nehru. Courtesy of the Delhi Crafts Council.

Kamaladevi in Kolkata with younger craft advocates: Irani Sen, Subhashini Kohli and Roopa Mehta of SASHA and Bunny Page and Laila Tyabji of DASTKAR. Courtesy of Laila Tyabji and the Dastkar Archives.

It was rare to capture Kamaladevi smiling. Courtesy of the Delhi Crafts Council.

In March 1982, the Sangeet Natak Akademi honoured Ragini Devi. Here, Kamaladevi is presenting the award to Ragini Devi's daughter, Indrani Rahman. Courtesy of Sukanya Rahman.

Asaf Ali, Ama Naidoo and Kamaladevi at Gopal Gandhi's home in October 1988. Courtesy of Gopal Gandhi.

Kamaladevi with grandchildren. Courtesy of Nina Menon and Neel Chatto.

women took on leadership roles in response to the refugee crisis. Students and young people were also active, and Kamaladevi worked to empower them. In the first week of November 1947, she was in Bombay at the All India Conference of Social Work, where she chaired the 'Youth Organisation' section. One young student, Lakshmi Chand Jain, quickly became a central figure at Kingsway Camp, one of the largest refugee camps in Delhi. It was Jain who showed the camp to Kamaladevi in February 1948. 'All this is very well,' she told him, acknowledging the emergency resources being offered to the refugees. 'But what about their future?' Jain was impressed with Kamaladevi's focus on long-term solutions and, in the years ahead, would dedicate himself to working under her leadership.[25]

In her memoir, Kamaladevi recalled the idea of working with refugees as 'a spark ignited in the darkness'. Partition had left her dispirited and unsure of how to direct her energies. 'I decided to apply myself to the rehabilitation of some of these uprooted families,' she wrote. She began with the question of land. Many of the refugees were farmers who, more than anything, hoped to acquire land. Vast tracts had been left behind when Muslim landowners had fled to Pakistan, but it remained unclear when and how that land would be distributed. One argument was that refugees should be given land in proportion to what they had lost. Thus, wealthy landowners fleeing Pakistan would gain vastly more than poor labourers. Kamaladevi rejected such an approach. She argued that if the Indian government was serious about addressing poverty and inequality, it would allocate land in a way that empowered as many poor farmers as possible.[26]

Kamaladevi's first efforts to gain land for refugees ended in failure. A young refugee named Mulk Raj had approached her on behalf of 400 farmers who had fled West Punjab. After struggling to find them land, Kamaladevi turned to Gandhi for support. According to Kamaladevi, the Mahatma became 'very keenly interested in the Scheme and discussed even details with zest with Mulk Raj and the rest of us'. With Gandhi's blessing, Kamaladevi was able to secure some 4,000 acres for the refugees, but the arrangement hit a bureaucratic wall and eventually the refugees decided to leave Delhi. 'With a gnawing pain in my heart,' Kamaladevi later wrote, 'I saw them depart for East Punjab. In this first round I had drawn a blank. It whetted the fighter in me. I was now determined to succeed.'[27]

It was with that determination that Kamaladevi travelled to P-Block—that massive government building described in the opening pages of this book. She was determined to help refugees gain access to a large stretch of land at Chhatarpur, some 20 kilometres from Delhi. 'The gentleman who allotted the land was an old friend and colleague of mine,' Kamaladevi later wrote. 'Together we had dreamed and planned to rebuild this country anew.' Her old colleague was not the same, however. 'He had now ceased to be the man of dreams,' Kamaladevi lamented. 'He was now very much the administrator, conscious of the weight of his files.' Unwilling to again be thwarted by bureaucratic headaches, Kamaladevi made the threat with which this book began—to lead the refugees in occupying the land illegally.[28]

The fact that the land was allotted the very night before her plan was to unfold suggests that her success in supporting refugees was a result of her determination and her willingness to defy authority—both virtues she had long demonstrated. But her success depended just as much on her talent for networking and coalition-building. Kamaladevi worked with Ram Manohar Lohia to establish a socialist refugee organization in Delhi. She convened an 'all-party political convention' and secured a resolution demanding that the government's refugee policy provide 'land to the tiller'. She worked closely with dozens of political figures. What would distinguish her approach to refugee resettlement was not her penchant for stubborn rebellion; it was her belief in cooperation.[29]

She knew that just giving refugees land would not be enough. They needed seeds, fertilizer, tools and a range of other resources. Given the state of the government's finances and the many demands on those resources, it was unlikely the government would be able to offer much. Kamaladevi wanted the refugees to be able to thrive without government support. The solution, she came to believe, lay in cooperatives. As a young woman, she had learnt about cooperatives from a family friend. During her travels abroad, she had been impressed with cooperative societies in Scandinavia and in China. She came to see cooperatives not just as 'an economic lever for providing a means of livelihood or raising the income, but rather as a social factor, and a way of life'. In August 1945, she told readers of the *Modern Review* that 'the superiority of co-operative effort has already been established wherever it has been attempted'. Her vision of 'co-operative effort' was simultaneously local and global. 'The same institution and technique,' she wrote, 'needs to be expanded from the small group-functioning to the nation and from each national area to the entire world'. It was with an expansive hope that she strove to build a cooperative union for the millions of refugees whose lives had been upended by Partition.[30]

She took her plans to Gandhi—a decision that reflects his continuing influence, their growing personal closeness and the fact that her own approach to development had become increasingly Gandhian. In an essay on 'The Village and the Future', she had declared in distinctly Gandhian terms that 'each village should grow into a little republic and the people made aware of their civic duties and responsibilities'. Equally Gandhian was her statement that 'experiments in agricultural improvement must go hand in hand with prohibition and simpler marriages'. She had good reason to hope that Gandhi would support her vision of refugee cooperatives.[31]

Gandhi studied the plans and agreed to support them on one condition—that the farmers would depend on their own labour and 'not lean on the administration'. 'For, as you know,' he added, 'the first principle of cooperation is self-reliance.' She agreed but reminded the Mahatma that the farmers would need government support to secure land. Gandhi then agreed to help convince Nehru. According to Kamaladevi, Nehru had dismissed the idea of a cooperative union as 'one of the impractical new fangled plans the socialists would think up'. If anyone could change Nehru's mind, it would be Gandhi.[32]

On 30 January 1948, Gandhi was shot and killed by a religious extremist who believed that the Mahatma had been too supportive of Muslims. It was about five-thirty in the evening when Kamaladevi learnt that Gandhi had been killed. 'At first I couldn't believe it,' she later recalled. She phoned a police officer she trusted and received confirmation of the tragic news. She then rushed to the site of the assassination, where she gazed on Gandhi's dead body in shock and disbelief. 'It seemed that Bapu was sleeping, and even then I could not believe that he was no more,' she recalled. 'I put my hand on his body, as if he were still alive! He could not die. He did not appear dead.'[33]

As the most prominent figure in India's freedom struggle, Gandhi had earned criticism from many Indians, including from Kamaladevi herself. But in the wake of his assassination, India united in grief. Kamaladevi attended Gandhi's cremation ceremony and found meaning in the shared sorrow. She later recalled watching Jayaprakash Narayan staring at the funeral pyre, 'as though the flames were a part of him and he could not be torn away from them'. For Kamaladevi, as for Narayan, the loss was deeply personal. Despite their many clashes or perhaps because of them, Kamaladevi and Gandhi had developed a strong bond. They had grown closer through their shared opposition to Partition and through their shared commitment to serving those left homeless in its aftermath. 'It was humanism and the idealism in Gandhiji that drew me to him,' she later reflected. She praised 'his interpretation of freedom in terms of the masses of people, his identification with the common man, his message of constructive work, his giving of equal opportunity to women, above all the importance with which he endowed each individual'.[34]

Kamaladevi did not wait until Gandhi's assassination to offer such praise. In the 1940s, she published a series of tributes to the Mahatma that reveal how close she had come to him. In one essay, published on Gandhi's seventy-fifth birthday in 1944, Kamaladevi praised the Mahatma for his support for child widows. 'The ancient is not sacrosanct to Gandhiji,' she wrote. 'His heart bleeds for those who suffer under the burden of traditions. Amongst these, perhaps, the child widow takes the first place. All through his life he had pleaded movingly, passionately, vigorously for justice for these helpless victims.' Kamaladevi quoted Gandhi at length in support of widow remarriage, but never mentioned own experience as a child widow. It was clear, however, that she felt personal gratitude for all Gandhi had done.[35]

The socialists were not known for their warmth towards the Mahatma. Yet, in June 1946, Kamaladevi told a socialist gathering that it was, in part, as a result of Gandhi's leadership that 'the long forgotten peasant in the remote village became somebody who mattered, a potential factor in the concept of freedom'. That same year, she contributed to an edited volume a chapter entitled 'What Gandhiji Has Done for Women'. She offered an insightful link between Gandhian nonviolence and social reform. 'Non-violence can be the expression of only a well adjusted society,' she wrote, 'and this can only come out of a unit whose every constituent is free and untrammeled, where one section does not dominate over the other.' Kamaladevi would never be one of Gandhi's disciples nor was she one to regularly invoke nonviolence. Yet her link between nonviolence and social justice reveals that she found a way to connect Gandhi's message with her own. His human fallibility served as another connection. Gandhi was 'too human to be superhuman,' she wrote. 'That is the secret of his greatness. He is just one of us, he is Bapu. He is not God the father, handing down tablets from Mount Sinai. He is shot through with our own weakness and sentiments. He suffers and he rejoices with us. That is why he is so close to us.'[36]

While Kamaladevi grieved Gandhi's death as a personal loss, the assassination became a source of tension between the Socialists and the more conservative members of the Congress. On 4 February 1948, Kamaladevi joined Lohia and JP in issuing a joint statement demanding that the government resign and Sardar Patel be replaced as Home Minister. 'The assassin is not one person, not even a team of persons,' they wrote, 'but a big and wide conspiracy of a foul idea and of organizations that embody it.' They blamed all communal organizations, including the 'Hindu Mahasabha, Rashtriya Swayamsevak Sangh and Muslim League', and declared that 'the State must crush these organizations'. They did not believe that Patel would undertake that task. 'The Home Ministry must be entrusted to the care of a minister,' they wrote, 'who will be able and willing to curb and crush the organizations of communal hate.' They tried to soften their criticism of Patel by adding, 'We have no doubts about the ability of the Home Minister. But a man of 74 has got departments which even a man of 30 probably would find it difficult to bear the burden of.'[37]

The following day Kamaladevi, Lohia and JP issued another statement offering 'some clarifications'. 'We have been attacked as seeking party advantage out of a national calamity,' they explained. They walked back their demands and suggested that they did not actually want Patel to resign from the government. 'He is indispensable to the Government,' they now admitted, while insisting that 'the attitude of Sardar Patel, till at any rate the great tragedy that overtook us, towards the danger of Hindu and Sikh communalism was not in accord with Congress policy'. Coming close to blaming Patel for the assassination, they added, 'The result was an unchecked growth of this danger.'[38]

One day after this 'clarification', Patel wrote Nehru enclosing a secret report alleging that the Socialist Party had 'decided to exploit' Gandhi's assassination in order to 'gain power both in the Congress organization and the Government'. According to Patel, a group of Socialist Party leaders had gathered at the Delhi home of Jayaprakash Narayan and had developed a 'scheme' that involved a 'a regular crusade' against Patel and an effort to get Narayan, Lohia and Kamaladevi elected to Parliament.[39]

Kamaladevi's position was delicate. She remained dedicated to socialism and to her fellow socialists but also valued her ties to Nehru and to many others who had stayed in the Congress camp. After the death of Patel in December 1950, it seemed as if a rapprochement might be possible. Kamaladevi arranged meetings at her Delhi apartment where JP could meet M.O. Mathai, Nehru's personal secretary. The goal was to find a way to bring JP into the cabinet and ultimately to shift the government towards the more transformative social and economic programmes the Socialists had long advocated. That effort failed, at least in the short term. JP did not enter the government, and the divide between Nehru and the Socialists remained.[40]

Nehru was not opposed, however, to working with individual Socialists, and he offered Kamaladevi a variety of government positions. She declined each offer, in part because none was at the level she expected. 'I was too proud to take it,' she later admitted. Rajkumari Amrit Kaur had been designated the Minister for Health. 'If Rajkumari was to be of cabinet rank—and quite rightly—I saw no reason why . . .' She left the sentence incomplete, perhaps embarrassed by her feelings. 'In any case,' she concluded, 'there was so much to do outside government!'[41]

~

In 1948, Kamaladevi founded the Indian Cooperative Union (ICU). The goal of the ICU was to support local cooperatives by offering coordination, best practices and help in securing financial support from the government. The government was not always supportive. Because of bureaucratic red tape it took eight months to register the ICU. Kamaladevi decried 'the tardy slowness, general apathy and the complacency of the administration'. It was not just apathy and complacency that was an issue. The government's cooperative department saw the ICU as a threat. As Kamaladevi explained, an 'independent cooperative body was an anachronism and a deadly challenge to its established authority'.[42]

Kamaladevi saw the ICU as an extension of her socialism, and many Socialists shared her enthusiasm for cooperatives. In October 1949, JP asked Kamaladevi to preside at a meeting in Calcutta focused on establishing the cooperative movement in that city. He also asked her to stay on for a few days to help set up the organization. Kamaladevi was not able to make the journey as her mother was sick. The historical record contains little information about her relationship with her mother at this point in their lives, but there is evidence that the two women grew closer as Girijabai approached the end of her life. In June 1950, nearly a year after Kamaladevi declined JP's invitation, she was still restricting her travel in order to help care for her mother.[43]

The challenges of travel help to explain why Kamaladevi's efforts to develop cooperatives at first centred on Delhi and the refugee communities immediately surrounding the capital city. With ICU support, the refugees at Chattarpur formed themselves into a cooperative. 'There were ugly men in the Secretariat who were doing their best to smash up the experiment,' Kamaladevi later wrote, and the land—arid and with no easy opportunities for irrigation—was itself a challenge. Kamaladevi lobbied the Food and Agriculture Ministry and eventually secured a boring drill and water storage tanks. She also set up a rural health service. The farmers were determined to thrive—not just as individual families but as a community—but Kamaladevi knew that they would need help if their 'experiment' was to succeed.[44]

To secure the necessary support, she included powerbrokers on the advisory board of the ICU, including several wealthy industrialists and Nehru's daughter, Indira Gandhi. It was Nehru himself who, despite his initial scepticism, proved to be the most important supporter. On 10 December 1948, JP wrote Nehru that the refugee crisis was a 'golden opportunity' to redistribute land and to establish cooperatives and thus 'to build up a sector of the national economy on a basis of Socialism'. The authorities were failing to seize that opportunity. 'If you want to know how keen your Government has been to develop such colonies,' JP told Nehru, 'you have only to enquire from Kamaladevi who has a heart-breaking story to tell.' While JP shamed Nehru, Kamaladevi tried a more upbeat form of persuasion. She arranged for farmers from Chattarpur to present the Prime Minister with a selection from their first harvest.[45]

Nehru demonstrated his growing support when the ICU launched a milk cooperative for refugee widows in Delhi. Kamaladevi first approached the Ministry of Rehabilitation but was told that the ministry was planning a similar milk cooperative. It was unclear when, if ever, the government scheme would be launched yet, as L.C. Jain later wrote, 'the Ministry was reluctant to help this small group of women who were in great distress and needed relief urgently'. Frustrated by the ministry's inaction, Kamaladevi sent the ICU's proposal to Nehru who then forwarded it to Mohanlal Saksena, the head of the Ministry of Rehabilitation. A veteran Congressman from the United Provinces, Saksena might have been the 'old friend' whom Kamaladevi wrote was no longer 'the man of dreams,' having become too 'conscious of the weight of his files'. Nehru anticipated such bureaucratic hesitancy. 'No doubt your office people will put up long notes,' Nehru wrote Saksena, 'and I will not be impressed by these notes. I should like to take advantage of every effort made by every group and individual in India for the rehabilitation of these unhappy displaced persons.'[46]

Those 'unhappy displaced persons' were actively fighting for their own future. While courting the support of Nehru and other powerful figures, Kamaladevi knew that it was the refugees themselves who would determine the fate of the cooperative movement. Consider the history of one of the government's largest and most celebrated refugee settlements, the 'model city' of Faridabad. Located some 32 kilometres south of Delhi, Faridabad was initially under the direct management of the government. From the beginning, however, the refugee residents were much more than passive beneficiaries. When the government proposed to house Faridabad residents in mud huts, a refugee named Sukh Ram launched a hunger strike against the proposal. The Public Works Department (PWD) of the government offered to build houses for the settlement, but the refugees decided to build their own homes. In the process, they would earn wages and would have more control over the design of the homes. When the government refused to allow the refugees to build their own homes, a group of Faridabad residents protested outside Nehru's residence. 'In a typically Indian compromise,' the historian Ramachandra Guha has written, 'the refugees were allowed to build about 40 per cent of the houses, with the PWD constructing the rest.'[47]

Nehru became closely involved in the future of Faridabad. On 10 June 1949, at a meeting of the Faridabad Development Board, he decided that 'a scheme for organizing cottage industries at Faridabad should be prepared'. He urged that Kamaladevi be consulted. On 18 June, he wrote Mohanlal Saksena that involving others would make people feel that 'they are sharing in the work' which would generate 'public goodwill' towards the government. 'That is why I think we should help the Indian Cooperative Union or other similar schemes run by Kamaladevi,' Nehru added. 'It may be that they fail, but it will be [a] far greater failure on our part if the news spreads that we are reluctant to help efforts at self-help.' Saksena tried to dissuade Nehru from supporting the ICU. He told the prime minister that the ICU's Chattarpur Dairy Farm, an enterprise that Nehru had supported, was losing money. Nehru remained adamant. He insisted that Saksena forward Rs 10,000 to Kamaladevi. 'If she wants more money,' he added, 'I will advance it to her.'[48]

Nehru invited Kamaladevi and the ICU to assume a major role within Faridabad. The government's efforts had failed to produce the social and economic transformation that both Nehru and Kamaladevi believed was possible. In July 1950, a reporter for the *Times of India* found 'wailing widows and ill-clad children' scattered among 'clusters of tattered, low tents sprawled across a water-logged stretch of land'. Of the 20,000 refugees living in Faridabad, only half had houses. 'As one passed among the rows of improvised tents,' the reporter wrote, 'one saw a shocking sight of humanity, huddled together like cattle, surrounded by filth and squalor.'[49]

To empower the refugees in the face of such dire circumstances, the ICU organized a variety of cooperative enterprises and self-help groups. Conditions improved dramatically. The 'tattered, low tents' were replaced by 'a neat, modern town, with 4,500 two-room houses, 16 kilometres of streets, its own electric powerhouse, schools, a 150-bed hospital, a hundred stores, a small buffalo dairy, a busy carpenter shop, a hosiery factory, flour mill, button factory, and a large weaving factory that furnishes cloth to Delhi, automobile workshop, and a polytechnic training center'. That description came in a glowing tribute, headlined 'Refugees in India Erect Model City', published by the *New York Times* in October 1951. The *Times* reported 'some 30,000' residents in Faridabad and declared that the city had proved 'that India can overcome her ancient curse of poverty if the people receive the inspiration to help themselves and are taught how to do it'. According to the *Times,* 'All the commercial aspects are run cooperatively under direction of the Indian Cooperative Union, Ltd., a private organization headed by Mme. Kamaladevi Chattopadyaya, Indian Socialist Leader.' The *Times* credited the ICU with giving agency to the refugees themselves. 'The remarkable thing about the new town,' readers learnt, 'is that it was built with their own hands by the people who live in it.' The *Times of India* echoed this narrative, telling readers that Faridabad had been 'built entirely by the inhabitants themselves—by men and women who quite apart from house-building, have never done manual labour before, but who have first grudgingly then gratefully learnt the dignity of labour'.[50]

Such an emphasis on the 'dignity of labour' dovetailed with the government's focus on preventing dependency, obscuring government inaction in regards to economic inequality. Why worry about undoing the vast inequities in landownership if the real solution resided in the dignity of labour? Kamaladevi echoed the celebratory narrative in which dependent refugees became independent farmers. 'They were helpless refugees three years ago,' she wrote. 'They were full of despair, and sorrow was written in poignant letters on their countenances.' Such a description might seem condescending, but Kamaladevi emphasized the increasing independence of the refugees in a way that did not absolve the government of continued responsibility for the poverty that marred India's freedom.[51]

Consider how she described a signal moment in the history of the ICU. In December 1951, some 4,000 former refugees gathered for a meeting of the ICU at the Constitution Club in Delhi. 'On that day,' Kamaladevi wrote, 'they spoke as proud citizens, cultivators and artisans, the men of the land and plough and those of the machines and the tools.' This gathering was not a celebration of past achievements. It was an opportunity to press the government to take action. 'These men and women who lifted the Cooperative Movement from the Secretariat files and red tape to a dynamic movement of the people,' Kamaladevi wrote, 'demanded to see the Minister for Planning and present their grievances and ask for redress.' The range of their 'grievances' is evident in the signs they produced at the gathering. While one sign declared 'Kisans want wells, tractors, engines, pumps', another offered the more sweeping message: 'Land to the tillers, factory to the workers.'[52]

Perhaps the most radical facet of the gathering was the demand to directly communicate with the Minister for Planning. When the minister replied that he was too busy to meet with the former refugees, they threatened to march to his office. The minister came to them. At first, he demanded a closed-door meeting with the leaders. When they refused, he agreed to speak in front of the full assembly. As a reporter later commented, 'They hammered in the brass tacks. They knew what they wanted and how to ask for it.' As for Kamaladevi, she concluded,

'We believed that Cooperation was a people's movement', a movement that would 'grow out of their faith and experience'.[53]

Kamaladevi saw cooperative labour as especially suited to women. 'When a woman becomes a member of the cooperative, and understands its business,' she wrote, 'she will contribute more than men to their organisation.' She did not, however, frame her efforts on behalf of the ICU in terms of gender. In keeping with her long-standing approach to the unity of India—and echoing the limitations of that approach—she also ignored the religious and caste-based identities of the refugees. As the scholar Ravinder Kaur has argued, the Indian state's refugee policies reproduced existing inequities of caste and class. Low-income and Dalit migrants were often housed in camps with inferior housing and given inferior jobs. Kamaladevi's efforts did not deliberately reproduce such inequities but neither did she confront them.[54]

In Gandhian fashion, Kamaladevi's belief in the fundamental unity of the community could lead her to ignore internal divisions—regardless of whether the community in question was Faridabad, an anonymous Indian village or all of India. But that vision of unity could also inspire her to protect the autonomy of the community from outside meddling. When the Minister for Rehabilitation argued that 'widows and unattached women and children' should be relocated from Faridabad, Kamaladevi replied that the 'segregation of such persons from the main body of community in which their friends and relations and co-villagers accepted some responsibility for them was hardly human'.[55]

In December 1951, an ICS officer offered a formal report on Faridabad. He interviewed Kamaladevi, visited the settlement, and left 'very impressed with the work being done at Faridabad'. 'A township has been built there by displaced persons themselves,' he wrote. 'What was previously just waste land has been converted into a thriving colony. Not only has this been a tremendous achievement in itself, but it has been a sort of pilot scheme showing the way in which the country can be developed.'[56]

Kamaladevi wanted Faridabad to demonstrate the power of cooperatively owned and operated enterprises. Yet while the government was willing to allow small-scale cottage industries to be cooperatively run, Kamaladevi's efforts to give the workers ownership of the larger enterprises ran into a wall of official opposition. According to L.C. Jain, 'They argued that the workers were penniless and could not be entrusted with the ownership of factories involving substantial government investment.' Kamaladevi enlisted the support of Faridabad Development Board members, including the President of India, Rajendra Prasad. The government remained firm. As Jain recalled, 'The factories were auctioned away to private enterprises; and the workers, who till an hour before were still hoping and longing to become owners, were reduced to wage-earners at the will of the new owners. This was a blow—the shattering of a social dream—from which Kamaladevi nor her fond instrument, the Co-operative Union, ever recovered.'[57]

Just as quickly and dramatically as Faridabad had emerged as a model city, its reputation declined over the course of 1952. Whereas Jain blamed government resistance to worker-owned enterprise, Kamaladevi's biographer, Reena Nanda, suggested that Kamaladevi herself 'displayed a lack of critical assessment of her workers and unquestioning trust which was detrimental for the future of the ICU'. What is clear is that many of the enterprises based at Faridabad floundered. At the same time, the end of active building deprived many refugees of work in construction, and unemployment surged. In July 1952, only seven months after that ICS officer had offered a glowing portrait of Faridabad, another government report offered a darker assessment that charged financial mismanagement and blamed the ICU for Faridabad's growing problems. On 19 September, Nehru wrote to the Minister for Rehabilitation defending Kamaladevi and making clear that she needed to be consulted on actions related to Faridabad. But Kamaladevi had herself realized that it was time for the ICU to withdraw from the city. What had been heralded as a model community was now seen as a cautionary tale.[58]

The failure of the ICU's efforts in Faridabad could be seen to reflect the weaknesses of Kamaladevi as an institution-builder. The Government of India also deserves a large share of the blame, and any assessment of Faridabad must recognize the profound challenges involved in creating a city from scratch and empowering refugees—many of whom lacked capital, formal education and managerial experience—with the opportunity to run their own businesses. In the years ahead, Kamaladevi would found many institutions that would outlive her. Indeed, the ICU itself outlasted the Faridabad experiment and contributed to community development efforts throughout India. As the historian Sunil Purushotham has written, 'Cooperative settlements that initially pioneered as refugee rehabilitation projects served as the model and inspiration for fifty-five community projects that were launched in 1952 and covered about seventeen thousand villages.'[59]

Faridabad must be seen as a failure but one that improved thousands of lives. Just because an initiative does not last does not mean that it was not meaningful. In Chattarpur and in Faridabad, Kamaladevi helped empower refugees to claim their own lives and futures. Even more than the immediate livelihoods they earned, it was that idea—the idea that poor people could and should take ownership of the struggle to end poverty—that would prove most impactful. It was an idea that risked obscuring the necessity of transformative social change—whether in regards to causes Kamaladevi had long supported, such as land redistribution or union rights, or in regards to the anti-caste movements that Kamaladevi largely ignored. At its best, however, Kamaladevi's vision of the ICU and of cooperative community-based development combined a focus on immediate improvements in the livelihoods of the poor with a radical challenge to the social, political and economic inequality that survived the end of British rule and continued to mock the very idea of India's freedom.[60]

~

In June 1949, an African American journalist named P.L. Prattis spent seventeen days in India. He wrote a daily report that was published in the African American newspaper the *Pittsburgh Courier*. Kamaladevi emerged as the hero of his story. Prattis explained his respect for Kamaladevi, whom he described as a 'woman of immense power', by offering his readers a breathless account of a conversation he shared with her one evening after dinner. It was a hot summer night, and Prattis and Kamaladevi were sitting outside in her garden. 'There, with the faintest of breezes,' Prattis wrote, 'we talked and talked and talked until it was midnight.' He heightened his readers' anticipation by noting that he would think of that conversation for many months to come. 'We had mused over the color problem all over the world,' he explained, 'and I had sought to obtain from her something of her feeling.' Prattis introduced Kamaladevi's view on 'the color problem' by stating, 'The quiet response of this remarkable woman was something wonderful to which to listen.'

Kamaladevi offered a transnational vision of antiracist solidarity. 'Not as an Indian,' she declared, 'but as a human being, my innate self-respect would suffer if I were not moved by the sufferings of others who are persecuted because of their color.' Kamaladevi's expansive humanism coincided with her commitment to antiracist solidarity. She held out her arm, pointed to her skin and declared, 'Every time prejudice is shown against any colored people, I look at myself and I know that I am a victim, too.' Colourism had long divided Indians and inspired many to purchase 'skin-whitening' creams. Rejecting such an obsession with whiteness, Kamaladevi embraced her identity as a 'colored woman', just as she had on that train in Louisiana years earlier. Her conception of racial solidarity was not anti-White. She linked conceptions of what would later be called Third World solidarity or the Global South to an expansive humanism. 'There can be no peace in the world until there is freedom of all people,' she concluded. 'Freedom is indivisible.'[61]

Prattis arranged to have the *Courier* publish a message from Kamaladevi to the newspaper's readers. In her message, Kamaladevi again combined an inclusive humanism with an expression of solidarity between people of colour throughout the world. She reached out to African Americans who, she explained, 'like ourselves in this vast continent of Asia are waging the great battle of humanism'. Connecting struggles against racism and imperialism, and linking both to the necessity of combating economic inequality, she added, 'As long as one part of humanity stands condemned to a slum life, world conflict is bound to continue.' She concluded, 'The Indian people have pledged to work and strive for a world order from which the vestiges of tyranny and exploitation be it racial or territorial are banished. For our own freedom assumes a reality only when the rest of mankind becomes genuinely free.'[62]

Kamaladevi's global vision of freedom was one of her most important contributions to the Indian freedom struggle. She demonstrated that global vision via her solidarity with African American struggles—and also via her condemnation of White supremacy within Africa. In a long piece on 'Racial Discrimination in South Africa', published in the *Modern Review* in June 1947, she declared that 'the saga of the White Man's rule in Africa is one of ignominy and inhumanness'. 'The children of the soil have been made aliens in their own land,' she wrote. Kamaladevi located Apartheid in relation to European imperialism in Africa and White supremacy worldwide. 'The African problem is a world problem,' she wrote, 'a problem which divides the world between the White and the Coloured, the dominating and the exploited, a basic human problem that can only be overcome with a radical change in our social and economic values.'[63]

Such a 'radical change' did not preclude national pride. Kamaladevi remained a fierce defender of India even as she advanced transnational Afro-Asian solidarities. Her commitment to Indian nationalism was on display in 1949, when she travelled to Kashmir to visit Indian soldiers locked in a tense stand-off with their Pakistani counterparts. Upon returning to Delhi, she raised 22,000 rupees for the soldiers and gave the cheque to Nehru in a public ceremony. After the photos had been taken, she then asked for the cheque back so that she could send it directly to the General she believed most likely to get the money to the troops quickly.[64]

Kamaladevi's Indian nationalism coincided with a strong interest in world government. On 31 August 1949, she inaugurated the Bombay Association for the World Federal Government. According to the *Times of India,* she criticized the UN for failing to eliminate 'the causes of conflict between the nations of the world' and condemned both the US and the Soviet Union for talking of peace even while they 'piled up their armaments'. As we have seen, she had long denounced American economic and racial inequality. She was equally critical of the USSR, but for different reasons. In a piece on 'Socialism and Moral Values' that she published in 1947 in an edited collection of her writings and then republished in the *Modern Review* in March 1948, she rejected 'ruthless "short-cuts" to achievement' and defended 'the dignity and nobility of personality'. 'Where a socialist State is not at the same time liberal and democratic,' she wrote, 'it is bound to become exploitative and oppressive.'[65]

Kamaladevi dreamt of a postcolonial world free of domination by Europe, the United States or the Soviet Union. In 1951, she travelled to East and Central Africa where she met Jomo Kenyatta and other anticolonial leaders. Upon returning to India, she told journalists, in the words of the *Times of India,* that 'the crux of the African problem' was 'that the Western Powers regard that continent as more or less an extension of Europe'. She criticized White settlers for 'resorting to crude and primitive methods to maintain what they called the western way of life'. Although she never used the term 'global south', writes the historian Vinay Lal, 'she was among the earliest exponents of the idea and perhaps had a more expansive conception of it than any of her contemporaries or even those who have elaborated upon the idea in recent years'. There were at least three pillars to Kamaladevi's 'expansive conception' of antiracist solidarities: her identification with transnational notions of colour; the intersectionality of her politics and, in particular, the way she connected anti-racism with anti-imperialism and struggles against sexism and class inequity; and her blend of nationalism, socialism and a broad humanism.[66]

Kamaladevi's humanism inspired her to champion the idea of human rights while criticizing the limitations of international human rights frameworks. In 1952, Nehru asked her to represent India on the UN Human Rights Commission. She agreed and travelled to Geneva that spring. When the US decided not to ratify the UN covenant on human rights, she told the other members of the commission that she 'had always regarded the concept of an international covenant on human rights as one of the highlights of the Charter of the United Nations'. She expressed disappointment 'that the United States representative should have raised such serious doubts about the practical value of the

Commission's work on the covenants'. To reporters, she was more blunt, stating that the American decision 'knocks the bottom out of the Commission's work'. Despite American inaction, she partnered with the Egyptian representative to put pressure on the European empires to grant 'self-determination'. Even those efforts came to feel hollow. In her memoirs, she wrote, 'For weeks we wrangled over punctuation marks in our meticulous drafts on notional decisions.'[67]

Kamaladevi lost faith in the UN but remained committed to building connections across national borders. Increasingly, those connections would take cultural forms. In May 1954, she travelled to the Soviet Union as the guest of the Soviet Society of Cultural Relations. She visited schools, model farms and daycare centres but spent the majority of her trip visiting museums and attending plays. Her love for Russian theatre, undiminished by her criticism of Soviet politics, would last throughout her life.[68]

On 7 October 1954, Kamaladevi presided over the inaugural celebration of the Indo-Arab Society. The event, held in Bombay, included a minister from Sudan, representatives from Ceylon and a variety of other distinguished figures. Nehru gave the keynote address, in which he celebrated the long history of connections between colonized peoples. After mentioning the upcoming Asian African conference in Bandung, Indonesia, Nehru asked, 'Are we in Asia or in Africa, who are close together, banding ourselves together against anybody?' 'Certainly not,' he answered. He did not want India to 'be pushed and harried about and made to participate in other people's conflicts and troubles. We have enough troubles of our own.' Thus, he defended nonalignment, a policy that would come to be identified with Nehru but that also resonated with Kamaladevi given her long-standing opposition to war, her strong connections to both the United States and the Soviet Union, and her belief in both national sovereignty and anticolonial solidarity.[69]

Kamaladevi rarely used the term 'nonalignment'. Nor did she favour phrases like 'Afro-Asian solidarity', the 'Third World' or the 'Global South'. But she had long advanced connections between anticolonial movements across Asia and Africa, and she offered a vision of future solidarities that was rooted in history. In October 1954, she published an article in the *Times of India* honouring the historic links between India and the Middle East. 'While the West still slumbered,' she wrote, 'Arabs and Indians had already made long voyages into unknown realms to fathom the mysteries of nature and reveal the wonders of man himself.' Links between India and the Arab World had 'endured over a great many centuries,' she continued, 'until the dark pall of political slavery fell over a large part of Asia and Africa.' Now that 'the long era of bondage' had come to an end in the subcontinent, she held up 'the common ideal of freedom' and declared, 'India cannot rest until freedom comes to all of Asia and to Africa.' Like Nehru, Kamaladevi celebrated the Bandung Conference and the kind of Afro-Asian solidarities it embodied. 'Such groupships, closer undertakings and working together of those with a common ideal and purpose, especially adhering to peace and keeping clear of the two mighty Power Blocs,' she wrote, 'is a happy augury and should go a long way in heartening and emboldening all those who do not share the tension between the Big Two, and wish to steer the ship of the world in waters of peace and amity.' It would prove difficult to achieve such 'peace and amity', not only on the global stage, but also within India itself. Whereas her commitment to nonalignment and Afro-Asian solidarity brought her closer to Nehru, their political differences at home became increasingly pronounced and heated.[70]

~

In June 1949, Kamaladevi brought P.L. Prattis, the *Pittsburgh Courier* reporter, to an unusual trial. The accused included Ram Manohar Lohia and forty-six members of the Socialist Party who had been arrested for conducting a nonviolent protest. Lohia had led the protest but it was Kamaladevi who attracted attention at the trial. Prattis was struck by how authority figures deferred to her and by how she used that deference to stage her own protest. Prattis described Kamaladevi's protest using the present tense: 'A chair is indicated for her. She won't move toward it. The judge has the chair brought over and placed beside her. She completely ignores it.' Discussing her decision to stand, Prattis explained, 'Her friends and followers are on trial, they have been beaten. She will accept no favor from such authorities.'[71]

Kamaladevi had spent decades fighting British rule only to find the government of 'free India' employing many of the same draconian methods. Despite her need for Nehru's support when it came to refugee resettlement, Kamaladevi did not hesitate to confront him and his government for its neocolonial tendencies. For his part, Nehru offered his own strident critiques of Kamaladevi's politics. In 1949, he attacked the Socialists as a 'bunch of reactionaries'. Kamaladevi responded with biting sarcasm. In 'Socialists, a Bunch of Reactionaries? Reply to Pandit Nehru', a pamphlet published in Hyderabad in 1949, she wrote that 'the Socialists are decidedly out of tune with the pomp and the pageantry the leaders sport about; the mansions where money and food is flung around to provide a setting for discussing secretarial promotions and the latest fashion in nail paint. Instead they hang around the smelly slums and pore over the grimy workmen's budgets.' She decried the arrest of Lohia and the other protesters, writing that 'nothing can be more cruel than the thought that a government headed by those who call themselves followers of the Mahatma and who proudly proclaim that the State is pledged to carry out Gandhian policies, should still indulge in the same old ignoble practices which are a complete negation of all that Gandhiji stood for and taught his people'. In a separate piece, entitled 'In Defence of R Lohia and Others', Kamaladevi wrote, 'At a time when the Constituent Assembly is engaged in the preparation of the first Constitution of free India, the Government's pursuing its present oppressive policies takes all the reality away from this very significant, nay sacred task.'[72]

Kamaladevi's opposition to authoritarian rule had long shaped her socialism. In 1947, in an article entitled 'The Simple Case for Democratic Socialism', she distinguished her vision from the authoritarian nature of the Soviet Union. 'In democratic socialism,' she wrote, 'the ideal is to evolve only such techniques and institutions as will smoothen out the frictions with *a minimum of coercion*, overt or implicit, and a *maximum of collective participation*.' The goal was 'a society of creative personalities, not mere automatons that conform to an ordered plan'. That is why 'democracy must be an indivisible quality of real socialism'.[73]

It did not take long after Independence to realize that both socialism and true democracy remained to be achieved. In 1950, Kamaladevi pulled together a variety of her writings on democratic socialism and published a book entitled *Socialism and Society.* She authored chapters on education, medicine and 'social insurance' policies like social security and unemployment benefits. She rejected tepid reformism. 'Where those who pursue the Socialist objective content themselves with trying to reform capitalism, instead of trying to replace it,' she wrote, 'there the positive Socialist purpose is surrendered.' Hers was a global vision. She connected 'restrictive capitalism and the narrow limits of a Nation-State' and linked a 'classless society' to the achievement of a 'World State'. She declared that 'imperialism abroad is but the reflection of monopoly at home.' Yet despite her sweeping vision, she remained committed to democracy and refused to endorse violence. In a chapter entitled 'Road to Socialism: Freedom from Want', she analysed the debate between 'constitutional methods or revolution by violence'. She quoted Lenin in favour of revolution but concluded that 'brutal military weapons' were less important than 'the strength the movement derives from the moral sanction behind the positive social purpose it is to serve'.[74]

Kamaladevi put her belief in democracy into action in 1951 when she ran for a seat in the Lok Sabha. The seat was based in the suburbs of Bombay. Kamaladevi ran for the Socialist Party and the Congress fielded its own candidate. Many Congress officials and women's advocates took issue with the idea of the Congress opposing Kamaladevi, and they besieged Nehru with complaints. The Prime Minister's relationship with Kamaladevi was, as we have seen, complex and multifaceted. For decades, they had worked together, sharing a global vision of India's freedom, a cosmopolitan and pluralistic understanding of diversity within India, and a commitment to both democracy and the fight against poverty and inequality. After Independence, Nehru had been a strong supporter of Kamaladevi's work with refugees. They had often disagreed, as we have seen, but remained close despite their disagreements. On 25 April 1950, Rajendra Prasad, the President of India, wrote Nehru to decry one of Kamaladevi's essays, an essay that had attacked Sardar Patel. Nehru replied that he disliked the article, but he refused to publicly criticize Kamaladevi. But now that she was running for office under the aegis of a different party, he had good reason to side with the Congress conservatives who had long disliked Kamaladevi—or, at the least, to avoid getting involved.[75]

Instead, Nehru sent out a series of letters arguing that the Congress should not oppose Kamaladevi. To the chief minister of West Bengal, Bidhan Chandra Roy, Nehru wrote that he was 'receiving all kinds of representations from all kinds of persons, chiefly Congressmen and women about Kamaladevi Chattopadhyaya. All these people tell me that it will be highly improper for us to oppose her . . . I think that there is a great deal in these arguments,' Nehru concluded, 'and our opposing Kamaladevi would bring discredit and a great deal of criticism on us.' That same day, he wrote Morarji Desai, the future Prime Minister and soon-to-be Chief Minister of Bombay. Nehru told Desai that Kamaladevi was 'an outstanding figure' from both 'the national and the international points of view' who had 'played an important role in the Congress' and had 'done extraordinary good work in Delhi and elsewhere to develop cooperatives for the refugees'. The Congress candidate, Jayashri Raiji, was a veteran of the Quit India movement and a leading member of the AIWC. 'I know that Mrs Raiji is a good woman,' Nehru wrote Desai, but it was 'difficult to compare her from the point of view of work with Kamaladevi'. Desai responded that Kamaladevi's identity as a member of the Socialist Party trumped the other considerations Nehru had mentioned. He also noted that the key figure in the decision was the local Congress leader S.K. Patil, who was firmly opposed to letting Kamaladevi win the seat. Nehru wrote back that he supported Kamaladevi 'not because she was a Socialist, but because she was one of the founders and leaders of the women's movement in India'. But when Desai and Patil remained firm, Nehru conceded, and the Congress continued to support Raiji in opposition to Kamaladevi.[76]

Kamaladevi lost the election. As she had in 1926, she found meaning in her defeat by embracing new roles outside of elected office. 'Politics did not come to me as a vocation or a career,' she later reflected. 'It came as a great cause, as organizing and training for a big liberation movement and filled my being with a thrill.' By contrast, she wrote, 'Politics as a career did not interest me.' Would she have felt differently had she won the election? We cannot know. What we do know is that she responded by embracing an identity outside of party politics. 'Temperamentally, I am not cut out to be the party champion,' she wrote. 'On many things I am open minded. Ideology to me is too rigid a circumference within which to grow and function.' She added, 'Gandhiji in his great wisdom had laid down that constructive workers should not enter politics.' It was with Gandhi in mind that she 'left the highway of politics to step into the side lane of constructive work'. For the remainder of her life, she would be focused on 'field work with the artisans, the artists, those who create and produce that mankind may live and grow, not on bread alone, but on things of beauty which uplift and raise us above the petty things of everyday life'. Her shifting focus should not be seen as a step away from politics; indeed, as L.C. Jain would later note, she would remain 'absorbed in politics of a different kind'.[77]

On 1 March 1953, the *Times of India* published a glowing interview with Kamaladevi, an interview that revolved around her commitment to socialism. Readers learnt that 'socialism to Mrs Kamaladevi Chattopadhyaya is not a creed but a way of life'. That way of life started early, at least according to Kamaladevi herself. 'Socialism became part of my life from my earliest girlhood in South India,' she explained. 'I couldn't help noticing and being distressed by the undesirable differences between my own comfortable middle-class life and the life of other people around me.' Kamaladevi rejected abstract, academic approaches to socialism. 'In fact,' she stated, 'I'm not an intellectual Socialist at all.' One is tempted to point out that she was most certainly an original thinker as well as a socialist, but her point concerned her path to socialism and the way that path influenced her ongoing commitments. 'I didn't read Karl Marx until I was well over 30,' she explained, 'and then only because I felt I ought to, as everyone was always talking about him.' Socialism was not a bookish thing for her, nor a series of cold principles; it was a living faith in the prospect of equality and dignity for all people. 'She thinks of India and its problems today not in terms of statistics,' readers learned, 'but in terms of suffering borne by human beings like herself. It is the humanity in her character that makes her instinctively want to relieve this suffering.'

As the promise of political independence crashed into the brutal realities left behind by colonial rule—religious division, caste oppression, crushing poverty—many of Kamaladevi's fellow freedom fighters began to lose faith in the government of Jawaharlal Nehru. In the words of historian Taylor Sherman, the economic policies of Nehru's administration 'aimed not to demolish existing hierarchies, but to invest them with new emotional foundations and then redeploy them for benevolent, developmentalist ends'. This was not the socialism Kamaladevi envisioned, but she maintained close relations with the government and with Nehru himself. Her career demonstrates the challenge of leveraging state power without being co-opted by that power, of reimagining a socialist India without accepting the limitations of what passed for 'socialism' within the bureaucracy.[78]

Kamaladevi's turn towards arts and crafts—the main focus of the next two chapters of this book and of Kamaladevi's life from the 1950s through the 1980s—could be understood as a response to the frustrations of high politics. Asked by the *Times* interviewer where she most enjoyed being in Delhi, Kamaladevi replied, 'Nowhere!' 'I'm much happier in the country or in Bombay,' she explained, 'where my only son is an engineer and where my granddaughter, Neena, lives.' When the topic of conversation shifted to the theatre, Kamaladevi's 'usually serene expression showed sudden animation'. Her joy for theatre and for art more broadly should not, however, obscure her continued passion for politics and grassroots social change. 'There are no half measures about this active woman Socialist,' readers learned. Asked what allowed her to persevere despite so many challenges, Kamaladevi replied, 'I suppose it is the knowledge that things could be better than they are.' That knowledge would continue to animate Kamaladevi in the decades ahead, as she travelled 'the side lane of constructive work', moved simultaneously by her love for India and Indian culture and by her deep conviction that India's freedom remained a work in progress.[79]

7

Crafting a Nation

IN 1944, KAMALADEVI TRAVELLED TO WEST BENGAL TO VISIT AN orphanage in Bankura, a small town about 170 kilometres northwest of Calcutta. Japanese forces controlled Burma at the time, but the largest threat to Bengal was not military invasion but famine. While the colonial government focused on the war effort, millions were dying of hunger and famine-related disease. As president of the AIWC, Kamaladevi rallied local women's groups to provide relief, but her trip to Bankura would not be remembered for its humanitarian purpose. Rather, it was a small, seemingly inconsequential discovery that would echo through Kamaladevi's future. Outside a modest home, Kamaladevi happened to spot two terracotta horses. She was struck by their beauty. After enquiring with the owner of the horses, Kamaladevi managed to acquire a pair that she brought back with her to Delhi. In the years ahead, the Bankura horse would become a symbol of India's craft renaissance, the emblem of India's most renowned department store and the namesake of that store's popular café. In 1957, the horse would earn its own postage stamp. By that time, the Bankura horse had become indelibly associated with Kamaladevi herself, a tribute to her commitment to recovering, preserving and celebrating the crafts of India. Largely forgotten was the fact that it was Kamaladevi's ability to see beauty in the midst of tragedy that defined the story of the Bankura horse—and much of Kamaladevi's life.[1]

The history of India's craft renaissance is rich with beauty and with tragedy. It is a history of heroic dedication to cultural preservation and regeneration, in which Kamaladevi and her colleagues strove to enhance the livelihoods of millions of Indian artisans and enrich the homes and lives of the millions of people—in India and abroad—who came to treasure Indian crafts. This is a history about the empowerment of women not only as producers and consumers of crafts but also as development visionaries routinely forgotten in narratives that ignore the crafts sector when discussing the economic development of postcolonial India. But this is also a history in which the majority of artisans remained in poverty, a history in which the markers of success were too often defined by elite consumers in Delhi and Manhattan. In the words of the scholar Anita Cherian, 'The middle classes presented themselves as saviours of the arts, liberating one form after the other from imminent depravation and sure extinction.' What does it mean to save an art form if most of the artists remain impoverished? To her credit, Kamaladevi stayed focused on the dignity and livelihood of crafts-makers. She recognized her own failures and linked them to the larger failures of postcolonial India. Just as she had when she was fighting for India's independence, she maintained hope in the face of epic challenges, and kept struggling to do as much good as possible. Even if she could not fully redeem the promise of India's freedom, she could support thousands of artists whose work carried forward that promise.[2]

'Beauty is the soul of freedom,' Kamaladevi told the All Bengal Students' Conference in 1931. That is why the 'cultural conquest of India' was bound up with India's economic and political enslavement. India would not be truly free until 'the artistic starvation of millions of people' had been ended. In Ceylon that same year, Kamaladevi decried the fact that 'the children of the people that created the wonderful works of art at Polonnaruwa and Anuradhapura are today feeding their hungry souls on Dunlop tyre advertisements and match labels that adorn the walls of the huts in the villages'. This was a great loss for those children and for humanity. 'Art is not a luxury or the privilege of the rich few,' Kamaladevi asserted. 'It is the life-giving force that touches all ordinary things of everyday common use with its vitality transforming them into sublime things of joy.' Kamaladevi linked such a democratic vision of art to a sharp critique of colonialism. In a speech in Meerut in 1936, she lamented the fact that when the East India Company came to power, 'the handicrafts were ruthlessly destroyed, throwing hundreds of thousands out of employment and abruptly converting the country into a purely agricultural one'. Some economic historians have challenged the idea that the onset of colonial rule devastated handicrafts industries. In the 1930s, however, that idea was an article of faith among most anticolonial activists. In the years ahead, Kamaladevi would repeatedly denounce the cultural devastation caused by colonialism and would link the struggle for beauty to the struggle for freedom.[3]

Indian anticolonial activists had long cherished crafts as emblems of Indian culture and resistance to foreign rule. The annual gatherings of the Indian National Congress often included handicraft demonstrations. By 1944, a 'Handicraft and Swadeshi Exhibition' had become a regular feature of the AIWC gatherings as well. In her presidential address that year, Kamaladevi called for 'training women in handicrafts and fostering hand industries'. Such training would benefit women and the economy. Moreover, such work would yield 'delicate creations in word, song and colour in which the dreams of mankind find expression'. Here we see the multifaceted nature of Kamaladevi's belief in crafts. A way to support women's advancement and India's economy, crafts were also charged with the power and potential of all art.[4]

According to Kamaladevi, her love for crafts had many roots: from her childhood in Mangalore to the influence of her longtime friend, the art critic G. Venkatachalam. 'But it was only after I met Gandhiji,' she wrote, 'that I came to understand the deep relationship of handicrafts with our daily life.' During one of her first visits with Gandhi, she found the Mahatma sitting next to James Cousins, the husband of Margaret Cousins, with 'a few handicraft objects lying before them'. Gandhi spoke passionately about the importance of using one's hands to create, a belief he would famously illustrate with the spinning wheel. Despite her love for homespun saris, Kamaladevi never embraced spinning with true

Gandhian zeal. Yet her commitment to creating with her hands brought her close to the Mahatma in a way that distinguished her from many veteran freedom fighters. When it came to handicrafts, one could argue that Kamaladevi was Gandhi's most devoted and impactful disciple.[5]

Kamaladevi's belief in handicrafts was linked to a vision of self-sustaining communities, a vision that she understood as simultaneously Gandhian and socialist. 'Whilst we insist on our right to things of beauty and comfort,' she wrote in 1947, 'we rarely assume any conscious responsibility as to how those things are produced, by what immoral methods, sweating, child labour, ugly conditions of work, exploitation, and a whole train of human degradations and sorrow.' That statement came in a piece entitled 'Socialism and Moral Values', but her concern for the exploitation at the heart of the anonymous modern economy was equally Gandhian in origin. While many of her socialist colleagues focused on large-scale industrialization, Kamaladevi championed crafts and other 'village industries' as part of the solution to rural unemployment. 'In such a thickly populated country as India,' she declared, 'cottage industries and handicrafts will undoubtedly play a decisive role.'[6]

Kamaladevi's Gandhian socialism is also apparent in her concern with the impact of competition on the arts. In an essay on the 'Social Evaluation of Art' that she published as a 'prelude' to *Towards a National Theatre* in 1945 and then republished in different form in *At The Cross-Roads* and in *Socialism and Society*, Kamaladevi wrote, 'Art in the ancient human society was a social expression.' One did not need advanced training to become an artist. 'Every man and woman was an artist,' Kamaladevi declared, 'and each created out of the joy of giving shape and form to dreams and inspirations.' Capitalism divided art from community. The artist became 'a tradesman selling his works as wares to those who could afford to buy them'. Kamaladevi might have linked this critique of capitalist competition to Gandhi. Instead, she quoted Marx and Engels that capitalism had 'stripped of its halo every occupation hitherto honoured and looked up to with reverent awe'. While embracing a socialist vision of art, she rejected approaches to 'Proletarian Art' that 'exploited' artists and their art 'for sectarian and factional propaganda in the name of the people, while in reality toeing what is called the "Party line"'. Rejecting the distinction between (high) art and (mass) crafts, she declared, 'The aim should be to create conditions for the masses to fashion their own instrument of expression.'[7]

Kamaladevi's vision of art and crafts was wedded to her Indian nationalism and to her transnational humanism. When she praised Mexican painters like Diego Rivera for maintaining 'their links with the community', her vision of 'community' was simultaneously local, national and global. 'We must realise,' she wrote, 'the fundamental fact that art is the appeal to the instinct of communion, the indivisible unity of mankind.' Art was more than a source of individual expression; it was a kind of solidarity. As she put it, 'We recognize each other with a growing awareness of our oneness by the echoes beauty awakens in us.' Her use of "we" transcended cultural and national borders. 'The very language an artist employs is universal,' she wrote. 'It overlaps all narrow boundaries and divisions.' To communicate her expansive vision of art, she offered a vivid metaphor. 'Art has to be like a free, large building,' she declared, 'where men and women can congregate and feel their communal oneness, their large physical and social unity.' It matters that Kamaladevi first wrote these words before 1947 and then reprinted them afterwards. Her vision of human unity was only deepened by the scars of Partition.[8]

It was in trying to heal those scars that Kamaladevi claimed the arts as her true vocation. It was in the refugee camps of Delhi that she reinvented herself as a champion of crafts and of the people who made them. In striving to provide refugees with a path to long-term recovery, Kamaladevi worked alongside a team of talented and dedicated social workers, many of whom volunteered their time and most of whom were women. Rajesh Nandini, who had fled Lahore as a refugee, organized a survey of the women at Kingsway Camp that identified sewing and embroidering as widely shared skills. Rameshwari Nehru, with whom Kamaladevi had worked on behalf of abducted women, helped organize women at Kingsway to sew and embroider clothing. Also vital to this effort was Kitty Shiva Rao, the Austrian-born activist who had written that glowing assessment of Kamaladevi and the Abrama camp in 1942.

Sucheta Kripalani, a veteran of the Quit India movement, arranged for twenty sewing machines to be donated to the women. Fori Nehru, a Hungarian Jew who had married a relative of Jawaharlal Nehru, convinced the owner of Pandit Brothers, the largest linen store in central Delhi, to provide a counter from which the refugees could sell their wares. Through word of mouth, a great demand was generated and the refugee women were soon supporting their families with the profits they were earning. This approach to the employment of refugee women revealed, in the words of the historian Anjali Bhardwaj Datta, 'clear assumptions and biases about the kind of work that was appropriate for them: women were offered training in embroidery, stitching, tailoring, and weaving, as these are associated with feminine and household-based skills'. The project also demonstrated the resilience of refugee women and the power and connections of the more affluent women who supported them—including Kamaladevi herself.[9]

In 1951, under Kamaladevi's direction, the Indian Cooperative Union opened a shop selling refugee handicrafts. A few years earlier, the Government of India had opened its own handicrafts store, but the effort floundered, and in 1952 Nehru asked the ICU to take control. Kamaladevi agreed and turned her focus to the new store, the Central Cottage Industries Emporium (CCIE). That same year, Nehru asked Kamaladevi to become the chair of the newly created All India Handicrafts Board (AIHB). Both the AIHB and the ICU opened offices at the CCIE. Kamaladevi now directed three organizations—the CCIE, the ICU and the AIHB—all three of which worked to expand the production and sale of crafts in a way that would benefit artisans and help end the poverty that continued to haunt so much of India.[10]

These organizations provided Kamaladevi with purpose and with power, as well as with a supportive community. The CCIE, widely known as 'the Cottage', became for Kamaladevi a kind of home; its staff became, in many ways, family. According to Gopalkrishna Gandhi, when Kamaladevi was at the Cottage she was 'like a queen would be in a durbar'. Kamaladevi told Gandhi that the CCIE was 'where she felt most at home'. A vibrant social space, it had the elegance and bustle of a durbar but the warmth of a home. Visitors first encountered a flower shop, stocked with blossoms grown by refugee farmers in Chattarpur. They might then be attracted to the bookshop or the art gallery. Perhaps the most popular scene was the café, appropriately called Bankura. According to a longtime supporter of the CCIE, Gulshan Nanda, many Delhi residents would make plans by saying 'see you at Cottage'.[11]

The CCIE was arguably the first department store in India. 'Although there are cases of jewelry, ceramics, enamels, metalwork, ivory, and woodcarvings,' one American craft expert wrote, 'the majority of space is given to textiles: sarees of silk and cotton, shawls, scarfs, purses, sandals, Western-styled clothing, dress goods, household linens. There are also large stocks of carpets and fabrics for interior decoration.' Sales were brisk—boosted by the social caché that was attached to the store, by the hard work of many volunteers, and by several high-profile visits, including from Jackie Kennedy and Queen Elizabeth.[12]

A cultural icon, a vibrant social space and a thriving business, the Cottage was also a source of employment for women. It was a rare place where single women from 'respectable' families could work and find meaning, purpose and a supportive community. One of the most dedicated managers, Mrs Vir Singh, was a war widow with several young children. Her daughter later recalled that the Cottage was 'like one big family'. If the CCIE was a family, Kamaladevi was its matriarch, providing support and mentoring to many of the women employees. In reminiscing on her time at the CCIE, Singh remembered Kamaladevi as 'the mother of the whole place'.[13]

Kamaladevi's ties to her own family had become richer as well, especially after Rama returned to India in 1951. He had married an American woman, Doris, and had a daughter with her. Doris had two children from a previous marriage, and all three children came with them to India. Rama and Doris had another child in 1953. Kamaladevi became very attached to her grandchildren. They became a major source of joy and purpose in her life. She also came to love Doris. The two women travelled together through rural India looking for crafts. Rama had become an expert in colour film processing and helped to launch a pioneering lab in Worli, Bombay. Together, Rama and Doris founded a media company,

RAMNORD, which combined Rama's first name with Doris's maiden name: Norden. The company had a preview theatre in Worli, where Kamaladevi and Doris would together host special screenings of children's films. Kamaladevi's granddaughter, Nina, remembered her as a 'warm and loving grandmother' who smelt of sandalwood and never failed to bring fireworks for Diwali.[14]

Kamaladevi embraced her identity as a grandmother and as something of a 'mother' to all those she worked with in the crafts world. But she chafed when people referred to her as 'amma' and often expressed a bittersweet awareness of her age. The dancer Sukanya Rahman remembered Kamaladevi visiting her in Delhi in the 1950s. 'I'm a boring old lady,' Kamaladevi said. 'But I've known your Mummy since she was a baby, so you must come and sit and talk with me for a few minutes.' It was Rahman's grandmother, Ragini Devi, who had eloped with Harin during the salt satyagraha. It's unclear if Kamaladevi was reminded of Harin when she visited Rahman. In her family memoir, Rahman recalled that Harin himself would often come to those gatherings in Delhi 'with some pretty young dancer attached to his arm'. Kamaladevi maintained cordial relations with Harin, but their different paths must have rankled at times, bound up as they were with the sexist inequality that shaped prevailing understandings of gender, beauty and age.[15]

Those unequal understandings were at play when Kamaladevi introduced herself as 'a boring old lady'. 'I hardly found her boring,' Rahman recalled. 'Draped in bright silk saris, richly woven shawls, heavy jewelry, and glass bangles up to her elbows, she was a walking advertisement for the Indian handicrafts she treasured.' Kamaladevi became known for her beautiful, vibrant clothes and jewellery—none of which were expensive but all of which were carefully selected and tastefully arranged. She loved to cut off the border of one sari and sew it on to another. She did not consider herself a maker of crafts, but her attention to dress and jewellery was itself a form of art that shaped how many people saw her—and how she saw herself—a way for her to embrace her own beauty as she aged.[16]

~

In 1953, an insurance agent living in Madras decided to give a special gift to the new queen of England, Elizabeth II. He commissioned the weavers of Pattamadai to produce a mat that would include both his name and that of the new queen. Hearing of this unusual gift, Kamaladevi decided to pay her own visit to Pattamadai, a small town near the southern tip of India. Her mission was not to order a gift for the queen—Kamaladevi had never been a fan of the British Crown—but to urge the weavers to market their goods cooperatively. They took her advice and formed a cooperative that was supported by the newly founded AIHB, which Kamaladevi directed. In the years ahead, the weavers were able to gain many forms of government support, including new looms as well as land and money to build homes. According to the anthropologist Soumhya Venkatesan, some of the oldest members of the Pattamadai Labbai Fine Mat Weavers' Co-operative Society still remember Kamaladevi's visit and her transformative support.[17]

While she was deeply committed to the CCIE, Kamaladevi knew that one store would never come close to creating the kind of demand necessary to support the millions of artisans struggling throughout India. Given the fact that India was still a poor country, only recently free of colonial rule, Indian crafts would need to find markets abroad. In March 1952, the ICU created an exports section to market Indian handicrafts in London and New York. Kamaladevi's international connections proved vital, as did the connections of many of the women who supported the ICU and the CCIE. The process of developing the export market, by pulling the ICU into collaboration with foreign department stores and philanthropists, sat uneasily with Kamaladevi's desire to empower grassroots collaboratives within India. In the same years that she strove to link Indian artisans to the global economy, she also ran for Parliament as a socialist who was fiercely critical of capitalism and the inequities of the market within India and abroad. If such inconsistencies bothered her, she did not allow them to prevent her from doing what she thought was best for the crafts-makers of India. She still hoped for a revolution in the social and economic order, but until that revolution arrived, she focused on supporting as many artists as possible. Thus, with the combination of idealism and pragmatism that defined so much of her life, Kamaladevi set out to be a capitalist and a socialist, whose travels took her from Manhattan to Pattamadai.[18]

She demonstrated her pragmatism when it came to what was perhaps the most surprising partnership that the ICU developed—a partnership with the American philanthropist Nelson Rockefeller. In 1946, in *America: The Land of Superlatives,* Kamaladevi denounced the millionaire philanthropists who used the cloak of charity to escape taxes and to 'influence the attitude of professional and technical people' in order to ensure that they would 'rarely challenge the present social order'. But in 1952, when Rockefeller offered to provide the ICU with a full-time consultant, Kamaladevi agreed. In part, this decision reveals her faith in individual people. The consultant in question, Thomas Keehn, had spent four months in India, much of it visiting ICU initiatives. He 'certainly won our hearts', Kamaladevi wrote when accepting Rockefeller's offer. 'We shall welcome him in our midst and hope for a long period of close collaboration and comradeship.' Her decision to accept Rockefeller's support also came from her pragmatic realization that the scale of India's problems called for as many resources as possible. She maintained her suspicion of big philanthropy and required that the Cooperative League of the USA be included in the collaboration between Rockefeller's organization and the ICU.[19]

The first major focus of the collaboration was a massive research project: a national handicrafts survey that took Keehn, L.C. Jain and several other ICU officials on a six-month, 56,000 kilometre journey across India. They talked with artisans, distributors, shop owners and government officials, and gathered data on costs, margins, publicity and all other facets of the crafts industry. The CCIE also sent its own team, headed by Mrs Vir Singh, to visit artisans throughout India and to place orders directly with craftsmakers. Despite her persistent health problems and her heavy workload, Kamaladevi made her own trips to meet with artisans, trips that she described as a 'voyage of discovery'.[20]

At the heart of that voyage was Kamaladevi's love for crafts and her respect for the people who made them. Consider her time in Chamba, a small town perched in the Himalayas some 600 kilometres north of Delhi. Kamaladevi had heard of a particular woman who was renowned for producing the embroidered handkerchiefs or coverlets known as rumals or Chamba rumals. Local officials told her not to bother with visiting the woman given the high elevation and the fact that it was 'a very poor and dirty locality'. Kamaladevi went anyway. Her assistant, Sita Kirpal, later recalled Kamaladevi sitting side by side with the woman on a bed, the only piece of furniture in the room, drinking tea and talking. After her visit, Kamaladevi helped establish a new centre for Chamba rumals and arranged for the woman she had met to receive an award for her skills.[21]

Decades earlier, Yusuf Meherally had praised Kamaladevi by noting that 'in a peasant's dilapidated hut, she feels as much at home as in a Maharani's glittering palace. And what is more, she knows how to make both the peasant woman and the Maharani feel at ease.' That talent for connecting across class divides drove Kamaladevi's success as an advocate for crafts. Recognizing her ability to connect with impoverished artisans like that woman in Chamba, we might laud Kamaladevi for her compassion and her long-standing commitment to ending poverty. But Kamaladevi did not see such visits as acts of charity. They were opportunities for her to learn more about the artwork she loved, and to pay tribute to the master craftsmakers who had preserved sacred traditions.[22]

The crafts advocate and Kamaladevi biographer Jasleen Dhamija recalled travelling with Kamaladevi to Srikalahasti, a bustling town in Andhra Pradesh, known for its Shiva temple and for the hand-painted cotton textile known as kalamkari. Kamaladevi met with 'the last surviving master' of kalamkari and convinced him to train younger artists. While arranging government funding, Kamaladevi also used her own funds to buy cloth and natural dyes which she gave to the master. In Hyderabad, Kamaladevi came upon saris of exceptional weave and design. She learnt that they were being produced in Poochampally, a small town in what is now the state of Telangana, and that the weavers there were struggling. It was May and blazingly hot but she immediately set out on the journey in a jeep with a wet towel on her head. After meeting with the weavers, she arranged for the government to procure saris at a rate that would support the expansion of the art.[23]

Like the AIHB's nationwide surveys, Kamaladevi's journeys could be understood as part of the Indian state's efforts to unify and control the country. As the scholar Chandan Bose has written, 'Nation-wide surveys and studies conducted by the Handicraft Board developed a new system of recording and documenting craft skills and knowledge, which gave bureaucratic power a new dimension.' Wary of such bureaucratic power, Kamaladevi believed in democratizing the research and planning process as much as possible. 'Planning of projects is not a compiling of figures or tabulation of needs,' she later wrote. 'It is very definitely a social act. It can succeed only with the active responsible participation of the widest range of individuals and groups.' She lamented how often 'research at higher levels has little or no contact with the members of the community for whose use and benefit this precious knowledge is sought'. To avoid such a colonial approach to knowledge and planning, Kamaladevi held AIHB meetings across India, from Trivandrum in the south to Srinagar in the north. Before each meeting, she invited craftsmakers from the region to attend in order to share their problems and ideas. Still, the ultimate decisions were made in typical bureaucratic fashion—with Kamaladevi usually having the final word.[24]

In 1956, Kamaladevi took the lead role in establishing the National Handicrafts and Handlooms Museum, often known as the National Crafts Museum. The museum collection included thousands of artefacts, ranging from dolls and puppets to jewellery and textiles. From its inception, the museum was designed not only to preserve crafts but also to contribute to India's crafts renaissance. As Kamaladevi wrote in 1959, the museum was 'meant not so much for collecting and preserving old crafts as for encouraging the revival and reorientation of this precious Indian heritage'. The museum contributed to such a 'revival' by running training sessions for artisans, by providing in its collection a reservoir of traditions from which new work could emerge and by boosting demand for handicrafts.[25]

Expanding the domestic market for handicrafts was central to Kamaladevi's long-term vision for the industry. On 7 January 1954, at the first Mysore Handicrafts and Cottage Industries Conference, she expressed concern about focusing too much on exports. With that concern in mind, she placed handicrafts on the list of consumer goods rather than the list of art objects destined for export. She believed that crafts needed to be a part of daily life. Yet she also wanted to provide as many markets as possible for the work of Indian artisans and wanted their work to be treasured and respected throughout the world.[26]

In the spring of 1955, Kamaladevi served as an adviser for what would become one of the most celebrated exhibits of Indian art outside of the subcontinent: *Textile and Ornamental Arts of India* at the Museum of Modern Art in New York. The exhibit would attract hundreds of thousands of visitors. One of the organizers, Edgar Kaufmann Jr, wrote Kamaladevi that he was delighted to have objects that were 'truly Indian in design' unlike the 'export' items that had 'dominated Western collections up to now'. Such an emphasis on the authentic nature of the objects risked an 'orientalist' exotification. As the scholar Farhan Karim has noted, the exhibit was designed as 'a magical setting for equally exotic and mysterious objects'. Kamaladevi was not opposed to deploying India's 'exotic' image. Asked to attend the launch of an India exhibition at the Neiman Marcus flagship store in Dallas, Kamaladevi suggested that a baby elephant be brought in to increase publicity.[27]

That same year, an ICU report to the Government of India recognized the challenge of positioning handicrafts as simultaneously authentic and pleasing to modern tastes. The report expressed concern that handicrafts would remain frozen by 'the sentiment of traditionalism' or would be replaced by 'the cheap, blank smoothness of the machine-made, mass-produced article or have handicraft designs revolutionized by foreign experts'. The solution, as Kamaladevi saw it, was to build bridges between the Indian and the international, the urban and the rural, the traditional and the modern. Such bridging was not easy, but Kamaladevi had been striving to achieve such connections for much of her life. One of the greatest challenges facing independent India—how to 'modernize' in a way that was Indian—was bound up with many of the struggles that had long defined Kamaladevi's career, especially the women's movement and the fight to end poverty and class inequality. As usual, Kamaladevi saw these struggles as deeply interconnected—nowhere more so than in regard to the vexed question of population control.[28]

~

In November 1952, a crowd of over 500 people filled Bombay's Sir Cowasji Jehangir Hall for the Third International Conference of Planned Parenthood. The conference was organized by Kamaladevi's former AIWC assistant, Avabai Wadia, who had become a leading supporter of population control. The birth control advocate, Margaret Sanger, attended the gathering, as did many of the most influential figures in the international movement to limit population growth. Kamaladevi chaired the reception committee for the conference and had the honour of being the first to formally address the assembled delegates. Despite her admiration for Sanger and her strong ties to Wadia, Kamaladevi did not hesitate to diverge from several of the foundational tenets held by many advocates of population control.

'The world has to be treated as one unit,' Kamaladevi declared. Such a statement might not seem controversial, especially at an international gathering at which delegates would launch the International Planned Parenthood Federation. By asserting the interconnectedness of the world, however, Kamaladevi rejected the common presumption that 'overpopulation' was primarily a national problem that should be confronted within the borders of independent nation-states. Her global vision suggested that population control was not even the main issue. The global community should treat 'all the world's resources as the birthright of every citizen', she declared. Many countries had ample land and resources and yet refused to allow migrants to enter from less wealthy parts of the world. The root problem, Kamaladevi suggested, was not overpopulation but global inequality. 'One cannot hope to find the solution to population control or regulation through merely contraceptives or other methods of birth control,' she asserted. 'It can only be through better living conditions for all, greater opportunities for creative work and more scope for the realization of human ambitions.'[29]

During her time in the United States, Kamaladevi had met with Margaret Sanger in Arizona. It remains unclear exactly what the two women discussed. In her memoirs, Kamaladevi praised Sanger for her 'relentless fight against the blind laws of bigoted conservatism'. There is good reason to believe that Sanger was equally impressed with Kamaladevi. In 1936, Margaret Cousins had told Sanger that Kamaladevi was 'paying for her championship of Birth Control and other Social Reforms by being denied inclusion in the Working Committee of the Congress'. Sanger would later call Kamaladevi 'an old friend' and praise her leadership. Sanger and Kamaladevi shared not just a belief in birth control but a willingness to rebel against convention—a willingness Kamaladevi herself demonstrated by distinguishing herself even among advocates of population control.[30]

Kamaladevi sometimes shared in the more troubling aspects of the population control movement. In 1938, in her piece on the 'Future of Indian Women's Movement', she reproduced the eugenicist strain popular among many advocates of birth control. She wrote, for example, that 'mere breeding adds neither to the quality nor the greatness of a nation, it merely lowers vitality, spreads diseases and brings unsound citizens into the world'. In reproducing such eugenicist rhetoric, Kamaladevi was participating in one of the most popular lines of thought among social reformers of that era, a line of thought that would later contribute to inhumane forced sterilization campaigns within India. As the historian Mytheli Sreenivas has written, 'the Indian government's family planning programs would eventually sacrifice women's bodies and reproductive autonomy in favor of a relentless drive to meet population targets'. That tragic future would mock Kamaladevi's vision of birth control as empowering women.[31]

Despite her occasional endorsements of eugenicist thinking, Kamaladevi saw birth control as a vital facet of women's freedom. 'No woman can call herself free,' she wrote in 1938, 'who cannot own and control her body and who can be subdued and enslaved through that very quality of fertility which once raised her to the altar as a deity in the dawn of early civilisation.' In 1939, in *The Awakening of Indian Women*, she noted that a 'masculine-dominated society always stresses the importance of women as a breeder'. By freeing women from 'the penalty of undesired motherhood', birth control had the potential to 'deal a death blow' to patriarchy. Men would no longer be able to 'chain and enslave' women. When a conservative Congress member denounced birth control, Kamaladevi replied that birth control was 'the sacred and inalienable right of every woman to possess the means to control her body and no God or man can attempt to deprive her of that right without perpetrating an outrage on womanhood'. As the scholar Sanjam Ahluwalia has written, Kamaladevi's advocacy of birth control as a way for 'women to control their sexuality' distinguished her 'from women who demanded the use of birth control on grounds of declining women's health, degeneration of national race, or Malthusian dread of overpopulation'. Kamaladevi's belief that women should have 'control' over their own sexuality led her, in 1947, to denounce 'the double standard of sexual morality that still plagues Indian society'. This was a dangerous view for a single woman to take, especially given how rumours regarding her own personal life had long been used against her.[32]

She took the safer and more established position when it came to prostitution. In Chandigarh on 20 November 1954, Kamaladevi gave the presidential address to the fourth annual gathering of the All-India Conference of the Association for Social and Moral Hygiene (ASMH), an organization that focused on ending prostitution. She was one of several prominent women—including Sushila Nayar, Rajkumari Amrit Kaur and Indira Gandhi—to serve a year as president of the ASMH. In her presidential address, Kamaladevi located prostitution alongside other 'degrading customs, outmoded rotting vestiges of the past that cling to present social modes and need to be swept away'. According to the *Times of India*, 'she admitted that the economic factor was important and often dominant in the problem, but pointed out that by rejecting the other aspects, we would only serve in distorting the real picture'. As the historian Rohit De has argued, Kamaladevi positioned herself in the mainstream by suggesting 'that the existence of prostitution as a social fact had very little to do with the exercise of choice by the woman involved'.[33]

Her differing approaches to birth control and prostitution reveal a tension in Kamaladevi's evolving views on women's struggles—a tension between her commitment to women's independence and her desire to embed women's activism within larger struggles for social progress. In 1955, she contributed a chapter on the 'Welfare of Women in India' to a volume published by the Planning Commission of the Government of India. She praised the creation of the Central Social Welfare Board and argued that the Board should 'plan and promulgate a comprehensive scheme to provide welfare services to the community of which women form but a part'. That framing reveals the persistence of her old antipathy to 'feminism', an antipathy that led her to disregard sexism by stating that 'opportunities for women doctors are the same as for men doctors'. Her analysis lacked the fire of her socialist radicalism and, in its place, exuded the bland detachment of a government bureaucrat. Contrast her earlier comments on birth control with the tepid statement that 'in view of the continuing increase of the population of India . . . the Planning Commission and the Government of India consider that schemes for regulating the size of individual families and control of population is essential'.[34]

Kamaladevi reiterated her opposition to 'feminism' in 1957 in the introduction to Neera Desai's *Women in Modern India*. Kamaladevi praised the book as 'perhaps, one of the most comprehensive books on the Indian women'. After dampening her praise with that 'perhaps', she added, 'there is one great regret that I feel . . . The approach, the slant and the emphasis is very "feminist".' She added that 'feminism, as known in the West, has never really been a feature of the national evolution of this country'. Kamaladevi hoped to keep it that way. 'Feminism like all "isms" tends to isolate and spotlight one particular phase or feature,' she wrote, 'and thereby rather distort the larger perspective.' It was imperative that 'the many disabilities that women suffer from in modern India' be located 'in the larger context of a society which still has many ugly general features, economic as well as social.' Progress necessarily cannot be only on one front,' she asserted, and that was why the Indian women's movement 'was not and never can have a feminist character'.[35]

In the 1920s and 1930s, Kamaladevi criticized feminism from the vantage point of a radical socialist. Now, she was something of an establishment figure, and her writings at times risked toeing the government line. In 1958, she contributed to an edited volume, *Women of India*, published by the Government of India with a foreword by Nehru. In addition to authoring the chapter on 'The Struggle for Freedom', Kamaladevi was also cited in three other chapters. She had become both a historian and a historical figure, and there was reason to worry that Kamaladevi had lost her willingness to denounce the failures of the government and the inequities of Indian society. For one thing, much of her chapter was backward-facing. She decried the impact of British rule on 'hand industries' and praised women as 'the repositories' of Indian culture. When she turned to the present, she offered an upbeat story of progress. 'Today large numbers of women hold important posts in the home as well as the foreign services,' she wrote. 'Their rise to responsibility and positions of importance has been remarkable.' Her chapter could have been written by a government official eager to present India in the most positive light.[36]

Kamaladevi was not a government official, and she was far from uncritical of those in power. Despite her many connections to the government, she came to believe strongly in the importance of a thriving civil sector. Indeed, one could argue that Kamaladevi was among the most important leaders in the development of non-governmental organizations (NGOs) in post-Independence India. Consider the way she fiercely defended the independence of the ICU and of cooperatives more generally. In 1956, the Government of India established a Committee on Cooperative Law which issued a report the following year proposing a series of rules and laws for various cooperative societies. In January 1959, Nehru wrote Ajit Prasad Jain, the Minister for Food and Agriculture, forwarding a letter from Kamaladevi that complained cooperatives were being subsumed within the bureaucracy. Nehru added that 'some of the criticisms made by the Indian Cooperative Union deserve serious notice.

The whole object of the cooperative movement, as we envisaged, is for non-officials to work it and for the present restrictions to be removed.' Nehru also wrote Kamaladevi directly explaining that the Planning Commission would look into the problem, and asking her to correspond directly with several ministers, including Jain and the Ministers for Law and for Community Development and Cooperation. Nehru himself wrote A.K. Sen, the Minister for Law, forwarding Kamaladevi's letter and adding, 'The objective we have set before us is to spread cooperatives, remove restrictions on them and make them non-official.'[37]

In 1958, Kamaladevi founded the Association of Voluntary Agencies for Rural Development (AVARD), an umbrella organization for rural NGOs. To help lead AVARD, she recruited the Gandhian activist Dharampal, a figure who was, like Kamaladevi, generally known by only one name. Dharampal had worked with Kamaladevi on refugee rehabilitation and within the ICU, and he would continue to help lead AVARD after Kamaladevi handed formal control to another old friend and colleague, Jayaprakash Narayan, whose political evolution mirrored Kamaladevi's in many ways. They both abandoned electoral politics and both believed in the importance of grassroots community organizing outside the aegis of the government. Kamaladevi was more directly involved in the arts, but JP respected that emphasis and his respect meant a lot to her. It was with pride that she included in her memoir the following note that JP had written for her: 'It is essential that all national development should include the preservation and continuation of cultural forms and pursuits. The present trend of deculturization does great damage to our national life. The core of all progress must be based on our practicing arts and crafts.' In the years ahead, Kamaladevi would grapple with how to link the arts and crafts to 'national development' without narrowing the definition of development or infringing on the independence of artists. At the heart of this challenge was another dilemma that would define Kamaladevi's post-Independence career—how to deploy state power without being constrained or corrupted by that power.[38]

~

On 28 January 1953, Maulana Azad, the scholar and veteran freedom fighter, spoke at the inauguration of a new governmental body dedicated to the arts, the Sangeet Natak Akademi (SNA). 'In a democratic regime,' Azad declared, 'the arts can derive their sustenance only from the people, and the state, as the organized manifestation of the people's will, must, therefore, undertake its maintenance and development.' Azad left unclear how the state should contribute to the 'maintenance and development' of the arts without exercising too much influence over what kinds of arts should be supported. He was speaking in his capacity as head of the Ministry of Education, which had been tasked with creating the SNA. Many of the key figures involved in its creation believed that the SNA needed to be independent of the ministry and of the government more generally. The importance of such independence was defended by Jawaharlal Nehru, but it was Kamaladevi who, as the vice chair of the SNA from its founding in 1953 until 1958, would play the most direct role in defending the independence of the institution and of the artists it was meant to serve.[39]

On 14 August 1955, Nehru sent Azad a revealing note about the complexities of government relations to the arts, a note that revealed Kamaladevi's awkward position as both a government insider and a perpetual outsider. In addition to serving as the vice chair of the SNA, Kamaladevi was also the founding president of the Bharatiya Natya Sangh/Theatre Centre India, which had some 250 local groups affiliated with it and was, in turn, itself affiliated with the International Theatre Institute (ITI), an offshoot of UNESCO. It was at a UNESCO conference in Beirut in 1948 that Kamaladevi learnt about the ITI and developed the idea of founding what became the Bharatiya Natya Sangh. Ignoring this history, the education ministry, under Azad's control, wrote the ITI requesting that it end its affiliation with the Bharatiya Natya Sangh and instead establish relations with the SNA. In effect, the ministry demanded that an NGO be replaced by an organization that was designed to be independent of government but that, in practice, was a branch of it. On learning of this effort, Kamaladevi went directly to Nehru who then wrote Azad. 'I think that it was unfortunate that such a letter should have been sent without the courtesy of consulting the President of the Theatre Centre India, who happens also to be the Vice President of the Sangeet Natak Akademi,' Nehru wrote. He stressed 'that these Akademis should be completely autonomous bodies and that there should be no Government interference in them'. 'In communist countries,' Nehru added, 'all such organisations are controlled by Governments. This is not so elsewhere and I do not think it should be so in India.'[40]

The following year, at the first Drama Seminar of the SNA, Kamaladevi had a unique opportunity to defend artistic autonomy and to warn about excessive government interference. Held in Delhi in 1956, the seminar brought together some forty eminent practitioners and producers to discuss the future of drama in India. The novelist Mulk Raj Anand called for the establishment of one hundred new theatres 'of the people and for the people' that would be 'thrown open both to the amateurs and the professionals'. Another participant challenged Anand: 'who is going to give you those theatres?' 'Well, to be frank,' Anand replied, 'I really do not know that.' It was Kamaladevi who offered the most detailed roadmap. She called for substantial government funding of the arts, but did not want the government to directly control artists or their work. 'Again and again I hear, not only in this Seminar but also outside it,' she stated, 'how nice would it be to have a Ministry of Culture. God forbid, if such a thing happens there will be an end to all cultural activities in this country.' 'I firmly believe that no cultural activity can be carried on by a Ministry,' she explained. 'All the time they will be busy in collecting data, statistics, blueprints, and hundred and one theories.' She made clear her decentralized and democratic vision of arts funding when she suggested that the Sangeet Natak Akademi finance a theatre in each state in order to support the creation of 'brilliant plays in all Indian languages'.[41]

Part of the danger of governmental control was the risk that the authorities would narrowly define what constituted Indian culture. According to the scholar Dia Da Costa, the Akademis privileged 'the regional languages, histories, and folk cultural practices of north India over those of southern India'. Kamaladevi was sensitive to that bias, and strove to support the arts throughout India. In November 1954, she organized a National Drama Festival in New Delhi. Twenty-two plays were performed, at least one in every major Indian language. Kamaladevi had a special passion for what she often called 'folk theatre'—theatrical forms with deep roots in rural India and among the indigenous peoples known in India as tribals or adivasis ('original inhabitants'). Often, cultural elites embraced a form of 'folk drama' that was, as the scholar Rustom Bharucha has written, 'essentially an urban construct' that was designed 'to win the approval of urban audiences'. For Kamaladevi, however, events like the National Drama Festival were an opportunity to win recognition (and funding) for diverse cultural forms from across India—forms that should also be supported in their local communities. Art need not be brought to Delhi to be art.[42]

In 1955, she began an essay on the future of the Indian theatre by celebrating 'folk theatre' not targeted at urban audiences. 'The Indian classical theatre was created and developed by masters who were of the people,' she declared. As she often did in regards to handicrafts, she offered a romanticized vision of the distant past. She imagined 'long summer nights' during which 'the villagers would sit under the scintillating stars, drinking in the gaiety, the music and philosophic thought'. While such a vision risked exotifying rural people, it was designed in opposition to a conception of art and theatre as essentially urban and modern. Kamaladevi acknowledged that 'new moulds and forms must arise with the new forces, out of the fresh experience of a people in the making', but these new forms needed roots in tradition. 'Our traditional theatre must not be allowed to decay through neglect,' Kamaladevi wrote. 'It must be revived and preserved as the rich heritage from which we shall build the theatre of tomorrow.' She envisioned theatre as 'an arena where all are free to exercise their dynamic powers and creative impulses, where the walls that have confined their lives into little, dank unlit chambers crumble away and they are no longer puny automata at the mercy of superior forces, but personalities of meaning and importance in the picture of contemporary history'.[43]

It matters that Kamaladevi published such a celebration of rural, local theatre in a bilingual edition of *World Theatre*, produced by the International Theatre Institute with the assistance of UNESCO. Kamaladevi continued to travel widely, crossing the borders of both nations and cultures and, in the process, revealing the fluid and contingent nature of cultural borders. In September 1955, she went to West Germany to attend an opera festival. In 1956, she led a cultural delegation, sponsored by the Government of India, on a two-month visit to Egypt, Sudan and Libya. That same year, she visited Ghana and Nigeria where, as chair of the All India Handicrafts Board, she helped open exhibitions of Indian industries.[44]

While serving as an ambassador of Indian culture abroad, Kamaladevi also strove to bring the cultures of the world to India. In October 1956, under the aegis of the Bharatiya Natya Sangh, Kamaladevi organized the first World Theatre Conference, which was held in Bombay. Some fifty delegates, mostly from Europe and Asia, elected her president. The gathering was sponsored by UNESCO's International Theatre Institute, and Kamaladevi saw the gathering as an opportunity to broaden that institution 'in order to make it truly international in character'. She had long criticized Western organizations that claimed to speak on behalf of the world. During the World Theatre Conference, the delegates resolved to found, in Kamaladevi's words, an 'Asian Centre for theatre study which would strengthen the roots of the theatre movement in the countries of Asia'. To Kamaladevi, there was no conflict between fostering solidarities within Asia while aiming to contribute to a global organization. Just as her Indian nationalism supported her transnational universalism, so her vision of pan-Asian collaboration was a bridge between the local and the global.[45]

The Asian Theatre Institute (ATI) was formally opened on 20 January 1958 by the President of India. The objectives of the institute were largely educational: conducting research and offering 'advanced post-graduate courses in dramatic arts'. With only twenty-six students and a fairly academic mandate, it might seem a relatively modest undertaking, but Kamaladevi had grand visions for its future. She saw it as an extension of generations of anticolonial struggle and of 'the upsurge in the Asian countries, particularly since the advent of freedom'. In keeping with her expansive vision, she wrote that the ATI should eventually extend out 'towards the rest of the world' and towards 'music and dance as well'. Hers was a global vision for a centre that would 'serve to draw closer together the most powerful and popular ties that can tie countries and people together'.[46]

Her dreams for the ATI would not be realized. In July 1958, only six months after the ATI had been founded, the SNA assumed control of the ATI and, over the course of the following year, merged it with the newly created National School of Drama. It remains unclear if Kamaladevi was disappointed by this turn of events. In any case, she continued to envision the arts as a bridge between the domestic and the transnational. In 1958, she served on a committee, chaired by M.C. Chagla, the chief justice of the Bombay High Court, that focused on how to celebrate the sixtieth birthday of Paul Robeson. As the founding president of the All-India Federation of Theatre Groups, she worked to support the creation of new theatres and drama academies and to democratize both the production of theatre and its audiences. She developed a plan in which productions would be offered across the country with admission costing no more than one rupee. In collaboration with the Gujarati playwright Adi Pherozeshah Marzban, she helped to found the Indian Academy of Dramatic Arts. She also mentored artists and producers like Moneeka Misra, who worked with her at the Bombay Natya Sangh, and Qudsia Zaidi, who founded the Hindustani Theatre. In August 1958, Kamaladevi was in Bombay inaugurating the Natya Academy and celebrating the importance of education in the performing arts. She saw education as a vital link across cultural and artistic forms.[47]

Arts education was also a bridge between the past and the future, between tradition and innovation. In March 1957, Kamaladevi travelled to Madras for the National Seminar on the Role of Arts and Crafts in Education and Community Development, where she chaired a session on the 'present situation of arts and crafts in general education and in community centres'. She made clear that her vision of arts education did not entail merely transmitting the techniques of the past. Craftsmakers should be offered 'training in the new techniques to evolve new patterns for different crafts'. As she explained, 'Mere imitation leads to bad art and kills the creative instinct.' She often lamented that the educational system did not give children the opportunity to create art and crafts. In the 1920s, under the aegis of the AIWC, she had worked to introduce more emphasis on music, dance and crafts in schools. Her vision for education was not limited to the arts. In 1961, she headed an advisory committee to the Ministry of Education that recommended grants to a variety of educational institutions. In 1964, a working group 'on the problems of training and employment prospects of museum personnel and teaching of history of art in Indian universities' was established by the Ministry of Education. Kamaladevi was one of four people on the committee.[48]

Whereas Kamaladevi believed in education, she loved crafts and the theatre. Ebrahim Alkazi, the longtime director of the National School of Drama, recalled her climbing six flights of steps in order to attend performances in his Bombay theatre. She would always stay after the show to congratulate the performers. She had a special love for puppet theatre—an artform in which crafts and theatre came together. She served as a vice president of UNIMA, an international puppet organization, and collaborated with puppet masters from Czechoslovakia and the United States. She also had a special interest in theatre architecture, and organized an exhibition on that field under the aegis of the Bharatiya Natya Sangh.[49]

Bridging her passion for crafts, the theatre and museums, Kamaladevi established a theatre crafts museum, which eventually became the Srinivas Mallya Memorial Theatre Crafts Museum. Much of the collection consisted of costumes, masks and puppets that Kamaladevi had gathered herself. The Theatre Crafts Museum merged with Naika, a theatre crafts workshop that she had founded. In keeping with the deeply personal nature of these initiatives, the museum was named after her close friend U. Srinivas Mallya, a member of the Constituent Assembly of India who later served as a member of Parliament from 1952 to 1965. Mallya was, like Kamaladevi, from Mangalore. Despite the fact that Mallya was a stalwart Congressman while Kamaladevi was a socialist, the two remained close—bonded through their shared love for theatre and for southern India. Kamaladevi donated all of the property she had inherited and a large sum of money to the Theatre Crafts Museum.[50]

Kamaladevi left few records of her financial situation, and it remains unclear which of her various responsibilities generated income for her and how much she depended on familial wealth or other sources of support. As she aged, her financial situation became a source of anxiety, in part because her generosity left her with fewer resources. Unlike many of the artists she strove to support, however, Kamaladevi did not need to worry about her basic expenses. Like many social reformers, it was from a position of relative economic security that Kamaladevi strove to transform India's economic landscape and to create sustainable paths out of poverty for artisans and artists. One could argue that Kamaladevi's retreat from the fiery socialism of her youth—from her demand for land redistribution and state control of the economy—could be attributed to her own class position. Yet Kamaladevi's class status did not change over time, and it would be a mistake to suggest that Kamaladevi's ultimate vision for India's economy became less radical as she aged. Her approach to realizing that vision did, however, change—and it remains unclear how much Kamaladevi grappled with the difference between her early and late politics and how much she questioned whether her emphasis on arts and crafts could, given the persistence of poverty and inequity, achieve the kind of sweeping economic transformation she had long envisioned.

~

In October 1960, Jawaharlal Nehru sent Kamaladevi an ambivalent note regarding her work promoting Indian handicrafts abroad. 'When I was in New York recently,' Nehru wrote, 'I got a message which I think you had sent me about visiting an Indian handicrafts depot with which John D. Rockefeller is connected.' Nehru visited the depot and left with mixed feelings. 'It was good in its way,' he explained. 'But I felt that it could have many more articles which would be appreciated in America. In fact, I am sure that the market for Indian handicrafts in America is a very big one.' Nehru's enthusiasm was sincere. On the same day that he wrote Kamaladevi, he also wrote Gulzarilal Nanda, the head of India's Planning Commission. He enclosed a letter from Kamaladevi and again stated that there was 'a very big market in America for many of our handicrafts'. But even while he expressed enthusiasm at the prospect of marketing Indian handicrafts abroad, Nehru also communicated doubts regarding the current approach to such efforts, an approach that Kamaladevi had long shaped.[51]

From the outset, Kamaladevi had misgivings about an export-oriented approach to handicrafts. Those misgivings grew with time, even while she continued to believe in building demand for crafts wherever possible. To help artisans produce crafts that could be marketed and sold in urban India and abroad, the ICU founded design centres in Delhi, Calcutta, Bangalore and Bombay. The design centres garnered praise within India and from foreign experts such as Margaret Patch, an American craft enthusiast who would become one of Kamaladevi's closest friends. In a laudatory article published in the American journal *Craft Horizons*, Patch highlighted the achievements of the Calcutta Design Centre, where a German ceramics expert had helped to spark a burst of productive experimentation 'in a wide range of forms so international, so un-Indian'. The fact that the work was 'so un-Indian' would have concerned Kamaladevi. Also of concern was the way Patch contrasted the traditional and the modern, the rural and the urban, when praising the head of the design centre for bringing two rural craftsmakers into the city 'to give them a feel of contemporary life'.[52]

By the time Patch visited India in 1962, Kamaladevi's authority within the world of Indian handicrafts had begun to wane. In 1959, the Government of India relocated the oversight of India's massive textiles industry from the AIHB to a new agency chaired by Pupul Jayakar. Born in Etawah in 1915, Jayakar had served as Mridula Sarabhai's assistant when Mridula and Kamaladevi were both working for the Kasturba Trust. She was also a close friend of Indira Gandhi. After Independence, she gained renown as an expert on textiles. Jayakar was later quoted as calling Kamaladevi 'a woman of incomprehensible imagination and knowledge' but for most of their lives the two women were seen as rivals and their personal relationship was frosty. According to Gopalkrishna Gandhi, 'Friends tried to "carve out" territories for them. "Kamaladevi is the first word on handicrafts, Pupul the last word on handlooms." But that turfing did not help.'[53]

Kamaladevi's role within the world of crafts was also threatened by success. By March 1962, the CCIE's revenues exceeded the equivalent of $400,000. These earnings attracted competition from private companies. It was not, however, direct competition that proved to be the greatest challenge. What became a major problem for Kamaladevi was the way in which those private companies compensated their managerial staff. In 1963, several CCIE staff members argued that they should be paid higher salaries, in line with what their counterparts were making in the private sphere. Kamaladevi and L.C. Jain replied that the CCIE had a social mission and that the staff should share profits equally with the artisans. 'We tried to explain to them that the Cooperative Union had undertaken this project for the craftspeople,' Jain later recalled. 'We could not compromise our core beliefs.' Unconvinced, the staff unionized and elected Rajkumari Amrit Kaur as president of their union. A stalwart of the freedom struggle, Kaur had been granted a cabinet position at precisely the time Kamaladevi was denied one. To add to Kamaladevi's troubles, the Ministry of Commerce audited the ICU's financial arrangements and published a highly critical report without allowing Kamaladevi or L.C. Jain the opportunity to challenge the findings. In the fall of 1963, under assault from within and without, the ICU ceded control of the CCIE.[54]

While stepping away from the CCIE, Kamaladevi deepened her commitment to the world of crafts by turning to one of her oldest passions—writing. The same year that the ICU withdrew from the CCIE, the Indian Council for Cultural Relations published *Indian Handicrafts,* a major synthesis of history and analysis that served as a kind of summation of all that Kamaladevi had learnt about crafts. Chapters covered pottery, metalware, textiles, embroidery, carpets, jewellery, mats and basketry, and woodwork. Kamaladevi argued that cottage industries encouraged 'the decentralisation of social and economic power' by 'providing ample employment to the rural folk'. They also fostered social cohesion. 'If the cottage industries taught the village independence in its ordinary life from the exactions of the Capital,' she wrote, 'they also taught the people in the village interdependence.' This blend of economic independence and social interdependence 'later inspired in Gandhiji the dream of Sarvodaya—a self-supporting community which stood for the good of all'.[55]

In such a Gandhian vision of handicrafts, Kamaladevi found a new direction for her work: away from marketing, especially international marketing, and towards preservation, especially national preservation. Yet Kamaladevi would continue to see economic development as central to her work with artisans, and her vision of crafts would remain bound up with the international. She had long seen herself as an ambassador of Indian culture abroad. In 1959, for example, she helped organize a special all-India edition of the American journal *Craft Horizons*, in which she wrote that Indian crafts 'express the great tradition and cultural heritage of our country from which beauty and utility were never divorced'. That same year, the American crafts scholar Allen Eaton, often called the 'dean of American crafts', travelled to India with the potter Gerry Williams. Eaton met with Kamaladevi and presented several books to her and to the AIHB. Hosting such visitors was a regular part of Kamaladevi's work. She saw herself as a cultural ambassador who fostered exchange in both directions—expanding knowledge of Indian crafts abroad while also helping Indian artists, consumers and members of the general public deepen their understanding of foreign crafts and cultures.[56]

On 15 April 1960, surrounded by dignitaries and photographers, Kamaladevi pushed a shovel into an open patch of ground near the heart of New Delhi. She was within sight of the famed Lodhi Gardens, where towering fifteenth-century tombs stood amidst lush greenery, but it was not a monument to the past for which she wielded that shovel. She was breaking ground for the India International Centre (IIC), an institution that would replace the CCIE as her second home—physically and emotionally. The idea for this international centre is often traced to a conversation the vice president of India, Dr S. Radhakrishnan, shared with John D. Rockefeller III in 1958. Rockefeller had been impressed by the International House of Japan and offered to help fund a similar institution in India. But the roots of the IIC go deeper into the history of two overlapping ideas that Kamaladevi had long championed: the idea of India as a global meeting place and the idea of an Indian public sphere that was open to cultural and intellectual exchange. Both of these ideas had enemies—particularly among those who viewed Indian culture in narrow and parochial ways. Both also had powerful supporters, including Jawaharlal Nehru, with whose backing the IIC was founded in December 1958. Dr C.D. Deshmukh, the chair of the University Grants Commission and a former finance minister in Nehru's cabinet, was selected to lead the new institution. Kamaladevi became the first vice president and a lifetime trustee. While many people deserve credit for creating the IIC, no one did more than Kamaladevi to cultivate the roots of the institution or to shape its character.[57]

In November 1960, a few months after Kamaladevi ceremonially turned the first earth at the site, the Crown Prince of Japan served as the chief guest at another official ceremony—the laying of the cornerstone. Kamaladevi attended the celebration and sat next to Nehru. She listened as he declared, 'The world today is so constituted that there can be no escape from international cooperation.' For Kamaladevi, international cooperation was more than a diplomatic necessity—it was a cultural and artistic opportunity. In the years ahead, a range of political figures would visit the IIC, from Tanzania's Julius Nyerere to Singapore's Lee Kuan Yew. They would be joined by intellectuals, artists and social activists including the novelist Pearl Buck, the poet Octavio Paz, the priest and social critic Ivan Illich, the French obstetrician Frédérick Leboyer and South Africa's Archbishop Desmond Tutu. Kamaladevi was delighted to meet many of these visitors and to learn from them. As Gopalkrishna Gandhi has noted, 'Kamaladevi's amazingly large international constituency equalled only that of the Nehrus.'[58]

More than a place where foreigners brought new ideas to India, the IIC became a community in which many people—from across India and abroad—could experience the subcontinent at its cosmopolitan best. It became a gathering place for Indian artists and intellectuals who looked beyond the borders of religion, caste, race and nation. Kamaladevi did not want the IIC to become an exclusive club for the Delhi elite. She wanted artists, journalists and social activists to have access to the IIC—and to be honoured members of its community. The dining hall, which quickly became famous for providing delicious food at budget prices, proved key to the success of that vision, as did Kamaladevi herself. She insisted on taking visitors to eat there, and especially enjoyed treating guests to idli, dosa and other South Indian fare that she personally requested of the IIC chefs. Bridging the global and the local through a plate of idli sambar, Kamaladevi again found a way to transcend borders and to be her full self. That would prove more challenging when it came to the most global organization she helped to create, an organization that would loom over the last decades of her life and would connect her transnational vision to her belief in crafts in ways that were exciting, empowering, and ultimately frustrating.[59]

8

Cultural Revolutions

At eleven in the morning on 12 June 1964, Kamaladevi sat in a large room in Ferris Booth Hall at Columbia University in New York. Representatives from over forty-five countries had gathered to incorporate a new organization, the World Crafts Council (WCC). Kamaladevi was selected as one of sixteen directors and was also elected one of the vice presidents. The president of the WCC and the main force behind its founding was an American woman named Aileen Osborn Webb. Like Kamaladevi, Webb was passionate about crafts. Also like Kamaladevi, she was an institution-builder. She founded *Craft Horizons* magazine in 1941, the American Craftsmen's Educational Council in 1943, the School for American Craftsmen in 1944 and the Museum of Contemporary Crafts (now known as the Museum of Arts and Design) in 1956. Unlike Kamaladevi, Webb was wealthy. She lived on East 72nd Street in New York in a penthouse apartment filled with art—from 'a spectacular Monet on a deep purple wall' to works by contemporary American artists like Paul Aschenbach and Lenore Tawney. Webb used her fortune to support a range of artists and artistic initiatives. As important as the money she donated was the passion she brought to making the WCC a vibrant space for personal, cultural and intellectual exchange—a space that echoed Kamaladevi's vision for the India International Centre in New Delhi.[1]

The founding of the WCC occurred as part of the First World Congress of Craftsmen, a ten-day gathering that included a special exhibition at the Museum of Contemporary Crafts; a gala dinner in the Rainbow Room of the RCA Building; and workshops, panels and lectures that attracted some 650 crafts-makers from forty-six different countries. Like Kamaladevi, Webb advanced a broad vision of crafts, and the gathering featured a range of artists and intellectuals, including the social critic Dwight MacDonald, the architect Louis Kahn and the writer Ralph Ellison. The president of CBS, Frank Stanton, spoke, as did René d'Harnoncourt, director of the Museum of Modern Art (MoMA) and Stanley Marcus of Neiman-Marcus, the high-end department store. In the foreword to the official record of the congress, Webb stated that 'the purpose of the Congress was to bring together craftsmen from the world over—both the village artisan and the urbanized designer-craftsman—for a creative, technical, economic and social exchange'. The goal was not only to advance crafts but also to cultivate a certain cosmopolitan inclusivity. According to Webb, 'The Congress proved that when confronted with each other as artists people could meet in a friendly spirit and with deep understanding no matter what their race or politics. This is the first road toward bringing peace to the world.'[2]

In the keynote address to the Congress, Dr D'Arcy Hayman, the director of arts education and cultural development at UNESCO, defended the importance of the 'aesthetic level of human awareness' in a world increasingly dominated by machines. Rejecting the distinction between arts and crafts, she declared that the 'artist-craftsman' served 'both the physical and the spiritual-aesthetic needs'. She was not opposed to technology. In some parts of the world she declared, 'The machine has liberated the old slave labor forces, has made the working day shorter, has increased literacy and raised the standards of living.' But technology had also fed 'the fragmented, specialized, compartmentalized, and uniform lives of men in automated societies'.[3]

Like D'Arcy, Kamaladevi framed her comments in response to modern technology and mass culture. 'There is a growing anxiety about traditional cultures that are dying or have already disappeared,' she stated.

Her talk was called the 'Preservation of the Cultural Values of a Society Through Craftsmanship'. Her vision of preservation was not static; rather, she called for cultural conservation via continual reinvention, a process that she linked to decolonization. 'The regeneration of crafts was made part of the national freedom movement by Mahatma Gandhi,' she explained. 'The national regeneration of the people, as Gandhi visualized it, was to come through the recreation of ideals, aspirations and dreams shaped partly through objects of craftsmanship with which they lived.' To explain the connection between craftsmanship and 'national regeneration', Kamaladevi offered a revealing definition of the word 'Swadeshi'. 'Although normally it means "products of the land",' she argued, 'in Gandhi's connotation it was a way of life, conforming to and upholding enduring values that enjoined gracious living and rejected unlovely utilities.'[4]

Kamaladevi distinguished herself from the other speakers by connecting the importance of 'enduring values' and 'gracious living' to the politics of decolonization. 'The long centuries of political and economic rule of some regions by others are giving way,' she declared, 'and now, as the less industrially developed areas emerge from the old suppressions, they come to a proper perspective, with a growing realization of the significance of their own cultures and their contribution to a world culture.' She did not draw hard boundaries between different cultures. Indeed, she framed the decolonization of culture as a gift to the entire world. 'The people of the former ruling countries, too, are waking up to a greater discernment and appreciation of the gifts and qualities that the newly freed have to offer,' she asserted. 'While we do not desire to be steam-rolled into one common expression,' she concluded, 'we could gradually grow to the happy realization of a common and universal heritage.'[5]

Kamaladevi made clear that she was not opposed to technology. 'The problem posed is not man versus machine,' she declared, 'but rather a harmony and cohesion between the two.' She also refused to contrast craft traditions with modernity. 'Craftsmanship need not,' she made clear, 'be bound up wholly with tradition. While it continues to draw strength from the past, it has also to be tuned to the present, evolve a new relationship with the current flow of life and thus create a new tradition.' In accord with her socialist emphasis on cooperation and her distrust of the market, she offered an idyllic image of the past in which 'craft-oriented society was based on personal relationships' and 'not contract and competition'. In her view, 'good taste and good opportunity to live in intimacy with beauty should not be the privilege of the few, but the common inheritance of all'. Kamaladevi's blending of tradition and creativity resonated with many others. Daniel F. Rubin de la Borbolla, director of the Museum of Popular Arts in Mexico City, distinguished between 'past' and 'living tradition', and declared, 'We are not dealing with obsolescence or decay, but with what is living and vital, dynamic and satisfying to man's material and aesthetic needs.' 'Tradition is not a static point,' added Pupul Jayakar. 'The moment a tradition becomes static and tends to imitate its past or present, it is dead.' Yet neither Borbolla nor Jayakar linked the evolution of crafts to decolonization or to a critique of the market. The political framing Kamaladevi brought to the WCC was largely unique.[6]

In January 1965, Aileen Webb travelled to India, where Kamaladevi arranged for her to take a national tour under the aegis of the AIHB and the Indian Council for Cultural Relations. In the pages of *Craft Horizons,* Webb celebrated 'the extreme kindness shown me by Mme. Chattopadhyay' and praised the AIHB for 'its emphasis on quality and its research into techniques of the past'. Such a focus on quality resonated with Kamaladevi, who wanted Indian crafts to be respected throughout the world. Whenever she travelled to London, she would visit the Victoria and Albert Museum. While other activists demanded that the UK return Indian artefacts that had been taken during the colonial period, Kamaladevi was 'quite happy that those things are there', where they could be cared for and remained 'open to world view'. They remained Indian wherever they were displayed. 'Even if they are in London,' she explained, 'they belong to the Indian people.' While embracing the opportunity to raise India's profile on the world stage, Kamaladevi remained committed to her vision of a crafts renaissance that would bring beauty into the homes of villagers throughout India. When it came to the development of crafts, she wanted to increase quality and quantity.[7]

It was to support both kinds of craft development that she founded the Crafts Council of India in 1964—the same year that the WCC was created. Unlike the AIHB, which was a government agency, the Crafts Council was an NGO driven by volunteer labour. Most of the key leaders were women, many of whom came to play a major role in Kamaladevi's life. When she visited Kanpur, Kamaladevi would stay in the home of Mrs Santosh Mahendrajit Singh, a dedicated supporter of the Crafts Council. The two women would take the family's Dodge to visit crafts-makers across Uttar Pradesh. In Chennai, Kamaladevi often stayed with Vijaya Rajan; in Calcutta with Ruby Palchoudhuri; in Nagpur with Leela Ramanathan. Kamaladevi was grateful for the hospitality and friendship of these younger women, all of whom were leaders in the Craft Council. In June 1963, she told delegates to the Far East Regional Workshop in Manila that 'women's response' to handicrafts had 'been the greatest' and that the consumption choices of women were key to the present and future of the sector. Her work with the Crafts Council demonstrates that it was also women volunteers who were at the forefront of the movement to protect and expand the making of Indian crafts.[8]

Her work with the Crafts Council took her on trips across India. In 1967, she travelled to Bastar, a remote district in the present-day state of Chhattisgarh, with another craft advocate, Mohana Ayyangar. Their goal was to help establish a craft exhibition. All of the hotel rooms had been booked by political figures, and so the two women were housed in a school. Heavy rains began to fall and the school flooded. According to Ayyangar, Kamaladevi remained stoic throughout the ordeal and insisted that they continue their work. On another occasion, Ayyangar recalled, Kamaladevi was delighted to attend a shadow puppet performance in a village in Andhra Pradesh. 'The performance took place under a tree; the accessories were only a couple of oil lamps and a big piece of cloth that was both the theatre and curtain,' Ayyangar remembered. 'We sat among the village people and enjoyed the show.'[9]

While developing the Crafts Council, Kamaladevi continued to use the AIHB as a tool to advance grassroots development—sometimes one artisan at a time. In Hyderabad, Kamaladevi was introduced to an artist who specialized in miniature Mughal-style paintings. The artist was finding it difficult to sell his work and was struggling to provide food for his family. Kamaladevi travelled with him to his village along with several AIHB field officers, whom she then instructed to provide the painter with raw materials and to send the finished work to the Shilpi Kendra exhibition hall in Bombay where the work would find eager buyers.[10]

Kamaladevi knew that such lone acts could never come close to ending the poverty of many of India's artisans. She continued to use her pen to advance knowledge of Indian crafts—and to argue for increased state support for the arts. In 1964 and 1965, she collaborated with Jasleen Dhamija to edit two issues of *MARG*, a journal run by Mulk Raj Anand. In the second issue, which was focused on the carpets of India, she wrote, 'It is a ridiculous irony that wherever objects of art wither and die people should sigh and grow nostalgic for feudal lords, the backbone of landed aristocracy, a system we strenuously fought and did our best to liquidate. Has all our struggle for democracy and socialism been in vain?' The key, in her opinion, was for 'the nation and its worthy leaders to offer a liberal and generous patronage to our great heritage of arts and crafts'. While many of her writings argued for such support, her main focus remained on celebrating the crafts themselves. In 1966, she published *Indian Carpets and Floor Coverings*, a sweeping overview that combined history, art analysis and technical details about carpet-making across different regions of India. Largely devoid of social critique, the book overflowed with the passion and attention to detail of a craft aficionado.[11]

Kamaladevi was not becoming apolitical, but her engagement with politics was changing and, in some ways, becoming less radical. Consider, for example, how she used her passion for crafts and other forms of art to advance solidarities between recently decolonized countries. In April 1966, she travelled to Dakar, Senegal, for the first World Festival of Negro Arts. She was selected as one of the few official invitees to the festival based on her ability to discuss, in the words of the deputy director general of UNESCO, '*les liens qui existent entre l'art indien et l'art africain*' ('the ties that exist between Indian art and African art'). Her flights were covered by UNESCO and her local expenses were paid by the Senegalese government, with the approval of the Senegalese president and pan-African visionary Léopold Sédar Senghor. In Dakar, she met a range of artists and intellectuals, including Langston Hughes who later remembered her as 'charming'. She gifted Hughes a copy of her book *Indian Handicrafts*, which he praised as 'lovely'. Hughes and Kamaladevi were both veteran socialists who had spent decades fighting racism and fascism throughout the world. It is possible that they discussed the ongoing struggle against White supremacy and other forms of inequity, but there is no evidence that Kamaladevi used her time in Senegal to link her cultural cosmopolitanism to the social and political challenges facing much of the postcolonial world.[12]

Kamaladevi continued to believe in the importance of Afro-Asian solidarity, but her focus on crafts increasingly narrowed her understanding of such solidarities. In June 1966, Kamaladevi travelled to Montreux, Switzerland, for another session of the WCC. Some 1,255 people from thirty-two countries attended. According to *Craft Horizons*, 'The most significant contribution was the clear demarcation of differences in the problems of craftsmanship among the developing nations of Asia, Africa, the Near East, and South America and those of Europe and North America.' Kamaladevi rejected the idea of India or other recently decolonized nations as less advanced than the so-called 'developed' world, but she was very aware of the unique challenges facing less wealthy regions.[13]

That summer, she travelled to Manila to receive the Ramon Magsaysay Award, a prestigious prize that honoured community activists and public servants in Asia. 'Among architects of modern India,' the award citation declared, 'few have been so broadly effective as Kamaladevi Chattopadhyay in challenging orthodoxy and then giving substance to the innovation.' In the process, 'she has helped realize the hopes of her countrymen that independence would be more than political, allowing them that added dimension of greater freedom in total life concerns'.

The award recognized 'her enduring creativity with handicrafts and cooperatives, as in politics, art and the theater'. In accepting the award, Kamaladevi declared that 'what fortifies and ensures long and effective service is the capacity to win and sustain love and confidence'. Service was the path to 'self realisation', she continued, 'because one can really find oneself only by serving one's fellow-beings.'[14]

In 1967, Kamaladevi founded the Delhi Crafts Council and the Crafts Council of West Bengal. That same year, she stepped down as chair of the AIHB. Kamaladevi believed in the power of government, but her dedication to the Crafts Councils as an independent movement of organizations marked a final stage in a long shift in her view of the government. She was returning to her role as a critic of the government and did not waste time before she put pressure on the Handicrafts Board, publicly demanding that it support a new crafts emporium in Bombay. Her status as an outsider also became more central to her role within the WCC, as she came to be increasingly critical of the Western-focused orientation of the organization and its disengagement from grassroots activism.[15]

Kamaldevi had long been an outsider. Forty years earlier, she had challenged gender norms by running for elected office. Thirty years earlier, she had brought her socialist politics into Congress meetings full of conservative elders, and she had travelled the world, harassed by the very government that should have protected her. Twenty years earlier, she had raised her voice against Partition and, in its wake, had challenged her own government to do more for refugees and all those whose struggles belied the promise of independence. In the 1950s and 1960s, Kamaladevi had continued to be an outsider in some ways, but she had become an insider in many others. Now, some sixty-five years old, Kamaladevi was returning to her roots as a rebel—at least in part. Her shifting relationship with the organizations she had helped to build would be incomplete, episodic and often painful.

~

In 1968, Kamaladevi travelled to Peru to attend a WCC conference. Eight hundred people from forty-five countries filled Huampani, a hotel located in Chaclacayo, a small town in the mountains outside of Lima. After the President of Peru opened the conference, Kamaladevi gave a short speech entitled 'Attributes of Traditional Craftsmanship'. She asserted that 'every human being is endowed with creative talent'. Poverty, inequality, racism, sexism and other forms of oppression robbed people of their ability to develop and enjoy that creative talent, but Kamaladevi did not dwell on such structural inequities in her speech. It remained unclear how a gathering of hundreds of artists and intellectuals, most of whom were among the cultural elite in their home countries, could contribute to extending opportunities to the masses. It also remained unclear how the work of the WCC intersected with the larger political struggles roiling much of the 'Third World'. A few months after he opened the WCC conference, the President of Peru was ousted in a military coup. Kamaladevi would be increasingly troubled by the limitations of the WCC, but in the late 1960s she continued to believe in the power of cross-cultural exchange as a path to a more just and unified world.[16]

Kamaladevi's closest friend in the world of crafts was Margaret Patch, the American woman who had written on the Indian design centres and who worked for many years on the staff of the WCC. On 23 September 1968, Kamaladevi wrote Patch from Los Angeles. She was about to spend two weeks in Mexico, where she would stay with the Indian ambassador's wife. She was then going to travel to New York, where she would stay at an apartment on Central Park West with Mrs Asoka Bhavnani, the wife of a successful Indian architect. Her letter demonstrates how Kamaladevi relied on the Indian diaspora to make her travels possible. It also revealed her growing closeness with Patch.[17]

In December 1968, Kamaladevi wrote Patch from her Delhi home at 2 Canning Lane. She explained to Patch that she had written Aileen Webb 'that if year after year the meetings are held in Europe and America, it becomes too much strain on people like me'. A few weeks later, she again wrote Patch in frustration. 'I am sorry that I have failed to convince the WCC of the validity of my pleas,' she wrote. 'In the opinion of some, Europe and north America may be very important. But they must also remember that regions like Asia, Africa, South America are the ones which are rich in Crafts. India alone has about a couple of million traditional Craftsmen who make their living by Crafts.' To be fair, the WCC had just met in Peru, and the organization would make efforts to spread its meeting sites to locations across the world. Kamaladevi had good reason to challenge the dominance of the United States and Europe within the WCC, but perhaps the more important divide separated the WCC from the social and political struggles of social activists throughout many of the less affluent countries of the world. Consider Kamaladevi's stay in Mexico City in 1968. Invited by the Mexican government as an official guest at the Olympics, she established ties with a range of arts organizations and spoke to women's groups, but there is no evidence that she protested the brutality with which the Mexican government had recently crushed a student movement.[18]

The political narrowness of her focus on crafts was matched by the cultural breadth with which she approached art of all kinds. While arguing against favouring Europe and North America, Kamaladevi rejected any dichotomy between the 'West' and the rest of the world. She appreciated the many ways cultural flows mocked such dichotomies. In July 1969, she sent Patch a sari and invited her to attend the WCC gathering in Delhi in November. 'Your knowledge and understanding of Asia, its people, and crafts would be a great asset,' she wrote Patch. Like the gift of the sari, her praise of Patch's knowledge of Asia demonstrated Kamaladevi's cosmopolitan vision of culture. For her part, Patch encouraged Kamaladevi to establish 'an independent and aggressive regional organization' that would serve as 'the voice of Asia to the Secretariat'.[19]

In 1969, Kamaladevi contributed to a UNESCO publication devoted to 'The Arts and Man'. Other contributors included the Italian architect Pier Luigi Nervi, the Argentinian poet Basilio Uribe, the American artist and futurist Buckminster Fuller and the violinist Yehudi Menuhin, who was born in the United States but spent much of his childhood in Europe. In her introduction to the book, D'Arcy Hayman wrote that 'a major objective of this publication is to give evidence in words and visual images of the way in which the arts embody the universal qualities of mankind as well as the endless individual and cultural differences which exist within the family of man'. The challenge of that dual objective—recognizing universality while respecting difference—echoed through many of the contributions. Yehudi Menuhin declared that through music 'we are welded into one group sharing each other's sense of sorrow or exhilaration'. The Russian filmmaker Grigory Kozintsev added that 'it is not only the artist who speaks to the audience but one people which speaks to another'. What remained unclear was how art could bring people together across cultural divides while also respecting their differences. In her essay entitled 'The Crafts: An Embodiment of the Great Folk Tradition', Kamaladevi drew upon her earlier writings, particularly *Indian Handicrafts* and her 1959 essay 'A Forceful Art', in order to outline her vision of crafts as 'a dynamic manifestation of man's endeavour to express universal human emotions and interests'. Kamaladevi linked the power of intercultural connections to the importance of democratizing access to art. 'Good taste and greater opportunity to live in intimacy with beauty should not be the privilege of the few,' she declared, 'but the common inheritance of all. This is what the crafts have to teach and offer us.'[20]

Like her selection as a vice president of the WCC, Kamaladevi's participation in the UNESCO forum reveals her international reputation. More important to her, however, was the respect she garnered from many crafts-makers within India. In 1969, she attended a crafts conference in Jaipur. The governor of Rajasthan was in attendance, as was the chairman of the handicrafts board and other dignitaries. 'As they were all entering into the arched portal,' one witness recalled, 'the craftspersons from either side of the decorated pathway surged forward, some with flower bouquets and a few with sandalwood garlands in hand, some with their own craft creations.' The VIPs seemed pleased by such a reception, but the artisans walked past them to garland Kamaladevi.[21]

In November 1969, Kamaladevi organized a WCC conference in New Delhi. The Crafts Councils of India and of Delhi played a key role in making the arrangements. According to Aileen Webb, this was the first conference 'ever held by Asian countries to discuss their joint craft problems'. The gathering, funded by the Rockefeller Foundation, brought delegates from twelve countries: Australia, Ceylon, Taiwan, India, Indonesia, Iran, Japan, South Korea, Malaysia, New Zealand, Sikkim and Thailand. Kamaladevi would later take issue with the inclusion of Australia and New Zealand within the WCC's definition of Asia, but she remained eager to collaborate with anyone—including those based in the West.[22]

These were years of nearly constant travel for Kamaladevi—both within India and abroad. In the fall of 1969, she toured Bhutan, where she advised the king on craft development and marketing. That winter, she took a monthlong trip through the south of India, then headed to Shantiniketan, in Bengal, where Rabindranath Tagore had established a school; there, she received a distinguished award. In the spring of 1970, she took another eight-week tour of southern India. That summer and fall, she travelled to London, Paris, Geneva and Iran, where she stayed with a friend, Farangis Yeganegi, who also combined a long career on behalf of women's rights with a strong dedication to crafts.[23]

Her many travels took a toll on Kamaladevi's health. Her hostess in Mexico City, Kamala Ratnam, later recalled that Kamaladevi 'looked extraordinarily old and weak' during that visit. Her weakness did not prevent her from working, however. 'The speed and force with which she worked,' Ratnam recalled of Kamaladevi, was 'astonishing'.[24]

In December 1970, Kamaladevi became acutely ill, and had surgery to remove what she called 'an abscess on the bone'. She wrote Patch, 'It has really been a very bad experience.' Her health continued to trouble her into the new year. On 29 March, she told Patch, 'I told you I had not been well the last three months. I seem to get better, then get a set-back.' Her health had improved enough by the fall that she was able to travel to India's eastern border for ten days to continue what she called her 'long wanderings' in search of crafts to protect and promote. She remained concerned that the WCC was not providing sufficient resources for Asian countries. 'Personally,' she wrote Patch, 'I am rather diffident about any progress in the Asian Region unless these countries feel they are getting something out of this.'[25]

In May 1972, Kamaladevi was in a car accident in Delhi. Thrown from her car, she fractured her left arm. Her hand and fingers were crushed. Her injuries kept her bedridden for months. 'These weeks of continuous pain have been like a nightmare,' she wrote Patch in July. 'But I am now on my way to recovery.' In August, she was well enough to travel to Istanbul for the fifth international meeting of the WCC. At a seaside resort, she mingled with some 240 representatives from thirty-nine countries. But her injuries had not fully healed. In April 1973, she was still visiting the hospital for treatment.[26]

When she was not travelling, Kamaladevi spent much of her time writing. In 1973, she completed two manuscripts, one on Indian crafts and the other on Indian embroidery, and also worked on a third book on indigenous 'tribal' cultures within India. 'I have worked very, very hard—start at 4am and work through the day,' she wrote Patch.[27]

On 31 October 1973, Kamaladevi inaugurated the nineteenth National Exhibition of Art at the Lalit Kala Akademi (National Academy of Art) in Delhi. Some 292 works by 206 artists from across India had been selected for exhibition. Kamaladevi linked her passion for crafts with her commitment to art of many kinds. She often noted that many Indian languages used the same word for both arts and crafts.[28]

In addition to her intellectual labour, she also worked to support the Crafts Councils. In 1973, the councils sought help from the AIHB in preparing the Indian contribution to the upcoming WCC exhibition in Toronto. 'I saw the minister over 8 months ago and got his o.k.,' Kamaladevi wrote Patch. 'Nevertheless, there were continuous delays at every stage,' she fumed. 'It is so frustrating,' she concluded. It must have been especially frustrating given that she had once controlled the AIHB.[29]

The WCC was similarly disappointing her. In June 1974, Kamaladevi was in Toronto for the tenth-anniversary conference of the WCC. *Craft Horizons* printed a photo of Kamaladevi with the Australian potter Marea Gazzard, and celebrated the size and breadth of the event, with some 1,200 people from fifty-six countries in attendance. Kamaladevi's doubts about the true reach of the organization had grown stronger. Aileen Webb arranged for Kamaladevi to have a single room, and the WCC covered all of her expenses during the conference. Yet while the organization supported Kamaladevi personally, it remained unclear what it was doing to support crafts-makers in India, the vast majority of whom could not afford to travel to such gatherings.[30]

After the Toronto gathering, Kamaladevi headed to the US, where she planned to spend time at the country home that Rama and Doris maintained in the small town of Hoosick in upstate New York. She was thrilled to see her grandchildren, but she could not stay long. In July, she spent two weeks in California visiting crafts-makers. A week of that time was spent in Ojai with the potter Beatrice Wood. In Toronto, Kamaladevi had stayed next door to Wood and the two women had become close. Theirs had not always been an easy relationship. The two women had met some ten years earlier. Wood later recalled this meeting with Kamaladevi. 'Although India meant nothing to me then,' Wood wrote, 'I wore a spectacular turban.' Kamaladevi did not seem to approve this sartorial fancy. 'Opposite me at table sat a middle-aged, stern faced Indian woman wearing a crimson sari,' Wood recalled. 'I smiled, but she did not smile back. I decided it was the turban.' Later, Kamaladevi visited Wood's exhibition room. According to Wood, Kamaladevi exclaimed, 'This is the most beautiful pottery I have seen. We must have it in India. Would you like to come to India?' Wood visited India in the winter of 1961–62. Her tour, arranged by the AIHB under Kamaladevi's direction, took her to fourteen cities. She visited Kamaladevi in her office and 'again found her as unresponsive as a sphinx'. Determined to break through Kamaladevi's stern demeanour, Wood devised a plan. The next time she saw Kamaladevi she was ready: 'I threw my arms around her, held her tight and told her how grateful I was for what she had done for me.' According to Wood, Kamaladevi 'melted, and from that moment became my friend. I soon discovered that she was a truly remarkable person.' In 1965, Kamaladevi returned to Ojai and again visited with Wood, who expressed a desire to return to India to 'photograph folk art'. Kamaladevi arranged for the visit through the Handicrafts Board. By the time they met again in 1974, they had become old friends.[31]

During her visit with Wood in Ojai, Kamaladevi was interviewed by a local reporter. Asked about the purpose of the WCC, she replied that crafts 'have an essential role to play in full human development. They are the expression of the creative urge in human beings.' The reporter asked, 'Are you an artist or craftsman?' 'I learned weaving,' Kamaladevi replied, 'but never kept it up. I was on stage at one time and loved it. I am still closely connected with the theatre movement, organizing programs, experimental work and training.' She could have added that her 'creative urge' had long infused all of her work. Kamaladevi approached her crafts advocacy as she had political movements in colonial India—with the vision and imagination of an artist.[32]

While on the west coast, Kamaladevi also spent a day with the artist and curator Edith Wyle in Los Angeles. In 1965, Wyle had founded an innovative art gallery and café, The Egg and the Eye, on Wiltshire Boulevard. Edith hosted a luncheon at The Egg and the Eye, where Kamaladevi met Kirpal Singh, a crafts-maker from Jaipur. Always eager to support an artist, Kamaladevi also met with the Indian consul in Los Angeles about gaining government support for Singh. She then flew to San Francisco and from there to New York, where she stayed with her niece Asha Puthli at 145 Central Park West. Kamaladevi had arranged for Puthli to audition with Martha Graham. After securing a dance scholarship from Graham, Puthli went on to earn fame as a jazz singer. It was as a successful musician that Puthli picked up her aunt Kamaladevi from the airport in a limousine. Kamaladevi was obviously amused yet tried to maintain her usual stern demeanour, and chastised Puthli for going to such expense.[33]

From New York, Kamaladevi flew to London and then to eastern Europe and Russia. From Budapest, she wrote Patch about her time in Moscow, where she had met with Yekaterina Furtseva, the Soviet culture minister, who had expressed scepticism regarding the WCC. Furtseva told Kamaladevi that the organization did not do 'any concrete work'. Kamaladevi told Patch that the Soviets were 'not in touch and not fully informed', but she shared Furtseva's criticism of the WCC. Rather than sit in conference rooms talking about crafts, Kamaladevi preferred to travel to rural areas to meet directly with artisans. 'This visit here has been inspiring and most instructive,' she wrote Patch from Hungary. 'The people are delightfully friendly and kindly.'[34]

In February 1975, she settled in Bombay to spend a month with her grandchildren. Her health was not good, and she found time with family the best form of recuperation. She did not stay long. In May, she was in Sydney, from where she wrote Patch about her health problems. 'I have been ill off and on for months,' she explained. 'Every relapse leaves me weaker and more shaken. So I get exhausted.' She was also frustrated by the direction of the WCC, as well as the challenge of advancing real change within India. She continued to believe in the power of grassroots activism and of cooperatives in particular. In a paper she prepared for the International Cooperative Alliance on 'Women's Participation in Industrial Co-operatives in India', she wrote about the power of cooperatives to 'maintain the dignity of artisans' by endowing them with 'equal rights and duties' and including them as 'Joint Partners of the Enterprise'. But the cooperative movement in India had stalled, and the government seemed uninterested in real change. The prime minister, Indira Gandhi, claimed to be a socialist yet seemed more interested in concentrating power in the state than in creating the kind of grassroots transformation Kamaladevi had long associated with socialism.[35]

In June 1975, the prime minister suspended the Constitution and declared a state of Emergency. Despite Kamaladevi's close ties with Indira's father, Jawaharlal Nehru, she had never been close to Indira herself. During a visit to the Cottage Industries Emporium, Indira once chose to 'walk right past' Kamaladevi, treating her as if she did not exist. Kamaladevi later returned the favour during another official visit, sending an assistant to 'greet her and show her around' instead of going herself. In the midst of the Emergency, much more was at stake than good manners. Indian democracy was facing its greatest threat since the struggle for Independence. The opposition to the Emergency rallied around Jayaprakash Narayan, who strove to mobilize a grassroots revolt against Indira Gandhi's authoritarian rule. Kamaladevi later recalled her sympathy for JP's 'total revolution', which Kamaladevi called the 'Unfinished Revolution'. As she and JP both saw it, the problems facing India went much deeper than Indira Gandhi. In an edited volume on the status of women that was published in 1975, just as the emergency was proclaimed, Kamaladevi lamented 'that the political leadership which had so long been denied power with prosperity, who had for decades been ruled by vigour generated by Gandhiji and an idealism which a long line of venerated leaders had inspired, now felt free to indulge their petty ambitions and often a thwarted greed'. This rot had begun soon after Independence. 'Gandhiji with his unerring intuition expanded and finalized the constructive programme to provide content and substance to the idea of a free country,' she wrote. But while 'Nehru talked of the great new adventures, most others who were now the rulers of the country were content with a tidy income and a smug abode'.[36]

Kamaladevi did not hide her disdain for the state of Indian politics, but there is little evidence that she dedicated much time to resisting the Emergency. This could be explained as a result of her age, but JP was just as old as Kamaladevi, and it seems strange that a radical like Kamaladevi would continue to focus on crafts development while the democracy she had spent decades struggling to achieve was facing an existential threat. A better explanation for Kamaladevi's inaction during the emergency is her ill health. On 23 August 1975, Kamaladevi wrote Margaret Patch from Bangalore where she was recuperating from an illness. 'I have really been ill since the beginning of the year,' she wrote, 'the last three months just confined to my room, mostly in bed. I almost feared I was going to be invalid for life.' Kamaladevi was 'feeling very much better but not quite normal yet'. She had been struggling with anaemia and her haemoglobin counts remained low. 'I tire very easily,' she wrote Patch, 'so have to go slow.' Her ill health helps to explain her absence from the resistance to the Emergency.[37]

She was also deeply enmeshed in family life—the family life she had long missed. Her decision to relocate to Bangalore was driven, in part, by climate. 'I knew I could not face Delhi summer,' Kamaladevi wrote

Patch. But the most important factor was the prospect of spending time with her grandchildren and with Doris, who had 'fixed up' the Bangalore home Kamaladevi would be staying in and who also 'did all the moving,' according to Kamaladevi. 'These three months I have had here in Bangalore have been relaxing,' Kamaladevi wrote Patch. 'The climate is beautiful,' she added, 'we are quite out of the city, quiet and restful. We have an independent bungalow, plenty of room and a garden.' Kamaladevi's use of 'we' is telling. This was a family home, one it would have been very hard for her to leave in order to join a political struggle that might very well have returned her to an Indian prison.[38]

Kamaladevi's Bangalore home was full of art and children. The dining table would often become a studio space, especially when a local expert on natural dyes would arrive with a variety of samples. Kamaladevi would give the grandchildren wood blocks and white cloth and let them create. According to Arundhati Chattopadhaya, 'Even our dog Velvet would step in the dye sometimes and leave colourful pawmarks all over the house.' The grandchildren loved to play rock music. At first, Doris worried they were bothering Kamaladevi. But the august grandmother emerged from her room during an especially loud session and, instead of asking them to turn off the music, requested that the volume be raised so that she could hear it better. 'Kamaladevi looked extremely happy when I visited her in her house in Bangalore,' the feminist economist Devaki Jain later recalled. 'She was back in her "homeland"—Kannada speaking, jasmine flowers in the hair of women of every class, rangoli in the front yard of homes—and all the flavours of Karnataka were present.' And she was with family. Along with Doris and the grandchildren, Kamaladevi's Bangalore home also hosted Seetha, also known as Sitamma, who had long ago served as Rama's nanny before eloping with Harin. According to Arundhati Chattopadhaya, 'Sitamma was a major part of the Chattopadhyaya household.' When Kamaladevi divorced Harin, she had urged him to marry Seetha. 'The injustice you have been doing to us,' she told him, 'you can't do the same with that orphan and helpless girl.' Harin did eventually marry Seetha, but his infidelities continued and eventually they separated. According to Kamaladevi, it was Harin's treatment of Seetha that eventually led Rama to stop taking his father's side and to stop blaming his mother for the divorce. It was not, however, Rama's affection for Seetha that led Kamaladevi to welcome her once again into her home. Indeed, at this point in Kamaladevi's life her ties with Rama had frayed once again after he divorced Doris and married a woman who, in a strange twist, happened to be the daughter of one of Harin's former lovers. Harin himself moved into her home and soon father and son were once again awkwardly arrayed in tension with Kamaladevi, who continued to embrace Doris. Nothing testifies more clearly to Kamaladevi's deep solidarity with other women than the way she embraced both Sitamma and Doris. If her support for Sitamma demonstrates her ability to forgive the past, her love for Doris reveals her ability to remain true to her own convictions. Her tolerance and her strength were both embodied in the family she fostered and the home she helped to build.[39]

Kamaladevi had many places she might consider home. Although she continued to spend long periods in Delhi, she increasingly felt drawn to the south, usually staying in Bombay or Bangalore but at times also visiting Mangalore. She once described Mangalore as a 'secluded little spot, unknown and unobserved by the usual traveller', like a 'lovely fawn lingering shyly' in the shadows of 'mighty mountains'. She told Gopalkrishna Gandhi that 'Mangalore is the most beautiful patch on Indian earth', but there is no evidence that she ever considered moving back to her ancestral grounds. For one thing, she was able to bring some of Mangalore with her wherever she went. Her love for the Konkani language and her native cuisine was renowned—and she made a point of partaking of both as often as she could.[40]

Kamaladevi still had too much of what Nehru had called 'the wanderlust' to settle anywhere—especially somewhere as provincial as Mangalore. As she entered her seventh decade, she continued to travel—and not just within India. Her voyages revealed the resilience of her body (despite her physical ailments) and the resilience of her vision for India and the world (despite the many disappointments of postcolonial politics). It would be a mistake, however, to overlook the degree to which she struggled with the burdens of ageing and with her many disappointments—from the failures of the Indian government to the failures of her former husband and of her son. It would also be a mistake to overlook the degree to which she had changed. The young Kamaladevi would not, for example, have let illness or the allures of home keep her from protesting the Emergency. India was no longer the same country, and she was no longer the same person, but the fire of her youth still burned—and she had a few more rebellions to claim as her own.

~

In 1974, Lord David Eccles, an English politician who had served as minister for education as well as minister for the arts, became president of the WCC. Kamaladevi was not happy. She complained to Patch that Eccles 'talked too much wasting time, mostly about himself, the posts he held, achievements etc'. Although he had some 'feeling for Crafts', he was 'ignorant about Craftsmen and their life'. Kamaladevi was especially concerned that Eccles would exacerbate the disconnect between the WCC and 'the current situation in practically all Asian and African States, barring India & Japan', where there were '*no* Craft Councils at all'. When the WCC put out a call for a conference, Kamaladevi explained that 'representatives are sent by Govt. depts. who are administrative men. The actual workers never get a chance.' 'The WCC is meant to be a *movement*,' she declared, not an excuse for government bureaucrats to attend lavish gatherings. Even the AIHB, the organization she spent over a decade building, had become 'completely export oriented' and so focused on 'foreign markets' that it neglected the preservation and development of crafts within India.[41]

Frustrated with the direction of the WCC and the AIHB, Kamaladevi threw her energy into the Crafts Councils. Seventy-two years old and not in great health, she did not have as much energy as she would have liked. On 30 December 1975, she wrote Patch from Madras. 'My health is not too good and I have to often slow down,' she explained. She was busy helping to relocate the headquarters of the Crafts Councils to Madras, where the organization would have 'permanency and stability'.

Recognizing her age and increasingly limited energy, she had begun to devolve leadership to a new generation.[42]

Her health did not prevent her from travelling. In the summer of 1976 she was back in the US, where she spent time in Texas and Vermont before visiting with Webb in New York. During her early trips to the US, she had been a sharp critic of American inequality and racism. Now, her travels were focused on crafts and she largely avoided discussing social or political struggles. The same was true of many of her foreign journeys. In September, she was in Teheran, where she had 'the most interesting and pleasant visit as the guest of the Iran Govt'. A young Kamaladevi might have challenged the autocratic nature of the Iranian government. Instead, she celebrated Iranian craft development. From Teheran, she travelled to Moscow and Central Asia where again she focused on crafts rather than discussing the broader social and political situation in her host countries or in India.[43]

It was not as if Kamaladevi had lost her critical edge or her belief in the importance of politics, broadly understood. Rather, she had focused her energy in the direction of crafts development—and what she saw as the failures of craft advocates and of the WCC in particular. In September 1977, she wrote Patch that 'the WCC seems to move further and further away from me'. At the previous meeting of the WCC in Mexico, India had been removed from the inner circle of the WCC's leadership. 'Probably India is about the richest in Crafts,' she wrote, 'but in recent years India has counted for little in the Councils of the WCC. Now we are fully out.'[44]

Her view of craft organizations within India was equally bleak. In 1977, she published a piece on 'The Ecology of Folk Art' for *Indian Horizons.* She called the early 1950s 'the heyday of the Indian crafts', a time during which 'the buoyancy surging from the coming of freedom enveloped them' and crafts 'became marks of freedom'. By the late 1960s, however, crafts had been 'turned into commercial commodities, mere instruments for making money'. In Kamaladevi's view, 'those interested in crafts either run boutiques or export these "goods". Gone is the old concept of creative work being an act of self realisation.' She lamented the division between 'fine art' and 'folk craft'. 'As the foreign influence on aesthetics began to wax,' she explained, 'this unnatural division so alien to our culture began to get more and more accentuated.' Even while she criticized the West for dividing arts and crafts, she found hope in trends that originated there. In particular, she celebrated the growing interest in 'folk art'. 'Even though it may have been generated by a wave from the West,' she added, 'it is nevertheless a very welcome and encouraging sign.'[45]

Kamaladevi's belief in 'folk art' was linked to her respect for rural traditions and, in particular, for the crafts of India's indigenous peoples. In 1978, she published a wide-ranging book called *Tribalism in India*. The book contained nineteen chapters, each focused on a particular indigenous community, from the Bhils of Gujarat and Rajasthan to the Nagas of Nagaland to the Kurichyas of Kerala. While recognizing diversity among these communities, she asserted that 'the basic affinities are far more impressive and convincing than the less important dissimilarities'. She also saw commonality between adivasi peoples and other Indians. 'As I came to know the tribals,' she wrote, 'I began to realize that there is basically not so much difference between them and us. A most fundamental tie is the universal concept of godhead and divinity and the belief that there is life in everything.' While recognizing such commonality, Kamaladevi often distinguished adivasis from other Indians, as when she lauded indigenous peoples for managing to 'preserve and cherish some of the elements and values that have faded out of our lives'. She celebrated tribal culture as 'an integrated all-pervading element' and contrasted such an organic culture with 'our concepts of culture' that are 'exclusive and the privilege of a few'. She discussed the widespread theft of tribal land, British policies that labelled certain peoples as 'criminal tribes', the destruction caused by liquor dealers, and the poverty created as a result of all of these assaults on tribal life. Overall, however, hers was a celebration of tribal cultures.[46]

Her interest in tribal cultures was shaped by the anthropologist Verrier Elwin, who Kamaladevi called 'one of the most lovable persons I had known'. In 1962, she toured Nagaland as chair of the Handicrafts Board and organized an exhibition of 'Tribal Crafts of the North East' that Elwin opened. Her views on adivasi cultures were also shaped by the anthropologist and social worker B.K. Roy Burman. In a tribute to Roy Burman, Kamaladevi wrote that 'those who are not familiar with the distant villages, assume that these inhabitants are simple'. She noted that the publisher of *Tribalism in India* urged her to avoid the term 'tribal', as 'he said I had pictured them as "civilised beings". For, to him tribals were wild people.' Her own approach to tribal cultures did not fully escape the 'noble savage' myth, as she made when describing the 'tribal artist' a few years later. 'Continuing to be an intimate child of nature,' she wrote, 'he was conditioned to following certain natural laws, which taught techniques and guided processes, sensitivity to right proportions and balances which nature so exuberantly portrays'. Her praise for tribal art was sincere and vivid. 'One gazes with wonder on the objects the tribals turn out,' she wrote. 'Their products vibrate with life, as though the maker infused some of his own self into his creation.' Yet by reproducing patronizing stereotypes, Kamaladevi risked undermining indigenous claims for cultural and political sovereignty. Her celebration of tribal culture obscured the degree to which the marketing and consumption of tribal art failed to benefit the communities in which that art was produced.[47]

Despite the poverty and state-sanctioned violence that plagued many adivasi communities—and much of rural India in the late 1970s and early 1980s—Kamaladevi maintained her belief in the social and economic potential of Indian crafts. It helped that her relations with the AIHB improved, largely as a result of a shift in the leadership of the board. Celebrating new possibilities for collaboration between the AIHB and the Crafts Councils, Kamaladevi wrote Patch, 'We are working out a programme of fellowships, exchange of craftsmen, periodical workshops and to make the Technical Development Centre we have into a regional one.' While Kamaladevi's connections to the AIHB grew stronger, her relations with the WCC remained strained. At first, she planned to skip the WCC gathering planned for Kyoto in the fall of 1978. 'I do not propose to go to Japan,' she wrote Patch. 'In fact, at the moment I have no desire whatsoever to involve myself with the world body.' In August

1978, she complained again that the WCC was 'so West dominated'. But after the Indian government decided to fund her trip, she decided to travel to Kyoto after all, and left in early September. The event attracted 2,400 people from fifty-four countries. For Kamaladevi, it was the chance to reconnect with old friends, and especially with Patch, that made the journey worthwhile.[48]

On 13 December 1978, Kamaladevi wrote Patch, 'I feel very hesitant and extremely diffident about these meetings. So far as our work here, or our problems here are concerned, they do not mean a thing and this continued domination of the west is very disheartening.' In Kyoto, she had been elected the vice president for Asia of the WCC. She was sceptical that she would be given the power necessary to pull the organization away from its long-standing domination by Europe and the United States. Things did not start off well. She wrote Patch that she had 'received three letters from Sydney telling me how to run the Asian Regional Office'. Such neo-imperial overreach was rooted in old stereotypes about the backwardness of Asia. 'The young lady who came was also trying to show her superiority and knowledge,' Kamaladevi told Patch. 'One of the first things she asked was if we had such a thing as toothpaste in this country.'[49]

Kamaladevi's deep concerns regarding the WCC coincided with a growing awareness of the challenges of travel given her health and age. Still, she did not give up on the WCC and she did not stop travelling. A month after attending the WCC gathering in Kyoto, she was in Greece conducting a 'comparative study of the arts and crafts of Greece and India'. She loved connecting with crafts-makers but wrote Patch that 'travel has become so difficult'. In January 1979, she visited the US again, staying with Patch in Florida and traveling to Riverdale, New York, for a meeting of the WCC directors. She then launched an ambitious tour through Asia on behalf of the WCC, a tour that included stops in Sri Lanka, the Philippines, Hong Kong, South Korea and Fiji. 'I think one can achieve something by working in one's own little sphere,' she wrote Patch, 'only mine has grown to be very large at the moment.'[50]

Kamaladevi's tour reinforced her concerns about the dominance of the WCC by government bureaucrats. She wrote Patch, 'These governments gladly pay the affiliation fee because they like to belong to an international organization and some of the officials are happy to get the opportunity to attend an international conference.' What Kamaladevi envisioned as a social movement to transform art and economic opportunities had become an opportunity for government officials and wealthy collectors to jet off to lavish conferences. 'A movement can only be built up and strengthened by voluntary non-government bodies,' she concluded.[51]

Kamaladevi strove to foster such a movement within Asia. As the WCC's vice president for Asia, she focused, in her words, 'on the need for closer cultural contacts, particularly collaboration and cooperation between the craftsmen of the various *Asian* countries, to build up a more closely knit Craft Community, and bridge the isolation of the long colonial period'. She rejected 'looking to the west for inspiration and models for what is vaguely called development'. She noted that 'those countries which are less mechanically industrialised are loosely termed "underdeveloped" but have often the richest and best developed crafts and should be accepted as leaders in the larger cultural world'. She stressed that 'national entities like Craft Councils are very necessary for they alone can build up national and international craft movements as distinct from institutions and establishments'. Kamaladevi told Patch that serving as vice president for Asia was 'the toughest job I ever did but it has shown promise and some results'. Those results included the Asian Assembly, held in Manila, in which, according to Kamaladevi 'for the first time the delegates seemed aware of the identity of their region, their heritage, and the need to give a proper direction to it'.[52]

The highlight of her time as vice president for Asia was a workshop she organized in Bangalore at the Design and Development Centre of the AIHB. Held from 23 April–4 May, 1980, the workshop included some seventy-one crafts-makers from sixteen countries across Asia and the Middle East. Compared to the size of the WCC gatherings, this workshop was tiny. Kamaladevi celebrated the intimacy of connections between the artisans, and explicitly rejected formal conference proceedings. When she travelled to Bangkok to get funding from various UN agencies, she later explained, 'it was difficult for them to understand the need for a gathering in which formal speech and clever debates would have no part at all. Seminars, Symposia, Conferences—yes. But simply for a lot of craftsmen made to work together, without so much as a raised stadium or a mike?' She refused to give up, and the costs were eventually covered by the AIHB as well as a variety of UN agencies including the International Labour Organization, the Economic and Social Commission for Asia and Pacific, and the Asian and Pacific Centre for Women and Development.[53]

The workshop began with 'a ceremonial dance performance' involving a Nandi Dhwaja, 'a 30 feet tall decorated pole, embellished with gold- and silver-gilted symbolic figurines'. After the performance, the delegates began producing art. According to one witness, 'Kalamkari panels were taking shape effortlessly; wooden pieces changed into deities; sawdust and rags took on the shapes of gorgeously clad kings and queens; charming shapes got conjured up from clay between the moving fingers of potters; bland leather pieces became epic characters; the loom moved majestically in centimetres, revealing complicated designs.' Kamaladevi celebrated the transnational and transcultural links fostered by acts of co-creation. It was an 'intriguing sight', she wrote, to see 'the Indian veteran, Parmeshwarachar, scooping out elegant figures from sandalwood along with Edith Ratna of Indonesia.' If only all WCC gatherings were so focused on the actual production of crafts, and so inclusive of crafts-makers from beyond Europe and the United States, Kamaladevi might have chosen to remain with the organization.[54]

A few months earlier, in February 1980, Kamaladevi had written to Patch from London after attending a WCC executive meeting in Paris. 'It was an even more distressing affair than the last year's New York one,' Kamaladevi wrote. 'I raised the need for making the WCC a real world body with office bearers from various regions. But nobody supported me.' She decided to resign as vice president for Asia. The workshop in Bangalore would serve as a culmination of the many years of hard work she had given the WCC. Later that year, the Australian potter Marea Gazzard would become the president of the WCC. Kamaladevi and

Gazzard had clashed repeatedly, often over what Kamaladevi saw as Gazzard's refusal to grant autonomy to the Asian Secretariat. Gazzard's presidency served as the proverbial final straw, and Kamaladevi severed her ties with the WCC permanently.[55]

Such a separation must have been painful. Kamaladevi had dedicated much of the previous sixteen years to supporting the WCC and helping the organization grow. Like the AIWC, Faridabad, the ICU, the Socialist Party and many other organizations and initiatives she helped to establish over the years, the WCC had thrived and had given Kamaladevi many reasons to feel proud of her efforts. Her passion was not, however, directed at the WCC as an organization. Kamaladevi was an institution-builder but her fidelity was not to the institution but to the cause and to the people touched by that cause. 'She always cared deeply about craftspeople,' the crafts advocate Laila Tyabji recalled. 'For her, they always came first.'[56]

Kamaladevi was aware that she had not been able to help crafts-makers nearly as much as she had wanted. Her Gandhian dream of a radical realignment of the Indian economy was still but a dream, and the majority of craftsmakers remained poor and marginalized. The scholar Dia Da Costa has criticized the 'flattering self-image of humanitarian nationalist elites' that was achieved 'by projecting employment generation as the chief outcome of artisanal modernization, even though artisanal exploitation remained its foundation'. Crafts themselves became regarded all too often as the kind of cheap commodities Kamaladevi had hoped to displace. 'Although Chattopadhyay was loath to commercialize craft,' Da Costa concluded, 'craft markets had just that effect.' As we have seen, Kamaladevi saw national and international markets as necessary given the limited purchasing power of many Indians and of rural Indians in particular. Her ambivalent relationship with capitalism and the market economy was a kind of compromise, bound up with a larger awareness that crafts development—like true swaraj—remained a distant goal.[57]

Kamaladevi never abandoned her hope that the Indian economy could be radically transformed, but in the meantime she wanted to support and empower crafts-makers—as many as she could and as much as she could. One could write many pages describing the impact Kamaladevi had on specific artisans, such as Jonnalagadda Gurappa Chetty, the kalamkari artist, or Kallu Hafiz, the master weaver. Many of Kamaladevi's colleagues have written about her remarkable generosity. Consider this account from Jasleen Dhamija:

> When a master-craftsman of the Blue Pottery lay ill from tuberculosis, it was [Kamaladevi] who arranged for his hospitalisation. When a musician broke his violin and did not have the money to buy another, she paid for it. When a Kalamkari man was afraid of ruining the cloth because he had not worked for 30 years, she paid for the cloth. When Shamadas Sengupta's wife was seriously ill, she sent money to him, and when I had nowhere to go she offered me shelter.

Another supporter of crafts recalled, 'When my wife was lying sick in Bangalore and my finances had dwindled, Smt. Chattopadhyay visited our residence and left me an envelope full of banknotes for my wife's treatment.' In addition to such direct acts of generosity, many of Kamaladevi's administrative efforts were driven by a deep concern for crafts-makers, a concern that fuelled her determination in the face of bureaucratic obstacles. It took Kamaladevi three years of determined effort to establish an official award for craftsmakers, for example, but she refused to give up.[58]

Not long after the Emergency, the designer Rajeev Sethi approached Kamaladevi to help organize the 'Bhule Bisre Kalakaar Cooperative' or 'Forgotten Artists Cooperative' for the hundreds of street performers and crafts-makers who had been evicted by 'slum clearance' initiatives. She immediately agreed. On 1 June 1978, Kamaladevi hosted a celebration at her home at which hundreds of street artists gathered to celebrate the cooperative. Sethi once asked Kamaladevi what originally drew her to arts and handicrafts: was it 'politically motivated' or more a matter of 'aesthetic feeling'? She replied that it was 'very definitely aesthetic feeling'. It was 'the beauty and the warmth that they brought into our life'. Yet as she continued to answer the question, she blurred the distinction between the aesthetic and the political. She was moved, she recalled, by a 'sense of pride in things made in India', a sense that had been inspired by 'the great swadeshi movement'. She noted that Gandhi had a profound impact on her appreciation for the handmade. While she made clear that crafts 'have an aesthetic value of their own', her understanding of that value was steeped in the expansive conception of politics she had long championed.[59]

In 1980, the Government of India published *India's Craft Tradition*, a book in which Kamaladevi drew upon several of her earlier writings to provide an overview of the history and variety of crafts in India. 'Handicrafts are valuable not merely as beautiful heritage,' she wrote, 'but because we need to live with them, touch them, feel them, use them, have intimate communion with them, so that our life is enriched by their grace.' Like *India's Craft Tradition*, many of her later works drew on her earlier writings. Consider the essay 'Crafts and the Future', which was published by the London-based arts journal *Temenos* and republished in the *India International Centre Quarterly* in 1984. The essay was largely based on her 1969 UNESCO essay, which itself drew heavily on her book *Indian Handicrafts*. Such intellectual recycling reveals the fact that Kamaladevi was busy and wanted to communicate her message to as many people as possible. It also testifies to the fact that, at least when it came to crafts, her basic message remained largely the same throughout her life.[60]

Her approach to craft was shaped by her rejection of three dichotomies: utility versus beauty, local versus global and traditional versus modern. Her rejection of these dichotomies often overlapped, as can be seen in her relationship to technology. She was deeply troubled by automation. 'Often when a machine takes over the tasks of thousands of men, these men find themselves uprooted,' she wrote in 1947, 'with no props to maintain themselves or their families, with complete loss of their social position and prestige.' While recognizing the dangers of mechanization, however, Kamaladevi did not reject all technological change. 'To frown upon the aeroplane and sing of the creaking country cart is not even poetic justice,' she wrote. 'It is sheer conservative sectarianism. The plough was as outlandish an innovation once as the tractor is today. To ignore man's inexhaustible genius for forging new implements is to ignore the very laws of social change, and no true artist can afford to do that.' From her typewriter to cordless phones (which she greatly enjoyed), Kamaladevi made the most of technology. In her eighties, she took pleasure in asking her grandson questions about sound-recording technologies.[61]

Kamaladevi was not opposed to changing traditions to fit changing needs. She encouraged Madhubani painters to shift from the traditional practice of painting on walls and floors to painting on paper and cloth so that the artwork could be sold. In Peru in 1968, she asserted that crafts 'cannot become fossilized into rigidity, because the crafts must reflect the common experiences of the community. Change must occur to reflect the flow and movement of life itself. To be meaningful, tradition must be a live force.' Such a dynamic approach to the relationship between the past and the future shaped how Kamaladevi approached the evolution of all art—and of herself too. As she aged, she embraced her role as an elder but continued to value the ideas and energy of younger generations—and to see herself as an innovator, a visionary and a dreamer. The question remained, however, whether a new generation of radical activists would see in Kamaladevi a fellow freedom fighter or a symbol of the establishment and whether India still had room for Kamaladevi's dreams.[62]

9

Homecoming

IN THE SUMMER OF 1987, KAMALADEVI TRAVELLED TO PUNE AS THE guest of honour at the diamond jubilee celebration of the All-India Women's Conference. Sixty years had passed since, at the age of twenty-four, she had been selected as the organizing secretary of the AIWC. Now she was eighty-four. India had changed in countless ways, and so had Kamaladevi, but her distaste for hierarchy had remained the same, as had her rebellious streak. Offered a seat of honour on the stage at the front of the room, she refused. 'I have never gone on to a raised platform,' she explained. 'It connotes hierarchy, distance.' The chief minister of Maharashtra was waiting on the stage. Next to him, a special seat had been prepared for Kamaladevi. She sat down in the last row of the hall and refused to move. The organizers of the event entreated her to come forward and asked her to light a ceremonial lamp to inaugurate the occasion. Still, she would not move. Realizing they could not change her mind, the organizers carried the lamp to the back of the hall, where Kamaladevi happily lit the flame.[1]

She gave her speech from the back of the hall too. According to the *Times of India*, she lamented that the women's movement had created a 'sex war' by attacking men. 'Men should not be treated as enemies of women,' she told the AIWC gathering. She had made similar arguments ever since the founding of the AIWC six decades earlier. While she remained steadfast in her opposition to what she saw as Western feminism, the women's movement in India had continued to evolve. By the 1980s, Kamaladevi was seen as a historical figure by a younger generation of feminists, many of whom were critical of her approach to women's rights. According to Devaki Jain, 'Kamaladevi was considered old-fashioned, if not outright disdained, by my feminist colleagues, particularly those in the left-leaning Women's Studies movement, who saw deep divides between what was considered revolutionary, as opposed to merely reformist, and deemed the ideas of a previous generation of women's rights activists reformist.'[2]

Kamaladevi's writings seemed dated in the eyes of many younger feminists. In June 1972, she published an essay entitled 'Some Thoughts on Women's Education'. 'If education is the acquisition of valuable knowledge and the building up of a personality,' she wrote, 'it should be open equally to women along with men, for they too are human beings and entitled to what is termed as our birth-right.' Such a defence of women's education was not especially radical in 1972, but neither was it likely to be seen as reactionary. In the same article, however, Kamaladevi wrote, 'The need for an enlightened wife as an intelligent companion to the husband and an understanding and sympathetic mother cannot be minimised.' We could explain such a statement as an effort to win male support for women's education or as a reflection of Kamaladevi's desire for women to be free to achieve in all fields of endeavour—including, if they chose, as wives and mothers. She celebrated the success of women scientists in the Soviet Union and argued that India should follow the Soviets in providing equal opportunities for women in all fields of knowledge. Still, it is difficult to reconcile Kamaladevi's own life choices—her decision to divorce Harin, her commitment to her own vocation—with the idea that women should be educated in order to serve as good wives and mothers.[3]

Asked by an American reporter in 1974 whether India had 'women's lib', Kamaladevi replied, 'Women in India don't need any liberation movement. They are quite free.' As evidence, she noted that 'a large number of women are doctors and lawyers', as if the professional achievements of certain women demonstrated the absence of sexism and patriarchy throughout all of India. In 1974, a government report offered extensive evidence that the status of women had in many ways either declined or remained the same since Independence. Entitled 'Towards Equality', the report was submitted to the United Nations World Conference on Women, held in Mexico City in 1975. Its greatest impact was within India, where it added fuel to a resurgent feminist movement, a movement from which Kamaladevi would remain largely estranged.[4]

Around the same time, Devaki Jain edited a volume entitled *Indian Women.* Jain had come to know Kamaladevi well. When Jain needed space for her Institute of Social Studies Trust, an organization dedicated to research 'on women and their work', Kamaladevi had offered space in the Theatre Craft Museum. When Jain developed the idea for an edited volume, Kamaladevi 'took the project to heart'. She authored a chapter for the volume and helped recruit other authors, including India's Foreign Minister, Lakshmi Menon, and the novelist Qurratulain Hyder. In the introduction to the volume, Jain celebrated Kamaladevi as her 'wise counsellor' and added that 'she indicated the areas which needed investigation and guided me to persons who were interested in the subject'.[5]

In her chapter of Jain's volume, Kamaladevi lamented that the Indian women's movement had lost the 'vigour, drive and adventure' that marked the activism of many women during the freedom struggle. Part of the problem, she suggested, was that the earlier struggle had already achieved so much. 'Today practically all doors are open to them,' she wrote, 'and women are seen filling a variety of posts and positions.' Overstating the importance of legal changes that were often honoured in the breach, she asserted that 'the early fifties also saw the elimination of their legal disabilities and the adoption of the convention of equal pay for equal work for all'. In January 1976, the feminist scholar Jashodhara Bagchi attacked Kamaladevi's 'glowing account of the legal privileges given to women in Modern India'. In a dual review of 'Towards Equality' and *Indian Women* published in the *Economic and Political Weekly,* Bagchi criticized Kamaladevi, Devaki Jain, and others for offering 'an extremely watered down version of the plight of Indian women'. To be fair,

Kamaladevi recognized that India continued to suffer from gender-based inequity, and her emphasis on class divisions among women was far from 'watered down'. She criticized women leaders for failing to forge 'links with the wide mass of women, who are only approached briefly at voting time to secure their ballot papers'. Still, even when compared to Jain and the other contributors to *Indian Women*, Kamaladevi understated sexism and patriarchy while advancing an upbeat narrative of collaboration between men and women.[6]

In her book *Indian Embroidery*, published in 1977, Kamaladevi wrote that 'for women living very sheltered lives, cut off from fuller participation in the larger social activities outside their immediate domestic precincts', embroidery provided 'a very suitable vehicle for self-expression as well as a welcome diversion'. Whereas she had once focused on challenging the inequities facing women, here Kamaladevi was celebrating the ability of women to live within those inequities. Such a framing was not entirely new. In 1964, Kamaladevi had published an article on embroidery in which she had heralded the 'feminine art' that allowed 'women in purdah and confined to the secluded precincts of the zenana' to 'shed in their twilight corridors and dim chambers the lustre of their burning and melting inside'. Kamaladevi's respect for the power of craft led her to obscure the physical and social barriers faced by many women—and not just the elite women who were forced to live 'very sheltered lives'.[7]

To be fair, Kamaladevi saw crafts as an opportunity for women to take control of their own economic fortunes. In the late 1970s, the Government of Bangladesh asked her to provide guidance on how to encourage crafts development and women's cooperatives. Kamaladevi arranged for a group of Bangladeshi women to travel to New Delhi to receive training in 'block printing, doll making and folk toys' at Naika, the craft centre she had established. Such training had the potential to provide new economic opportunities—as well as new venues for creativity—but it did little to challenge the prevailing status quo, whether in regard to inequities of gender or class. Kamaladevi's belief in women's cooperatives seemed a pale echo of the radical dreams with which she had first envisioned the women's movement.[8]

In 1983, she published her own history of the movement entitled *Indian Women's Battle for Freedom.* She had been working on the book for over five years, and elements of her argument were the result of decades of hard-earned wisdom. Take, for instance, her criticism of male leaders who tended 'to treat social evils as different malfunctioning constituents of society'. Such a fractured outlook misjudged society and human psychology. 'Even as they failed to see a human personality as an integrated whole,' she wrote, 'they failed equally to realise that human life too is an integrated single unit.' By contrast, women 'took their sphere as an integrated whole covering all aspects of social living'.[9]

Kamaladevi criticized younger feminists for failing to recognize such interconnectedness. She complained that 'the emphasis on *equal* rights, and no demands for favours' had given way to 'making sex a claim for special consideration'. Looking towards the past, she stated, 'The women's problems were never sought to be treated on a sex basis but as social maladies of a common society to be cured by the efforts of all members of society, men and women alike.' Younger activists were, according to Kamaladevi, too focused on 'the sensational assaults on women and the spectacular dowry burnings'. Kamaladevi recognized these atrocities as 'excruciatingly grievous' but urged her readers to remember 'that these are not accidental carbuncles erupting on the body of our society'. They reflected fundamental inequities. 'The social revolution remains unfinished,' she declared. 'We still lack a common civil code.' Reena Nanda called the book 'a rather dull history of the social reform movement' and suggested that Kamaladevi responded to the 'condemnation of her generation' by ignoring 'her own critique of the "bourgeois" women's movement'. Kamaladevi's call to complete the 'social revolution' suggested something of that critique, but it is understandable why even sympathetic readers overlooked that radical message.[10]

In March 1987, a few months before travelling to Pune for the AIWC celebration, Kamaladevi published an article in the *Economic and Political Weekly* entitled 'Some Real Issues Facing Women'. Here, her radical vision emerged with fierce clarity. 'The benefits of development have accrued in some measure only to a small section of Indian women and have largely by-passed the great majority,' she wrote. For the majority of women, 'economic, social and political rights have remained more on paper'. She called for 'action by women and on behalf of women—to uphold, defend and enhance their rights'. She lamented 'the existing discriminatory patterns of both land ownership and land utilization' and 'irrational social divisions', most likely a reference to caste and religion, and located the struggle for the 'equal status for women including equal opportunities' within 'a wider area aimed at a basic reorganization of the social system'.[11]

Kamaladevi's persistent criticism of the term 'feminism' as well as her equally persistent critique of 'anti-men' forms of advocacy distanced her from many younger feminists. Yet her long-standing attention to the intersectionality of sexism with other forms of oppression—particularly colonialism, racism and class inequity—resonated across the postcolonial world with women's advocates who were crafting their own approaches to what came to be called 'Third World feminism'. For some of these women, Kamaladevi was a trailblazer whose limitations were understandable given the context of the anticolonial struggle. In *Feminism and Nationalism in the Third World*, published in 1986, the Sri Lankan feminist Kumari Jayawardena wrote that Kamaladevi's 'life reflected the many strands of activity in the women's movement of that time'. In addition to recognizing the breadth of Kamaladevi's activism, Jayawardena also credited her with being 'more radical than Sarojini Naidu'. The global reach of Kamaladevi's approach to women's activism extended beyond the 'Third World'. Gloria Steinem met Kamaladevi in India in the late 1950s and remained an admirer in the decades ahead. While there does not seem to have been any direct influence, many of the women who contributed to the pathbreaking 1981 volume *This Bridge Called My Back: Writings by Radical Women of Color* advanced an expansive conception of resistance that echoed Kamaladevi's self-identification as a 'coloured woman'.[12]

Within South Asia, Kamaladevi's support of women's collaboratives and cottage industries anticipated the flourishing of women's self-help groups in the 1970s and 1980s. Kamaladevi's legacy was advanced by a new generation of leaders such as Ela Bhatt, the founder of the Self-Employed Women's Association (SEWA). Bhatt's mother had worked with Kamaladevi at the AIWC, and Bhatt herself combined labour activism and women's struggles in ways similar to the work that Kamaladevi had done under the aegis of the AIWC. Yet while Bhatt focused on building an organization that gave women a collective voice with which to challenge the status quo, Kamaladevi became increasingly focused on supporting individual women as artists and artisans. In her *Economic and Political Weekly* article, Kamaladevi heralded crafts as 'instruments of social change' but left vague what kind of social change she had in mind. When she celebrated 'the field of performing arts' as 'most natural for women's participation', her emphasis was not on the arts as a platform for radical social change but as a source of 'creative satisfaction'. It would be a mistake, however, to draw too sharp a line between Kamaladevi's early radicalism and her later views—whether in regards to women's rights or arts advocacy. Throughout her life, Kamaladevi saw the creativity and imagination of women as a powerful source of social change. We might argue that her dedication to the arts was increasingly focused on artists and their art, rather than on the power of culture to transform society. Kamaladevi did not see it that way. She rejected the divide between culture and politics, just as she refused to choose between revolution and reform, between socialism and democracy, or between social progress and individual freedom. As a 'coloured woman', a socialist, an Indian and a human being, Kamaladevi never liked being put in boxes. That is part of what she loved about the arts—the ability to go beyond what others thought was possible, the ability to surprise even ourselves.[13]

~

On 1 August 1980, Kamaladevi wrote Margaret Patch a note that reveals how she responded to ageing. 'I have heavy commitments in India itself that keep me more than busy,' she wrote, 'and at my age I need to have very severe priorities because I simply do not know how much time I have in which I would like to do a number of things.' Seventy-seven years old,

Kamaladevi refused to retire from active engagement with the world. She recognized the limitations of time, however, and knew that she would need to prioritize.[14]

Chief among her priorities was serving as the chair of the Sangeet Natak Akademi, a position she held from 1977–82. It had been over two decades since she had helped establish the SNA. Since then, her main focus had been on crafts, but she had maintained her passion for the performing arts. On 11 March 1965, for example, she hosted a dance performance at her home in Delhi. That same year, she penned the foreword to Enakshi Bhavnani's *The Dance in India*. She called dance 'a spiritual experience, a medium of worship, an experience of the upliftment of the soul'. As she moved towards the end of her life, Kamaladevi found such a 'spiritual experience' increasingly meaningful. In a review of a book on Bharatanatyam, she wrote that 'creative expression is the outer form of an inner inspiring experience that could be called religion'. Kamaladevi rarely commented on her own personal experience of religion or spirituality. Asked in 1967 whether she was a 'believer, agnostic or an atheist', she replied, 'I would say that I am a believer. But . . . it has not always meant in the way of a personal God but a way of life one must live.' At the core of her 'way of life', Kamaladevi's passion for the arts was a form of devotion, an 'upliftment of the soul'.[15]

Kamaladevi approached the performing arts with the same preservationist urge she brought to crafts. In the spring of 1980, she celebrated the dancer Guru Kuppiah Pillai as 'one of those but for whose sincere dedication the country would have lost a great art'. The dancer Uma Sharma, known for reviving the Ras Lila, a traditional form of Kathak dance, credited Kamaladevi with inspiring her to protect the old style of devotional dance. 'It was Kamaladevi Chattopadhyay who encouraged me to do research on this and told me never to change the old form,' Sharma recalled. 'I can still see her sitting in the open air, on the moonlit night watching Brindavan Raas.'[16]

Her love for the arts inspired Kamaladevi to champion arts education. She wanted younger generations to experience the power and beauty of art, as well as to have the opportunity to contribute to new forms and new creations. In 1979, she helped to found the Centre for Cultural Resources and Training, an organization with the 'objective of integrating the arts with the values and skills they embodied into the educational system'. In January of that year, she attended a 'Magic World of Toys' exhibition in Delhi. One of the organizers later recalled her 'sharing her joy with children and motivating them to play with rattles, crazy cobras, wriggling snakes, magic flowers and the like'.[17]

Whereas Kamaladevi found joy in watching Brindavan Raas on a moonlit night or delighting children with magic flowers, leading the SNA involved a variety of administrative tasks that were decidedly less joyful. Kamaladevi told Patch that it was 'an arduous task and a great responsibility', one that 'pressure from the artists and cultural organisations' persuaded her to accept. The SNA had gone 'into the doldrums', she explained, and it was 'a herculean task now to revive it'. The workload remained heavy throughout her term of service. 'I am kept so terribly busy,' she told Patch in January 1981. 'There is so much to do and so little time.'[18]

Despite her heavy workload and the exhaustion she often felt, Kamaladevi found the time and energy to travel, both within India and abroad. In 1978, she returned to Sri Lanka where she was hosted by the High Commissioner and introduced to other dignitaries. She insisted on taking a jeep village to village so she could speak with crafts-makers and attend folk theatrical performances. She requested a meeting with the master painter L.T.P. Manjusri, who promptly came to see her, in the words of one witness, 'in an ecstasy of joy'.[19]

Speaking in 1981 at the SNA Annual Awards, Kamaladevi admitted her 'continuing distress' that she couldn't do more to support artists. In her view, the work of the SNA was but 'a drop in the ocean' compared to the kind of support that the Indian state should provide to artists. The awards themselves made her 'feel great anguish' and 'deeply distressed' because they were 'a very small inadequate recognition of a great gift and service which the artists render'. At one SNA award function, Kamaladevi seized an opportunity to demonstrate her deep respect for artists and, as she would at that AIWC gathering in Pune, to stage a frontal assault on archaic hierarchy. When another speaker thanked the President of India for attending and thus honouring the artists, Kamaladevi took the microphone to say, 'I don't know who is honouring whom? It is an honour for the President of India to be in the company of such great artists.'[20]

In March 1982, Kamaladevi presented an award to Indrani Rahman, a classical dancer and former Miss India. Rahman had earned her own award from the SNA, but it was a posthumous award that Kamaladevi presented, an award for Rahman's mother, Ragini Devi, the same woman who had eloped with Harin and whom Kamaladevi had supported from jail. In giving that award, Kamaladevi built upon the generosity she had first offered Ragini Devi some fifty years earlier. She demonstrated yet again her ability to forge solidarities across divides of many kinds—and her belief in seeing people as people and forgiving their mistakes.[21]

In 1987, Kamaladevi praised Gopalkrishna Gandhi's novel *Refuge* for being 'free from grim shades of dyed-in-the-wool villains'. She preferred complex characters, she explained, 'for shadow is inevitably a part of light'. Gandhi later said of Kamaladevi that, 'above all, she was a theatre person'. In his view, 'her mind was that of a playwright,' and like Shakespeare or Kalidasa, 'she understood the human stage and all the players on it with compassion and without judgment'. Kamaladevi's view of human nature inspired her remarkable tolerance. Decades after her detention in the princely state of Travancore, she bumped into the man who had ordered her arrest, Sir C.P. Ramaswami Aiyer. One of Kamaladevi's grandchildren happened to be in the room, and Aiyer was introduced to her as 'the gentleman who sent your granny to jail'. The child demanded to know why Kamaladevi spoke with him. According to one account, Kamaladevi and Aiyer 'exchanged quizzical smiles'. She had forgiven him long ago.[22]

Perhaps her greatest act of forgiveness involved Harin. It was not easy for her to forgive him—not just for all the ways he failed her but for the harm he caused Rama. Kamaladevi was especially angered by Harin's role in the dissolution of Rama's marriage. 'A person who has failed in his own marriage,' she told Kamala Ratnam, 'who has suffered the sorrows of a broken family, should never be helpful in destroying his son.' She wondered if Harin had deliberately intervened as a 'way to take revenge on me'. 'To isolate me,' she explained, 'he made even our son separated from his family.' Yet Kamaladevi still forgave him. For his part, Harin had always been capable of expressing love—if never good at doing so consistently. When Kamaladevi was in the hospital after her car accident, Harin came to visit her and the two watched a Hindi film in which Harin was one of the lead actors. In their seventies and eighties, Harin would visit Kamaladevi at the IIC. They would have lunch together, often laughing at old jokes no one else understood.[23]

In her later years, Kamaladevi took to staying in a guest room at the IIC whenever she was in Delhi. Even when she was living elsewhere, she often spent much of the day at the IIC, attending lectures or sharing a meal with guests. The American scholar Diana Eck warmly recalls Kamaladevi greeting her at the IIC when Eck was a young student. Eck remembers Kamaladevi as 'an impressive, imposing, and kind woman' who graciously invited the young student to share tea in her guest room.[24]

Kamaladevi spent much of her life alone—in solitary confinement in Vellore Jail, on long sea voyages, on trains crisscrossing India, Europe and America. Her later years can be framed as a period of extended aloneness, but she was never without friends. As we have seen, many of the women whom Kamaladevi inspired in the crafts world became something akin to disciples—devoted to her as a person as well as to the causes for which she fought. Those relationships were infused with love. Kamaladevi wrote one younger craft advocate that they shared 'an exhilarating friendship'. She remained close with many of her old friends, as well, including Mohan Bhavnani, the director of her first film, and Badruddin Tyabji, a member of the Indian Civil Service who had seen Kamaladevi perform on the stage in Hyderabad in the 1930s. Tyabji liked to tease Kamaladevi by recalling that when he first saw her, she was 'lying in silks and jewels on a tiger skin'. According to Laila Tyabji, Kamaladevi 'used to giggle and quite enjoy being teased about this long-ago moment of youth, beauty, and fun, especially at a time when so many things she had passionately strived for seemed to be disintegrating and in decay'.[25]

Many friends have painted a similar picture of an ageing Kamaladevi, finding joy in community even while confronting the many ways independent India had failed to live up to its promise. According to Devaki Jain, the last decade of Kamaladevi's life was 'difficult, personally and otherwise'. 'She had retained her courage and vibrancy,' Jain wrote, 'but the institutions that she had spent so many years nurturing had not.' The decline of those institutions challenged Kamaladevi's sense of purpose. 'I think she was disappointed by the turn India had taken,' Jain added, 'and disappointed by how totally her principles, and perhaps that of the Gandhian ethos in general, had been twisted, marginalised and forgotten.' Jasleen Dhamija offers a similar portrait of Kamaladevi struggling with disappointment. 'She was a private person,' Dhamija wrote, 'and no one, but no one, could fathom her loneliness and the anguish in her heart.' That anguish did not, however, define fully Kamaladevi's days or diminish her ability to laugh. 'Despite everything,' Dhamija continued, 'she had a fantastic sense of humour. She was a superb raconteur and a devastating mimic.'[26]

Towards the end of her life, Kamaladevi was routinely feted. In December 1977, she won a national UNESCO award. In 1979, the Ministry of Information produced a film by B.D. Garga, the film historian and documentary filmmaker, entitled *Kamaladevi Chattopadhyay: A Tribute to Her Life and Work*. Featuring archival footage and an interview with Kamaladevi herself, the film offers a short but moving summary of her life. In June 1986, the *Times of India* published a long celebration of Kamaladevi entitled 'A Vivid Tapestry'. That same year, the Crafts Council of Karnataka launched a Kamaladevi Chattopadhyay Viswakarma Award, and invited Kamaladevi to preside over the first award ceremony. The Delhi Crafts Council did something similar, launching a scholarship programme for youth interested in crafts, the Kamaladevi Puraskar, and inviting Kamaladevi to present the awards. In December 1987, she received the first Charles Eames Award from the National Institute of Design. The citation called her 'a symbol and a conscience' who embodied 'Mahatma Gandhi's ideal of an India open to world influences, yet able to withstand being blown off its feet by any one of them'. That year, she was also presented with the Padma Vibhushan, the country's second-highest civilian honour. 'Kamaladevi was human enough to be greatly pleased,' Gopalkrishna Gandhi recalled. With 'barely concealed joy', she told him, 'I am getting it for my contribution to Letters!'[27]

None of her awards meant as much as the deep bonds she formed with her friends and family. 'For me,' she explained in her memoirs, 'the warmth and companionship of my comrades is basic and lasting.' She had a special connection with her grandchildren. When she won the Padma Vibhushan, Kamaladevi invited Arundhati Chattopadhaya to travel with her to Delhi, where she was to receive the award. Despite her packed schedule, Kamaladevi made time to take Arundhati on a tour of Delhi that included sharing vegetarian dhaba kababs.[28]

Two biographies of Kamaladevi were published during her lifetime. She told one of her biographers, Jamila Brijbhushan, 'Don't make it too complimentary,' but both volumes were overwhelmingly complimentary. In the foreword to the Hindi-language biography by Kamala Ratnam, Kamaladevi wrote, '*Apane badanaapravan jeevan mein bujhe saamaany aur asaamaany sabhee tarah ke anubhav hue he,*' which might be translated as follows: 'In my eventful life, I have experienced both significant and insignificant things.' The word '*badanaapravan*' could also be rendered 'ill-fated', and the Ratnam book, more than other works about her, delved into Kamaladevi's most personal struggles, from her divorce to her relationship with her son. Even in Ratnam's account, however, the element of exposé was limited. Kamaladevi herself made clear her boundaries when, in her preface, she wrote, 'Regardless of the demands of appearing contemporary, fresh, and interesting, in my view, a biography need not necessarily expose all those solitary and private moments that bring meaning to one.' She did not want a book in which 'one's solitude and privacy is breached'. As she asserted, 'Life is a series of complex events—some bringing cheer, others not so—and who and what amongst these events have left lasting impressions in my life may be decided only by me.'[29]

In 1986, Kamaladevi published her memoirs, *Inner Recesses, Outer Spaces.* The beauty of the prose and the epic sweep of the narrative made it fitting that it was a novelist, Raja Rao, who authored the preface. It was in that preface that Rao celebrated Kamaladevi as 'firmly Indian and therefore universal'. The statement deserves quoting in full: 'Firmly Indian and therefore universal, highly sophisticated both in sensibility and intelligence, she walks with everyone in city and country with utter simplicity.' She walks with everyone—this was a statement about her life and also about her memoir, which blends a remarkable cast of characters, many vividly drawn, with an equally remarkable silence when it comes to the personal life of the narrator. We might say that the book offers more of the 'outer spaces' than the 'inner recesses', but that would not be accurate. L.C. Jain later suggested that Kamaladevi emerged as 'more of a narrator than an actor'. That is also not entirely accurate. It is true that the book abounds with other remarkable figures, but Kamaladevi is very much an actor and readers encounter many of her emotions—if only in regards to the public developments of her life. We learn how she felt about the women's struggle, the salt satyagraha, Partition, and the challenges and achievements of the crafts movement. We also learn about how she confronted ageing. What we don't see is how she felt about having a child or leaving her husband. In the words of the scholar Annie Devenish, her silences provided 'a form of self protection from the public gaze'.[30]

Despite such self-protection, *Inner Recesses, Outer Spaces* offers a window on Kamaladevi's life and, in particular, on how she looked back on that life near its end. One striking feature is the way the narrative jumps back and forth in time. As Kapila Vatsyayan noted in a review of the book, 'The past and the present imperceptibly merge: through narration of an incident which occurred fifty years ago a problem or concern of the present is illumined.' In the vividness of her account, we see the older Kamaladevi relishing her memories. But there is also what Vatsyayan called 'a quiet pain, a pain born from the maturity of one who has seen too much, and who continues to hold ideals dear to her heart and sheds a silent tear on aspirations unfulfilled'.[31]

Kamaladevi lived through so many chapters in the making of modern India—from the early freedom struggle through the Nehru years to the

Emergency and the early stages of economic liberalization. The India she confronted in her twilight diverged radically from the country she had entered as a child—and from the country she had long envisioned. Kamaladevi did not stop fighting to realize her vision for her country. Even in the twilight of her life, she continued to confront injustice wherever she encountered it. Having learnt that a young woman had been attacked with acid in Meerut, she approached Gopalkrishna Gandhi to raise money to pay for the young woman's surgery. Together, they were able to raise a large sum, including a substantial donation from Vice President R. Venkataraman. In another incident, she learnt that two Indian boys had accidentally wandered across the border to Pakistan while picking berries. They had been arrested and were being held in jail in Pakistan. The arrests made news, and many Indians worried for the boys. Kamaladevi did more than worry. She wrote a personal letter to the President of Pakistan, Muhammad Zia-ul-Haq, and within a few days the boys were released. They visited Kamaladevi to thank her personally. Gopalkrishna Gandhi later recalled the pride on her face and the tears in her eyes, the kind of tears 'which don't actually escape the eyes' and 'are actually the most powerful'.[32]

The young woman attacked with acid, the boys who wandered into Pakistan—these young people were not artists or crafts-makers; they had no direct connection to the causes that were closest to Kamaladevi's heart in the last years of her life. Yet they were human beings who needed help, and so Kamaladevi helped them. Her empathy and her determination were revealed yet again by her response to one of the most painful and controversial events in post-Independence India—Prime Minister Indira Gandhi's decision to send the Indian army into the Golden Temple in Amritsar in June 1984 in order to capture heavily armed Sikh separatists. The ensuing battle left at least 500 casualties. Some estimates range much higher. Hundreds of prisoners were taken, including a large number of women and children who happened to be visiting the temple. When Kamaladevi learnt that many of those civilian prisoners remained in jail, she petitioned the Supreme Court to gain their release. The case, officially known as *Kamaladevi Chattopadhyay v. State of Punjab and Another*, led the

Supreme Court to direct the district judges of Ludhiana and Amritsar 'to personally visit the jails and to verify whether any children were detained in the jails and if so to forthwith take steps for their removal from the jails and further to arrange for their safe custody and well being'. The district judge of Ludhiana found three women and eleven children ranging in age from one to sixteen who had been 'caught by circumstances in the action that took place in the Golden Temple'. Another fifteen children were being held in various special security jails. The Supreme Court demanded their immediate release.[33]

While many octogenarians were withdrawing from the world, Kamaladevi continued to fight for justice—and to expand the number of causes she held dear. She developed, for example, a profound concern for the destruction of the natural environment. Kamaladevi had grown up surrounded by natural beauty. Her family's 'huge garden', larger than 3 acres, contained coconut trees surrounded by coffee bushes and tropical flowers. Perhaps her memories of that beauty informed the environmental concerns she developed later in life. As early as 1944, she had attacked 'large scale industrialization' for destroying 'priceless natural resources'. In her view, production should not be the primary measure of economic health. 'It is not enough to produce more,' she argued. 'It is more important to determine its basis, and the principles that will guide the distribution, in short, who controls and directs the economy.' In 1986, at the age of eighty-three, Kamaladevi published an article on puppetry in which she noted that 'scientists are studying intensively the relationship of every organism to its environment. The life chain that reaches from the tiniest organism in the human being affects each manifestation of life along the way.' Rejecting the idea of 'art for art's sake', she encouraged the use of puppet theatre to galvanize environmental action and to overcome 'public apathy and ignorance, corporate greed, economic pressure, administrative ineptitude'. 'In every community,' she wrote, 'there are local threats to the environment which citizens must fight: a proposed highway through a park, an unnecessary dam, an unwelcome subdivision, inadequate wildlife protection laws, air and water pollution from industries.'[34]

Kamaladevi loved puppets and puppetry. In 1965, she made a point of taking her niece, Asha Puthli, to meet the American puppeteer Bill Baird. Later in life, she arranged for a performance of Bengali rod puppetry at Pragati Maidan in New Delhi. Puppets bridged her two greatest artistic passions: handicrafts and theatre. Her love for puppets makes it even more remarkable that when she chose to write an essay on puppetry, she focused not on the magic of the art itself, but on the power of the art to attract attention to environmental degradation. 'Man's concern for the Earth is no passing fad,' she concluded. 'It is one of the most urgent problems which we face today and will continue to face into the forseeable [sic] future.'[35]

On 14 January 1987, she gave the fourth C.D. Deshmukh Memorial Lecture at the IIC. She praised Deshmukh as one of 'those whose vision and wisdom had enabled them to break out of their narrow grooves and signify their identity with all humanity'. The same could be said of Kamaladevi, as her talk made clear. She held up 'that ancient spirit of tolerance we always prized as our richest heritage' and lamented that 'the problem of Hindu–Muslim relations' had become 'an everlasting phantom'. She celebrated the cosmopolitan strands of Indian thought and culture, noting that 'Gandhiji aptly said that he kept his window open so that new breezes may come in, otherwise we would stifle'. She worried that 'colonialism still prevails but through another medium—technology, which rules today through large industries, specially multi-national organization'. She again demonstrated her growing ecological concerns by lamenting threats to the environment 'from dams for irrigation, genetic engineering, to toxic fertilisers and, above all, to nuclear power for energy'.[36]

She concluded by connecting beauty and tolerance, and by linking both to the traditions she had long championed. 'We belong to a region of great and noble traditions,' she declared. 'They teach us that life is not made rich by simply cluttering it up with acquisitions, but rather by self-expression; that beauty is not determined by the possession of expensive objects but rather by making everything we use in our daily life, no matter how mundane, beautiful.' Bridging her social vision and her own personal philosophy, she explained that 'the art of living, like all arts, is a moving, flowing and changing thing. It is like life itself, inclusive, not exclusive; it teaches us to identify our interests with one another.' It was both for society and for each of us and the richness of our lives that 'we need to cultivate tolerance and a respect for those whose ways are different from ours'. 'If we wish to revive and relive the genuine art of living,' she declared, 'we must adopt once again the law of reason—relive our old faith in humanity'.[37]

Kamaladevi never lost her faith in humanity, a faith grounded in her respect for the ancient past. In 1988, in an essay on 'Handicrafts of Tamilnadu,' she invited the reader to imagine an ancient scene set at the seaside city of Kaveripattinam: 'One sees almost a sea of faces, thousands of hands and arms briskly moving, some preparing colours, some dying, others embroidering on fine silk or cotton or doing applique, lapidaries, stringing corals, agate and pearls, setting gems, carving on sandalwood and conch shell, making garlands of flowers.' By celebrating such artistic abundance, Kamaladevi used the past to imagine a utopian future, a world of unending creation and abiding beauty. Here is where she differed from Gandhi. She was never interested in austerity. She was too much in love with the world—the world as it was and the world as it could be.[38]

~

In the fall of 1988, the crafts advocate Ruby Palchoudhuri visited Kamaladevi in New Delhi. She had come with a request, but found Kamaladevi 'quite ill'. Kamaladevi was eighty-five years old. Her health had challenged her for over a decade, and the last year had been especially difficult. Fortunately, the request Palchoudhuri brought with her to Delhi was one that Kamaladevi was delighted to grant regardless of her health. Palchoudhuri had helped to organize a folk theatre festival focused on traditions from eastern and northeastern India, and she wanted Kamaladevi's blessings for the event. Kamaladevi smiled when hearing of the festival and warmly extended her blessings. 'You never know,' she added with a smile, 'I may be there for your show.'[39]

Kamaladevi died at 3.45 in the afternoon of 29 October 1988. She had flown to Bombay to attend a craft exhibition. After showing signs of a heart attack, she was rushed to Breach Candy Hospital. Her assistant, Mohana Iyengar, immediately telephoned Rama, who was living in Bombay at the time. He rushed to the hospital and was at his mother's side when she passed away. Rama accompanied his mother's body when it was flown to Delhi the following morning, as did Sunil Dutt, the actor and member of Parliament. Hundreds of people, including the President of India, Ramaswamy Venkataraman, visited Kamaladevi's residence on Canning Lane to lay wreaths on the body and to pay their respects.[40]

Tributes poured in. In Bombay, the governor, K. Brahmananda Reddy, presided over a gathering to honour her. In Kolkata, the *Telegraph* published a United News of India (UNI) obituary that deemed Kamaladevi 'the commander-in-charge of women's volunteer corps in the national struggle' and 'the high priestess of Indian culture, arts, theatre and literature'. In *American Craft*, her old mentee Roshan Kalapesi celebrated her 'stamina' and her 'totally contemporary' thinking. From Copenhagen, John Vedel-Rieper, the secretary general of the World Crafts Council, sent a letter to WCC branches throughout the world mourning Kamaladevi's death. 'We have all lost a unique personality,' he wrote, 'a friend of the craft and a guardian patron to the last day of life.' At a memorial fittingly held at the IIC, Kamaladevi's old friend, President Venkataraman, called her 'a Ganga in purity and power'. 'Kamaladevi made every one of her friends feel that she had a special interest in each of them,' Venkataraman noted. 'There was in Kamaladevi an astonishing gift for identification. She seemed to belong to every part of India which she travelled.' As if echoing this insight in India's northeast, Ruby Palchoudhuri and some 250 performers and crafts-makers dedicated their folk theatre festival to Kamaladevi.[41]

L.C. Jain published an obituary in the *Economic and Political Weekly*. 'Even two days before she had the fatal heart attack,' he wrote, 'she expressed deep distress that despite official pronouncements, nothing had been done to ensure regular availability of good yarn to the handloom weavers at proper prices.' Her tireless determination was contagious.

'Kamaladevi was not a solo actress,' Jain wrote. 'She was a magnet who drew hundreds of men and women, young and old, to every social movement or cause she stirred or stepped into.' Kamaladevi did not suffer fools gladly. 'For those who showed superficial interests,' Jain explained, 'the encounter was brief, sometimes chilling—for she had no patience with passive observers of the scene. But in those who showed even a little spark, she lit the fire; she was all inspiration, light and rock-like support when the occasion demanded.'[42]

Tributes to Kamaladevi continued well beyond her death. More than two decades later, Bhagirathi Bai created a play in Kamaladevi's honour and performed it in both Kannada and Hindi. 'Once, after a performance in Bangalore,' Bai recalled, 'an old man of 92 was quietly looking at me as I mingled with the audience. I approached him and asked how he found the performance. He said Kamaladevi revived puppetry and one of the hand puppets she picked out was his and ended up encouraging him to bring back the art.' Kamaladevi had helped the man win an award from the Sangeet Natak Akademi and had continued to support his art and his career for years.[43]

Kamaladevi's legacy extends beyond India. In 1995, the Irish poet John Montague published a poem entitled 'On Hearing Kamaladevi Speak Again'. In 2016, the American dancer and choreographer Anjal Chande created a dance drama based on Kamaladevi's radical anti-racism. Entitled 'Out of the Shadows, a Colored Solidarity', the work debuted at the Smithsonian Institution in Washington, DC. Also in the United States, the artist and writer Shebani Rao created a graphic work entitled 'Kamaladevi: The Hero We Need'.[44]

Kamaladevi was a hero in her lifetime, and there are many reasons why new generations of activists are turning to her for inspiration: her concern for the intersection of multiple forms of injustice; her blend of radical rebellion and pragmatic reform; her ability to embrace multiple identities—as a woman, an Indian, a person of colour, an Asian, a socialist—while rejecting hard boundaries and any form of chauvinism. Kamaladevi offers heroic lessons for anyone concerned with ongoing struggles against sexism, racism, economic inequality, environmental calamity or any of the other injustices and existential threats facing our world today. Yet just as Kamaladevi celebrated Gandhi as a human being and reminded us that it was his humanity that made him such a powerful leader, so we must strive to understand all of Kamaladevi if we are to do her justice as a human being and as a hero.

To many people, Kamaladevi appeared so stoic as to seem almost inhuman. In 1966, her old friend G. Venkatachalam wrote that Kamaladevi 'lives in a world of her own, which has all the quietness and peace of a mountain lake, and no crisis or calamity, either domestic or personal, upsets her mental equilibrium'. This statement seems more like a description of Kamaladevi's public facade than of her inner state. Venkatachalam admitted as much when he wrote, 'Even while intensely agitated she puts on a serene expression and conducts herself so coolly that you would wonder if she was a woman with any feeling or emotions!'[45]

Venkatachalam was not alone in being struck by Kamaladevi's calm bearing. According to the Israeli dancer Deborah Bartonoff, there was 'something about her that is all her own, her stillness, her reticence, both of a singular kind'. That stillness was both inviting and imposing. 'You want to talk to her, to ask her many questions and she has time for you and for them,' Bartonoff explained. 'But when you look her in the face you do not dare.' Bartonoff traced that forbidding demeanour to self-control. 'Her stillness, her command of stillness as if it were mobilized stillness,' she explained, 'this is not calmness, it is self-control.'[46]

While many remember Kamaladevi's apparent 'self-control', she was equally well-known for being stern, demanding and—at times—difficult. In her eighties, Kamaladevi was introduced to Vaidehi, who had translated one of Kamaladevi's books into Kannada. 'Looking sharply at me,' Vaidehi later recalled, Kamaladevi asked a mutual friend if the translation had done justice to the work. 'Her eyes were gleaming like the edge of a sword,' Vaidehi remembered, 'sending a slight shiver down the spine. Smiles were infrequent visitors on this aristocratic visage.' As Gopalkrishna Gandhi noted, Kamaladevi 'had a commanding presence' and 'she was not afraid of anyone, but everyone was . . . not afraid, but nervous in her presence'. According to her niece, Asha Puthli, 'Everyone was a little fearful of her because of her presence, her strength.'[47]

In her memoir, Kamaladevi explained her stoic exterior as a defence mechanism. 'I discovered from an early age that my emotional responses were generally quick and deep,' she wrote. She was 'continuously hurt' when those responses were misunderstood. 'I have come to develop rather a stern exterior,' she explained, 'so even if I were touched within, I would not show. Those who do not know me take me as cold, proud, and distant, none of which I really am.'[48]

Asked at age sixty-four if she had any regrets, Kamaladevi replied, 'Sometimes I do feel that perhaps I need not have spent so much of my time in politics . . . I think there were other valuable things that one gave up and one wonders whether it was really worth doing that.' She would echo that sentiment throughout the last two decades of her life. 'If I were twenty-one again,' she declared on All-India Radio, 'I would hold the little things to my bosom and let the big things go by.' 'I would never get involved in a hurried, rushing life,' she said, before offering a vivid portrait of what she held most dear:

> I would keep loads of time for reading and writing. Above all I would keep plenty of time to fling about with the family—just to thrill at my son's eyes bent fondly on me; to play with him—to exchange with the household the sweet nothings; to write long rambling letters to friends, to pour out one's self and to indulge in the little gossips about myself to make the letters spicy; then, as twilight crept up with its lengthening shadows, to watch the sharp contours soften and fade, watch the play of light and darkness on the wall, on the floor, on the surrounding landscape, on the hill in front of me, so reminiscent of life with its joys and sorrows, hopes and fears, triumphs and failures; to relax on the balcony and watch the moon journey lazily across the sky with its cool mocking light; close one's eyes and listen to music; of a clear evening saunter to the playground for a game of tennis or shuttlecock; call on friends to argue out the insoluble problems of life and sharpen the teeth of one's wits; have lots and lots of music, play

> and sing and dream music. I would pour out my creative spirit into producing plays and acting in them. Theatre, the synthesis of all art, would be the most perfect vehicle of expression for a many-sided person like me. I would fill my life with arts and crafts. When my spirit took wing I would take the car to go for a spin—or more likely to go out for a long, long walk away from the beaten path, into the woods, along flowing water, sail boats down the stream and watch them vanish beyond the bend . . . Yes, it is these little things that keep one human, preserve the human qualities and human values. It is the big things that have come my way, many a time strangling the smaller things. The small things are soft like tender birds, little birds that need warm fur, that can so easily be bruised. In the rough and tumble of life they get pushed around, behind the high walls of demands and duties. But if I were twenty-one, starting life, I would hold them to my bosom and let the big things go by.

Equally full of regret and nostalgia, of gratitude and yearning, this celebration of 'little things' says much about the life Kamaladevi lived and the life she chose not to live. Hers was often 'a hurried, rushing life'. Surely, there were many days when she longed 'to thrill' at her son's eyes or to 'relax on the balcony and watch the moon'. Ageing made her more aware of the choices she had made, the paths she had left unexplored. As one ages, Kamaladevi explained in her memoir, 'one suddenly becomes aware of an emerging end to what had seemed a continuing burgeoning. Each day, each year, one grows acutely aware, is taking that much of time out of the short span left. How long or short, it is not given to any of us to guess or know—something within only keeps warning you that it is getting shorter, quickly, fatally.'[49]

Kamaladevi lived her eighty-five years with exceptional energy and passion. Towards the end of her life, she recognized the shortness of time but, as one would expect from someone who rebelled against nearly every boundary, she never stopped fighting for a better future. 'The past is a dead thing,' she wrote in 1938, 'the present a chain that seeks to bind us; but the future—it is the free untrammelled wonder.' Asked towards the end of her life whether she had achieved a sense of fulfilment, Kamaladevi replied, 'Somehow the idea of a sense of fulfilment sounds like a full stop, as though you had come to the end of a journey. I think as long as one is really alive there can't be a full stop.' To be 'really alive' required motion and change and desire. 'One has certain objectives,' Kamaladevi explained. 'One wants to reach certain goals. One doesn't really achieve all that. And there is so much more it seems to be done.'[50]

Epilogue

The Art of Freedom

TRAVELLING THROUGH EUROPE AS A YOUNG WOMAN, KAMALADEVI attended a performance of Chekhov's *The Three Sisters*. The lead role was played by the actress Maria Germanova. More than sixty years later, Kamaladevi still recalled Germanova declaring in her concluding monologue, 'Time will pass and we shall be gone forever, but our sufferings will turn into joy for those who will live after us—and they will remember those who live now and will bless them.' Kamaladevi is remembered with great love by many who continue her legacy. She deserves to be remembered even more widely—because of her contributions to the making of modern India and because her life offers lessons for all those fighting to create a better India and a better world.[1]

Kamaladevi was a fighter—a rebel—who believed in collective struggle and individual acts of rebellion. Writing in 1947, Yusuf Meherally traced Kamaladevi's life as a series of insurrections:

> The school-girl-widow, defying age-old conventions. The restless student crossing the far seas in search of knowledge. The first society lady to go on the stage not for money or fame, but for a new artistic ideal. The first woman to contest a legislative election, laughing at the great odds against her. The tireless and persevering organizer,

> knocking at inertia, apathy and indifference, spreading encouragement and sunshine around her. The fearless crusader, criticizing Japanese invasion of China, in the heart of Japan itself, without caring for the consequences. The unassuming political worker, facing prison after prison, with a radiant smile. Such is Kamaladevi.

If Meherally had written some forty years later, he might also have described Kamaladevi as a supporter of refugees, a defender of the arts and a champion of handicrafts—a rebel struggling against the persistent inequities and bureaucratic indifference of independent India just as she had long rejected any system of power that stood in the way of justice.[2]

As important as her rebellions were the solidarities Kamaladevi forged between those struggling to reimagine the world. In the introduction to this volume, I discussed three key lessons that Kamaladevi's life reveals about the making of modern India: (1) that bridges between organizations, communities and social causes empowered the freedom struggle; (2) that those bridges extended beyond the borders of the nation; and (3) that the process of bridge-building required the imagination of artists of many kinds. This last point bears repeating: the solidarities Kamaladevi advanced were acts of imagination. According to the former president of India, R. Venkataraman, Kamaladevi's 'entire life was a continuous dialogue with either questions of justice or creativity'. It was in the connection between justice and creativity—in the art of freedom—that Kamaladevi made her most enduring contributions.[3]

Kamaladevi understood that India's freedom entailed much more than the end of British rule; freedom entailed ending sexism, poverty and other forms of injustice and inequity. Consider again what Kamaladevi told the Bombay Presidency Youth Conference in December 1929: 'Freedom or Swaraj can mean but one thing: absolute freedom for each individual as well as collective growth and evolution.' Kamaladevi knew that the 'absolute freedom' of the individual at times conflicted with 'collective growth and evolution' but she also knew that social movements, by combating oppression, had the power to enhance the liberty of the individual and the freedom of society as a whole. That power depended on a kind of radical inclusivity—what today is often known as intersectional politics. The liberty of the individual and of the nation depended on attacking the intersection of different forms of oppression. That is why Kamaladevi's 1939 article 'Freedom' called for solidarities across 'the socially dominated classes'; such solidarities were at the core of her vision of freedom. That is why coalitions between different organizations and causes proved so central to India's freedom struggle—both before and after 1947—and why Kamaladevi forged links with those fighting oppression across the world.[4]

Kamaladevi's global conception of freedom was forged in the 1920s and 1930s, but it was in the 1940s, as India moved towards Independence, that her transnational vision of freedom became fully realized. Earlier in this volume, we heard Kamaladevi tell AIWC delegates in 1944 that 'the world cannot be divided into islands of slavery and freedom'. We saw her defend interconnected social movements that transgressed multiple borders. 'Just as national freedom is but an extension of the social freedom the Conference is fighting for,' she declared, 'the establishment of the same principle all the world over is of equal interest to us.' Like the many African American subscribers of the *Pittsburgh Courier,* we encountered Kamaladevi's statement that 'the Indian people have pledged to work and strive for a world order from which the vestiges of tyranny and exploitation be it racial or territorial are banished'. 'Our own freedom assumes a reality,' she argued, 'only when the rest of mankind becomes genuinely free.' It matters that Kamaladevi's global vision of freedom extended across the moment of Indian independence. It matters that it was only a few years after the violence of Partition that Kamaladevi declared that 'freedom is indivisible'.[5]

Kamaladevi's belief in the indivisibility of freedom shaped her radical vision for what would come to be called the Third World or the Global South. What made her vision of the Global South uniquely radical was the way she grounded both her nationalism and her transnationalism in grassroots social and political struggles against a range of oppressions. In attacking the intersection of multiple injustices, Kamaladevi positioned herself alongside pioneering women of colour like the South African anti-

Apartheid activists Ida Mntwana, Annie Silinga and Amina Cachalia, as well as the African American civil rights leaders Pauli Murray, Ella Baker and Septima Clark. She could also be compared with environmental activists like Berta Cáceres of Honduras or Wangari Maathai of Kenya—women who pursued sustainable development and social justice, women who refused to be pigeonholed. Unlike many of the (male) leaders most often associated with Third World or Afro-Asian solidarities, Kamaladevi distinguished between national sovereignty and true freedom—and demanded emancipation for women, the poor and all oppressed or marginalized people. As the historian Carolien Stolte has demonstrated, Kamaladevi was not alone in seeking grassroots conceptions of Afro-Asian solidarity. As scholars of the African diaspora have revealed, such alternative geographies have deep roots in the resistance to slavery and colonialism. Kamaladevi's life—from her radical travels in the 1920s to her work with the WCC in the 1960s and 1970s—offers a unique vantage point on the continuities and discontinuities of the long struggle to forge solidarity in the face of White supremacy and in support of an inclusive freedom.[6]

It was Gandhi whom Kamaladevi most often cited when explaining the breadth of her conception of freedom. In 1966, in an edited volume entitled *Mahatma Gandhi and One World,* Kamaladevi wrote that Gandhi 'never conceived of freedom and independence for India in a narrow, exclusive sense'. He believed in the 'fundamental unity between all peoples and classes'. That belief drove his internationalism, Kamaladevi explained, as well as his opposition to religious chauvinism and to what he called 'the poison of untouchability'. As Kamaladevi noted, 'To him, freedom conveyed a state where such indignities and religious animosities ceased to exist.' In tracing the links between Gandhi's internationalism, religious pluralism and egalitarianism, Kamaladevi mapped her own expansive conception of freedom.[7]

For Kamaladevi, as for Gandhi, freedom did not entail the absence of any restraints but rather the human flourishing possible only within a society. The word 'swaraj' uniquely captures the social dimensions of freedom—'self-rule' entailed checking one's own excesses in order to support the larger community. True swaraj required responsibility as well as liberty, and that responsibility was bound up with a sense of national belonging and a belief in the importance of national unity. Kamaladevi's nationalism was never chauvinistic. Like Gandhi, Kamaladevi embraced what the scholar Leela Gandhi has called 'an ethics of moral imperfectionism'. She recognized her limitations and her mistakes—and those of her country. Kamaladevi was not a narrow nationalist, but she was a patriot. She loved her nation enough to recognize its imperfections and to fight for real change.[8]

From the anticolonial theatre of the 1920s and 1930s to the crafts conventions of the 1960s and 1970s, Kamaladevi advanced a conception of freedom bound up with a belief in the importance of national unity. Her life reveals the complex relationship between national unity and postcolonial freedom and, in particular, the danger that national unity will be defined and achieved through majoritarian rule. In the words of the scholar Karuna Mantena, 'Majoritarianism has been a consistent feature of post-colonial politics, and one that has proved hard to separate from the inner logic of popular sovereignty.' Kamaladevi's approach to the politics of caste and religion reveals the challenge of advancing unity while respecting diversity and recognizing inequity. Like many socialists, Kamaladevi hoped that an end to class inequity would do away with the other divisions that marred India's unity. Even late in life, when the prospect of a socialist revolution had dimmed, Kamaladevi did not prioritize struggles against caste inequity or religious discrimination. At the core of her politics, however, Kamaladevi rejected chauvinistic conceptions of India and Indian culture, and she fought for a society that respected the rights and the freedoms of all people.[9]

In broadening the scope of freedom, Kamaladevi reimagined the relationship between self and society. She blended a socialist commitment to the broader good with the fierce independence of a lifelong rebel. Her radical egalitarianism at times conflicted with her belief in the importance of organized action. As the scholar Shruti Balaji has argued, Kamaladevi embodied 'the tension between elite postcolonial leaders' imagined worlds rooted in abstract notions of equality and the often hierarchized social organizing tactics required to bring these worlds to life'. Ultimately, Kamaladevi prioritized the freedom of the individual, even while recognizing the importance of solidarity and organized struggle. Her views on the autonomy of the self manifested in 'private' acts such as her decision to divorce Harin as well as more 'public' dramas such as the salt march. Feminist scholars have long rejected neat distinctions between private and public, and Kamaladevi's life demonstrates the futility of such distinctions, even if she herself fought tenaciously to protect her privacy whenever possible. From her first marriage as a child to her struggles as a single mother, Kamaladevi's life offers a vantage point on larger histories that shaped the lives of countless other women. Even if we put aside her participation in social movements and other public spectacles, Kamaladevi's story explodes the old myth that biography as a genre fails to examine questions of social, cultural or political change. As the historian Dinyar Patel has noted, 'Historians of South Asia, who are very prone to the vagaries of academic fashion, have been loath to accept biography as a legitimate form of scholarship.' This is especially true when it comes to biographies of Indian women. 'While women's autobiographies have been of quite extraordinary importance to feminist scholarship in India,' the scholar Supriya Chaudhuri has noted, 'biographies of women are relatively scarce and, with some notable exceptions, unremarkable.' While Kamaladevi's autobiography deserves to be widely read, the breadth of her life and work demonstrates the importance of expanding the number of biographies of the many dynamic women who fought for the freedom of India—and for their own freedom as well.[10]

Kamaladevi identified the self as the locus of freedom without being trapped in narrow individualism or hollow nationalism. In that way, she joined many anticolonial thinkers and activists around the world for whom the idea of 'self-determination' involved a variety of selves within and beyond the nation-state. Kamaladevi's vision of freedom traversed borders much as she had in her many travels. This is more than just an analogy. Indeed, the sprawling geography of her life helped inspire her inclusive understanding of freedom. Travelling overseas deepened her identity as an Indian, while simultaneously strengthening her ties to transnational struggles. It was abroad that she honed her ability to embrace multiple identities and to oppose multiple injustices, to see India as a unified whole as well as a fractured and profoundly unequal society within a fractured and profoundly unequal world. Her travels within India were equally extensive and impactful. From her days as a teenager into her eighties, Kamaladevi was on the move. She journeyed from the Himalayas to the southern tip of the subcontinent, 'where the dry land ends, and the high waves of the sea were banging their heads on the shore with all their might'. She lived many of her days in Delhi, Bombay, Madras and Bangalore but was equally at home in the remotest of villages. Kamaladevi did not just speak about the rural masses. She travelled village to village, talking with people, learning from them and offering her love and respect.[11]

She could not offer—try though she did—the kind of economic stability she hoped would become the birthright of all Indians. Nor was she able to empower women to achieve full equality, whether socially or financially. If casteism and religious discrimination confounded Kamaladevi's vision of Indian unity, it was the persistence of poverty and patriarchy that most directly challenged Kamaladevi's lifework. Tracing the arc of her struggles for socialist equality and gender equity, one could use Kamaladevi's life as a marker for the profound gap between the freedom dreams of the anticolonial era and the realities of postcolonial India. It would be a mistake, however, to assess the efforts of Kamaladevi or her generation in relation only to their radical dreams. Compared to the revolutionary ideas she championed in the 1920s and 1930s, Kamaladevi's post-Independence politics—and particularly her work on behalf of crafts—could be seen as a kind of tepid gradualism. She did not see it that way, however, and neither did most of the artisans she supported. Throughout her career, Kamaladevi balanced radical dreams with a pragmatic desire to achieve results. While she failed to achieve her dreams for India, Kamaladevi's work on behalf of artists and artisans empowered marginalized people—many of them poor and indigenous women. Our challenge is to recognize the power of Kamaladevi's dreams and the limitations of her achievements and to find new ways to extend her legacy in the fight against poverty, inequity and injustice and on behalf of the arts broadly understood.[12]

For Kamaladevi, art was more than a tool to achieve freedom; art embodied freedom. Art constituted freedom. As the scholar Annie Devenish has written, Kamaladevi 'sought to embed creativity as freedom into her vision of a political and economic order'. Kamaladevi recognized that the freedom to create was bound up with all other kinds of freedom. In 1944, she offered delegates to the AIWC convention in Bombay a vivid metaphor for the life-giving power of freedom dreams: 'Weighed down though we may be by chains, we continue to live on dreams and thoughts of freedom.' In August 1945, she defined 'freedom' as 'the fullest opportunity for development and the realisation of the gifts, talents, potentialities inherent in man'. For Kamaladevi, freedom meant much more than mere license. 'The quality which lends the highest moral value to life is freedom,' she wrote in 1947. 'Freedom is the essence of life.'[13]

Kamaladevi expressed her freedom by rebelling against the constraints of doctrine. Asked in 1967 to describe her 'philosophy of life', Kamaladevi replied, 'I never felt a need that I should have a philosophy.' Kamaladevi was a thinker and an institution-builder—but her ultimate faith was in people. She played a central role in the creation of many of India's most impactful organizations: the AIWC, the Congress Socialist Party, the Indian Cooperative Union, the Sangeet Natak Akademi, the All India Handicrafts Board, the Crafts Councils of India, the India International Centre. In most of these cases, she dedicated years of labour to establishing the organization only to walk away when she was called to new endeavours. As L.C. Jain noted, 'This is her special ability—to get people together, start the idea, and little by little withdraw.'[14]

Kamaladevi's life was full of creating and of letting go, of hope and of loss. In her private life and in her public adventures, her resilience is as impressive as her ambition. She struggled and suffered but did not give up, whether fighting for India's freedom or for her own. In our historical moment, at a time in which truth, democracy and tolerance are all under assault across much of the world, many of the goals for which Kamaladevi fought remain but dreams—dreams that the next generation must struggle to realize and to reimagine. In the late 1930s, Kamaladevi visited the poet and artist Rabindranath Tagore at his home. They took a long walk together at sunrise. Decades later, she would still remember the last thing he told her: 'Now as I keep coming to the end of my life, all I am left with are my dreams.' It was Kamaladevi's dreams that linked her activism to her passion for art. It was at the intersection of empathy and creativity, determination and imagination that she lived the wisdom she shared with students in Bengal in 1931: 'Beauty is the soul of freedom.'[15]

Acknowledgements

LIKE MOST AMERICANS, I LEARNT VERY LITTLE ABOUT INDIA AS A child. I knew nothing about Kamaladevi Chattopadhyay when, some twenty years ago, I first read her memoir, *Inner Recesses, Outer Spaces*. I had just begun my graduate studies, and had developed an interest in how Indian radicals viewed African American freedom struggles. I was deeply moved by Kamaladevi's account of being harassed on a racially segregated train in Louisiana—moved by her refusal to leave her seat and by her self-identification as a 'colored woman' fighting against racism throughout the world.

My first book, *Colored Cosmopolitanism*, begins with Kamaladevi on that train. Her life and work shaped *Colored Cosmopolitanism* and my self-understanding as a historian. I chose to dedicate a recent book, *Lord Cornwallis Is Dead*, to Kamaladevi and to the African American civil rights advocate Pauli Murray. Kamaladevi and Murray both embody a radicalism that refuses to be bounded. As they fought for the rights of others, they also fought to be themselves. That expansive radicalism is what I have found most inspiring about Kamaladevi—her refusal to limit her love, her life or her imagination.

I am grateful to Ramachandra Guha for inviting me to contribute to this series, for believing in my work for many years and for the inspiration of his scholarship. We first met in the reading room of the Nehru Memorial Museum and Library. I was working in the papers of Kamaladevi when Ram invited me to share tea. I was struck by the sincerity of his interest in my work and have been grateful for his mentorship ever since. Like Kamaladevi, Ram is a thinker and a writer whose love for ideas and books is linked to a passionate determination to serve his country and the world.

Kamaladevi spent much of her life travelling across national borders, and I am delighted that this book is being published both in South Asia and in the United States. At HarperCollins India, Udayan Mitra believed in this book from the outset. At the University of Pittsburgh Press, William Masami Hammell guided the book towards publication with a rare combination of care, skill and kindness. I want to thank everyone at HarperCollins India and at the University of Pittsburgh Press.

Ellen DuBois and Vinay Lal both played a vital role in this book. They invited me to contribute to their outstanding volume, *A Passionate Life*. Ellen connected me with several potential interviewees. Her thoughts on Kamaladevi's feminism were foundational to my own understanding. Vinay shared a treasure trove of materials on Kamaladevi and also shaped my thinking on Kamaladevi's socialism and her vision of the Global South. Both Ellen and Vinay have been generous and deeply supportive colleagues, and I am grateful to them both.

I also feel deep gratitude to Mrs Santosh Mahendrajit Singh, who drafted a biography of Kamaladevi but passed away before being able to publish it. I want to thank Gita Mithal and her husband, Arvind, for sharing the unpublished manuscript with me. Gita also shared with me many of her own memories of Kamaladevi's visits to her home.

Gopalkrishna Gandhi spoke with me at length on multiple occasions. His memories of Kamaladevi were matched by his deep understanding of her. He shared photos and helped me track down correspondence with his grandfather, Mahatma Gandhi. I came to look forward to every opportunity we had to speak—not just because I knew I would learn more about Kamaladevi but also because Gopalkrishna Gandhi's knowledge of Kamaladevi is itself a form of love and a source of beauty.

I am grateful to the authors of the existing biographies: Reena Nanda, Jasleen Dhamija, Sakuntala Narasimhan, Kamala Ratnam and Jamila

Brijbhushan. I have cited their works throughout the text and am grateful for all I learnt from them and from the many other scholars whose works are cited in the notes. I extend special thanks to Sanjam Ahluwalia, Shruti Balaji, Julie Laut Barbieri, Aparna Basu, Manu Bhagavan, Anita Cherian, Dia Da Costa, Rohit De, Annie Devenish, Aparna Bhargava Dharwadker, Geraldine Forbes, Abigail McGowan, Rosalind Parr, Gail Pearson, Sunil Purushotham, Barbara N. Ramusack, Nicole Sackley, Gouri Salvi, Uditi Sen, Mrinalini Sinha, Mytheli Sreenivas, Carolien Stolte, Soumhya Venkatesan.

I thank Dinyar Patel for sharing many rich archival documents and for the example of his own scholarship. Vanessa Han conducted extensive research for this volume. Arko Dasgupta and Rashid Abbasi offered invaluable translations. Benno Weiner and Ricky Law provided thoughts on Kamaladevi's writings about China and Japan. I am grateful to them all.

Many archivists were vital to my research. I especially want to thank Beth Goodrich, the librarian of the American Craft Council.

For sharing memories or reflections about Kamaladevi, I want to thank Suneet Aiyar, Bhagirathi Bai, Adam Chattopadhya, Rub Pal Chaudhuri, Neelam Chiders, Ruchira Gupta, Anuradha Kapur, Purnima Mankekar, Nina Menon, Neel Menon, Manjari Nirula, Veena Talwar Oldenburg, Anand Patwardhan, Asha Puthli, Purnima Rai, Vijaya Rajan, Gita Ram, Shekhar Sen, Rajeev Sethi, Laila Tyabji and Romulus Whitaker. A special thanks to Purnima Rai for help locating appropriate images.

I had the great pleasure of sharing my research on Kamaladevi with the Oxford South Asian Intellectual History Seminar. For making that possible, I would like to thank Faisal Devji, Zobia Haq and Alizeh Paracha. I also greatly enjoyed sharing my research via an online seminar organized by Dinyar Patel and Sanjay Kumar for the The Lakshmi Mittal and Family South Asia Institute at Harvard University. I also had the pleasure of discussing Kamaladevi's life via an online lecture organized by Iftikhar Dadi and Daniel Bass of the Cornell South Asia Program. I am grateful for all that I learned from these conversations.

One of the great joys of working on Kamaladevi's history has been the opportunity to explore that history with artists. I was honoured to work with Anjal Chande as she created her powerful dance performance, 'Out of the Shadows, A Colored Solidarity', and to have played a very small role in helping to inspire the graphic story, 'Kamaladevi: The Hero We Need', by Shebani Rao. Nicole Hamilton inspired me to respect craft of many kinds. Her creativity is matched only by her generosity of spirit, and I am honoured to know her.

My brother, Peter Slate, was a singer, rapper and screenwriter. Like Kamaladevi, he reimagined himself many times as he pursued a range of artistic callings. My mother, Karen Slate, came with me to Delhi and spent hours in the archives reading through Kamaladevi's letters and papers. Like Kamaladevi, she was a single parent who worked long hours while still finding ways to be a loving and caring mother.

To my children, Kai and Lucia, and to my wife, Emily Mohn-Slate: thank you for inspiring me to live, as Kamaladevi lived, with kindness, curiosity and joy. Thank you for your love. Thank you for being who you are.

Notes

Introduction: Homeless

1. Kamaladevi Chattopadhyay, *Inner Recesses, Outer Spaces: Memoirs* (New Delhi: Niyogi Books, 2014), 317.
2. *Inner Recesses,* 317–18.
3. L.C. Jain, *The City of Hope: The Faridabad Story* (New Delhi: Concept Publishing Company, 1988), 106; 'Refugees in India Erect Model City', *New York Times,* 21 October 1951; Taylor C. Sherman, *Nehru's India: A History in Seven Myths* (Princeton: Princeton University Press, 2022), 92–95.
4. Ellen Carol DuBois and Vinay Lal, editors, *A Passionate Life: Writings by and on Kamaladevi Chattopadhyay* (Delhi: Zubaan, 2017); Jasleen Dhamija, *Kamaladevi Chattopadhyay* (New Delhi: National Book Trust, 2007); Reena Nanda, *Kamaladevi Chattopadhyaya: A Biography* (New Delhi: Oxford, 2002); Sakuntala Narasimhan, *Kamaladevi Chattopadhyay: The Romantic Rebel* (New Delhi: Sterling Publishers, 1999); Kamala Ratnam, *Kamaladevi: Eka Samarpita Vyaktitva* (Delhi: Alekh Prakashan, 1979); Jamila Brijbhushan, *Kamaladevi Chattopadhyaya: Portrait of a Rebel* (Abhinav Publications, 1976).
5. On the 'intersectionality' of injustice, see Leslie McCall, 'The Complexity of Intersectionality', *Journal of Women in Culture and Society* (26 November 2007): 1771–1800, and Kimberlé Crenshaw, 'Mapping the Margins: Intersectionality, Identity Politics, and Violence against Women of Color', *Stanford Law Review,* Vol. 43, No. 6 (1991): 1241–299. For a review of recent scholarship on post-Independence India, see Ornit Shani, 'India's

Democracy Before the Democratic Discontent, 1940s–1970s', *History Compass*, Vol. 20, No. 6 (June 2022). Also see Ramachandra Guha, 'The Other Liberal Light', *New Republic*, 22 June 2012, and 'Indians Great, Greater, Greatest', *The Hindu*, 21 July 2012.

6. Raja Rao, 'Preface', in *Inner Recesses*, ix; Vinay Lal, 'Kamaladevi Chattopadhyay and the Idea of the Global South', *Groniek*, No. 220 (Zomer 2019), 349–59; Carolien Stolte, '"The People's Bandung": Local Anti-imperialists on an Afro-Asian Stage', *Journal of World History*, Vol. 30, No. 1–2 (2019): 125–56; Anne Garland Mahler, *From the Tricontinental to the Global South: Race, Radicalism, and Transnational Solidarity* (Durham: Duke University Press, 2018); Vijay Prashad, *The Darker Nations: A People's History of the Third World* (New York: New Press, 2007).
7. For a recent volume that centres the creative and imaginative dimensions of modern Indian history, see Manu Goswami and Mrinalini Sinha, *Political Imaginaries: Rethinking India's Twentieth Century* (London: Bloomsbury, 2022). Also see Sharmistha Saha, *Theatre and National Identity in Colonial India: Formation of a Community Through Cultural Practice* (Delhi: Aakar, 2018); Abigail McGowan, *Crafting the Nation in Colonial India* (Palgrave, 2009); Vasudha Dalmia, *Poetics, Plays, and Performances: The Politics of Modern Indian Theatre* (New Delhi: Oxford University Press, 2008); Aparna Bhargava Dharwadker, *Theatres of Independence: Drama, Theory, and Urban Performance in India since 1947* (Iowa City: The University of Iowa Press, 2005); Manu Goswami, *Producing India: From Colonial Economy to National Space* (Chicago: University of Chicago Press, 2004).
8. *Inner Recesses*, 19 and 77; KC, *At The Cross-Roads*, edited by Yusuf Meherally (Bombay: The National Information and Publications Ltd, 1947), 5.
9. *Inner Recesses*, 2 and 401. Also see Archana Venkatesh, 'Marriage, Love, and the Nation: The Private Life of an Indian Freedom Fighter', *Journal of Women's History*, Vol. 32, No. 2 (Summer 2020): 89–112.

1. Born to Rebel

1. *Inner Recesses*, 18; Brijbhushan, 7.
2. Some government documents list her birth year as 1901. See Nanda, 4, 21.
3. Oral History interview with Kamaladevi Chattopadhyay conducted in New Delhi by Shri K.P. Rungachary and Dr Hari Dev Sharma, 6 December 1967, for the Nehru Memorial Museum and Library, Oral History Project (KC Oral History), 2; Aparna Basu, 'Feminism and Nationalism in India,

1917–1947', *Journal of Women's History*, Vol. 7, No. 4 (Winter 1995): 95–107; Nandini Deo, 'Indian Women Activists and Transnational Feminism over the Twentieth Century', *Journal of Women's History*, Vol. 24, No. 4 (Winter 2012): 149–74, quote on 153–54; Bharati Ray, *Early Feminists of Colonial India: Sarala Devi Chaudhurani and Rokeya Sakhawat Hossain* (New Delhi: Oxford University Press, 2002); Geraldine Forbes, *Women in Modern India* (Cambridge: Cambridge University Press, 1996), 66–73.

4. *Inner Recesses*, 17–18; Govindraj Venkatachalam, *My Contemporaries* (Bangalore: Hosali Press, 1966); Brijbhushan, 2.
5. *Inner Recesses*, 15–16.
6. Frank F. Conlon, *A Caste in a Changing World: The Chitrapur Saraswat Brahmans, 1700–1935* (Los Angeles: University of California Press, 1977), 95–96; *Inner Recesses*, 27; Nanda, 10; 'KC to JP', JP Papers, Nehru Memorial Museum and Library.
7. *Inner Recesses*, 25, 27.
8. Accounts vary regarding the year in which Kamaladevi was married and the year in which she was widowed. See *Inner Recesses*, 7; KC, *The Awakening of Indian Women* (Madras: Everyman's Press, 1939), 19; Dhamija, viii, 4; Brijbhushan, 8; Nanda, 11.
9. 'Saraswats and Social Reform', *Indian Social Reformer* (3 June 1944): 308–09; Conlon, *A Caste in a Changing World*, 96, 149–51, 163; B. Pandukumar, 'Social Reform Movements and Emancipation of Women in Karnataka: 1840–1947', *Proceedings of the Indian History Congress*, Vol. 71 (2010–2011): 822–28.
10. *Inner Recesses*, 18, 38, 40–41; KC Oral History, 11–12. Also see Sharleen Mondal, 'Hindu Widows as Religious Subjects: The Politics of Christian Conversion and Revival in Colonial India', *Journal of Women's History*, Vol. 29, No. 3 (2017): 110–36; Kamaladevi Chattopadhyaya, 'A Tribute to Annie Besant', *Kamaladevi Chattopadhyaya Papers, Speeches and Writings by Her*, File 79, 1, Nehru Memorial Museum and Library.
11. KC, 'I Remember', in *1921 Movement: Reminiscences* (Delhi: Publications Division, Government of India), 57; KC interviewed by Charles Allen, 1975–76, British in India Oral Archive, British Library Sound Archive reference C5/103, India Office reference MSS EUR R87; *Inner Recesses*, 24.
12. *Inner Recesses*, 24, 27–28.
13. *Inner Recesses*, 27–28; Ratnam, 34; Dhamija, 6–7.
14. Kamaladevi's words are translated from the Hindi biography produced by Kamala Ratnam. I am grateful to Rashid Abbasi for translating the Ratnam text. Ratnam, 45–46.

15. Harindranath Chattopadhyay, *Life and Myself* (Bombay: Nalanda, 1948), 141–42.
16. Dhamija, 14; Ratnam, 47.
17. Ratnam, 50.
18. Ibid.
19. Ibid.
20. *Inner Recesses*, 47; KC, 'I Remember', 57–61. Also see Guha, *Gandhi: The Years that Changed the World*, 74–76.
21. *Inner Recesses*, 47; KC, 'I Remember', 57–61.
22. Kim A. Wagner, *Amritsar 1919: An Empire of Fear & the Making of a Massacre* (Yale: Yale University Press, 2019); Faisal Devji, *The Impossible Indian: Gandhi and the Temptation of Violence* (Harvard University Press, 2012); Dennis Dalton, *Mahatma Gandhi: Nonviolent Power in Action* (Columbia University Press, 2003); KC, 'I Remember', 57–61.
23. KC interviewed by Charles Allen; Brijbhushan, 28; KC, 'I Remember', 57–61.
24. Kumari Jayawardena, *The White Woman's Other Burden: Western Women and South Asia During British Rule* (Taylor & Francis, 1995), 147–56; James H. Cousins and Margaret E. Cousins, *We Two Together* (Madras: Ganesh & Co., 1950).
25. B.D. Garga, 'Kamaladevi Chattopadhyay: A Tribute to Her Life and Work', A film produced by Ministry of Information, Films Division, 1979, https://archive.org/details/dli.MoI.KamaladeviChattopadhyay_Eng; Brijbhushan, 11.
26. *Inner Recesses*, 64–65; Cousins and Cousins, *We Two Together*, 377–78, 380.
27. Ibid.
28. Brijbhushan, 13.
29. Ratnam, 52, and Chattopadhyay, *Life and Myself*, 179–80 and 188.
30. Yusuf Meherally, *At The Cross-Roads*, 1.
31. *Inner Recesses*, 51–52; Brijbhushan, 15.
32. *Inner Recesses*, 54–55; KC Oral History, 19. Also see Barooah Nirode Kumar, *Chatto: The Life and Times of an Anti-Imperialist in Europe* (Oxford, 2004).
33. Chattopadhyay, *Life and Myself*, 196.
34. *Inner Recesses*, 53–54 and 57.
35. *Inner Recesses*, 60–64; KC Oral History, 24–25; Brijbhushan, 17–18; Garga, 'Kamaladevi Chattopadhyay'.

36. Venkatachalam, *My Contemporaries*; 'An Indian Poet', *Times of India*, 15 September 1926; 'Abu-Hassan', *Times of India*, 26 March 1927.
37. Rumya Sree Putcha, *The Dancer's Voice: Performance and Womanhood in Transnational India* (Durham, NC: Duke University Press, 2022); Shailaja Paik, *The Vulgarity of Caste: Dalits, Sexuality, and Humanity in Modern India* (Stanford: Stanford University Press, 2022); Rimli Bhattacharya, *Public Women in British India: Icons and the Urban Stage* (Delhi: Routledge India, 2018); Bishnupriya Dutt and Urmimala Sarkar Munsi, *Engendering Performance: Indian Women Performers in Search of an Identity* (Sage, 2010); Anupama Rao, *The Caste Question: Dalits and the Politics of Modern India* (Berkeley: University of California Press, 2009).
38. *Inner Recesses*, 60–64, 86–87; Brijbhushan, 17–18; Garga, 'Kamaladevi Chattopadhyay'.
39. Copy of Ramakrishna Chattopadhyay's passport, in author's possession courtesy of Nina Menon; KC Oral History, 10, Ratnam, 32.
40. Ratnam, 57, 61 and 73.
41. Ratnam, 73.
42. Nanda, 17; Ratnam, 73.
43. *Inner Recesses*, 74; Shruti Balaji, 'From Colonial Subjecthood to Shared Humanity: Social Work and the Politics of "Doing" in Kamaladevi Chattopadhyay's International Thought,' *Global Studies Quarterly*, Vol. 3, No. 1 (2023): 1–12; L.C. Jain, 'Kamaladevi: An Epochal Life', *Manushi*; V.S. Narayana Rao, *Dr N.S. Hardiker* (New Delhi: Publications Division, Government of India, 1985); Jyotsna Kamat, 'Umabai Kundapur', http://www.kamat.com/kalranga/women/kundapur.htm.
44. 'Report of the Thirty-Eighth Indian National Congress held at Cocanada on the 28th, 29th, 30th, and 31st December 1923 and 1st January 1924' (Cocanada: Cocanada Printing Works, 1924), 187; *Inner Recesses*, 74–75; Brijbhushan, 28; S.R. Bakshi, 'Gandhi and the Belgaum Congress—An Assessment', *Proceedings of the Indian History Congress* 55 (1994): 522–26.
45. N.S. Hardiker, 'To Our Friends', *Young India* (January 1919), 7; *Inner Recesses*, 19, 74, 79; Ratnam, 56–57.

2. Bridging Revolutions

1. Kamaladevi rejected the historical narrative that undergirded the imperial project, a narrative in which India had been hopelessly backward until the British arrived. On the relationship between British imperialism and the discipline of history, see Priya Satia, *Time's Monster: How History Makes*

History (Cambridge, MA: Belknap Press of Harvard University Press, 2020). Also see 'India's Needs: Shrimati Kamala Devi's Election Speech', *New India in Equal Rights,* 25 December 1926, 365–66, reprinted in *A Passionate Life,* 53–56.

2. Gail Pearson, 'Tradition, Law and the Female Suffrage Movement in India', in *Women's Suffrage in Asia: Gender, Nationalism and Democracy,* eds. Louise Edwards and Mina Roces (New York: RoutledgeCurzon, 2004), 200–01; Geraldine Forbes, '"Votes for Women": The Demand for Women's Franchise in India 1917–1937', in Vina Mazumdar, ed., *Symbols of Power: Studies of the Political Status of Women in India* (Bombay, 1979), 3–23; Annie Devenish, *Debating Women's Citizenship in India, 1930–1960* (New Delhi: Bloomsbury Publishing India, 2019); Sumita Mukherjee, *Indian Suffragettes: Female Identities and Transnational Networks* (Delhi: Oxford University Press, 2018).

3. 'India's Needs'.

4. Katherine Mayo, *Mother India* (London: Jonathan Cape, 1927); Mrinalini Sinha, *Specters of Mother India: The Global Restructuring of an Empire* (Durham, N.C.: Duke University Press, 2006); Lata Mani, *Contentious Traditions: The Debate on Sati in Colonial India* (Oxford: Oxford University Press, 1998); Antoinette M. Burton, 'The Feminist Quest for Identity: British Imperial Suffragism and "Global Sisterhood" 1900–1915', *Journal of Women's History,* Vol. 3, No. 2 (Fall 1991): 46–81; Barbara Ramusack, 'Catalysts or Helpers? British Feminists, Indian Women's Rights and Indian Independence', in *The Extended Family: Women and Political Participation in India and Pakistan,* ed. Gail Minault (Missouri: South Asia Books, 1981), 109–50.

5. 'India's Needs'.

6. Cousins and Cousins, *We Two Together,* 446–47; Margaret Cousins, *Indian Womanhood Today* (Allahabad: Kitabistan, 1941), 66–67; *Inner Recesses,* 82–83; Cousins, 'Women Candidates for the Legislative Council', in Muthulakshmi Reddi, *Margaret Cousins and Her Work in India by One Who Knows* (Madras: WIA, 1956) and quoted on page 170 of Catherine Candy, *The Occult Feminism of Margaret Cousins in Modern Ireland and India, 1878–1954,* Dissertation for the Degree of Doctor of Philosophy, Department of History, Loyola University Chicago (1996), https://ecommons.luc.edu/luc_diss/3614; Nanda, 32.

7. Kamaladevi told Kamala Ratnam she had lost by 200 votes. Other accounts range from 500 to 55. 'Women in the New Legislative Councils', *International Woman Suffrage News,* December 1926, 25; 'Heroic Defeats', *International Woman Suffrage News,* February 1927, 57; Ratnam, 58;

Indian Social Reformer, 27 November 1926; 'Hindu Social Reform League, Madras,' *The Indian Social Reformer*, December 4, 1926, 21; Cousins and Cousins, *We Two Together*, 446–47; Nanda, 25.

8. 'The First All-India Women's Conference', *Indian Social Reformer*, 15 January 1927, 313–14.
9. Mrinalini Sinha, 'A Global Perspective on Gender: What's South Asia Got to Do with It?' in *South Asian Feminisms*, eds., Loomba and Ritty (Duke University Press, 2012), 347–48.
10. Mrinalini Sinha, 'Reading Mother India: Empire, Nation, and the Female Voice', *Journal of Women's History*, Vol. 6, No. 2 (Summer 1994): 6–44; Aparna Basu and Bharati Ray, *Women's Struggle: A History of the All India Women's Conference 1927–1990* (Delhi: Manohar, 1990).
11. *Inner Recesses*, 83; Ratnam, 59.
12. *Inner Recesses*, 83; Barbara N. Ramusack, 'Cultural Missionaries, Maternal Imperialists, Feminist Allies: British Women Activists in India, 1865–1945', *Women's Studies International Forum*, Vol. 13, No. 4 (1990): 309–21.
13. *Inner Recesses*, 85; Brijbhushan, 38.
14. *A Passionate Life*, 7–8; Forbes, *Women in Modern India*, 158; Madhu Kishwar, 'Why I Do Not Call Myself a Feminist', *Manushi* (November–December 1990), 2–8; Anupama Roy, *Gendered Citizenship: Historical and Conceptual Explorations* (Hyderabad: Orient Longman, 2005); Chandra Talpade Mohanty, *Feminism without Borders: Decolonizing Theory, Practicing Solidarity* (Durham: Duke University Press, 2003); Tanika and Sumit Sarkar, eds., *Women and Social Reform in India* (Bloomington: Indiana University Press, 2008).
15. *Inner Recesses*, 94, 121–22; Nanda, 19–20; Ratnam, 59.
16. KC Oral History, 69; Brijbhusan, 35.
17. Nanda, 32; KC Papers, NMML; Brijbhushan, 55–56; Ratnam, 106–07.
18. KC Oral History, 65; Brijbhushan, 31 and 53; Julie Laut Barbieri, 'Kamaladevi Chattopadhyaya, Anti-Imperialist and Women's Rights activist, 1939–41', A Thesis Submitted to the Faculty of Miami University in Partial Fulfilment of the Requirements for the Degree of Master of Arts Department of History, Miami University Oxford, Ohio, 2008.
19. KC Oral History, 123; Brijbhushan, 39.
20. Forbes, *Women in Modern India*, 81.
21. *Inner Recesses*, 111; KC interviewed by Charles Allen.
22. Margaret E. Cousins, 'Impressions of the Second All-India Women's Conference: The Women's Assembly in Delhi', *Times of India*, 6 March 1928.

23. Quoted in Savel Zimand, *Living India* (New York: Longmans, 1928), 115–16.
24. Cousins, 'Impressions of the Second All-India Women's Conference.'
25. *Inner Recesses,* 117; Cousins, 'Impressions of the Second All-India Women's Conference'; Mrinalini Sinha, 'Reading Mother India.'
26. 'Age of Consent Inquiry', *Times of India,* 15 September 1928; Philippa Levine, 'Sovereignty and Sexuality: Transnational Perspectives on Colonial Age of Consent Legislation', in *Beyond Sovereignty: Britain, Empire and Transnationalism, c. 1880–1950,* eds., Frank Trentmann, Philippa Levine and Kevin Grant (New York: Palgrave Macmillan, 2007), 16–33. Also see Ishita Pande, *Sex, Law, and the Politics of Age: Child Marriage in India, 1891–1937* (Cambridge: Cambridge University Press, 2020).
27. Kamaladevi Chattopadhyay, 'Co-Education', a review of B.A. Howard, *The Mixed School* (University of London Press, 1928), *Servant of India,* 22 November 1928, 615–16.
28. *Inner Recesses,* 115.
29. 'Social Reform and Women', *Times of India,* 14 January 1929.
30. 'All-India Women's Conference, Leaders' Impressions', *Times of India,* 11 January 1929; Barbieri, 'Kamaladevi Chattopadhyaya'; 'The Women's Educational Conference', *Indian Quarterly Register,* January–June 1929, 419–24.
31. 'All-India Women's Conference, Leaders' Impressions'.
32. *Inner Recesses,* 113–14.
33. 'World Educational Conference', *International Woman Suffrage News,* February 1929, 69; *Inner Recesses,* 125–26; Rosalind Parr, 'Citizens of Everywhere: Indian Nationalist Women and the Global Public Sphere, 1900–1952', Doctor of Philosophy (History), University of Edinburgh, January 2018, 240.
34. *Inner Recesses,* 125–26; 'All-India Women's Conference, Its Value to India', *Times of India,* 30 October 1929; 'The Annual Report of the All-India Women's Conference 1929–30', 26.
35. Barbieri, 'Kamaladevi Chattopadhyaya', 11–12; *Inner Recesses,* 127–28; *Stri Dharma,* Vol. 12, November 1928–November 1929, 565; Leila Rupp, *Worlds of Women: The Making of an International Women's Movement* (Princeton, NJ: Princeton University Press, 1997), 151; Jayawardena, *The White Woman's Other Burden,* 266–67.
36. Keshavjee Luckmidas, *Modern India Thinks* (Bombay: D.B. Taraporevala Sons & Co., 1932), 126; *Inner Recesses,* 126.

37. 'The Elsinore Educational Conference', *Modern Review*, Vol. 46, No. 5 (November 1929): 580.
38. *Inner Recesses*, 125, 128–30.
39. Vaidehi, 'A Voice for Women', translated by Sumathi Niranjan Karody, *The Hindu*, 26 October 2017, https://www.thehindu.com/books/a-voice-for-women/article19924223.ece; *Inner Recesses*, 128–30; Secretary of Government to Home (Pol) Department, 29 January 1930, quoted in Mrs Santosh Mahendrajit Singh, Untitled and Undated Draft Biography of Kamaladevi in Author's Possession, Courtesy Gita Mithal (hereafter Singh), 19; KC Letter to Viren Chattopadhyaya, 16 November 1929, National Archives, Home Political, File 25/9/1930; Nanda, 40–4; Parr, 'Citizens of Everywhere', 275.
40. 'Local Engagements', *Times of India*, 23 September 1929; Singh, 19.
41. Janaki Nair, 'The Lateral Spread of Indian Feminist Historiography', *Journal of Women's History*, Vol. 20, No. 4 (Winter 2008): 177–84; 'The Annual Report of the All-India Women's Conference 1929–30', in All India Women's Conference, 4th Session, Bombay 1930 (Poona: Aryabhushan Press, n.d.), 24, https://dspace.gipe.ac.in/xmlui/handle/10973/28627.
42. Sinha, 'A Global Perspective on Gender', 347–48; Lakshmi Arya, 'The Uniform Civil Code: The Politics of the Universal in Postcolonial India', *Feminist Legal Studies*, Vol. 14, No. 3 (2006): 293–328.
43. Secretary of Government to Home (Pol) Department, 29 January 1930, quoted in Singh, 19; National Archives, Home Political, File 25/9/1930, quoted in Nanda, 44.
44. 'The All India Women's Conference, 17th Session—Bombay', *Indian Annual Register*, January–June 1944, vol. 1, 284–85; *Inner Recesses*, 134–35.
45. 'The Status of Women in India', from *Women in Modern India*, eds., Evelyn C. Gedge and Mithan Choksi (Bombay: D.B. Taraporewala, 1929), 1–13; Forbes, *Women in Modern India*, 158; Sulochanabai Hukalikar, 'Future of Indian Womanhood', *Servant of India*, 6 March 1930, 120.
46. 'The Bombay Youth Conferences', *Indian Quarterly Register*, July–December 1929, ed., Nripendra Nath Mitra (Calcutta: The Annual Register Office, 1930), 403–04; *Inner Recesses*, 136–37.
47. 'The Bombay Youth Conferences', 403–04; *Inner Recesses*, 330; Madhu Dandavate, *As the Mind Unfolds: Issues and Personalities*, ed., B. Vivekanandan (Delhi: Shipra, 1993), xii and 304.
48. 'The Bombay Youth Conferences', 403–04; 'Youth and the Fight for Independence', Address at the Bombay Presidency Youth Conference,

Ahmedabad, 14 December 1929, in *At the Cross-Roads*, 51–55; *Inner Recesses*, 136–37.

49. Compare the version in *At the Cross-Roads* with the version in the *Indian Quarterly Register*. In the *Register* version, she was quoted that 'the term "Red" is much abused'. See 'The Bombay Youth Conferences', 403–04; 'Youth and the Fight for Independence'; Singh, 23.
50. 'The Annual Report of the All-India Women's Conference 1929–30', 24–26.
51. *Inner Recesses*, 138.
52. KC to Viren, 16 November 1929, National Archives, Home Political, File 25/9/1930, cited in Nanda, 46.
53. 'C.P. Youth Conference', February 24, 1930, *Indian Annual Register*, January–June 1930, ed., Nripendra Nath Mitra (Calcutta: Annual Register Office, 1930), 27; Nanda, 45–46 and National Archives, Home Political, File 25/9/1930.
54. 'The All India Women's Conference', *India & Canada* (March 1930), 10 in Box 9, 'India and Canada', South Asians in North America Collection, MSS 2002/78 cz, Bancroft Library, University of California, Berkeley; Michele L. Louro, '"Where National Revolutionary Ends and Communist Begins": The League against Imperialism and the Meerut Conspiracy Case', *Comparative Studies of South Asia, Africa and the Middle East*, Vol. 33, No. 3 (2013): 331–44; Carolien Stolte, 'Bringing Asia to the World: Indian Trade Unionism and the Long Road Towards the Asiatic Labour Congress, 1919–37', *Journal of Global History*, Vol. 7 (2012): 257–78; eds., Ali Raza, Benjamin Zachariah and Franziska Roy, *Internationalist Moment South Asia, Worlds, and World Views 1917–39* (Delhi: Sage, 2014).
55. Dhamija and Nanda offer conflicting accounts. See Nanda, 45; Dhamija, 28–29.

3. Salt and Solitary

1. Garga, 'Kamaladevi Chattopadhyay'; *Inner Recesses*, 139.
2. *Inner Recesses*, 149; Basu, 'Feminism and Nationalism in India,' 102; Brijbhushan, 62–63; 'Impatient Sisters,' *Times of India*, 23 March 1930; interview with Gopalkrishna Gandhi, 23 April 2021. Also see Dinyar Patel, *Naoroji: Pioneer of Indian Nationalism* (Harvard, 2020).
3. *Inner Recesses*, 150–51.
4. Ibid.
5. 'Impatient Sisters', *Times of India*, 23 March 1930.

6. Rao, *Dr N.S. Hardiker*, 143–44; *Inner Recesses*, 141 and 151.
7. *Inner Recesses*, 152–53.
8. *Inner Recesses*, 153–54.
9. Patrick Kelly, Commissioner of Police (CP), Bombay, to G.F.S. Collins, Home Secretary, Government of Bombay, 8 April 1930, in K.K. Chaudhari, ed., *Source Material for a History of Freedom Movement: Civil Disobedience Movement, April–September 1930*, Vol. 11 (Bombay: Government of Maharashtra, 1990), 11–12; Garga, 'Kamaladevi Chattopadhyay'.
10. *Inner Recesses*, 152–53.
11. Bombay Presidency Police Abstract of Intelligence, 3 May 1930, in *Source Material*, 596–98; CP to Collins, 11 April 1930, in *Source Material*, 15–16.
12. CP to Collins, 12 April 1930, in *Source Material*, 17–18; CP to Collins, 14 April 1930, in *Source Material*, 19–20; *Inner Recesses*, 156; CP to Collins, 15 April 1930, in *Source Material*, 21.
13. CP to Collins, 14 April 1930, in *Source Material*, 19–20; CP to Collins, 16 April 1930, in *Source Material*, 22; CP to Collins, 17 April 1930, in *Source Material*, 24–25; CP to Collins, 18 April 1930, in *Source Material*, 25.
14. CP to Collins, 19 April 1930, in *Source Material*, 26–27; CP to Collins, 21 April 1930, in *Source Material*, 29–31; CP to Collins, 23 April 1930, in *Source Material*, 37–40.
15. CP to Collins, 23 April 1930, in *Source Material*, 37–40; interview with C.K. Narayanswami, conducted by Uma Shanker, 14 September 1969, Centre of South Asian Studies, University of Cambridge, https://www.s-asian.cam.ac.uk/archive/audio/collection/c-k-narayanswami/; Bombay Congress Bulletin, 22 April 1930 in CP to Collins, 23 April 1930, in *Source Material*, 37–40; CP to Collins, 24 April 1930, in *Source Material*, 40–41; CP to Collins, 25 April 1930, in *Source Material*, 45–46.
16. Bombay Congress Bulletin, 22 April 1930 in CP to Collins, 23 April 1930, in *Source Material*, 37–40.
17. CP to Collins, 17 April 1930, in *Source Material*, 24–25.
18. 'A Survey', *Young India*, 17 April 1930; CP to Collins, 17 April 1930, in *Source Material*, 24–25; CP to Collins, 18 April 1930, in *Source Material*, 25.
19. CP to Collins, 21 April 1930, in *Source Material*, 29–31; CP to Collins, 23 April 1930, in *Source Material*, 37–40; CP to Collins, 24 April 1930, in *Source Material*, 40–41; CP to Collins, 28 April 1930, in *Source Material*, 49–50.
20. Singh, 102; Bombay Congress Bulletin, 21 April 1930, CP to Collins, 22 April 1930, in *Source Material*, 32–35.

21. CP to Collins, 28 April 1930, in *Source Material*, 49–50; Bombay Presidency Police Abstract of Intelligence, 10 May 1930, in *Source Material*, 606–09.
22. CP to Collins, 30 April 1930, in *Source Material*, 56–58; Bombay Congress Bulletin, 29 April 1930 in CP to Collins, 30 April 1930, in *Source Material*, 56–58.
23. CP to Collins, 1 May 1930, in *Source Material*, 58–60.
24. Bombay Congress Bulletin, 28 April 1930 in CP to Collins, 29 April 1930, in *Source Material*, 55–56; CP to Collins, 2 May 1930, in *Source Material*, 60–62.
25. CP to Collins, 5 May 1930, in *Source Material*, 66–67; CP to Collins, 6 May 1930, in *Source Material*, 71–72.
26. Bombay Congress Bulletin, 6 May 1930, 73–75, in CP to Collins, 6 May 1930, in *Source Material*, 71–75.
27. CP to Collins, 3 May 1930, in *Source Material*, 62–64; Bombay Congress Bulletin, 8 May 1930, in CP to Collins, 8 May 1930, in *Source Material*, 81–83.
28. 'Salt Tax', *Young India*, 27 February 1930; CP to Collins, 9 May 1930, in *Source Material*, 84–85; CP to Collins, 13 May 1930, in *Source Material*, 90–91; Nanda, 51; CP to Collins, 14 May 1930, in *Source Material*, 94–95; CP to Collins, 15 May 1930, in *Source Material*, 97–98.
29. CP to Collins, 16 May 1930, in *Source Material*, 98–100.
30. Kaur, *Role of Women in the Freedom Movement*, 179.
31. CP to Collins, 16 May 1930, in *Source Material*, 98–100; *Inner Recesses*, 157–58.
32. 'To M.R. Jayakar', 16 May, 1930, Digitized Private Papers, M.R. Jayakar, National Archives of India, File No.: Roll_00071_File_No_482, https://indianculture.gov.in/archives/civil-disobedience-correspondence-mrs-kamaladevi-chattopadya-nc-kelkar-mk-dixit-etc.
33. Bombay Presidency Police Abstract of Intelligence, Poona, 31 May 1930, in *Source Material*, 652; CP to Collins, 17 May 1930, in *Source Material*, 102–03; CP to Collins, 19 May 1930, in *Source Material*, 103–06.
34. Bombay Presidency Police Abstract of Intelligence, Poona, 7 June 1930, 664–68 and 670; Jawaharlal Nehru, 'Jail Diary', 17 May 1930, in *Selected Works of Jawaharlal Nehru* (SWJN), Series 1, Vol. 4, ed. S. Gopal (New Delhi: Jawaharlal Nehru Memorial Fund, 1973), 349; 'Women Demonstrators in India', *Evening News*, Rockhampton, Queensland, Australia, 20 May 1930; Francis Low, 'Britain Takes Firmer Stand against Rebels', *Mount Pleasant Daily Times*, 16 May 1930; 'Letter to John Haynes Holmes', 22 May 1930, *Jayaprakash Narayan: Selected Works*, Vol. 1,

1929–1935, ed., Bimal Prasad (New Delhi: Manohar, 2000), 46–47; Kaur, *Role of Women in the Freedom Movement,* 179; Brijbhushan, 67.

35. Singh, 75 and 102–05.
36. *Bombay Congress Bulletin,* 18 May 1930, in CP to Collins, 19 May 1930, in *Source Material,* 103–08; *Bombay Congress Bulletin,* 19 May 1930, in CP to Collins, 19 May 1930, in *Source Material,* 103–10; CP to Collins, 20 May 1930, in *Source Material,* 110–11.
37. *Inner Recesses,* 158–59.
38. Cousins, *We Two Together,* 537; Ratnam, 61; Bombay Presidency Police Abstract of Intelligence, Poona, Saturday, 4 October 1930, in *Source Material,* 243–44; Bombay Presidency Police Abstract of Intelligence, Poona, 30 August 1930, in *Source Material,* 819.
39. Erin Pineda, *Seeing Like an Activist: Civil Disobedience and the Civil Rights Movement* (New York: Oxford University Press, 2021).
40. *Inner Recesses,* 159; KC, 'Woman the Comrade', in *Gandhiji: His Life and Work,* eds., D.G. Tendulkar, M. Chalapathi Rau, Mridula Sarabhai and Vithalbhai K. Jhaveri (Bombay: Keshav Bhikaji Dhawale, 1944), 132–41.
41. 'All Bengal Students' Conference', *Indian Annual Register,* January–June 1931, Vol. 1, 359–62.
42. KC Oral History, 82; Brijbhushan, 74; Nanda, 59; Kama Maclean, *A Revolutionary History of Interwar India: Violence, Image, Voice and Text* (Delhi: Penguin, 2016): 192–93.
43. Ratnam, 64.
44. Sukanya Rahman, *Dancing in the Family: An Unconventional Memoir of Three Women* (New Delhi: HarperCollins India, 2001), 6–17.
45. Ibid., 18–21.
46. Ibid.; Nanda, 64.
47. Ratnam, 62.
48. Nanda, 64; 'All Bengal Students' Conference', *Indian Annual Register,* January–June 1931, Vol. 1, 359–62.
49. Handy Perinbanayagam, *A Memorial Volume* (Chunnakam: Thirumakal Press, 1980), 72–75; Wesley S. Muthiah and Sydney Wanasinghe, eds., *The Bracegirdle Affair: An Episode in the History of the Lanka Sama Samaja Party* (Colombo: Young Socialist, 1997), 25; *Inner Recesses,* 165; KC Oral History, 174.
50. Perinbanayagam, *A Memorial Volume,* 82; Minnette De Silva, *The Life & Work of an Asian Woman Architect* (Colombo: Smart Media, 1998), 49; Nanda, 64; Ratnam, 62–63.

51. Bhagwan Das Garga, *Silent Cinema, in India: A Pictorial Journey* (Noida: Collins, 2012), 104, 144–45; *Inner Recesses,* 208.
52. *Inner Recesses,* 166.
53. Kamaladevi to Gandhi, 26 July 1931, SN 17391, Sabarmati Ashram.
54. Jawaharlal Nehru, 'On Protection of Women Workers', *Bombay Chronicle,* 9 August 1931, in SWJN, Series 1, Vol. 5, 292; 'The All-India Congress Committee', Bombay, 6 August 1931, in *The Indian Annual Register* July–December 1931, Vol. 11, 73–75.
55. 'The All-India Congress Committee', Bombay, 6 August 1931. Also see Eleanor Newbigin, *The Hindu Family and the Emergence of Modern India: Law, Citizenship and Community* (Cambridge: Cambridge University Press, 2013).
56. 'The All-India Congress Committee', Bombay, 6 August 1931.
57. 'Hindustani Seva Dal Conference', in B.G. Kunte, ed., *Source Material for a History of the Freedom Movement in India,* Vol. 9, Mahatma Gandhi in Maharashtra, 1915 to 1946 (Mumbai: Government of Maharashtra, 1980), 205; G.F.S. Collins, Home Secretary, Government of Bombay to H.W. Emerson, Secretary to the Government of India, 24 September 1931, in K.K. Chaudhari, ed., *Source Material for a History of Freedom Movement: Civil Disobedience Movement,* October 1930–December 1941, Vol. 12 (Bombay: Government of Maharashtra, 1995), 99; V.S. Narayana Rao, *Dr N. S. Hardiker,* 160–61.
58. Collins to Emerson, 26 October 1931, *Source Material for a History of Freedom Movement: Civil Disobedience Movement,* October 1930–December 1941, 100–01; *Inner Recesses,* 168.
59. Singh, 117; Kaur, *Role of Women in the Freedom Movement,* 180.
60. Brijbhushan, 69; *Inner Recesses,* 169; 'To K.F. Nariman', 4 December 1931, SWJN, Series 1, Vol. 5, 335; 'The Maharashtra Youth Conference', in *Indian Annual Register,* July–December 1931, Vol. 11, 273–74.
61. Singh, 39–40; Nanda, 53.
62. 'Chronicle of Events', *Indian Annual Register,* January–June 1932, Vols. 1, 3 and 17; R.M. Maxwell, Home Secretary, Government of Bombay to Emerson, 22 April 1932, in Chaudhari, ed., *Source Material,* 209–10.
63. 'One Year's Jail for Mrs Chattopadhyaya', *Times of India,* 8 April 1932; *Inner Recesses,* 170–71.
64. *Inner Recesses,* 170–71.
65. *Inner Recesses,* 172; Mira Behn, *The Spirit's Pilgrimage* (London: Longmans, 1960), 159–60; Gandhi, 'Letter to Mirabehn', 22 April 1932, *The Collected*

Works of Mahatma Gandhi (CWMG), Electronic Book (New Delhi: Publications Division, Government of India, 1999); Ramachandra Guha, Rebels against the Raj: Western Fighters for India's Freedom (New York: Knopf, 2022), 121–24.

66. Gandhi, 'Letter to Mirabehn', 22 April 1932, CWMG; *Inner Recesses*, 172.
67. Suruchi Thapar-Bjorkert, 'Gender, Nationalism, and the Colonial Jail: A Study of Women Activists in Uttar Pradesh', *Women's History Review*, Vol. 7, No. 4 (1998): 583–615; Nanda, 61–63; Brijbhushan, 78; *Inner Recesses*, 174–75.
68. Venkatesh, 'Marriage, Love, and the Nation', 99; Aparna Basu, *Mridula Sarabhai: Rebel with a Cause* (New Delhi: Oxford University Press, 2003), 43–44; Cousins and Cousins, *We Two Together*, 580; *Inner Recesses*, 36–37, 172–73.
69. Ratnam, 47–48, 65, 76–77; KC Oral History, 93–94.
70. Ratnam, 53, 60.
71. Kamaladevi to Gandhi, 26 March 1933, SN 20712, Sabarmati Ashram.
72. KC, 'Enter Gandhi', from *India's Case for Swaraj*, edited and compiled by Waman P. Kabadi, 2nd edition (Bombay: Yeshanand and Co., 1932), in *A Passionate Life*, 132; Cousins and Cousins, *We Two Together*, 708.
73. Kamaladevi to Gandhi, 5 May 1933, SN 21184, Sabarmati Ashram.
74. Ratnam, 66; 'Letter to Mathuradas Trikumji', 15 October 1933, CWMG; 'Letter to Abbas Tyabji', 15 October 1933, CWMG; KC, 'Sarojini Naidu', in *At The Cross-Roads*, 35 and 37–38; Interview with Gopalkrishna Gandhi, 23 April 2021; KC, Review of *Sarojini Naidu: An Introduction to a Fascinating Personality*, by Khawaja Ahmad Abbas (Bharatiya Vidya Bhawan, Bombay, 1980) in *India Quarterly*, Vol. 37, No. 3 (1981): 482–83; Nanda, 56 and 64; Forbes, *Women in Modern India*, 113–14; Rohit De, 'The Two Husbands of Vera Tiscenko: Apostasy, Conversion, and Divorce in Late Colonial India', *Law and History Review*, Vol. 28, No. 4 (November 2010), 1011–41.
75. *Inner Recesses*, 181; Barbieri, 'Kamaladevi Chattopadhyaya'; Ratnam, 64–65.
76. 'Letter to Mathuradas Trikumji', 20 October 1933, CWMG; Nanda, 64; Ratnam, 66.
77. Singh, 133–35; Nanda, 2.
78. Jawaharlal Nehru, 'To N.S. Hardikar', 28 October 1933, SWJN, Series 1, Volume 6, 49.
79. Singh, 133–35.
80. Ibid.; Nanda, 65.
81. Ratnam, 64–66.

82. Ratnam, 70; *Kamaladevi Chattopadhyay: An Extraordinary Life*, by Delhi Crafts Council, 2017, based on exhibition "Kamaladevi Chattopadhyay and the Making of Modern India," at IIC in April 2016, Devaki Jain and Kapila Vatsyayan, research led by Prof. Aparna Basu.
83. Ratnam, 46–47.
84. Bhargava, *Leaders of the Left*, 20.
85. 'Letter to Vallabhbhai Patel', 27 February 1934; Nanda, 2, and Nehru to KC, 21 November 1933, Kamaladevi Papers, NMML; Nanda, 71 and 115.
86. *Inner Recesses*, 183–84; Ratnam 155–56.
87. Ratnam, 71.
88. Scholarship on the colonial prison is vast. See Mushirul Hasan, *Roads to Freedom: Prisoners under Colonial Rule* (Delhi: Oxford University Press, 2016); David Arnold, 'India: The Contested Prison', in *Cultures of Confinement: A History of the Prison in Africa, Asia, and Latin America*, eds., Frank Dikötter and Ian Brown (Cornell University Press, 2007): 147–84; Thapar-Bjorkert, 'Gender, Nationalism, and the Colonial Jail'; Satadru Sen, 'The Female Jails of Colonial India', *Indian Economic and Social History Review*, Vol. 39, No. 4 (2002): 417–38; Ratnam, 157; Thomas Weber, *On the Salt March: The Historiography of Gandhi's March to Dandi* (New Delhi: HarperCollins Publishers India, 1997), 429.
89. Singh, 137; Nanda, 67; and Letter to J.B. Kripalani, 1 June 1934, Dr N.S. Hardikar Papers, NMML; *Inner Recesses*, 183–84.

4. Democratic Socialism

1. 'The All India Socialist Conference', *Indian Annual Register*, July–December 1934, Vol. 2, 295–96.
2. 'The All India Socialist Conference', 293–96; 'Mr Gandhi's Mission', Western Mail (Perth), 25 October 1934.
3. 'Report of the 48th Annual Session of the Indian National Congress' held at Abdul Ghaffar Nagar, Bombay, in October 1934 (Bombay: Associated Advertisers Press, n.d.): 16–17, 50.
4. Ibid., 74 and 79–80.
5. Sunil Khilnani, *The Idea of India* (London: Penguin, 2003), 74; Taylor C. Sherman, '"A New Type of Revolution": Socialist Thought in India, 1940s–1960s', *Postcolonial Studies*, Vol. 21, No. 4 (2018): 485–504; Amartya Sen, *The Argumentative Indian: Writings on Indian History, Culture and Identity* (New York: Picador, 2006); Andrae Beachtiger, John S. Dryzek,

Jane J. Mansbridge and Mark E. Warren, *Oxford Handbook of Deliberative Democracy* (New York: Oxford University Press, 2007).

6. Jayaprakash Narayan, 'Evolution of My Own Thinking', in *Jayaprakash Narayan, A Centenary Volume*, ed., Sandip Das (New Delhi: Mittal, 2005): 4–5; Pranav Jani, 'Bihar, California, and the US Midwest: The Early Radicalization of Jayaprakash Narayan', *Postcolonial Studies*, Vol. 16, No. 2 (2013), 155–68; Ramachandra Guha, *India after Gandhi: The History of the World's Largest Democracy* (New York: HarperCollins Publishers, 2007): 145, 311, 408, 477–85; 'The League of the Oppressed Peoples', *Independent Hindustan*, Vol. 1, No. 2 (October 1920), 27, South Asian American Digital Archive (SAADA); Kris Manjapra, *M.N. Roy: Marxism and Colonial Cosmopolitanism* (New York: Routledge, 2010); Samaren Roy, *M.N. Roy: A Political Biography*, 16; Sohi, *Echoes of Mutiny*, 80–81; John Patrick Haithcox, *Communism and Nationalism in India: M.N. Roy and Comintern Policy, 1920–1939* (Princeton: Princeton University Press, 1971), 219.
7. Dandavate, *As the Mind Unfolds*, xii and 304.
8. Nanda, 83, and KC to Kripalani, June 1934, Hardikar Papers, NMML.
9. Nanda, 74.
10. Nanda, 77.
11. 'Avoiding Reality', *Servant of India*, 16 May 1935, 257; 'Karnatak Leads the Way', Karnatak Political Conference, Mangalore, May 1935, in *At the Cross-Roads*, 56–57.
12. V.S. Narayana Rao, *Dr N. S. Hardiker*, 183–84, 192–93 and 209–10; Nanda, 74 and 77.
13. Nanda, 78.
14. Singh, 44–45.
15. Kamaladevi, 'Vallabhbhai Speaks', in Singh, 45–47.
16. Umashankar Joshi, 'Inaugural Address', 'Symposium on Cinema in Developing Countries', Publications Division, Ministry of Information and Broadcasting, New Delhi, 1979; *Inner Recesses*, 209.
17. The Indian Annual Register, July–December 1935, Vol. II, 276–77; Nanda, 78–79.
18. 'Socialist Party Conference', *Indian Annual Register*, July–December 1935, Vol. 2, ed., Nripendra Nath Mitra (Calcutta: Annual Register Office, 1936), 260; 'Imperialism and Class-Struggle', Presidential Address, All-India Socialist Conference, Meerut, 1936, in *At the Cross-Roads*, 20–21.
19. 'Sex and Social Struggle', *Congress Socialist*, April 1936, in *At the Cross-Roads*, 131–36.

20. Bhargava, *Leaders of the Left*, 22.
21. 'The Indian National Congress, Third Day–Lucknow–14th April 1936', in *Indian Annual Register*, ed., Nripendra Nath Mitra, January–June 1936, Vol. 1 (Calcutta: Annual Register Office, 1936), 288–89; 'Socialist's Victory on A.I.C.C. Election Method', *Times of India*, 16 April 1936.
22. Haithcox, *Communism and Nationalism in India*, 242.
23. 'Jawaharlal Nehru', undated, *At The Cross-Roads*, 30–31.
24. Nanda, 101.
25. 'The All-India Women's Conference at Karachi', *Indian Social Reformer*, 5 January 1935, 295; 'The World Under Capitalism', *Times of India*, 9 August 1935.
26. H.M. Hood Esq., Secretary to the Government of Madras to the Foreign Secretary to the Government of India, Foreign and Political Department, New Delhi, 20 October 1936, in 'Refusal to Grant Passport Facilities to Mrs Kamaladevi Chattopadhyaya, a Member of the Socialist Party Executive Question and Answer in Parliament Regarding This Decision of the Government', File No.: Home_Political_NA_1936_NA_F-28-102, Identifier: PR_000003036043, Digitized Public Records, Home Political, https://indianculture.gov.in/archives/refusal-grant-passport-facilities-mrs-kamaladevi-chattopadhyaya-member-socialist-party.
27. 'Mrs Chattopadhyaya: Refusal of Passport', *Servant of India*, 29 October 1936, 506.
28. 'Question and Answer in Parliament dated the 30th November 1936 regarding refusal of a passport to Mrs Kamala Chattopadhyya [sic]' in 'Refusal to Grant Passport Facilities to Mrs Kamaladevi Chattopadhyaya'.
29. Muthiah and Wanasinghe, *The Bracegirdle Affair*, 25–33.
30. Ibid.
31. Singh, 84–85.
32. Jawaharlal Nehru, 'Election Activities in Mysore State', Statement to the Press, Allahabad, 20 February 1937, *The Hindu*, 22 February 1937, SWJN, Series 1, Vol. 8, 548; 'Mrs Chattopadhyaya: Ban in Bangalore', *Servant of India*, 21 January 1937, 25; *Inner Recesses*, 204–05.
33. Gandhi to Nehru, 'Silence-Day Note to Jawaharlal Nehru', before 5 April 1937, CWMG.
34. KC Oral History, 129; 'Letter to Jawaharlal Nehru', 5 April 1937, CWMG.
35. 'Gujarat Socialist Conference', *Times of India*, 27 April 1937; 'All India Congress Committee', *Indian Annual Register*, July–December 1937, Vol. 11, 352 and 356–58; Nanda, 87; L.C. Jain, 'Kamaladevi: An Epochal Life', *Manushi*.

36. Gandhi, 'The A.I.C.C.', *Harijan*, 13 November 1937, CWMG; Nehru to Gandhi, 14 November 1937, in Appendix XI, CWMG; Singh, 85–86.
37. 'Congress Enters Upon a New Phase', *Modern Review* 62 (August 1937): 208–09; 'All India Congress Committee', *Indian Annual Register*, July–December 1937, Vol. 11, 352 and 356–58.
38. 'The U.P. Students' Conference', *Indian Annual Register*, July–December 1937, Vol. 11, 471–72; 'The All India Students' Conference', 1 January 1938, *Indian Annual Register*, January–June 1938, Vol. 1, 411–12.
39. Jawaharlal Nehru, 'The Congress and Federation', Speech at the Haripura Congress, 18 February 1938, from *The Hindu* (evening edition), 18 February 1938, SWJN, Series 1, Vol. 8, 759–60.
40. 'Mrs Kamaladevi Arrested', *Times of India*, 22 August 1938; KC Oral History, 171–73; *Inner Recesses*, 206–07.
41. 'Travancore to the Fore', *Indian Social Reformer*, 10 September 1938, 20–21; Singh, 86–88.
42. Gandhi, 'Statement to the Press', 3 September 1938, published in *Harijan*, 10 September 1938, CWMG.
43. Kamaladevi Chattopadhyay, 'Recent Happenings in Mysore', *Indian Student* (January 1939), 10–11, copy in author's possession courtesy of Ramachandra Guha.
44. The Indian National Congress, Tripuri, 12 March 1939, Proceedings and Resolutions, in *Indian Annual Register*, January–June 1939, Vol. 1 (Calcutta: N.N. Mitra), 338–39.
45. 'Ban on Mrs Kamaladevi', *Times of India*, 17 April 1939.
46. Singh, 92.
47. Ratnam, 74–75; Nanda, 72 and 76; KC to JP, 1937, JP Papers, NMML.
48. Ratnam, 71–72.
49. The phrase 'separated from both the male and female genitalia' is a translation of '*nara aur naaree yonee se alag*'. The word 'yonee' is usually translated as vagina, but 'genitalia' seems more fitting given that Kamaladevi was referencing both male and female anatomy. See Ratnam, 105–06.
50. Nandini Deo, 'Indian Women Activists and Transnational Feminism over the Twentieth Century', *Journal of Women's History*, Vol. 24, No. 4 (Winter 2012): 149–74, quote on 154; All-India Women's Conference, Thirteenth Session, Delhi, 28 December 1938–1 January 1939 (Bombay: Wagle Process Studio & Press, n.d.). On contested definitions of the political, also see Goswami and Sinha, *Political Imaginaries*; Prathama Banerjee,

Elementary Aspects of the Political: Histories from the Global South (Durham, NC: Duke University Press, 2020).

51. Kamaladevi, 'Freedom', *Congress Socialist,* 1 January 1939 in ed., Mushirul Hasan, *Towards Freedom: 1939, Part 2,* 1168–70.
52. Kamaladevi, 'Keeping Step with Times', *Congress Socialist,* 15 January 1939 in ed., Mushirul Hasan, *Towards Freedom: 1939, Part 2,* 1186–187.
53. Kamaladevi Chattopadhyaya, 'Future of Indian Women's Movement', in Shyam Kumari Nehru, *Our Cause: A Symposium by Indian Women* (Allahabad: Kitabistan, 1938), xiv, 385–99, 401–02, 419.
54. Kamaladevi, 'Future of Indian Women's Movement'; Kamaladevi, 'Freedom.'
55. KC, *The Awakening of Indian Women,* 76–77, 85.
56. 'The Women's Movement', *Servant of India,* 7 September 1939, 446; Mrs A. Asaf Ali, 'Women in India', *Indian Social Reformer,* 19 August 1939, 808.
57. *Inner Recesses,* 217; Ratnam, 75.
58. On Nehru's internationalism, see Michele Louro, *Comrades against Imperialism: Nehru, India, and Interwar Internationalism* (Cambridge: Cambridge University Press, 2018); *Inner Recesses,* 217; H.M. Hood Esq., Secretary to the Government of Madras to the Secretary to the Government of India in the External Affairs Department, Simla, 1 August 1938, 'Grant of Passport to Mrs Kamaladevi Chattopadhyaya and Her Son', File No.: Home_Political_NA_1938_NA_F-28-99_38, Identifier: PR_000003037178, Digitized Public Records, Home Political, National Archives of India, https://indianculture.gov.in/archives/grant-passport-mrs-kamaladevi-chattopadhyaya-and-her-son.

5. Freedom Abroad, Prison at Home

1. Brijbhushan, 83–84. Also see Barbieri, '"Chasing Me Over the Globe" Kamaladevi and the Limits of Imperial Surveillance and Passport Controls, 1939–41', in *A Passionate Life,* 401–23.
2. Brijbhushan, 84–85; *Inner Recesses,* 218–20; 'Mrs Kamaladevi in Egypt', *Times of India,* 21 June 1939; 'All-India Women's Conference, Fourteenth Session', Allahabad, no publishing information, 27–31 January, 1940, 88.
3. Brijbhushan, 85 and 87.
4. *Report of the Thirteenth Congress: Copenhagen July 8th to 14th 1939* (Ashford, Kent: Alliance, 1939), 8; Barbieri, 'Kamaladevi Chattopadhyaya', 22; Brijbhushan, 86; *Inner Recesses,* 230.

5. Kamaladevi, 'Keeping Step with Times', *Congress Socialist,* 15 January 1939 in ed., Mushirul Hasan, *Towards Freedom: 1939, Part 2,* 1186–87.
6. Gandhi, 'India's Attitude', *Harijan,* 14 October 1939, CWMG.
7. 'Mr Gandhi's Mission of World Peace', *Times of India,* 4 October 1939.
8. Indian Political Intelligence (IPI) 16, Microfiche # 570, File 635 (1939), Oriental and Indian Office Collections, British Library; Menon's correspondence with his invitees is in Box 2, File 27 of the V.K. Krishna Menon Papers, NMML; *Inner Recesses,* 224–27, 230 and 232.
9. Sangulee to Lord Zetland and Note to 'Mr Silver', Indian Political Intelligence (IPI) 16, Microfiche # 570, File 635 (1939), Oriental and Indian Office Collections, British Library; *Inner Recesses,* 234.
10. Barbieri, 'Kamaladevi Chattopadhyaya'; Krishnalal Shridharani, *War without Violence: A Study of Gandhi's Method and Its Accomplishments* (New York: Harcourt, Brace and Company, 1939).
11. *Inner Recesses,* 238–40, Barbieri, 'Chasing Me Over the Globe', 416 and note 47 on 422; *America: The Land of Superlatives,* 42, 109, 111.
12. Elizabeth La Hines, 'India Advanced in Equal Rights: Mrs Kamaladevi, Visiting Here, Tells How Men and Women Cooperate', *New York Times,* 26 November 1939.
13. 'Britain is Assailed for Plight of India', *New York Times,* 18 December 1939, 18; 'Events Today', *New York Times,* 3 January 1940, 19; Barbieri, 'Kamaladevi Chattopadhyaya'.
14. J.J. Singh to Vijaya Lakshmi Pandit, 20 June 1944, J.J. Singh Papers, NMML; Roger Baldwin to JN, 31 January 1940, Vol. 6, JN Papers, NMML.
15. 'Kamaladevi's American Impressions', *Indian Social Reformer,* 25 October 1941, 91–92; *Inner Recesses,* 246; KC Oral History, 136.
16. KC, 'Women Reform India', *The Living Age* (January 1940), 418.
17. Cairine Wilson, 'Address to the Annual Meeting of Women's Teachers Federation', Windsor, Ontario, 27 February 1940, in Nancy M. Forestell with Maureen Moynagh, eds., *Documenting First Wave Feminisms: Volume II Canada—National and Transnational Contexts* (Toronto: University of Toronto Press, 2014), 64; Lloyd to KC, 12 January 1940, Box 7, Georgia Lloyd Papers (GLP), New York Public Library.
18. 'Forum Lecture Bureau Inc., Presents Mme Kamaladevi', MVK Papers, SSC; 'Kamaladevi', undated flyer, Box 7, GLP; Jessie Ash Arndt, 'India to Avoid War, Says Woman Leader', *Washington Post,* 29 November 1939; Hope Ridings Miller, 'Social Calendar Filled by Topflight Visitors', *Washington Post,* 19 March 1940; Barbieri, 'Kamaladevi Chattopadhyaya'.
19. *Inner Recesses,* 238–43, 250; Barbieri, 'Kamaladevi Chattopadhyaya', 11–12.

20. James Williams to Nehru, 6 March 1940, Vol. 103, JN Papers, NMML; John Evans, 'Called Key to Future', *Chicago Daily Tribune,* 19 March 1940; June Markert, 'Mme Kamaladevi Describes Indian Reform Moves', *Daily Illini,* 20 March 1940; KC to Georgia Lloyd, 26 March 1941, GLP.
21. 'British Imperialism in India Denounced', 16 December 1939 in Folder 1, Box A 379, NAACP Papers, Library of Congress, Washington, DC; *Inner Recesses,* 253; Kamaladevi Chattopadhyaya, *America: The Land of Superlatives* (Bombay: Phoenix Publications, 1946), iv; 'Mme Kamaladevi in Farewell Talk', *New York Amsterdam Star News,* 1 March 1941, 8; *Bombay Chronicle,* 17 June 1940, quoted in Brijbhushan, 91.
22. This anecdote and other parts of this chapter first appeared in '"I Am a Colored Woman": Kamaladevi Chattopadhyaya in the United States, 1939–41', *Contemporary South Asia,* Vol. 17, No. 1 (March 2009): 7–19 and in *Colored Cosmopolitanism,* 138–39. Also see *Inner Recesses,* 253.
23. Poster for Event, 'Culture and the Future of the Darker Races', Mary Van Kleeck Papers, Smith College; 'Events Scheduled for Today', *New York Times,* 8 March 1941, 17; *Chicago Defender,* 23 March 1940, 10.
24. Several of their letters are in Vol. 88, Jawaharlal Nehru Papers, NMML; Rajni Patel to JN, 6 May 1939, Vol. 80, Jawaharlal Nehru Papers, NMML; Rajni Patel to JN, 14 July 1939, Vol. 80, Jawaharlal Nehru Papers, NMML; Indian Political Intelligence (IPI) 16, Microfiche # 570, File 635 (1939), Oriental and Indian Office Collections, British Library; Jawaharlal Nehru, 'To Kamaladevi Chattopadhyaya', 25 September 1940, *Selected Works of Jawaharlal Nehru,* Series 1, Vol. 11, 432–33.
25. Hilda Wierum Boulter, 'Kamaladevi—Gentle Warrior', *Asia,* Vol. 42, No. 3 (1942): 180; Brijbhushan, 93–95; 'Radio Today', *New York Times,* 7 April 1941, 32; Annie Mae Brown, 'Gandhi's Country: Tells of Life in India', Charlotte News, 8 April 1941, Rose Florence Papers, SSC, quoted in Barbieri, 'Kamaladevi Chattopadhyaya', 13.
26. KC to Georgia Lloyd, 7 January 1941, GLP.
27. Ratnam, 74.
28. Brijbhushan, 92–93; Western Union telegram, MVK to Henry Sigerist and others, 31 March 1941, MVK Papers, SSC, quoted in Barbieri, 'Kamaladevi Chattopadhyaya', 22.
29. 'Britain Flayed by Indian Woman Leader in Talk', *Nippu Jiji,* 30 April 1941; *Inner Recesses,* 258 and 263.
30. KC to Georgia Lloyd, 18 May 1941, GLP; Kamaladevi to My Dear Friends, 22 May 1941, MVK Papers, SSC, and *A Passionate Life,* 228.

31. 'India May Be Next Arsenal for Britain in War against Germany', *Japanese American News*, 23 May 1941.
32. KC to 'My Dear Friends', May 22, 1941, in *A Passionate Life*, 225–29; KC to 'My Dear Friends', 24 May 1941, in *A Passionate Life*, 230–31.
33. KC to 'My Dear Friends', 7 July 1941, in *A Passionate Life*, 231–33.
34. 34 KC to 'My Dear Friends', 7 July 1941; Nanda, 83 and KC to Kripalani, June 1934, Hardikar Papers.
35. 'Paradox of the Far East', *Bombay Chronicle*, 2 November 1941; Kamaladevi, 'Birth of a New Imperialism', *Bombay Chronicle*, 25 January 1942, quoted in Brijbhushan, 99 and 113–14.
36. Kamaladevi Chattopadhyaya, *In War-Torn China* (Bombay: Padma Publications, 1942), 8; KC to Georgia Lloyd, 26 March 1941, GLP.
37. KC to Georgia Lloyd, 6 September 1941, GLP; KC to 'My Dear Friends', 5 September 1941, in *A Passionate Life*, 234–37.
38. *In War-Torn China*, 15–16; *Inner Recesses*, 275.
39. *Inner Recesses*, 264; Brijbhushan, 114; Kamaladevi, 'An Indian in War-Torn China', *Bombay Chronicle*, 10 May 24, and 14 June 1942 and 'Women of China', 22 February 1942; *Inner Recesses*, 275; *In War-Torn China*.
40. On connections between Indian and Chinese political struggles in these years, see Maria Framke, '"We Must Send a Gift Worthy of India and the Congress!" War and Political Humanitarianism in Late Colonial South Asia', *Modern Asian Studies*, Vol. 51, No. 6 (2017): 1969–98. Also see Jawaharlal Nehru, 'Prison Diary', Friday, 10 October 1941, SWJN, Vol. 11, 712–13.
41. KC to 'My Dear Friends', 5 September 1941; KC to Georgia Lloyd, 6 September 1941, GLP.
42. Bombay Chronicle, 2 November 1941, quoted in Brijbhushan, 105-06; 'A Woman's Way to a Better World', *Tribune* (Manila), 23 October 1941; *Inner Recesses*, 282.
43. KC to Georgia Lloyd, 24 September 1941.
44. KC to Georgia Lloyd, December 1941, GLP.
45. 'American Interest in India: Mrs Kamaladevi Impression About America, China and Japan', Amrita Bazar Patrika, 2 October 1941 in Amit Kumar Gupta and Arjun Dev, eds., *Towards Freedom, 1941, Part 1*, 194–95; 'India and America', editorial, *Amrita Bazar Patrika*, 6 October 1941, in *Towards Freedom, 1941, Part 1*, 197.
46. 'Kamaladevi's American Impressions', *Indian Social Reformer*, 25 October 1941, 91–92.

47. 'Report on CSP General Secretary's Speech at Bihar Provincial Congress Socialist Conference', *Amrita Bazar Patrika,* 1 November 1941, in *Towards Freedom, 1941, Part 1,* 552; Cousins, *Indian Womanhood Today,* 150 and 68–69.
48. KC Oral History, 130; 'Letter to Kamaladevi Chattopadhyaya', 3 October 1941.
49. 'Letter to Amrit Kaur', 9 October 1941, CWMG; 'Letter to Amrit Kaur', 10 October 1941, CWMG; 'Letter to Kamaladevi Chattopadhyaya', 8 November 1941, CWMG; 'Telegram to Jayaprakash Narayan', 17 November 1941, CWMG; *Inner Recesses,* 288; KC Oral History, 178–80.
50. All-India Women's Conference, Sixteenth Session, Cocanada, 29 December 1941–1 January 1942 (Bombay: All India Women's Conference, 1942), 12–14. On Pandit, see Anne Guthrie, *Madame Ambassador: The Life of Vijaya Lakshmi Pandit* (New York: Harcourt, Brace and World, 1962).
51. All-India Women's Conference, Sixteenth Session, Cocanada, 66–67, 73 and 89–90.
52. C.K. Narayanaswamy, 'Two Days in Women's Camp', *Bombay Chronicle,* 21 June 1942; Brijbhushan, 115; Nanda, 92–93; Kulsum Sayana article in Kamaladevi Papers, NMML; The All-India Women's Conference, Seventeenth Session, Bombay, 7–10 April 1944 (publishing information absent); Kitty Shiva Rao, 'Women Workers' Training Camp,' *Indian Journal of Social Work,* 226–30, http://ijsw.tiss.edu/greenstone/collect/ijsw/index/assoc/HASHe4c6.dir/doc.pdf; 'The Alumni Association: The Tata Graduate School of Social Work', Annual Report for 1941–42, 126–27, http://ijsw.tiss.edu/greenstone/collect/ijsw/index/assoc/HASH0197/81b1632d.dir/doc.pdf.
53. Narayanaswamy, 'Two Days in Women's Camp'; Rao, 'Women Workers' Training Camp'.
54. Rao, 'Women Workers' Training Camp'.
55. 'Letter to Kamaladevi Chattopadhyaya', 26 February 1942, CWMG; Nanda, 93; K.K. Chaudhari, *Quit India Revolution*; Guha, *Gandhi: The Years That Changed the World.*
56. 'Socialist Homage to M.K. Gandhi's Leadership: Will Line Up with Congress in Non-violent Struggle for Freedom', *Bombay Chronicle,* 7 August 1942 in ed., Bipan Chandra, *Towards Freedom, 1942, Part 1,* 541–42; Nanda, 94.
57. *Inner Recesses,* 291; Nanda, 99.
58. Nanda, 95.

59. 'As an Indian Sees It', *Pittsburgh Courier*, 17 October 1942, 12; 'Indian Woman Leader Who Toured U.S. Jailed', *Chicago Daily Tribune*, 8 September 1942; Singh, 94–96.
60. *Inner Recesses*, 290–92.
61. *Inner Recesses*, 292–93.
62. 'The All India Women's Conference, 17th Session–Bombay–7th to 10th April 1944', in *Indian Annual Register*, January–June 1944, Vol. 1 (Calcutta, N.N. Mitra).
63. Ibid., 284–88.
64. Avabai B. Wadia, *The Light Is Ours: Memoirs & Movements* (London: International Planned Parenthood Federation, 2001), 102–03; *Inner Recesses*, 294.
65. The All-India Women's Conference, Eighteenth Session, Hyderabad (Sind), 28 December 1945–1 January 1946 (Bombay: Associated Advertiser and Printers Limited, 1946), 3, 48, 83–84; *Inner Recesses*, 294; Wadia, *The Light Is Ours*, 109; 'Chronicle of Events', *Indian Annual Register*, July–December 1944, Vol. 2, ed., Nripendra Nath Mitra (Calcutta: Annual Register Office, 1945), 24.
66. Interview dated 26 May 1945 reproduced in Homi J.H. Taleyarkhan, *They Told Me So* (Bombay: Thacker, 1947), 69–74.
67. Written statement submitted to the Hindu Law committee: Vol. 1, 1945 (Madras: Government Press, 1947), 29–30.
68. 'All India Women's Conference', *Indian Social Reformer*, 8 April 1944, 243; 'A Bandra Diary', *Indian Social Reformer*, 22 April 1944, 261.
69. KC, 'Woman the Comrade'; 'Kasturba Gandhi', National Press Syndicate, 22 February 1947, in *At The Cross-Roads*, 38 and 40.
70. Neela Bhatt, 'The Kasturba Gandhi National Memorial Trust', *Indian Journal of Social Work*, http://ijsw.tiss.edu/greenstone/collect/ijsw/index/assoc/HASHc2b5/edd15a2e.dir/doc.pdf; 'Letter to Kamaladevi Chattopadhyaya', 19 June 1944, CWMG; 'Letter to Kamaladevi Chattopadhyaya', 18 July 1944, CWMG.
71. Ed., B.G. Kunte, *Source Material for a History of the Freedom Movement in India*, Vol. 4, Congress Activities, 1942–46 (1977), 120; Anonymous, 'A Bandra Diary', *Indian Social Reformer*, 16 June 1945, 251–53.
72. 'CID Report for April 1945, Gwalior State (Extracts)', in Bimal Prasad, ed., *Towards Freedom*, 1945, 589; Kunte, *Source Material*, 126–27, 129 and 135.
73. 'Note to Kamaladevi Chattopadhyaya', after 4 July 1945, CWMG; 'Note to Kamaladevi Chattopadhyaya', after 5 July 1945, CWMG; 'Silence-Day Note to Kamaladevi Chattopadhyaya', After 5 July 1945, CWMG.

74. T.L. Goodman, 'The Problem of India's Women', *Advertiser* (Adelaide), 30 December 1944.
75. Elisabeth Armstrong, 'Before Bandung: The Anti-Imperialist Women's Movement in Asia and the Women's International Democratic Federation', *Signs: Journal of Women in Culture and Society*, Vol. 41, No. 2 (Winter 2016): 305–31, quote on 313; Kamaladevi Chattopadhyay, *Uncle Sam's Empire* (Bombay: Padma Publications, 1944), 49; Reviews quoted in promotional materials for *Uncle Sam's Empire* attached to Vinayak Damodar Savarkar, *Indian War of Independence, 1857* (Bombay: Phoenix Publications, 1947).
76. Kamaladevi, *America*, 70, 113–41, 144–45, 171, 177–79, 185, 199–205 and 209.
77. 'The Bihar Provincial Conference', *Indian Quarterly Register*, July–December 1928, ed., Nripendra Nath Mitra, (Calcutta: Annual Register Office, 1929), 441; 'The All-India National Social Conference', *Indian Quarterly Register*, July–December 1928, 477; 'Youth and the Fight for Independence'; 'All Bengal Students' Conference', *Indian Annual Register*, January–June 1931, Vol. I, 359–62.
78. KC, *Women Reform India*; 'The All India Women's Conference, 17th Session—Bombay', 284–85.
79. Parr, 'Citizens of Everywhere', 244 and 483; 'The Indian Question Has a Vital Bearing on Future World Order', Kamala Devi Chattopadhyay's letter to Corbett Ashby, 11 May 1945, *Bombay Chronicle*, 12 May 1945, in ed., Bimal Prasad, *Towards Freedom*, 1945, 211–12.
80. Kunte, *Source Material*, 93–100.
81. KC, *Towards a National Theatre* (Aundh: Published for the All-India Women's Conference by Aundh Publishing Trust, 1945), 56; KC Oral History, 142; Brijbhushan, 19; Dhamija, 101–02; *Inner Recesses*, 294; Wadia, *The Light Is Ours*, 109; Narasimhan, 101.
82. *Towards a National Theatre*, 6, 9–10, 36.
83. *Towards a National Theatre*, 10 and 54–55; Huntly Carter, *The New Theatre and Cinema of Soviet Russia* (New York: International Publishers, 1925), 17 and 51; Aparna Bhargava Dharwadker, *Theatres of Independence*, 32–35; Sharmistha Saha, *Theatre and National Identity in Colonial India.* On contested citizenship, see Kalyani Ramnath, 'Review Essay: Histories of Indian Citizenship in the Age of Decolonisation', *Itinerario*, Vol. 45, No. 1 (2021), 152–73; Sarah Ansari and William Gould, *Boundaries of Belonging. Localities, Citizenship and Rights in India and Pakistan* (Cambridge: Cambridge University Press, 2020); Ornit Shani, *How India Became*

Democratic: Citizenship and the Making of Universal Franchise (Cambridge: Cambridge University Press, 2017); Niraja Gopal Jayal, *Citizenship and Its Discontents: An Indian History* (Cambridge, Mass.: Harvard University Press, 2013); Anupama Roy, *Mapping Citizenship in India* (Oxford: Oxford University Press, 2010).

84. *Towards a National Theatre*, 52–54.

6. Triumph and Tragedy

1. 'Need for National Theatre', *Times of India*, 27 August 1945; Interview dated 26 May 1945, reproduced in Homi J.H. Taleyarkhan, 'They Told Me So' (Bombay: Thacker, 1947), 69–74.
2. 'The Motion Picture Industry', *Modern Review*, May 1946, 340–42; 'The Principles of Health Insurance', *Roshni*, Journal of the All-India Women's Conference, June 1945; 'The Demand for Full Employment', *Modern Review*, November 1945, 275; 'Industrial Strikes', *Modern Review*, January 1947, 21–23; 'The Food Problem', *Modern Review*, November 1947, 357–60; 'The Struggle of Viet Nam against French Imperialism', *Modern Review*, March 1947, 189–92; 'The Trial of Democracy', *Modern Review* (February 1946): 93–96; 'The Spanish Issue', *Modern Review* (October 1946), 257–59; 'Current Political Trends in Europe', *Modern Review* (April 1947), 273–76; 'The Demand for Full Employment', *Modern Review*, November 1945, 275 and 'Full Employment', in *At The Cross-Roads*, 169–80.
3. 'Goals of Social Reconstruction', *Modern Review*, August 1945, 79–82; 'The Place of Women in the New Society', *Modern Review* (July 1946), 21–24.
4. 'All-India Congress Committee Proceedings', 23 September 1945, in *Indian Annual Register*, July–December, 1945, Vol. 2, 96–97; 'Issues Before All India Congress Committee', *Leader*, 22 September 1945 in Bimal Prasad, ed., *Towards Freedom*, 1945, 421–23.
5. Singh, 96–99.
6. 'Letter to Kamaladevi Chattopadhyaya', 14 December 1945, CWMG; 'Education and the New Society', Inaugural address at the Morris College Centenary, Nagpur, December 1945, in *At the Cross-Roads*, 115–16 and 121.
7. Wadia, *The Light Is Ours*, 104.
8. 'Srimati Kamaladevi', *Times of India*, 25 December 1945; 'The All-India Women's Conference, Eighteenth Session, Hyderabad (Sind)', 83–84.
9. 'Capitalism, Imperialism and Exploitation', Address at the Workers and Peasants' Conference at Jubbulpore, 26 April 1946, in *At the Cross-Roads*, 151; 'Indian National Movement', from the Address at the Socialist

Conference at Gadag, Karnatak, June 1946, in *At the Cross-Roads,* 45–48; '"No Dictatorship" for India', *Times of India,* 24 June 1946.

10. 'Karnatak Leads the Way', Karnatak Political Conference, Mangalore, May 1935, in *At the Cross-Roads,* 60; 'Issues Before All India Congress Committee'; Girja Shankar, 'Socialists and the Partition of India', *Proceedings of the Indian History Congress* 50 (1989), 539–46; Ashoka Mehta and Achyut Patwardhan, *The Communal Triangle in India* (Allahabad, 1942), 222.
11. Jawaharlal Nehru, 'The New Congress Executive', SWJN, Series 1, Vol. 15, 460.
12. *Jayaprakash Narayan: Selected Works, Volume 4, 1946–1948,* ed., Bimal Prasad (New Delhi: Manohar, 2003), 57; *Inner Recesses,* 299–300.
13. 'Proceeding of the Working Committee', 8–13 August, 27–30 August, 23–25 October and 19–22 November 1946, in *Indian Annual Register,* July–December 1946, Vol. 11, 104–05, 109–10, and 114–17.
14. 'Pakistan and the Shifting of Populations', *Blitz,* February 1947, in *At the Cross-Roads,* 76–82.
15. 'Princes Stand Condemned', *The Hindu,* 3 March 1947, in ed., Sucheta Mahajan, *Towards Freedom: 1947, Part 2,* 2132–133; 'States People Conference Demands Clean Out of Princely Autocracy', Extract from a report in *People's Age,* 4 May 1947, in *Towards Freedom: 1947, Part 2,* 2220–25.
16. 'Fascist Dictatorship in Portugal', *Modern Review* (November 1946), 341–43; B.G. Kunte, ed., *Source Material for a History of the Freedom Movement in India,* Vol. 8, Part 1, Goa Freedom Struggle (Mumbai: Government of Maharashtra, 1978), 86 and 98–99.
17. Kamala Devi Chattopadhyaya, *Status of Women in India* (New Delhi: Indian Council of World Affairs, 1947); 'The Awakening of Asia', written in conjunction with the Inter-Asian Relations Conference in Delhi, in *At The Cross-Roads,* 180–81, 185; Vineet Thakur, 'An Asian Drama: The Asian Relations Conference, 1947', *International History Review,* Vol. 41, No. 3 (2019), 673–95.
18. Narashimhan, 101–02.
19. 'The Communal Problem—A Socialist Perspective', Extract from the address at the Provincial Socialist Convention, Mangalore, April 1947, in *At The Cross-Roads,* 65–73.
20. 'Congress Deliberations on HMG's Statement', Extracts from the Proceedings of the Congress Working Committee, 31 May 1947–5 June

1947, AICC Papers, File No. G-43, NMML, in ed., Sucheta Mahajan, *Towards Freedom: 1947, Part 1,* 833–34; KC Oral History, 152–59.

21. *Inner Recesses,* 302; Shankar, 'Socialists and the Partition of India'; Haithcox, Communism and Nationalism in India, 247; 'To Jawaharlal Nehru', 3 May 1947, *Jayaprakash Narayan: Selected Works,* Vol. 4, 140.
22. *Inner Recesses,* 303–04.
23. Brijbhushan, 123–25.
24. 'Urgent Need for National Unity', *Times of India,* 2 March 1948; Anjali Bhardwaj Datta, 'Renegotiating the Self: Recovery and Restoration—The "Gendered" Histories of Partition', *Indian Historical Review,* Vol. 35, No. 2 (July 2008), 191–208; Urvashi Butalia, 'Community, State, and Gender: Some Reflections on the Partition of India', in *Women and the Politics of Violence,* ed., Taisha Abraham (New Delhi: Shakti Books, 2002): 90–106; *Inner Recesses,* 325 and 327–28.
25. L.C. Jain, 'Kamaladevi Chattopadhyay—My Long Journey with Her in the Realm of Handicrafts', in *Kamaladevi Chattopadhyay: A True Karmayogi,* ed., M.V. Narayana Rao (Bangalore: Crafts Council of Karnataka, 2003), 1; J.A. Panakal, 'All India Conference of Social Work', *Indian Social Reformer,* 6 December 1947, 108–09; Salvi, *Development Retold,* 5.
26. *The Ramon Magsaysay Awards,* published under the auspices of the Board of Trustees of the Ramon Magsaysay Award Foundation (Manila: Carmelo & Bauerman Printing, 1966), 56; Gulshan Nanda, 'Kamaladevi's Vision of Handicraft Cooperatives: A Personal Narrative', given as part of the programme, 'To Remember Kamaladevi Chattopadhyay', on 13 April 2013, reprinted India International Centre Occasional Publication 51; *Inner Recesses,* 307–08.
27. Kamaladevi, 'A Saga of the Uprooted', quoted in Brijbhushan, 130–31.
28. Kamaladevi, 'A Saga of the Uprooted', quoted in Brijbhushan, 132.
29. 'Annual Report of the General Secretary, Socialist Party Conference (Organizational), Nasik, 19–21 March 1948', *Jayaprakash Narayan: Selected Works,* Vol. 4, 443–51; L.C. Jain, 'Kamaladevi: Obituary', *Economic and Political Weekly,* Vol. 23, No. 48 (26 November 1988): 2520–521.
30. Jawaharlal Nehru, 'Prison Diary', Friday, 10 October 1941, SWJN, Vol. 11, 712–13; *Inner Recesses,* 27–28 and 306–07; 'Goals of Social Reconstruction', *Modern Review,* August 1945, in *At The Cross-Roads,* 144–45; Dhamija, 59–61.
31. 'The Village and the Future', in *At The Cross-Roads,* 89–90.
32. *Inner Recesses,* 307–08.
33. Ratnam, 181.

34. KC Oral History, 187; Brijbhushan 123–25.
35. 'Woman the Comrade'.
36. 'Indian National Movement' and '"No Dictatorship" for India', KC; KC, 'What Gandhiji Has Done for Women', in *What Gandhiji Has Done for India* (Lahore: Ilami Markaz, YMCA, 1946), 57–72.
37. 'Government Must Formally Resign and Home Minister Replaced, New Delhi, February 3, 1948', statement issued jointly by Jayaprakash Narayan, Rammanohar Lohia and Kamaladevi Chattopadhyaya, *Pioneer,* 4 February 1948 in *Jayaprakash Narayan: Selected Works,* Vol. 4, 211–12.
38. 'Demand for Reconstruction of the Government: Some Clarifications, New Delhi, February 5, 1948', statement issued jointly by Jayaprakash Narayan, Rammanohar Lohia and Kamaladevi Chattopadhyaya, *Searchlight,* 7 February 1948 in *Jayaprakash Narayan: Selected Works,* Vol. 4, 212–13.
39. Vallabhbhai Patel to Jawaharlal Nehru, 6 February 1948, in ed., Valmiki Choudhary, *Dr Rajendra Prasad Correspondence and Select Documents,* Vol. 8 (New Delhi: Allied, 1987), 198–99.
40. M.O. Mathai, *Reminiscences of the Nehru Age* (New Delhi: Vikas, 1978), 213.
41. Gandhi, *Of a Certain Age,* 96; Ratnam, 194–95.
42. Kamaladevi, 'A Saga of the Uprooted', quoted in Brijbhushan, 132 and 135; *Inner Recesses,* 307–08.
43. 'To Shakti Bose and Sibnath Banerjee', 16 October 1949, 'To Rohit Dave', 22 October 1949, 'To K.B. Menon', 20 June 1950, and 'To Kamaladevi Chattopadhyaya', 5 March 1950, all in *Jayaprakash Narayan: Selected Works,* Vol. 5, 1948–1950, ed., Bimal Prasad (New Delhi: Manohar, 2005), 297, 303, 356–57, 401–02.
44. Kamaladevi, 'A Saga of the Uprooted', quoted in Brijbhushan, 132–33; Brijbhushan, 136–37.
45. 'To Jawaharlal Nehru', 10 December 1948, *Jayaprakash Narayan: Selected Works,* Vol. 5, 1948–1950, ed., Bimal Prasad (New Delhi: Manohar, 2005), 113; Brijbhushan, 137–38.
46. L.C. Jain, *The Faridabad Story,* 108; 'To Mohanlal Saksena', 6 June 1949, SWJN, Series 2, Vol. 11, 81–84.
47. Guha, *India after Gandhi,* 87–88; Yasmin Khan, *The Great Partition* (New Haven: Yale University Press, 2007), 173.
48. 'Meeting of the Faridabad Development Board', 10 June 1949, SWJN, Series 2, Vol. 11, 109–11; 'To Mohanlal Saksena', 18 June 1949, SWJN, Series 2, Vol. 11, 92–94.

49. 'Co-operate with Government in Relief Work', *Times of India,* 10 July 1950.
50. Guha, *India after Gandhi,* 87–88; 'Refugees in India Erect Model City', *New York Times,* 21 October 1951; Lillian T. Mowrer, 'India: World's Worst-Fed Country', *World's News,* July, 1951; 'Experiments in Living: Faridabad–Nilokheri–Etawah', *Times of India,* 14 February 1952.
51. Kamaladevi, 'A Saga of the Uprooted', quoted in Brijbhushan, 127–30 and 135–36; Ian Talbot, 'Punjabi Refugees' Rehabilitation and the Indian State: Discourses, Denials and Dissonances', *Modern Asian Studies,* Vol. 25, No. 1 (2011): 109–30.
52. Kamaladevi, 'A Saga of the Uprooted', 128 and 135.
53. Kamaladevi, 'A Saga of the Uprooted', 135–36.
54. Ravinder Kaur, *Since 1947: Partition Narratives among Punjabi Migrants of Delhi* (Oxford: Oxford University Press, 2007), 24–25; Uditi Sen, *Citizen Refugee: Forging the Indian Nation after Partition* (Cambridge: Cambridge University Press, 2018).
55. L.C. Jain, *The Faridabad Story,* 183.
56. http://www.probashionline.com/faridabad-womans-vision-build-city.
57. Jain, 'Kamaladevi: Obituary'.
58. Jawaharlal Nehru, 'Faridabad Development Board', Note to the Minister for Rehabilitation, 19 September 1952, SWJN, Series 2, Vol. 19, 159–60; Nanda, 112–13.
59. Sunil Purushotham, *From Raj to Republic: Sovereignty, Violence, and Democracy in India* (Stanford: Stanford University Press, 2021), 138.
60. *Inner Recesses,* 322.
61. P.L. Prattis, 'Seventeen Days in Independent India', *Pittsburgh Courier,* 3 September 1949, 12; P.L. Prattis, 'Seventeen Days in Independent India', *Pittsburgh Courier,* 1 October 1949, 7.
62. Kamaladevi Chattopadhyay, 'Determining Social Status by Color . . . Antiquated: East Indian Woman Leader Decries Age of Irrationalism', *Pittsburgh Courier,* 1 October 1949, 8.
63. KC, 'Racial Discrimination in South Africa', *Modern Review* (June 1947), 441–43 and 'The People of Africa', in *At The Cross-Roads,* 186–95.
64. Brijbhushan, 149–51.
65. 'Bombay Association for World Government Formed', *Times of India,* 31 August 1949; 'Socialism and Moral Values', in *At the Cross-Roads,* 99–113; 'Restatement of Human Values', *Modern Review* 83 (March 1948), 189–94.

66. 'West's Attitude Towards Africa', *Times of India*, 23 August 1951; Brijbhushan, 154; Vinay Lal, 'Kamaladevi Chattopadhyay and the Idea of the Global South', 391.
67. 'Regret Expressed Over U.S. Stand on "Rights" Pact', *San Bernardino Sun*, 9 April 1953; 'Work on Human Rights in Vain', *Times of India*, 9 April 1953; Manu Bhagavan, 'Indian Internationalism and the Implementation of Self-Determination: Kamaladevi Chattopadhyay and the United Nations Human Rights Commission', in *A Passionate Life*, 424–44; *Inner Recesses*, 375; Manu Bhagavan, *India and the Quest for One World: The Peacemakers* (New York: Palgrave, 2013), 115.
68. *The Ramon Magsaysay Awards*, 62.
69. Jawaharlal Nehru, 'India and Neighbouring Countries', Speech while inaugurating Indo-Arab Society, Bombay, 7 October 1954, SWJN, Series 2, Vol. 27, 188–94.
70. Kamaladevi Chattopadhyay, 'Let the Two Streams Flow Together', *Times of India*, 7 October 1954.
71. P.L. Prattis, 'Seventeen Days in Independent India', *Pittsburgh Courier*, 1 October 1949, 7; Rajindar Sachar, 'Dr Lohia—Our Revolutionary Mentor', *Mainstream*, Vol. 47, No. 14, 21 March 2009.
72. 'Socialists, A Bunch of Reactionaries? Reply to Pandit Nehru (Hyderabad: Published for the Socialist Party by Chetna Prakashan, 1949),' in *A Passionate Life*, 108–18; *Inner Recesses*, 382–83; Devenish, 'Creativity as Freedom', 351; KC, 'In Defence of R. Lohia and Others', 1949, 'Speeches and Writings by Her', File 8, KC Papers, NMML.
73. 'The Simple Case for Democratic Socialism', *Caravan* (1947) republished in *At the Cross-Roads*, 7–14; 'The Case for Socialism Restated', undated, *At the Cross-Roads*, 15–16.
74. KC, *Socialism and Society* (Hyderabad: Chetana, 1950), 1–3, 9–15.
75. Ed., Valmiki Choudhary, *Dr Rajendra Prasad: Correspondence and Select Documents*, Vol. 12 (Bombay: Allied Publishers, 1989), 238.
76. Jawaharlal Nehru, 'To Morarji Desai', 22 October 1951, SWJN, Series 2, Vol. 16, Part 2, 47–48; 'To B.C. Roy', 22 October 1951, SWJN, Series 2, Vol. 16, Part 2, 49; 'To Morarji Desai', 27 October 1951, SWJN, Series 2, Vol. 16, Part 2, 55–57.
77. Kamaladevi, 'Reflections after Sixty', Bharat Jyoti, 23 January 1966; 'Shrimati Kamaladevi Was "Locked Up" By Family', *Times of India*, 27 August 1956; Jain, 'Kamaladevi: An Epochal Life'.
78. Sherman, *Nehru's India*, 117 and 122; Daniel Kent-Carrasco, 'A Battle Over Meanings: Jayaprakash Narayan, Rammanohar Lohia and the Trajectories

of Socialism in Early Independent India', *Global Intellectual History*, Vol. 2, No. 3 (2017): 370–88; Aditya Balasubramanian, 'Contesting "Permit-and-Licence Raj": Economic Conservatism and the Idea of Democracy in 1950s India', *Past and Present*, Vol. 251, No. 1 (May 2021): 189–227.

79. 'Mrs Kamaladevi Chattopadhyaya', *Times of India*, 1 March 1953.

7. Crafting a Nation

1. Ashoka Gupta, *In the Path of Service: Memories of a Changing Century*, translated from the Bengali by Sipra Bhattacharya with Ranjana Dasgupta (Kolkata: STREE, 2005), 79–84; Ellora De, 'Folktale of Indian Handicrafts', http://businesseconomics.in/folk-tale-indian-handicrafts; Nicole Sackley, 'The Bankura Horse as Development Object: Women's Work, Indo-American Exchanges, and the Global Handicraft Trade', in Harald Fischer-Tiné and Nico Slate, *Indo-US Entanglements: The United States and South Asia from the Age of Empire to Decolonisation* (Leiden: Leiden University Press, forthcoming).
2. Cherian, 'The First Drama Seminar Report', 38. Also see McGowan, *Crafting the Nation*; Goswami, *Producing India*; Saloni Mathur, *India by Design: Colonial History and Cultural Display* (Berkeley: University of California Press, 2007); Lisa Trivedi, *Clothing Gandhi's Nation: Homespun and Modern India* (Bloomington: Indian University Press, 2007).
3. On the debate concerning the 'deindustrialization' of India, see McGowan, *Crafting the Nation*, 4, and Tirthankar Roy, *Traditional Industry in the Economy of Colonial India* (Cambridge: Cambridge University Press, 1999). Also see 'All Bengal Students' Conference', *Indian Annual Register*, January–June 1931, Vol. I, 359–62; Perinbanayagam, *A Memorial Volume*, 76; *At The Cross-Roads*, 21; *The Awakening of Indian Women*, 171.
4. 'The All India Women's Conference, 17th Session—Bombay—7th to 10th April 1944', in *Indian Annual Register*, January–June 1944, Vol. 1 (Calcutta: N.N. Mitra), 286; McGowan, *Crafting the Nation*.
5. *Inner Recesses*, 66–67.
6. 'Socialism and Moral Values', in *At the Cross-Roads*, 106; 'Labour Problems', in *At The Cross-Roads*, 152.
7. *Towards a National Theatre*, 1–5; 'A Social Evaluation of Art', in *At The Cross-Roads*, 123–25; KC, *Socialism and Society* (Hyderabad: Chetana, 1950), 107–08, 113–15.
8. Ibid., 127–31.

9. Datta, '"Useful" and "Earning" Citizens? Gender, State, and the Market in Post-Colonial Delhi', *Modern Asian Studies*, Vol. 53, No. 6 (November 2019): 1924–1955; Uditi Sen, 'Social Work, Refugees, and National Belonging: Evaluating the "Lady Social Workers" of West Bengal', *South Asia: Journal of South Asian Studies*, Vol. 44, No. 2 (2021): 344–61; Gouri Salvi, *Development Retold: Voices from the Field* (Delhi: Concept Publishing, 1999), 98; Nanda, 'Kamaladevi's Vision'.
10. *Inner Recesses*, 319; Sackley, 'The Bankura Horse as Development Object'.
11. Interview with Gopalkrishna Gandhi, 23 April 2021; Purnima Rai, interviewed by author, 4 May 2021; Nanda, 'Kamaladevi's Vision'.
12. Margaret Patch, 'Craftsman's Odyssey', *Craft Horizons*, Vol. 22, No. 5 (September–October 1962), 53.
13. Suneet Aiyar, interviewed by author, 14 May 2021; Salvi, *Development Retold*, 107.
14. Gita Ram interviewed by author, 18 May 2021; Romulus Whitaker, correspondence with author, 24 April 2021; From the presentations by Arundhati Chattopadhaya and Nina Menon in 'Ode to the Glorious Past . . . Past Presidents of AIWC: Kamaladevi Chattopadhyaya', a webinar, Friday, 27 August 2021.
15. Rahman, *Dancing in the Family*, 93–94.
16. Rahman, *Dancing in the Family*, 93–94; Ruby Palchoudhuri, interviewed on 17 May 2021 and written correspondence in author's possession, including a compilation of memories compiled with the assistance of Shikha Mukerjee (Palchoudhuri compilation); Jain, 'Kamaladevi Chattopadhyay—My Long Journey with Her in the Realm of Handicrafts'; Asha Puthli interviewed by author, 1 July 2021.
17. Soumhya Venkatesan, 'The Social Life of a "Free" Gift', *American Ethnologist*, Vol. 38, No. 1 (February 2011): 47–57.
18. Sackley, 'The Bankura Horse as Development Object.'
19. *America: The Land of Superlatives*, 122–23; Sackley, 'The Bankura Horse as Development Object'; 'Project States for the India Program of the American International Association for Economic and Social Development and the Cooperative League of the USA', 12 March 1953, Rockefeller Family Archives, Public Relations Department Papers, Series 1, Box 5, Folder 50, Rockefeller Archives Center, Tarrytown, NY.
20. Nanda, 'Kamaladevi's Vision'; Sackley, 'The Bankura Horse as Development Object'; Tom Keehn to Mabel and Harper, 15 February 1954 in *India Ink*, 34; L.C. Jain and Karen Coelho, *In Wake of Freedom: India's Tryst with Cooperatives* (New Delhi: Concept Publishing, 1996), 352;

Ashoka Gupta, *In the Path of Service*, 80; 'A Relationship with Handicrafts', An Interview with Kamla Devi Chattopadhyay by Rajeev Sethi and Nalini Singh, Asian Heritage Foundation, https://www.youtube.com/watch?v=xbkCu5oYoIU; L.C. Jain, *Two Freedom Struggles, One Life*, 123–24.

21. Manjari Nirula interviewed by author, 5 May 2021; Brijbhushan, 143.
22. Meherally, *At The Cross-Roads*, 5–6.
23. Vijaya Rajan interviewed by author, 1 May 2021; Brijbhushan, 143; Dhamija, 92–93.
24. Chandan Bose, 'Authenticating the Craft: Geographical Indication as the New History of the Telangana Scroll', *India International Centre Quarterly*, Vol. 42, No. 1 (Summer 2015): 109–22, quote on 118; Kamaladevi Chattopadhyay, 'Of Reason Fragmented', *India International Centre Quarterly*, Vol. 14, No. 1 (Spring 1987), 29–36; R. Kalyana Sundaram, 'Some Thoughts on the "Mother of Handicrafts"', in *M. Rao, Kamaladevi Chattopadhyay: A True Karmayogi*, 43.
25. Paul Greenough, 'Nation, Economy, and Tradition Displayed: The Indian Crafts Museum, New Delhi', in ed., Carol Appadurai Breckenridge, *Consuming Modernity: Public Culture in a South Asian World* (Minneapolis: University of Minnesota Press, 1995), 216–17 and 222–23; KC Speech, Tenth Asian Assembly of the World Crafts Council, in M. Rao, *Kamaladevi Chattopadhyay: A True Karmayogi*, 98; Kamaladevi, 'A Forceful Art'.
26. 'Artisans Need Education', *Times of India*, 8 January 1954; Devaki Jain, 'Remembering Kamaladevi', *Indian Express*, 3 November 1988, in author's possession.
27. Farhan Karim, *Of Greater Dignity than Riches: Austerity and Housing Design in India* (Pittsburgh: University of Pittsburgh Press, 2019), 226; Sackley, 'The Bankura Horse as Development Object'; Saloni Mathur, 'Charles and Ray Eames in India', *Art Journal*, Vol. 70, No. 1 (Spring 2011), 34–53; Saraf, *D.N. Saraf in the Journey of Craft*; 29.
28. Research and Education Division, Indian Cooperative Union, *Report of the Marketing of Handicrafts*, New Delhi, 1955; Dhamija, 76–77; Sackley, 'The Bankura Horse as Development Object'.
29. Kamaladevi Chattopadhyay, 'Address of Welcome', in *The Third International Conference on Planned Parenthood: Report of the Proceedings* (Bombay: Family Planning Association of India, 1952), 7–8; Mytheli Sreenivas, *Reproductive Politics and the Making of Modern India* (Seattle: University of Washington Press, 2021), 82–83, 110–11; Avabai B. Wadia, *The Light Is Ours: Memoirs and Movements*, 122, 141–45;

Brijbhushan, 153; 'Excerpt from "Greetings from India",' Bombay, 20 November 1952, in *The Selected Papers of Margaret Sanger*, Vol. 4: Round the World for Birth Control, 1920–1966, eds., Esther Katz, Peter C. Engelman, and Cathy Moran Hajo (University of Illinois Press, 2016), 505–06; Sara Weydner, 'Reproductive Rights and Reproductive Control: Family Planning, Internationalism, and Population Control in the International Planned Parenthood Federation', *Geschichte und Gesellschaft*, Vol. 44 (January–March 2018), 135–61.

30. Margaret Cousins to Margaret Sanger, 15 May 1936, Box 48, Folder 426, MSP, SSC; Barbieri, 'Kamaladevi Chattopadhyaya'; 'Future of Indian Women's Movement', 399–401; *Inner Recesses*, 243.

31. 'Future of Indian Women's Movement', 399–401; Sreenivas, *Reproductive Politics and the Making of Modern India*, 7; Connelly, *Fatal Misconception: The Struggle to Control World Population.*

32. Sanjam Ahluwalia, *Reproductive Restraints: Birth Control in India, 1877–1947* (Champaign: University of Illinois Press, 2007), 104; Barbara N. Ramusack, 'Embattled Advocates: The Debate over Birth Control in India, 1920–1940', *Journal of Women's History*, Vol. 1, No. 2 (Fall 1989): 54; 'Future of Indian Women's Movement', 399–401; *The Awakening of Indian Women*, 32–33 and 83; 'Socialism and Moral Values', in *At the Cross-Roads*, 112.

33. KC, 'Presidential Address', All India Conference of the ASMH, Kamaladevi Chattopadhyay Papers, NMML; 'Mrs Chattopadhyaya Calls for Creation of Social Hygiene Bureau', *Times of India*, 21 November 1954; Rohit De, *A People's Constitution: The Everyday Life of Law in the Indian Republic* (Princeton: Princeton University Press, 2018), 169–214; Durba Mitra, *Indian Sex Life: Sexuality and the Colonial Origins of Modern Social Thought* (Princeton: Princeton University Press, 2020).

34. *Social Welfare in India*, issued on behalf of the Planning Commission, Government of India, New Delhi, 1955, eds., Smt. Durgabai Deshmukh, Chairman, and C.V.H. Rao, 149, 153–54, 156–57 and 162–63.

35. Kamaladevi Chattopadhyaya, 'Introduction', in Neera Desai, *Women in Modern India* (Bombay: K.K. Vora, Vora and Co. Publishers Pvt. Ltd, 1957), 1–3.

36. Kamaladevi Chattopadhyay, 'The Struggle for Freedom', in Tara Ali Baig, *Women of India* (Publications Division, Ministry of Information and Broadcasting, 1958), 14–31, also see pages 90, 169 and 251.

37. Jawaharlal Nehru, 'To Ajit Prasad Jain', 30 January 1959, SWJN, Series 2, Vol. 46, 426; Jawaharlal Nehru, 'To Asoke K. Sen', 30 January 1959, SWJN, Series 2, Vol. 46, 427.

38. Ed., Gita Dharampal, *Essential Writings of Dharampal* (New Delhi: Publications Division, Ministry of Information and Broadcasting, Government of India, 2015), 4; *Inner Recesses*, 331–32; Salvi, *Development Retold*, 26–34.
39. Anita Cherian, 'Institutional Maneuvers, Nationalizing Performance, Delineating Genre: Reading the Sangeet Natak Akademi Reports 1953–59', *Third Frame: Literature, Culture and Society*, Vol. 2, No. 3 (July–September 2009): 32–60; Dharwadker, *A Poetics of Modernity*.
40. Jawaharlal Nehru, 'To A.K. Azad', 14 August 1955, SWJN, Series 2, Vol. 29, 122–23; KC Oral History, 143.
41. Mulk Raj Anand, 'Indian Theare in the Context of World Theatre', *Sangeet Natak*, Vol. 38, No. 4 (2004), https://indianculture.gov.in/flipbook/10844; Rustom Bharucha, 'Anatomy of Official Cultural Discourse: A Non-Government Perspective', *Economic and Political Weekly*, 1–8 August 1992, Vol. 27, No. 31/32 (1–8 August 1992), 1667–676; Anita Cherian, 'The First Drama Seminar Report: Imagining a National Theatre', *Sangeet Natak*, Vol. 61, No. 2 (2007): 15–48.
42. KC Oral History, 147; Dia Da Costa, *Politicizing Creative Economy: Activism and a Hunger Called Theater* (University of Illinois Press), 42–43; Rustom Bharucha, *Theatre and the World: Performance and the Politics of Culture* (London: Routledge, 1993), 200; Nanda, 141.
43. 'Futre of the Indian Theatre/L'avenir du theatre Indian' in Le theatre en Inde (International Theatre Institute and Theatre Center, India, 1955), 1–8, also published as Kamaladevi, 'Future of the Indian Theatre', *World Theatre*, Vol. 5, No. 2 (Spring 1956), 93–100. Also see Vasudha Dalmia, *Poetics, Plays, and Performances: The Politics of Modern Indian Theatre* (New Delhi: Oxford University Press, 2008).
44. *The Ramon Magsaysay Awards*, 62; 'Report, 1956–57', Government of India, Ministry of External Affairs, 24–27, in author's possession courtesy Vinay Lal; 'Arabs Want Closer Ties with India', *Times of India*, 21 June 1956; 'Report, 1956–57', Government of India, Ministry of External Affairs, 29–30.
45. *The Ramon Magsaysay Awards*, 62; 'Aims and Objects of Asian Theatre Institute: Smt. Kamala Devi's Statement', *Sangeet Natak Akademi Bulletin* 9, July 1958, 22–24.
46. 'Aims and Objects of Asian Theatre Institute'; Anita Cherian, 'Institutional Maneuvers, Nationalizing Performance, Delineating Genre: Reading the Sangeet Natak Akademi Reports 1953–59', *Third Frame: Literature, Culture and Society*, Vol. 2, No. 3 (July–September 2009): 32–60.

47. Dharwadker, *A Poetics of Modernity;* Jawaharlal Nehru, 'To B.V. Keskar', 10 March 1958, SWJN, Series 2, Vol. 41, 253; *The Ramon Magsaysay Awards,* 62; Enakshi Bhavnani, 'Creative and Fine Arts', in Tara Ali Baig, *Women of India* (Publications Division, Ministry of Information and Broadcasting, 1958), 169; Habib Tanvir, '"It Must Flow": A Life in Theatre', *Seagull Theatre Quarterly,* 10 June 10 1996; 'Scientific Training in Theatre Arts', *Times of India,* 4 August 1958.
48. Kamaladevi Chattopadhyaya, Oral Transcript, 52, NMML, quoted in Candy, *Occult Feminism,* 192; Ministry of Education, Education in India: 1961–62 (New Delhi: Government of India, 1966): 157–58; Indian National Commission for UNESCO, 'Report of the National Seminar on the Role of Arts and Crafts in Education and Community Development', held at Kalakshetra, Adyar, Madras, 7–12 March 1957 (Faridabad: Government of India Press, 1957), 5 and 7; Ministry of Education, Annual Report, 1964–65 (Faridabad: Government of India Press, 1965), Publication no. 733 and 113.
49. Brijbhushan, 20–21.
50. Brijbhushan, 167.
51. Jawaharlal Nehru, 'To Kamaladevi Chattopadhyaya: Indian Handicrafts in USA', 23 October 1960, SWJN, Series 2, Vol. 63, 317; Jawaharlal Nehru, 'To Gulzarilal Nanda', 23 October 1960, SWJN, Series 2, Vol. 63, 318.
52. Margaret Patch, 'Craftsman's Odyssey', *Craft Horizons,* Vol. 22, No. 5 (September–October 1962), 53.
53. Gopalkrishna Gandhi, *Of a Certain Age: Twenty Life Sketches* (Penguin, 2011); Jayakar quoted in *Kamaladevi Chattopadhyay: A True Karmayogi,* 12; Malvika Singh, 'The Tapestry of Her Life', *Seminar,* https://www.india-seminar.com/2004/540/540%20malvika%20singh.htm; McGowan, 'Mothers and Godmothers of Crafts: Female Leadership and the Imagination of India as a Crafts Nation, 1947–67', *South Asia: Journal of South Asian Studies,* Vol. 44, no. 2 (2021): 282-297.
54. Jain, Civil Disobedience, 131–33; Nanda, 'Kamaladevi's Vision'; *The Ramon Magsaysay Awards,* 58–59.
55. KC, *Indian Handicrafts* (New Delhi: Indian Council for Cultural Relations, 1963), 1–8.
56. Kamaladevi, 'A Forceful Art', in 'India's Crafts Today', all-India issue of *Craft Horizons* (July–August 1959), 11–12; David B. Van Dommelen, 'Allen Eaton: In Quest of Beauty', *American Craft* June–July 1985 (Vol. 45, No. 3), 35–39.
57. https://iicdelhi.in/history.

58. Gandhi, *Of a Certain Age*, 97.
59. Gita Ram interviewed by author, 18 May 2021.

8. Cultural Revolutions

1. 'Minutes of the First Meeting of Incorporators of the World Crafts Council', Ferris Booth Hall, Columbia University, 12 June 1964, in author's possession courtesy of Beth Goodrich, the librarian of the American Craft Council; Joyce Lovelace, 'Who Was Aileen Osborn Webb?', *American Craft* (August–September 2011), https://www.craftcouncil.org/magazine/article/who-was-aileen-osborn-webb; Oral History interview with Ken Shores, 2007, 13–14 November 2007, Archives of American Art, Smithsonian Institution.
2. 'The First World Congress of Craftsmen', 8–19 June 1964, Columbia University, sponsored by American Craftsmen's Council, ed., Jacqueline Rice, published by American Craftsmen's Council, New York, 1965, 8.
3. 'The First World Congress of Craftsmen', 10–11.
4. 'The First World Congress of Craftsmen', 15–20.
5. Ibid.
6. 'The First World Congress of Craftsmen', 15–20, 23–24 and 34. Also see KC, 'Craftsmanship and Culture', *Times of India*, 14 June 1964.
7. 'The Craftsman's World', *Craft Horizons*, May–June 1965 (Vol. 25, No. 3), 4; KC interviewed by Charles Allen.
8. Gita Mithal interviewed by author, 6 July 2021; Vijaya Rajan interviewed by author, 1 May 2021; Palchoudhuri Compilation; Leela Ramanathan, 'Kamaladevi Chattopadhyay: Remembering the High Priestess of Indian Culture', in *M. Rao, Kamaladevi Chattopadhyay: A True Karmayogi*, 37; *The Ramon Magsaysay Awards*, 60.
9. Mohana Ayyangar, 'Kamaladevi Chattopadhyay: A Seer with a Vision', in M. Rao, *Kamaladevi Chattopadhyay: A True Karmayogi*, 52–53.
10. Taleyarkhan, 'In Fond Memory: Kamaladeviji', 10–11.
11. KC, 'Editorial: Carpets are Works of Art', *MARG: A Magazine of the Arts*, Vol. 18, No. 4 (September 1965), 2–3, and 'Origin of Pile Carpets and Their Development in India', 4–11; KC, *Indian Carpets and Floor Coverings* (New Delhi: All India Handicrafts Board, 1966).
12. Langston Hughes to T.K. Mahadevan, 28 December 1966, Folder 3727, Box 225, Langston Hughes Papers (Series IIV), JWJ MSS 26, Beinecke Rare Book and Manuscript Library, Yale University; L. Gomes Machado to Kamaladevi Chattopadhyay, 15 March 1966 and Malcolm S. Adiseshiah

to Léapold Sédar Senghor, 24 February 1966, both in author's possession courtesy of Cédric Vincent.

13. 'Montreaux: World Crafts Council', *Craft Horizons,* September–October 1966 (Vol. 26, No. 5), 16–17 and 49–50.
14. KC to Patch, 20 August 1966, Margaret Patch Papers, Folder 15, Box 5, Archives of American Art, Smithsonian Institution (hereafter MPP); *The Ramon Magsaysay Awards,* 49–51.
15. *Kamaladevi Chattopadhyay: An Extraordinary Life,* 143; Ruby Palchoudhuri, interviewed by author on 17 May 2021 and Palchoudhuri Compilation; Margaret Merwin Patch, 'Guide to World Crafts', in *The Crafts of the Modern World,* ed., Rose Slivka (New York: Bramhall House, 1968), 22–23; 'Kamaladevi's Plea for Handicrafts Emporium in City', *Times of India,* 7 June 1967.
16. Conference Proceedings, 23, in author's possession courtesy of Beth Goodrich; Rose Slivka, 'Peru Conference', *Craft Horizons,* November–December 1968 (Vol. 28, No. 6), 22 and 53.
17. KC to Patch, 23 September 1968, MPP.
18. KC to Patch, 15 December 1968, and KC to Patch, 11 January 1969, MPP; Ratnam, 14.
19. KC to Patch, 29 July 1969, MPP; Path to KC, 2 February 1970, MPP.
20. D'Arcy Hayman, 'The Arts and Man', *UNESCO Courier* (May 1969), 4, 10, 13; Kamaladevi Chattopadhyay, 'The Crafts: An Embodiment of the Great Folk Tradition', *UNESCO Courier* (May 1969), 15–17 and 33–36.
21. M.V. Narayana Rao, 'Kamaladevi: Journeying Back in Space and Time', in M. Rao, *Kamaladevi Chattopadhyay,* 103.
22. Aileen O. Webb, 'World Crafts Council', *Craft Horizons,* January–February 1970 (Vol. 30, No. 1), 6.
23. KC to Patch, 15 October 1969, MPP; KC to Patch, 22 January 1970, MPP; KC to Patch, 11 July 1970, MPP; KC to Patch, 6 September 1970, MPP.
24. Ratnam, 14.
25. KC to Patch, 26 January 1971; KC to Patch, 29 March 1971, MPP; KC to Patch, 9 February 1972, MPP; KC to Patch, 5 September 1971, MPP; KC to Path, 14 May 1971, MPP.
26. KC to Patch, 22 July 1972, MPP; KC to Patch, 4 August 1972, MPP; *Craft Horizons,* December 1972 (Vol. 32, No. 6), 6; KC to Patch, 25 April 1973, MPP.
27. KC to Patch, 22 May 1974; KC to Patch, 6 July 1974; KC to Patch, 26 July 1974, MPP.

28. Ministry of Education and Social Welfare, Report: 1973–74 (Faridabad: Government of India Press, 1974), 129; Kalapesi, Untitled Obituary, *American Craft*, Vol. 49, No. 3 (June–July 1989), 66.
29. KC to Patch, 12 December 1973, MPP.
30. KC to Aileen, 6 April 1974, in author's possession courtesy of Beth Goodrich; 'Mrs Vanderbilt Webb to Mme Kamaladevi Chattopadhyay, 6 Chateau Marine, Subhas Road, Bombay 20, India', 23 April 1974, in author's possession courtesy of Beth Goodrich; *Craft Horizons*, October 1974 (Vol. 34, No. 5), 12.
31. KC to Patch, 22 May 1974; KC to Patch, 6 July 1974; KC to Patch, 26 July 1974, MPP; Beatrice Wood, *I Shock Myself: The Autobiography of Beatrice Wood*, ed., Lindsay Smith (San Francisco: Chronicle Books, 2006), 146 and 149–50, 158; Denise Hare, 'The Lustrous Life of Beatrice Wood', *Craft Horizons*, June 1978 (Vol. 38, No. 3), 26–28 and 69–70.
32. Polly Bee, 'Indian Activist, Cultural Leader Visits Valley Artist', Ojai Valley New, 21 August 1974.
33. KC to Patch, 22 May 1974; KC to Patch, 6 July 1974; KC to Patch, 26 July 1974, MPP; Asha Puthli interviewed by author, 1 July 2021.
34. KC to Patch, 12 October 1974, MPP.
35. KC to Patch, 1 February 1975, MPP; KC to Patch, 24 May 1975, MPP; Devenish, 'Creativity as Freedom', 367 and 'Women's Participation in Industrial Co-operatives in India', paper prepared for the International Co-operative Alliance, 6 June 1975, in 'Speeches and Writings by Her', KC Papers, NMML.
36. Interview with Gopalkrishna Gandhi, 23 April 2021; Vijaya Rajan interview, 1 May 2021; *Inner Recesses*, 329–33; Kamaladevi Chattopadhyay, 'The Women's Movement: Then and Now', from *Indian Women*, ed., Devaki Jain (1975), 86; Gyan Prakash, *Emergency Chronicles: Indira Gandhi and Democracy's Turning Point* (Princeton: Princeton University Press, 2019).
37. 'Support for Kamala Devi Chattopadhyaya's Campaign for Cultural Development, Patna, 14 April 1978', *Jayaprakash Narayan: Selected Works*, Vol. 10, 1972–1979, ed., Bimal Prasad (New Delhi: Manohar, 2009), 735–36; KC to Patch, 13 July 1975 and 23 August 1975, MPP.
38. KC to Patch, 13 July 1975 and 23 August 1975, MPP.
39. Arundhati Chattopadhaya and Nina Menon, 'Ode to the Glorious Past'; Ratnam, 77; Devaki Jain, 'The Essential Freedom Fighter: Some Reminiscences of Kamaladevi Chattopadhyay', in *A Passionate Life*, 445–56.

40. 'Karnatak Leads the Way', Karnatak Political Conference, Mangalore, May 1935, in *At the Cross-Roads,* 55; Purnima Mankekar interview, 7 May 2021; Gopalkrishna Gandhi, 7 May 2021; Vijaya Rajan, 'Kamaladevi Chattopadhyay—My Fond Memories of the Great Lady', in *Kamaladevi Chattopadhyay: A True Karmayogi,* 32.
41. KC to Patch, 13 July 1975, MPP; KC to Patch, 22 September 1975, MPP; KC to Patch, 30 December 1975, MPP.
42. KC to Patch, 30 December 1975, MPP.
43. KC to Patch, 17 July 1976; KC to Patch, 28 July 1976; KC to Patch, 3 September 1976, MPP.
44. KC to Patch, 24 September 1977, MPP.
45. KC, 'The Ecology of Folk Art', *Indian Horizons,* 26, No. 2 (1977), 5–10.
46. KC, *Tribalism in India* (Delhi: Vikas Publishers, 1978), vii–vi, 1, 3, 30–32, 50–54.
47. *Inner Recesses,* 93; KC, 'Foreword', in *Social Science and Social Concern,* ed., S.B. Chakrabarti (Delhi: Mittal Publications, 1988), xii–xiii; *India's Craft Tradition* (New Delhi: Publications Division, Government of India, 1980), preface and 3–4. Also see Lydia Walker, 'Decolonization in the 1960s: On Legitimate and Illegitimate Nationalist Claims-Making', *Past and Present,* Vol. 242, No. 1 (February 2019): 227–64; Abhay Xaxa and Ganesh N. Devy, *Being Adivasi: Existence, Entitlements, Exclusion* (Vintage, 2021).
48. KC to Patch, 23 June 1978, MPP; KC to Patch, 20 August 1978, MPP; *Craft Horizons,* December 1978 (Vol. 38, No. 8), 46; KC to Patch, 12 October 1978, MPP.
49. KC to Patch, on 13 December 1978, MPP; KC to Patch, 23 June 1978, MPP.
50. KC to Patch, 12 October 1978, MPP; KC to Patch, 4 January 1980, MPP; KC to Patch, 17 February 1979, MPP; 'World Crafts Council Directors Meet', *Craft Horizons,* Vol. 39, No. 1 (February 1979), 34.
51. KC to Patch, 4 January 1980, MPP.
52. 'Report of the Asian Regional Office January 1979 to June 1980', in KC to Patch, 30 June 1980, MPP; *Asian Newsletter,* No. 1 (January 1979), MPP; KC to Patch, 30 June 1980, MPP.
53. 'Report of the Asian Regional Office January 1979 to June 1980', and 'Report on the Asian Crafts Workshop', in KC to Patch, 30 June 1980, MPP.
54. 'Report on the Asian Crafts Workshop', in KC to Patch, 30 June 1980, MPP.

55. KC to Patch, 9 February 1980, MPP; 'WCC News', *American Craft* August–September 1980 (Vol. 40, No. 4), 80.
56. Laila Tyabji, 'Remembering Kamaladevi', lecture offered at IIC on 14 May 2019, https://www.youtube.com/watch?v=R8-WPxe9CRE; Email from Laila Tyabji to author, 25 April 2021.
57. Da Costa, *Politicizing Creative Economy*, 37, 39 and 153.
58. Jasleen Dhamija, 'Remembering Kamaladevi', in *Kamaladevi Chattopadhyay: A True Karmayogi*, 17; S. Sen Gupta, 'Kamaladevi Chattopadhyay—My Reminiscences', in *Kamaladevi Chattopadhyay: A True Karmayogi*, 27; Palchoudhuri compilation.
59. Ratnam, 174–75; Shruti Dubey, 'Understanding Participation in a Heterogeneous Community: The Resettlement of Kathputli Colony' in *Space, Planning and Everyday Contestations in Delhi*, eds., Rohit Negi and Surajit Chakravarty (Springer India, 2016), 35–58; 'A Relationship with Handicrafts', https://www.youtube.com/watch?v=xbkCu5oYoIU.
60. *India's Craft Tradition*; Kamaladevi, 'Crafts and the Future', Temenos 4, London, reproduced in *India International Centre Quarterly*, Vol. 11, No. 4, (December 1984), 5–14 and then again in *India International Centre Quarterly*, Vol. 28, No. 4 (Winter 2001–Summer 2002), 112–21.
61. 'Socialism and Moral Values', in *At the Cross-Roads*, 101; 'A Social Evaluation of Art', in *At The Cross-Roads*, 123–25; Vijaya Rajan interviewed by author, 1 May 2021; Arundhati Chattopadhaya, 'Ode to the Glorious Past'; Email from Laila Tyabji to author, 25 April 2021.
62. Abigail McGowan, 'All that is Rare, Characteristic or Beautiful: Design and the Defense of Tradition in Colonial India, 1851–1903', *Journal of Material Culture*, Vol. 10, No. 3 (2005), 263–87; Eric Hobsbawm and Terence Ranger, eds., *The Invention of Tradition* (Cambridge: Cambridge University Press, 2012); Manjari Nirula interviewed by author, 5 May 2021; Conference Proceedings, 23, in author's possession courtesy of Beth Goodrich; Rose Slivka, 'Peru Conference', *Craft Horizons*, November–December 1968 (Vol. 28, No. 6), 22 and 53.

9. Homecoming

1. Jain, 'A Singular Woman: A Feminist's Friendship with Kamaladevi Chattopadhyay,' *Caravan*, 30 June 2015, https://caravanmagazine.in/essay/singular-woman-kamaladevi-chattopadhyay; Jain, 'Remembering Kamaladevi.'

2. 'Women's Movement Has Taken a Crooked Turn', *Times of India*, 5 June 1987; Devaki Jain, 'A Singular Woman'.
3. KC, 'Some Thoughts on Women's Education', *Indian Review* (June 1972), 17–21.
4. Bee, 'Indian Activist'; Nandini Deo, 'Indian Women Activists and Transnational Feminism over the Twentieth Century', *Journal of Women's History*, Vol. 24, No. 4 (Winter 2012): 149–74.
5. Devaki Jain, 'A Singular Woman'.
6. Kamaladevi Chattopadhyay, 'The Women's Movement—Then and Now', from *Indian Women*, ed., Devaki Jain (New Delhi: Publications Division, Government of India: 1975), 29–36; Jashodhara Bagchi, 'Killed with Kindness', *Economic and Political Weekly*, Vol. 11, No. 4 (24 January 1976), 101–03; Jain, 'A Singular Woman'.
7. KC, *Indian Embroidery* (New Delhi: Wiley Eastern Limited, 1977), 1 and 3; KC, 'Editorial', and 'Origin and Development of Embroidery in Our Land', *MARG: A Magazine of the Arts*, Vol. 17, No. 2 (March 1964), 1–10.
8. *Asian Newsletter*, No. 1 (January 1979), MPP.
9. KC to Patch, 30 December 1976, MPP; KC to Patch, 24 September 1977, MPP; KC, *Indian Women's Battle for Freedom* (New Delhi: Abhinav Publications, 1983), 2–3, 5, 7, 9, 18, 78 and 129–30.
10. Nanda, 36–37; KC, *Indian Women's Battle for Freedom*, 2–3, 5, 7, 9, 18, 78 and 129–30.
11. KC, 'Some Real Issues Facing Women', *Economic and Political Weekly*, 21 March 1987, Vol. 22, No. 12, 495–96.
12. Kumari Jayawardena, *Feminism and Nationalism in the Third World* (1986), 99–101; Gloria Steinem, Meenakshi Mukherjee and Ira Pande, 'A Conversation with Gloria Steinem', *India International Centre Quarterly*, Vol. 34, No. 2 (Autumn 2007), 90–105; Steinem, 'A Past and Future Teacher', in *A Passionate Life*, xi–xvi; eds., Cherríe Moraga and Gloria E. Anzaldúa, *This Bridge Called My Back: Writings by Radical Women of Color* (Watertown: Persephone Press, 1981).
13. KC, 'Some Real Issues Facing Women'.
14. KC to Patch, 1 August 1980, MPP.
15. KC, 'Foreword', in Enakshi Bhavnani, *The Dance in India* (Bombay: Taraporevala, 1965), vii; M.V. Narayana Rao, 'Kamaladevi—Journeying Back in Space and Time', in M. Rao, *Kamaladevi Chattopadhyay: A True Karmayogi*, 101; KC, 'The Language of Dance', *Times of India*, 27 April 1980; KC Oral History, 11.

16. 'Guru Kuppiah Pillai felicitated', *Times of India,* 20 April 1980; Leela Venkataraman, 'On Being One's Own Dancer', Narthaki, 5 September 2016, https://narthaki.com/info/taalam/taalam11.html; Divya Kaushik, 'Krishna at Close Quarters', *Pioneer,* 12 August 2014, https://www.dailypioneer.com/2014/vivacity/krishna-at-close-quarters.html; Anjana Rajan, 'Have Spirit, Will Dance', *The Hindu,* 19 August 2011, https://www.thehindu.com/features/metroplus/have-spirit-will-dance/article2373391.ece.
17. Kapila Vatsyayan, 'Education through the Arts: Values and Skills', First Kamaladevi Chattopadhyay Memorial Lecture, 29 May 2009, https://www.youtube.com/watch?v=EOywjhWSwMU; Brij Kul Deepak, 'My Mentor and Inspirer—Kamaladevi Amma', in M. Rao, *Kamaladevi Chattopadhyay: A True Karmayogi,* 71.
18. KC to Patch, 11 January 1978, MPP; KC to Patch, 23 June 1978, MPP; KC to Patch, 1 August 1980 and 6 January 1981, MPP.
19. Interview with Gopalkrishna Gandhi, 23 April 2021; Gandhi, seminar.
20. 'Sangeet Natak Akademi Annual Awards: Speeches Delivered by the Chairman, Smt. Kamaladevi Chattopadhyaya and vice-chairman, Dr Smt. Kapila Vatsyayan at the Awards Giving Ceremony on February 11, 1981', https://indianculture.gov.in/sangeet-natak-akademi-annual-awards-speaches-delivered-chairman-smt-kamaladevi-chattopadhyaya-and; Jain, 'Remembering Kamaladevi'.
21. Rahman, *Dancing in the Family,* 156.
22. Interview with Gopalkrishna Gandhi, 23 April 2021; Kamaladevi, 'Foreword', in Gopal Gandhi, *Refuge: A Novel* (Delhi: Penguin Books, 2010), ix; Singh, 93.
23. Singh, 93; Ratnam 66–67 and 79.
24. Palchoudhuri compilation; Purnima Mankekar interview, 7 May 2021; From Diana Eck, email to author, 19 May 2021.
25. Roshan Kalapesi, Untitled Obituary, *American Craft,* Vol. 49, No. 3 (June–July 1989), 66; Arundhati Chattopadhaya in 'Ode to the Glorious Past'; Laila Tyabji, 'Remembering Kamaladevi'.
26. Jain, 'A Singular Woman'; Dhamija, 'Remembering Kamaladevi', 19.
27. 'National UNESCO award for Kamaladevi', *Times of India,* 6 December 1977; 'Kamaladevi Chattopadhyay: A Tribute to Her Life and Work'; 'A Vivid Tapestry', *Times of India,* 8 June 1986; email correspondence with Purnima Rai, 5 May 2021; 'Kamaladevi Puraskar', Delhi Crafts Council, http://www.delhicraftscouncil.org/projects/2016/6/3/kamaladevi-puraskar; Manjari Nirula interviewed by author, 5 May 2021;

Gandhi, *Seminar*; *Karmayogi*, 42; 'Charles Eames Award to Kamaladevi Chattopadhyay', National Institute of Design Newsletter, March 1988, and the Charles Eames Award Citation, undated, courtesy Beth Goodrich.

28. *Inner Recesses*, 402; Arundhati Chattopadhaya, 'Ode to the Glorious Past'.
29. Brijbhushan, v; Ratnam, preface; KC to Patch, 23 June 1978, MPP.
30. L.C. Jain, 'Kamaladevi: An Epochal Life', *Manushi;* Annie Devenish, 'Performing the Political Self: A Study of Identity Making and Self Representation in the Autobiographies of India's First Generation of Parliamentary Women', *Women's History Review*, Vol. 22, No. 2 (2013): 280–94, quote on 290.
31. Kapila Vatsyayan, 'Endearing Encounters', *India International Centre Quarterly*, Vol. 13, No. 2 (June 1986), 251–55.
32. Gandhi, *Seminar*; Interview with Gopalkrishna Gandhi, 23 April 2021.
33. *Kamaladevi Chattopadhyay v. State of Punjab and Another* (Supreme Court of India), Criminal Writ Petition No. 1508 of 1984 | 21-09-1984; *A Passionate Life*, 32–33.
34. 'The All India Women's Conference, 17th Session—Bombay', 287–88; KC, 'The Media of Puppetry', *Indian Horizons*, Vol. 35, Nos. 1–2 (1986), 1–4.
35. KC, 'The Media of Puppetry', *Indian Horizons*, Vol. 35, Nos. 1–2 (1986), 1–4; Asha Puthli interviewed by author, 1 July 2021; Palchoudhuri compilation; Ratnam, 24.
36. KC, 'Of Reason Fragmented', 29–30 and 34–36.
37. KC, 'Of Reason Fragmented', 34 and 36.
38. KC, 'Handicrafts of Tamilnadu', *Indian Horizons*, Vol. 38, Nos. 3–4 (1988), 1–5.
39. Palchoudhuri compilation.
40. 'Kamaladevi, Champion of Arts, Dead', *Times of India*, 30 October 1988; 'Kamala Devi Chattopadhyaya dies at 85', *Telegraph*, 30 October 1988; 'Kamaladevi Cremated', *Telegraph*, 31 October 1988; 'Kamaladevi Chattopadhyay in the Afterlife' (Kamaladevi Chattopadhyay Paraloke), *Anandabazar Patrika*, 30 October 1988; 'Kamaladevi's Funeral Rites Completed' (Kamaldevi-r Antyesti Sampanna), *Anandabazar Patrika*, 31 October 1988; email to the author from Nina Menon, 6 June 2022.
41. 'Rich tributes to Kamaladevi', *Times of India*, 4 December 1988; 'High Priestess of Indian Culture', *Telegraph*, 30 October 1988; 'WCC Secretary General to WCC National Entities', 25 November 1988, in author's possession, courtesy Beth Goodrich; Ramaswamy Venkataraman, 'A Many Splendoured Life', address on 27 November 1988, reproduced in

India International Centre Quarterly, Vol. 15, No. 3 (Monsoon 1988), 1–5; Palchoudhuri compilation; Kalapesi, Untitled Obituary, *American Craft*.

42. L.C. Jain, 'Kamaladevi: Obituary', *Economic and Political Weekly*, Vol. 23, No. 48 (26 November 1988): 2520–521.
43. Bhagirathi Bai audio messages sent to author and translated from Hindi by Arko Dasgupta, April 2021.
44. John Montague, 'On Hearing Kamaladevi Speak Again', *Poetry Ireland Review*, Vol. 47 (Autumn–Winter 1995), 43; http://www.anjalchande.com/out-of-the-shadows-a-colored-solidarity; http://theaerogram.com/kamaladevi/.
45. Govindraj Venkatachalam, *My Contemporaries* (Bangalore: Hosali Press, 1966), 76.
46. Bartonoff quoted in Brijbhushan, 5.
47. Vaidehi, 'A Voice for Women', translated by Sumathi Niranjan Karody, *The Hindu*, 26 October 2017, https://www.thehindu.com/books/a-voice-for-women/article19924223.ece; Interview with Gopalkrishna Gandhi, 23 April 2021; Asha Puthli, interviewed by author, 1 July 2021.
48. *Inner Recesses*, 401.
49. *Inner Recesses*, 399 and 402; Brijbhushan, 169–71; KC Oral History, 176.
50. KC, 'Future of Indian Women's Movement', 385; 'Kamaladevi Chattopadhyay: A Tribute to Her Life and Work'.

Epilogue: The Art of Freedom

1. *Inner Recesses*, 53–54.
2. Meherally, *At The Cross-Roads*, 6.
3. Venkataraman, 'A Many Splendoured Life'.
4. 'The Bombay Youth Conferences', 403–04; 'Youth and the Fight for Independence', Address at the Bombay Presidency Youth Conference, Ahmedabad, 14 December 1929, in *At the Cross-Roads*, 51–55; Kamaladevi, 'Freedom', *Congress Socialist*, 1 January 1939 in ed., Mushirul Hasan, *Towards Freedom: 1939, Part 2*, 1168–70.
5. 'The All India Women's Conference, 17th Session—Bombay—7th to 10th April 1944', in *Indian Annual Register*, January–June 1944, Vol. 1 (Calcutta: N.N. Mitra), 284–88; Kamaladevi Chattopadhyay, 'Determining Social Status by Color . . . Antiquated', 8; P.L. Prattis, 'Seventeen Days in Independent India', *Pittsburgh Courier*, 3 September 1949, 12; P.L. Prattis, 'Seventeen Days in Independent India', *Pittsburgh Courier*, 1 October 1949, 7.

6. Lal, 'Kamaladevi Chattopadhyay and the Idea of the Global South'; Stolte, 'The People's Bandung'; Mahler, *From the Tricontinental to the Global South*; Prashad, *The Darker Nations*; Katherine McKittrick, *Demonic Grounds: Black Women and the Cartographies of Struggle* (Minneapolis: University of Minnesota Press, 2006); Frank A. Guridy, *Forging Diaspora: Afro-Cubans and African Americans in a World of Empire and Jim Crow* (University of North Carolina Press, 2010); Barbara Ransby, *Ella Baker and the Black Freedom Movement: A Radical Democratic Vision* (Chapel Hill: University of North Carolina Press, 2003); Katherine Mellen Charron, *Freedom's Teacher: The Life of Septima Clark* (Chapel Hill: University of North Carolina Press, 2009); Rosalind Rosenberg, *Jane Crow: The Life of Pauli Murray* (Oxford: Oxford University Press, 2017); Troy R. Saxby, *Pauli Murray: A Personal and Political Life* (Chapel Hill: University of North Carolina Press, 2020).
7. Kamaladevi Chattopadhyay, Untitled Chapter, *Mahatma Gandhi and One World* (New Delhi: Publications Divisions, Government of India, 1966), 5–7 and 11–12, republished as 'Mahatma Gandhi and One World', in ed., B.K. Ahluwalia, *Facets of Gandhi* (New Delhi: Lakshmi Publishing House, 1968), 48–55.
8. Leela Gandhi, *The Common Cause: Postcolonial Ethics and the Practice of Democracy, 1900–1955* (Chicago: University of Chicago Press, 2014), 4.
9. Onit Shani, 'India's Democracy before the Democratic Discontent'; Karuna Mantena, 'Popular Sovereignty and Anti-Colonialism', in eds., Richard Bourke and Quentin Skinner, *Popular Sovereignty in Historical Perspective* (Cambridge: Cambridge University Press, 2016), 297–319; Emily Rook-Koepsel, *Democracy and Unity in India: Understanding the All India Phenomenon, 1940–1960* (Routledge, 2019); Nazmul S. Sultan, 'Self-Rule and the Problem of Peoplehood in Colonial India', *American Political Science Review*, Vol. 114, No. 1 (2020), 81–94; Madhav Khosla, *India's Founding Moment: The Constitution of a Most Surprising Democracy* (Cambridge: Harvard University Press, 2020).
10. Balaji, 'From Colonial Subjecthood to Shared Humanity'; Patel, *Naoroji*, 10; Supriya Chaudhuri, 'Significant Lives: Biography, Autobiography, Gender, and Women's History in South Asia', The Oxford Centre for Life-Writing, https://www.youtube.com/watch?v=oToXw0b13EE; Judith M. Brown, '"Life Histories" and the History of Modern South Asia', *American Historical Review*, Vol. 114, No. 3 (June 2009), 587–95.
11. Adom Getachew, *Worldmaking after Empire: The Rise and Fall of Self-Determination* (Princeton, 2019); Ben Zachariah, 'A Long Strange Trip: The Lives in Exile of Har Dayal', *South Asian History and Culture*, Vol. 4,

No. 4 (2013): 574–92; ed., Neilesh Bose, *South Asian Migrations in Global History* (London, 2020); Ratnam, 76–77.

12. Sackley, 'The Bankura Horse as Development Object'; Daniel Immerwahr, *Thinking Small: The United States and the Lure of Community Development* (Cambridge, Mass.: Harvard University Press, 2015); Nikhil Menon, *Planning Democracy: Modern India's Quest for Development* (Cambridge: Cambridge University Press, 2022); Nikhil Menon, 'Developing Histories of Indian Development', History Compass, 24 August 2021.
13. 'The All India Women's Conference, 17th Session—Bombay—7th to 10th April 1944', in *Indian Annual Register*, January–June 1944, Vol. 1 (Calcutta: N.N. Mitra), 284–88; Annie Devenish, 'Creativity as Freedom: Kamaladevi Chattopadhyay and the Politics of Self-Expression', in *A Passionate Life*, 351–74, quote on page 369; 'Goals of Social Reconstruction'; 'Socialism and Moral Values', in *At the Cross-Roads*, 104.
14. KC Oral History, 176; Ruby Palchoudhuri, interviewed on 17 May 2021 and Palchoudhuri compilation; Neelam Chiders interview, 21 June 2021; email from Laila Tyabji, 25 April 2021; *The Ramon Magsaysay Awards*, 56; Jain, 'Kamaladevi: Obituary'.
15. *Inner Recesses*, 106; KC Oral History, 70; 'All Bengal Students' Conference'.

[illegible] Nepal [illegible] 2020, [illegible]

13. [illegible] [illegible] [illegible] Cambridge, Mass.: Harvard University Press [illegible]

14. [illegible]

15. [illegible]

16. [illegible]

Index

About the Author

Nico Slate is Professor of History and Head of the Department of History at Carnegie Mellon University. His research focuses on the transnational history of social movements in the United States and South Asia, with a particular focus on the history of struggles against racism and imperialism. He is the author of four books: *Colored Cosmopolitanism: The Shared Struggle for Freedom in the United States and India* (Harvard University Press, 2012), *The Prism of Race: W.E.B. Du Bois, Langston Hughes, Paul Robeson and the Colored World of Cedric Dover* (Palgrave Macmillan, 2014), *Gandhi's Search for the Perfect Diet: Eating with the World in Mind* (Washington University Press, 2019) and *Lord Cornwallis Is Dead: The Struggle for Democracy in the United States and India* (Harvard University Press, 2019).

HarperCollins *Publishers* India

At HarperCollins India, we believe in telling the best stories and finding the widest readership for our books in every format possible. We started publishing in 1992; a great deal has changed since then, but what has remained constant is the passion with which our authors write their books, the love with which readers receive them, and the sheer joy and excitement that we as publishers feel in being a part of the publishing process.

Over the years, we've had the pleasure of publishing some of the finest writing from the subcontinent and around the world, including several award-winning titles and some of the biggest bestsellers in India's publishing history. But nothing has meant more to us than the fact that millions of people have read the books we published, and that somewhere, a book of ours might have made a difference.

As we look to the future, we go back to that one word—a word which has been a driving force for us all these years.

Read.